MALE SUPREMACISM IN THE UNITED STATES

Male Supremacism in the United States is a timely editorial collection providing analysis of current patriarchal, misogynistic, and antifeminist threats in the United States.

The book theorizes how male supremacism—the system that disproportionately privileges cis men and subordinates women, trans men, and nonbinary people—and its accompanying ideology of male superiority undergird many of the most crucial phenomena of our time. The book examines how male supremacism manifests in three ways: as patriarchal traditionalism, as secular male supremacism, and in its intersections with other systems of oppression. From anti-abortion activism to misogynist incels to the Proud Boys, the collection illustrates how male supremacism plays a vital role in right-wing recruitment and organizing. The volume's contributions illuminate unique aspects of male supremacist ideology, practice, and culture. Together, they provide a sweeping overview of the development and deployment of male supremacism in the United States.

This book will be of value to anyone studying or researching male supremacism, gender, feminism, women's studies, hate studies, and the far right.

Emily K. Carian is Co-founder and Board Chair of the Institute for Research on Male Supremacism, USA, and Assistant Professor of Sociology at California State University, San Bernardino, USA.

Alex DiBranco is Co-founder and Executive Director of the Institute for Research on Male Supremacism, USA.

Chelsea Ebin is Co-founder and Treasurer of the Institute for Research on Male Supremacism, USA, and Assistant Professor of Politics at Centre College, Kentucky, USA.

Routledge Studies in Fascism and the Far Right
Series editors
Nigel Copsey, Teesside University, UK and Graham Macklin, Center for Research on Extremism (C-REX), University of Oslo, Norway.

This book series focuses upon national, transnational and global manifestations of fascist, far right and right-wing politics primarily within a historical context but also drawing on insights and approaches from other disciplinary perspectives. Its scope also includes anti-fascism, radical-right populism, extreme-right violence and terrorism, cultural manifestations of the far right, and points of convergence and exchange with the mainstream and traditional right.

Titles include:

The Blackshirts' Dictatorship
Armed Squads, Political Violence, and the Consolidation of Mussolini's Regime
Matteo Millan

Male Supremacism in the United States
From Patriarchal Traditionalism to Misogynist Incels and the Alt-Right
Edited by Emily K. Carian, Alex DiBranco and Chelsea Ebin

Fascism in Brazil
From Integralism to Bolsonarism
Leandro Pereira Gonçalves and Odilon Caldeira Neto

The Dynamics of Right-Wing Extremism within German Society
Escape into Authoritarianism
Edited by Oliver Decker, Elmar Brähler and Johannes Kiess

The Fascist Faith of Romania's Legion "Archangel Michael" in Romania, 1927–41
Martyrdom to National Purification
Constantin Iordachi

For more information about this series, please visit: www.routledge.com/Routledge-Studies-in-Fascism-and-the-Far-Right/book-series/FFR

MALE SUPREMACISM IN THE UNITED STATES

From Patriarchal Traditionalism to Misogynist Incels and the Alt-Right

Edited by Emily K. Carian, Alex DiBranco and Chelsea Ebin

LONDON AND NEW YORK

First published 2022
by Routledge
4 Park Square, Milton Park, Abingdon, Oxon OX14 4RN

and by Routledge
605 Third Avenue, New York, NY 10158

Routledge is an imprint of the Taylor & Francis Group, an informa business

© 2022 selection and editorial matter, Emily K. Carian, Alex DiBranco and Chelsea Ebin; individual chapters, the contributors

The right of Emily K. Carian, Alex DiBranco and Chelsea Ebin to be identified as the authors of the editorial material, and of the authors for their individual chapters, has been asserted in accordance with sections 77 and 78 of the Copyright, Designs and Patents Act 1988.

All rights reserved. No part of this book may be reprinted or reproduced or utilised in any form or by any electronic, mechanical, or other means, now known or hereafter invented, including photocopying and recording, or in any information storage or retrieval system, without permission in writing from the publishers.

Trademark notice: Product or corporate names may be trademarks or registered trademarks, and are used only for identification and explanation without intent to infringe.

Please note that this book contains some profanity which readers may find offensive.

British Library Cataloguing-in-Publication Data
A catalogue record for this book is available from the British Library

Library of Congress Cataloging-in-Publication Data
Names: Carian, Emily K., editor. | DiBranco, Alex, editor. | Ebin, Chelsea, editor.
Title: Male supremacism in the United States : from patriarchal traditionalism to misogynist incels and the alt-right / edited by Emily K. Carian, Alex DiBranco and Chelsea Ebin.
Description: Milton Park, Abingdon, Oxon ; New York, NY : Routledge, 2022. | Series: Routledge studies in fascism and the far right | Includes bibliographical references and index.
Identifiers: LCCN 2021053489 (print) | LCCN 2021053490 (ebook) | ISBN 9780367752583 (hardback) | ISBN 9780367754044 (paperback) | ISBN 9781003164722 (ebook)
Subjects: LCSH: Male domination (Social structure)--United States. | Sex discrimination against women--United States. | Misogyny--United States. | Anti-feminism--United States. | United States--Social conditions. | Equality--United States.
Classification: LCC HQ1090.3 .M234 2022 (print) | LCC HQ1090.3 (ebook) | DDC 305.420973--dc23/eng/20220125
LC record available at https://lccn.loc.gov/2021053489
LC ebook record available at https://lccn.loc.gov/2021053490

ISBN: 978-0-367-75258-3 (hbk)
ISBN: 978-0-367-75404-4 (pbk)
ISBN: 978-1-003-16472-2 (ebk)

DOI: 10.4324/9781003164722

Typeset in Bembo
by SPi Technologies India Pvt Ltd (Straive)

TABLE OF CONTENTS

Preface	*vii*
Acknowledgments	*xv*
Notes on Contributors	*xvi*

PART I
Foundations · 1

1 Mobilizing Misogyny · 3
Alex DiBranco

2 The Inversive Sexism Scale: Endorsement of the Belief That Women Are Privileged · 21
Emily K. Carian

3 The U.S. Far Right's Politics of Gender · 48
Matthew N. Lyons

PART II
Patriarchal Traditionalism · 65

4 "I Want to Thank My Husband Fred for Letting Me Come Here," or Phyllis Schlafly's Opportunistic Defense of Gender Hierarchy · 67
Amélie Ribieras

vi Table of Contents

5 Created Equal, but Equal in No Other Respect: Opposing
Abortion to Protect Men 94
Carol Mason

PART III
Secular Male Supremacism 115

6 Of Victims, Mass Murder, and "Real Men": The Masculinities of
the "Manosphere" 117
Ann-Kathrin Rothermel, Megan Kelly, and Greta Jasser

7 Men's Rights Activists, Personal Responsibility, and the End of
Welfare 142
Alexis de Coning and Chelsea Ebin

8 Misogynist Incels and Male Supremacist Violence 164
Megan Kelly, Alex DiBranco, and Julia R. DeCook

PART IV
Intersections 181

9 Fight Club: Gavin McInnes, the Proud Boys, and Male
Supremacism 183
Meadhbh Park

10 Watching Awakening: Violent White Masculinity in *Cuck* 202
Meredith L. Pruden

11 Trans Women and the Invisible Sisterhood 219
Katherine Cross

Bibliography 226
Index 250

PREFACE

In May 2020, a self-identified men's rights lawyer, well-known in antifeminist circles for filing dozens of lawsuits alleging discrimination against men, traveled across the country and, disguised as a package delivery driver, shot and killed the son and seriously wounded the husband of a New Jersey federal judge. The shooter's autobiography discussed his attraction to the judge and his belief that she was working "to convince America that whites, especially white males, were barbarians."[1] That same month, armed protesters stormed the Michigan State Capitol and voiced cries of "lock her up," referring to the state's woman governor, Gretchen Whitmer (later the subject of an attempted far-right kidnapping plot).[2] Four months later, then-president Donald Trump allied himself with the far-right group the Proud Boys during a national debate in nearly explicit terms, directing them to "stand back and stand by."[3] Several Proud Boys members were later arrested for their role in the violent January 6 attack on the Capitol, and the State Capitol invasion in Michigan began to look like a test run for this event.[4] In the first six months of 2021, an unprecedented 561 abortion restrictions were introduced in legislatures across the United States, 83 of which were enacted.[5] By mid-March 2021, 82 anti-transgender bills had been proposed, already outpacing the total count from the previous year (79).[6]

The through line in all of these events is male supremacism. We define a male supremacist system as a cultural, political, economic, and social system in which cisgender men disproportionately control status, power, and resources, and women, trans men, and nonbinary people are subordinated. Such systems are underpinned by an ideology of male supremacism: the belief in cisgender men's superiority and right to dominate and control others. While male supremacism also intersects with other axes of oppression, such as racism, xenophobia, antisemitism, and heterosexism, it motivates and undergirds the types of events described earlier. Male supremacism manifests in various ways, including physical

viii Preface

and sexual violence, militarism, and exertion of control over women's, trans men's, and nonbinary people's bodies.[7]

This volume derives from our work at the Institute for Research on Male Supremacism (IRMS), which advances the argument that male supremacism plays a vital role in right-wing mobilizations. We reject Christian Right language of "traditional moral values" and recognize opposition to abortion rights and LGBTQ rights as expressions of male supremacist and misogynist ideologies with political and social impacts that can and do often turn to violence. The relationship between male supremacist, white supremacist, Christian supremacist, and antisemitic ideology is complex, and there is a rich body of shared theories from which our analyses draw.

Scholarship on right-wing ideologies in the United States has expanded in recent decades, especially with regard to understanding their racist, xenophobic, and class appeals, through studies of movements ranging from the Ku Klux Klan to the Religious Right to the Tea Party to, most recently, the alt-right.[8] Earlier work has already identified some of the ways male supremacism works with these other systems, even when using other terminology for the ideology. For example, in analyzing white cis men who feel attacked by feminism and civil rights advances, Ferber writes that "central to this backlash is confusion over the meanings of both masculinity and whiteness, triggered by the perceived loss of white, male privileges."[9] Right-wing movements in historical and contemporary analyses capitalize on a perceived "decline in the political influence of white male [cis men] citizens," Rory McVeigh writes in his analysis of the Ku Klux Klan; Mitch Berbrier makes a similar point (see Chapter 10 by Meredith L. Pruden in this volume for more on Berbrier's frame of white male victimhood).[10]

Yet even as our understanding of the Right in the United States has expanded, insufficient attention has been devoted to theorizing misogynist ideologies. Research addressing "gender" most often focuses on women's participation in right-wing movements, like their involvement in the Ku Klux Klan, pro-fascist and isolationist movements, and anti-Communist organizing.[11] While this work is excellent, a gap exists in examining how ideology about gender motivates and mobilizes the Right. The presence of (predominantly white) women in right-wing movements is a worthy subject in and of itself, but too often, when attempting to discuss misogynist gender ideologies, the presence of women becomes a means of shifting the focus away from male supremacism. Studies of anti-abortion movements stand out for their interrogation of misogynist gender ideologies, but anti-abortion ideology has often been treated by the right-wing studies field as the only social movement ideology that targets women and sustains cis men's domination.[12] We strive to maintain a more holistic focus on male supremacism as an ideology that informs and structures social, political, and economic relations.

In addition, misogynist movements are often seen as conservative or "traditional" rather than part of the "right-wing," the umbrella under which white supremacist movements are placed. For instance, Blee and Creasap in 2010 defined "right-wing movements" as those "that focus directly on race/ethnicity and/or promote violence as a primary tactic or goal."[13] Not only does this definition exclude gender as a primary organizing principle for right-wing movements, but it also characterizes misogynist movements as non-violent, treating the existence of anti-abortion violence as the exception to the rule and leaving out secular male supremacist groups (e.g., the men's rights movement) that have perpetrated violence. This approach is common to the field and weakens the foundation for a robust analysis of anti-woman, anti-gay, or anti-trans ideologies in and of themselves. This further prevents scholars from examining how male supremacism works in conjunction with white supremacism, xenophobia, and antisemitism within right-wing movements.

Our advancement of the concept of male supremacism is part of encouraging a shift to "supremacism studies," a lens to look at how various forms of supremacist ideology threaten individuals and communities, structure society, and interact with one another. We developed the framework of male supremacism in engagement with the widely used framework of white supremacism and the less often used Christian supremacism. The concept of supremacism can be further developed to give us a more multifaceted understanding of other forms of oppression and domination. Cisgender supremacism, for instance, is touched on in this volume as an element of male supremacist ideology but can also be far more richly explored. Moving into an international context, there are other forms of religious and ethnic supremacisms to explore that may not be as prevalent in the U.S. context.

The purpose of this volume is to theorize male supremacism as a conceptual framework for understanding right-wing movements. This volume, therefore, begins with a section titled "Foundations," which opens with a reprint of the 2017 piece "Mobilizing Misogyny" written for *The Public Eye* magazine. This piece by Alex DiBranco, one of this book's co-editors and IRMS co-founder and executive director, significantly impacted perceptions of misogynist movements. The chapter operates as an introduction of sorts, describing how misogyny functions as a motivating principle across the Right. The following chapter, by co-editor and IRMS co-founder and chair Emily K. Carian, shows how "inversive sexism," the belief that men are discriminated against that is prevalent in male supremacist movements, is common in the United States and functions as part of patriarchal society. A third foundational article, excerpted from Matthew N. Lyons's 2018 book *Insurgent Supremacists*, shows how adopting male supremacism as a framework aids in our understanding of change over time within right-wing movements. Lyons argues for recognizing a distinctive misogyny in the alt-right beyond that of past white supremacist and neo-Nazi movements. Lyons lays out his conception of four distinct types of male supremacism found in right-wing movements, including patriarchal traditionalism, the framework for the next section in the volume.

A number of studies of the Christian Right have foregrounded how religious conservatives have operationalized the concept of "tradition" to promote patriarchal roles within marriage, the family, and social policy—even as they rewrite

x Preface

the past and construct the "traditional" according to modern social, economic, and political relations and norms.[14] The patriarchal traditionalist viewpoint in the United States is typically embedded in white, Christian supremacist attitudes about the family and the "proper" roles of women and men.[15] The second section of the volume, "Patriarchal Traditionalism," contributes to this scholarship with two chapters that explore religious forms of male supremacism. Amélie Ribieras's article examines prominent right-wing woman, Phyllis Schlafly, as a case study of how women can organize for male supremacism while navigating the contradictions of being movement leaders. In the second, Carol Mason continues her decades of scholarship on anti-abortion movements with an article examining how the anti-abortion group Created Equal casts men as the "real" victims. Through a critical reading of Created Equal's activities and media products, Mason demonstrates the ways in which white and male supremacism co-constitute an anti-abortion politics that erases women and instead centers the protection of white cis men.

The third section of the volume, "Secular Male Supremacism," focuses on ideologies and movements that have grown in significance in recent decades yet have received far less attention than the Christian Right. We recognize that the term "secular" has a complex history, often intertwined in the U.S. and European contexts with Christian domination, where a "secular" system is in fact shaped by hegemonic Christianity.[16] In more recent usage, "secular" is sometimes used interchangeably with the term "atheist." We use secular in its basic meaning as an ideology that is not primarily referring to religious beliefs, and we can see in U.S. secular male supremacist movements the coexistence of Christian and atheist participants and ideological influences from each. And so, while articulated in secular language, these forms of male supremacism in the United States often reflect conservative Christian beliefs. Nonetheless, we believe it is important to distinguish secular forms of male supremacism from those that are self-consciously religious. Our aim in this section, therefore, is to recognize the existence and influence of non-religious male supremacist actors and ideologies.

In the first chapter in this section, IRMS fellow Ann-Kathrin Rothermel and IRMS co-founders and fellows Megan Kelly and Greta Jasser analyze the five major secular misogynist groups active in the "manosphere," a term used to denote the internet communities and websites driven primarily by male supremacist ideology, to break down their differences and areas of overlap. This is followed by a historical piece investigating men's rights activists' attack on the welfare state before the ubiquity of the internet and social media written by IRMS fellow Alexis de Coning and IRMS co-founder and treasurer Chelsea Ebin. Drawing on a unique dataset from a newsletter messaging board popular in the 1990s, de Coning and Ebin explore how men's rights advocates understood the relationship between women, rights, and the welfare state as one that is controlled by women—who simultaneously are undeserving dependents, parasites, conniving, and capable of capturing the state—and systematically discriminatory against men. Next, an excerpt from Megan Kelly, Alex DiBranco, and Julia R.

DeCook's recent report, published by IRMS and New America, dives deeper into misogynist incel men's ideology and violence.

The final section ends with three pieces considering male supremacism and its intersections. Meadhbh Park's analysis of the rhetoric of Proud Boys' founder Gavin McInnes speaks directly to the problem of miscategorizing a group as white supremacist and analyzing it only through that frame, demonstrating the significance of male supremacism to its recruitment of both white men and men of color as an entry point to this discussion for future research. Meredith L. Pruden provides an analysis of the 2019 film *Cuck* that demonstrates how whiteness and masculinity interplay in the construction of a sympathetic portrait of a "lone wolf" killer. Finally, ending the collection, Katherine Cross's chapter provides a reminder of the centrality of anti-trans ideology to the biological essentialism of male supremacism and opens up further questions for exploration, such as how anti-trans feminists reinforce male supremacism.

This volume, the first collection of works around the theory of male supremacism, aims to help correct the failure to take misogyny as seriously as racism, xenophobia, and antisemitism, part of a broader neglect of male supremacist movements in research on the Right. Read individually, the chapters in this volume dive deep into unique aspects of male supremacist ideology, practice, and culture. Read as a whole, this volume provides a more sweeping overview of the development and deployment of male supremacist ideologies and practices across the Right. While male supremacism is the central ideology that ties these articles together, other linkages and overlaps exist. As these chapters show, male supremacism works in tandem with other forms of supremacism. The framework of male supremacism strengthens our analytical tool kit for understanding how misogyny, racism, homophobia, xenophobia, transphobia, and antisemitism intertwine and diverge in complex ways. Attention to male supremacism does not need to come at the cost of intersectional analysis; rather, it demands it.

The 11 chapters in this volume are but a small sampling of topics that could be analyzed using a male supremacist lens. Significant and substantial work has been done in this vein on the Christian Right in the United States, especially by Black women at the forefront of reproductive justice theory, and for this reason, our section on patriarchal traditionalism is briefer in this volume. We recommend work by Loretta Ross, Rickie Solinger, and Zakiya Luna, among others, which speak to misogynist attacks on the bodies and autonomy of women of color in particular, including forced and coerced sterilization, unequal access to reproductive health care and technologies, and the entwinement of white and male supremacism in the anti-abortion movement. Writers such as Heron Greenesmith and the researchers at the Center for Applied Transgender Studies address anti-trans ideology, including the collaboration of TERFs (trans-exclusionary radical feminists) with the Christian Right in fighting transgender rights. And research projects in the early stages being conducted by mentees at IRMS, such as Alexandria Onuoha's work on the impact of far-right messaging on Black girls in college, and research projects on racial narratives and politics in misogynist incel

xii Preface

forums conducted by Rina James and Ye Bin Won, promise a next generation of scholarship on male supremacism that includes increasingly diverse researchers and attention to a wide range of issues. Lastly, while the United States is particularly significant as an exporter of many male supremacist ideologies, this volume's limited geographical context leaves out the many ways male supremacism operates globally, and we intend to take a global perspective in future collections. As we look toward the future of male supremacist studies, we hope to see the field reflect the work of a more diverse group of scholars and activists, to advance more intersectional analyses, and to broaden the geographic scope of studies to include more international male supremacist movements and actors.

Notes

1 Nicole Hong, Mihir Zaveri, and William K. Rashbaum, "Inside the Violent and Misogynistic World of Roy Den Hollander," *The New York Times*, July 26, 2020, https://www.nytimes.com/2020/07/26/nyregion/roy-den-hollander-judge.html.
2 Allan Smith, "'Lock Her Up!': Anti-Whitmer Coronavirus Lockdown Protestors Swarm Michigan Capitol," *NBC News*, April 16, 2020, https://nbcnews.com/politics/politics-news/lock-her-anti-whitmer-coronavirus-lockdown-protestors-swarm-michigan-capitol-n1184426.
3 Reid J. Epstein, "Trump Refuses to Denounce White Supremacy in Chaotic Debate," *The New York Times*, September 29, 2020, https://www.nytimes.com/live/2020/09/29/us/presidential-debate-trump-biden.
4 Ryan Lucas, "4 Proud Boys Charged with Conspiracy Over Jan. 6 Capitol Riot," *NPR*, March 19, 2021, https://www.npr.org/2021/03/19/979304432/4-proud-boys-charged-with-conspiracy-over-jan-6-capitol-riot.
5 Elizabeth Nash and Lauren Cross, "2021 Is on Track to Become the Most Devastating Antiabortion State Legislative Session in Decades," April 29, 2021, https://www.guttmacher.org/article/2021/04/2021-track-become-most-devastating-anti-abortion-state-legislative-session-decades.
6 Wyatt Ronan, "2021 Becomes Record Year for Anti-transgender Legislation," *Human Rights Campaign*, March 13, 2021, https://www.hrc.org/press-releases/breaking-2021-becomes-record-year-for-anti-transgender-legislation.
7 The primary terms we use are "misogynist," "anti-women," and "male supremacist" as correlates to terms such as "racist," "antisemitic," and "white supremacist." We acknowledge the validity of Schilt and Westbrook's argument that

[t]he hierarchical gender system that privileges masculinity also privileges heterosexuality. Its maintenance rests on the cultural devaluation of femininity and homosexuality. [...] The gender system must be conceived of as *heterosexist*, as power is allocated via positioning in gender and sexual hierarchies.

However, white gay men have used misogyny to gain influence in contemporary right-wing movements, and our scholarship makes an analytical distinction to recognize ideology that is anti-women and anti-trans but makes space for gay men. Kristen Schilt and Laurel Westbrook, "Doing Gender, Doing Heteronormativity: 'Gender Normals,' Transgender People, and the Social Maintenance of Heterosexuality," *Gender & Society* 23, no. 4 (August 1, 2009): 443.

Preface **xiii**

8 See, for example, David Cunningham, *Klansville USA: The Rise and Fall of the Civil Rights-Era Ku Klux Klan* (New York: Oxford University Press, 2012); Rory McVeigh, *The Rise of the Ku Klux Klan* (Minneapolis: University of Minnesota Press, 2009); Randall Balmer, *Thy Kingdom Come* (New York: Basic Books, 2006); Sara Diamond, *Not by Politics Alone: The Enduring Influence of the Christian Right* (New York: The Guilford Press, 1998); Sara Diamond, *Spiritual Warfare: The Politics of the Christian Right* (Boston, MA: South End Press, 1989); Dan Gilgoff, *The Jesus Machine* (New York: St. Martin's Griffin, 2007); Esther Kaplan, *With God on Their Side* (New York: The New Press, 2004); Robert C. Liebman and Robert Wuthnow, eds., *The New Christian Right* (New York: Aldine Publishing Company, 1983); David G. Bromley and Anson Shupe, eds., *New Christian Politics* (Macon, GA: Mercer, 1984); Gary Wills, *Heart and Head: American Christianities* (New York: Penguin Press, 2007); Theda Skocpol and Vanessa Williamson, *The Tea Party and the Remaking of Republican Conservatism* (Oxford: Oxford University Press, 2011); Lauren Langman, "Cycles of Contention: The Rise and Fall of the Tea Party," *Critical Sociology* 38, no. 4 (July 2012): 469–94; Matthew Lyons, *Insurgent Supremacists: The U.S. Far Right's Challenge to State and Empire* (Oakland: PM Press, 2018).
9 Abby Ferber, "Racial Warriors and Weekend Warriors: The Construction of Masculinity in Mythopoetic and White Supremacist Discourse," *Men and Masculinities* 3, no. 1 (July 2000): 31.
10 Rory McVeigh, *The Rise of the Ku Klux Klan* (Minneapolis: University of Minnesota Press, 2009); Mitch Berbrier, "The Victim Ideology of White Supremacists and White Separatists in the United States," *Sociological Focus* 33, no. 2 (2000): 175–91, 187.
11 Kathleen M. Blee, "Women in the 1920s' Ku Klux Klan Movement." *Feminist Studies* 17, no. 1 (1991): 57–77; Linda Gordon, *The Second Coming of the KKK: The Ku Klux Klan of the 1920s and the American Political Tradition* (New York: Liveright, 2017); Glen Jeansonne, *Women of the Far Right: The Mothers' Movement and World War II* (Chicago, IL: University of Chicago Press, 1996); Michelle M. Nickerson, *Mothers of Conservatism: Women and the Postwar Right* (Princeton, NJ: Princeton University Press, 2012).
12 Ziad W. Munson, *The Making of Pro-life Activists: How Social Movement Mobilization Works* (Chicago, IL: University of Chicago Press, 2009); Carole Joffe, "Working with Dr. Tiller: Staff Recollections Of Women's Health Care Services of Wichita," *Perspectives on Sexual and Reproductive Health* 43, no. 3 (August 9, 2011): 199–204; Carol Mason, *Killing for Life: The Apocalyptic Narrative of Pro-life Politics* (Ithaca, NY: Cornell Press, 2002); Kristin Luker, *Abortion and the Politics of Motherhood* (University of California Press, 1984), http://www.jstor.org/stable/10.1525/j.ctt1ppck8.
13 Kathleen M. Blee and Kimberly A. Creasap, "Conservative and Right-Wing Movements," *Annual Review of Sociology* 36, no. 1 (2010): 270.
14 See, for example, Beth Allison Barr, *The Making of Biblical Womanhood: How the Subjugation of Women Became Gospel Truth* (Grand Rapids, MI: Brazos Press, 2021); Kristen Kobes Du Mez, *Jesus and John Wayne* (New York: Liveright, 2020); John P. Bartkowski, "Debating Patriarchy: Discursive Disputes over Spousal Authority among Evangelical Family Commentators," *Journal for the Scientific Study of Religion* 36, no. 3 (1997): 393–410; Margaret Lamberts Bendroth, "Fundamentalism and the Family: Gender, Culture, and the American Pro-family Movement," *Journal of Women's History* 10, no. 4 (1999): 35–54; Chelsea Ebin, "Tomorrow's Past Today: The Prefigurative Construction of Christian Right Belonging," in *American Examples: New Conversations about Religion*, Vol. 3, ed. Michael J. Altman (Tuscaloosa, AL: University

xiv Preface

of Alabama Press, forthcoming); Susan Jeffords, *Hard Bodies: Hollywood Masculinity in the Reagan Era* (New Brunswick, NJ: Rutgers University Press, 1994).

15 Sophie Bjork-James, *The Divine Institution: White Evangelicalism's Politics of the Family* (New Brunswick, NJ: Rutgers University Press, 2021); Anthea Butler, *White Evangelical Racism: The Politics of Morality in America* (Chapel Hill: The University of North Carolina Press, 2021).

16 Talal Asad, *Formations of the Secular: Christianity, Islam, and Modernity* (Stanford, CA: Stanford University Press, 2003); Tisa Wenger, *Religious Freedom: The Contested History of an American Ideal* (Chapel Hill: The University of North Carolina Press, 2017).

ACKNOWLEDGMENTS

We want to thank everyone who helped make this book possible, including all the people who have given advice, support, and contributions to the IRMS from which this volume was born. We are excited that the majority of the chapters in this volume come from our fellows or mentees.

We especially appreciate the hard work of our interns and fact-checkers: Jessa Mellea, Ha-Jung Kim, Devon Rodriguez, and Natalie Li.

We are also grateful to the Berkeley Center for Right-Wing Studies for its role in supporting the development of some of these chapters through its conferences and working group.

And, of course, we are incredibly thankful for all the contributors to this volume who have shared their excellent work in this format.

NOTES ON CONTRIBUTORS

Emily K. Carian is Co-founder and Board Chair of the Institute for Research on Male Supremacism, USA, and Assistant Professor of Sociology at California State University, San Bernardino, USA. Her research examines the mechanisms that sustain gender inequality, including male supremacism and backlash among men's rights activists.

Katherine Cross is a scholar and PhD student at the University of Washington's School of Information, USA, where she studies the dynamics of online harassment campaigns. At the time her chapter was originally written (2013), she was a board member of the Sylvia Rivera Law Project.

Alexis de Coning is a South African immigrant to the USA, and a doctoral candidate at the University of Colorado Boulder, USA. Her dissertation considers the history and development of the men's rights movement and focuses on the movement's transition from print to digital media from 1990 to 2010.

Julia R. DeCook is an Assistant Professor of Advocacy and Social Change in the School of Communication at Loyola University Chicago, USA. Her research interests include platform governance, online hate groups, race and gender, digital culture, and social justice and technology.

Alex DiBranco is Co-founder and Executive Director of the IRMS, USA. Her research focuses on male supremacist ideologies and violence, from the anti-abortion movement to misogynist incels, and on the development of rightist infrastructure over the past half-century.

Notes on Contributors **xvii**

Chelsea Ebin is Co-founder and Treasurer of the IRMS, USA, and Assistant Professor of Politics at Centre College, Kentucky, USA. Her research focuses on the relationship between American political development and the Right, with a focus on male, white, and Christian supremacisms.

Greta Jasser is a Research Associate at University of Hildesheim, Germany, and PhD student at Leuphana University Lüneburg, Germany. She researches far-right and misogynist online networks with an interest in technology, platforms, affordances, and ideologies.

Megan Kelly is a PhD candidate at the University of Basel, Switzerland. Her research examines the construction of masculinities and (de-)radicalization narratives among male supremacists.

Matthew N. Lyons writes regularly for *Three Way Fight*, a radical antifascist blog. He has written several books and for various journals, magazines, and websites. His work focuses on the interplay between right-wing movements and systems of oppression, and responses to these movements by leftists, liberals, and the state.

Carol Mason is University Research Professor at the University of Kentucky, USA, and affiliate faculty at Berkeley Center for Right-Wing Studies, USA. She is the author of three books on various aspects of the rise of the Right.

Meadhbh Park is an MA graduate of Peace and Conflict Studies from University College Dublin, Ireland, and specializes in the areas of the far right and masculinity. She has worked as a research consultant for U.S. and U.K. organizations, such as Life After Hate and Groundswell Project UK, and has helped develop training programs for practitioners, service users, and others who have been affected by far-right ideologies.

Meredith L. Pruden is a postdoctoral research associate at the University of North Carolina at Chapel Hill's Center for Information, Technology, and Public Life, USA, and a fellow with the IRMS, USA. Her work is rooted in feminist media studies, and she uses a combination of quantitative computational and qualitative techniques to explore white and male supremacy, violent misogyny, and far-right politics, as well as the mis/disinformation and conspiracy thinking associated with these groups.

Amélie Ribieras is an Associate Professor at Panthéon-Assas-Paris 2 University, France, where she teaches legal English. Her research focuses on conservative women's mobilization under the leadership of activist Phyllis Schlafly, as well as on their discourse on women, gender, and the family.

xviii Notes on Contributors

Ann-Kathrin Rothermel is a Research Associate, Lecturer, and PhD candidate at the Chair for International Relations of the University of Potsdam, Germany, and a research fellow with the Berlin Graduate School for Global and Transregional Studies, Germany, and the IRMS, USA. In her research, she uses feminist discourse approaches to analyze radicalization dynamics in online male supremacist groups, as well as gendered dynamics of change in international counterterrorism agendas.

PART I

Foundations

1

MOBILIZING MISOGYNY

Alex DiBranco

This chapter was originally published by Political Research Associates on March 8, 2017. The chapter has been edited from its original version in accordance with the No Notoriety campaign's recommendation not to name perpetrators of mass violence.

Unquestionably, President Donald Trump's demonstrated enthusiasm for catering to the Christian Right on abortion—and obliterating their memory of his pro-choice past—spells trouble for reproductive rights. But that's not the only threat to women under Trump's new order. Trump's campaign distinguished itself from those of other Republican candidates by its attacks on women: regularly insulting women's appearances or behavior and defending physical and sexual harassment and violence against them. Sometimes, Trump's threatening and offensive rhetoric directly targeted his Democratic opponent, Hillary Rodham Clinton, the first woman major party nominee for president, from calling her a "nasty woman" to suggesting there might be a Second Amendment "remedy" in case of her election.[1]

This rhetoric energized members of a secular misogynist Right—such as the men's rights movement and, more recently, the "Alt Right"—that has flourished online since the 1990s. And it found no pushback from a brand of conservative, libertarian "feminism"—another '90s development—that provides a dangerously legitimizing female face for misogynist ideology centered on overt hostility to women and the promulgation of rape culture.

Effectively fighting mobilizations like those emboldened by Trump's election requires accurately understanding their composition—one in which misogyny thrives alongside, and intertwined with, racism.

DOI: 10.4324/9781003164722-2

4 Alex DiBranco

Patriarchal Traditionalism from White Supremacy to the Christian Right

Male supremacism, enshrined in the nation's founding documents, is as fundamental to U.S. history as White Anglo-Saxon Protestant (WASP) nativism.[2] The same patriarchal stance—combining race, religion, and nativism—fuels conservative Christian ideology on appropriate gender roles. (Transgender women and men and genderqueer individuals also violate these designated roles.) Especially in the last 100 years, as some women have succeeded in pushing back against the sexist world they inherited, social and political movements have emerged to defend traditional gender structures.

Amid Second Wave feminism, the antifeminists Phyllis Schlafly (a Roman Catholic) and Beverly LaHaye (an evangelical) followed in this tradition when they organized a "pro-family" movement to stop the ratification of the 1972 Equal Rights Amendment (ERA). Though themselves prominent activists, LaHaye and the late Schlafly promoted submission to husbands and attacked women seeking careers.[3]

Abortion, contraception, and sexuality education all threaten the enforcement of traditional gender roles. After the *Roe v. Wade* decision legalizing abortion in 1973, conservative evangelicals joined with the existing Catholic "prolife" movement in the creation of the Christian Right, and abortion became "a vital component of [the Right's] fight to protect the bottom line of traditional family values—the dominance of white, male power and control," as PRA's Jean Hardisty and Pam Chamberlain observed. The anti-abortion movement drew together members of the Religious Right and White supremacists and neonazis, who contributed to the rising violence against clinic providers in the 1990s perpetrated primarily by White men.[4] (The legacy of White supremacy, Hardisty and Chamberlain continue, can be seen in how "the Right applies race and class criteria that distinguish between the rights of white, middle-class women and low-income women of color." This dynamic led to the 1990s stereotype of the "welfare queen" and welfare reform under Bill Clinton designed to discourage women of color and immigrant women from having "too many" children.[5])

But attacks on women's reproductive rights have often come wrapped in the guise of chivalry, framed as "moral issues" and "family values" rather than misogyny. To gain wider acceptance, the anti-abortion movement has adopted a framework of "protecting women," vilifying abortion providers as preying on weak women threatened by the physical and mental health consequences of abortion.[6] That effort has made significant legislative progress in recent years, with a slew of state anti-abortion bills in 2011. Despite this official strategy, clinic protesters on the ground expose their misogyny in calling women "murderers" and "whores" and sometimes resorting to physical intimidation.[7]

In 2012, contraception came under increased attack as immoral in the debate over healthcare reform. Anti-abortion groups have long denounced the "morning after pill" as an abortifacient yet had otherwise tended to avoid pushing an unpopular position against contraception, largely considered a settled issue.

When law student Sandra Fluke testified in favor of contraceptive coverage, Rush Limbaugh infamously ranted about her being a "slut" and a "prostitute" who should be required to post sex videos online.[8]

Set on proving that his "pro-choice" days were behind him, during the 2016 campaign, Trump denounced Planned Parenthood as an "abortion factory" and selected hard-line reproductive and LGBTQ rights opponent Indiana governor Mike Pence as his running mate. In his eagerness, Trump unknowingly violated the Christian Right's strategic deployment of a "kinder, gentler" image[9] when he announced that women who obtained an illegal abortion should face "punishment." Although Trump backpedaled to mollify anti-abortion groups that claim to protect women, his original statement was characteristic of the anti-woman vitriol of his campaign and may have appealed to the existing hatred demonstrated by clinic protesters.[10]

The Christian Right's attack on women isn't limited to reproductive issues. Schlafly frequently argued that women make false accusations of sexual assault and domestic violence—her grounds for opposing the Violence Against Women Act (VAWA) and suggesting that there exists a "war on men."[11] Concerned Women for America (CWA), a major Christian Right group founded by Beverly LaHaye, claims that the "wage gap" results from women's own choices and therefore opposes equal pay legislation.[12] In such respects, Christian Right ideology aligns with that of equity feminism and men's rights.

Equity Feminism and Men's Rights

In 1991, "Women for Judge Thomas" formed to defend conservative Supreme Court nominee Clarence Thomas against Anita Hill's sexual harassment allegations. The following year this group institutionalized itself as the Independent Women's Forum (IWF), under the premise that, as co-founder Anita Blair declared, feminism should have "declared victory and gone home" by 1978.[13] The idea that, at least in the U.S., women have achieved equality underlies the secular libertarian philosophy of "equity feminism" (also "individualist feminism").[14] In 2009, IWF's then-president Michelle Bernard explained, "[W]e have a philosophical belief that women are not victims … we believe that free markets are really the great equalizer, and will allow women to become truly equal with men in areas where we still may be unequal."[15] This ideology diverges from patriarchal traditionalism in applauding successful career women (and holding varied views on abortion), replacing it with a sexism that blames women's continuing underrepresentation in positions of influence on personal choices and intrinsic differences, and to protect this worldview, frequently dismisses contradictory evidence.[16]

By offering a provocative dissident women's voice, presenting "the other side," equity feminists can forego the grassroots organizing of Schlafly and LaHaye[17] while benefiting from extensive media dissemination of its ideas. As former IWF executive director Barbara Ledeen put it, "You can't have white guys saying you don't need affirmative action."[18]

6 Alex DiBranco

Of course, plenty of White guys have spoken out against affirmative action, developing a male victimhood ideology to complement equity feminism's rejection of female victims. In 1988, Warren Farrell, who had once been involved with feminist organizing of men's consciousness group, published the book *Why Men Are the Way They Are*,

> depicting a world where women—particularly female executives—wield vast influence. Even those women who are less successful have 'enormous sexual leverage over men.'[19]

When men think about women's gains, Caryl Rivers and Rosalind C. Barnett write in *The New Soft War on Women: How the Myth of Female Ascendance Is Hurting Women, Men—and Our Economy*, "There's a tendency to circle the wagons, to exaggerate how far women have come and how far men have fallen."[20] Alarm over women's advancement emerges repeatedly in U.S. history: as Danielle Paquette points out in the *Washington Post*, 30 years prior to Farrell's book, Harvard historian Arthur Schlesinger, Jr. worried over the trickle of wives into the 1950s workforce: "Women seem an expanding, aggressive force, seizing new domains like a conquering army, while men, more and more on the defensive, are hardly able to hold their own and gratefully accept assignments from their new rulers."[21]

Farrell, dubbed the "father of the men's rights movement," followed up in 1993 with *The Myth of Male Power: Why Men Are the Disposable Sex*, where he suggested that American (White) men were the new "nigger," threatened by women's ability to cry sexual harassment and "date rape." According to sociologist Michael Kimmel, this became the movement's "bible," awakening men to their status as victims of women's ascendancy.[22] Like White supremacist movements, men's rights ideology warns White men that they are losing their place in society. Where equity feminism thrives among elite women with access to major communications platforms, the men's rights movement is a decentralized "netroots" movement that draws men who feel less privileged, especially those with employment troubles and failures in romantic relationships.

Claiming rampant false accusations of rape and violence is one of the most prevalent men's rights and equity feminist talking points.[23] *Who Stole Feminism?*, a classic among conservative "feminists" published the following year by Christina Hoff Sommers, similarly argues that "gender" or "radical" feminists lie about rates of rape and domestic violence. Speaking on campus sexual assault in 2014, Sommers, a scholar at the conservative American Enterprise Institute, repeated the same themes of "false accusations" and "[i]nflated statistics," declaring, "I believe that the rape culture movement is fueled by exaggerated claims of intimacy and a lot of paranoia about men."[24] A spokesperson for A Voice for Men (AVFM), one of the most prominent men's rights organizations, rejected rape "hysteria...as a scam" and baselessly claimed that sexual assault affects only about 2% of women—far from the Centers for Disease Control and Prevention's one-in-five statistic.[25]

Although equity feminists reject the existence of structural constraints on women, like men's rights activists (MRA) they suggest that American boys and men suffer at the hands of gender feminists. In 2000, Sommers wrote *The War against Boys: How Misguided Feminism Is Harming Our Young Men*, and a flurry of concern over boys' educational achievements in 2013 landed her in major outlets including, *The New York Times*, *TIME Magazine*, and *The Atlantic*. Psychologist Helen Smith, one of IWF's "Modern Feminists," suggested in 2012 that "the deck is so stacked against men that they are 'going Galt,'" a reference to Ayn Rand's novel *Atlas Shrugged*, an MRA favorite.[26]

Equity feminism's depiction of women as liars with "victim mentalities" dovetails alarmingly with (and legitimizes) the online manifestation of the men's rights movement, which uses more virulent and hateful rhetoric to convey the same argument.

Male Supremacist Harassment and Violence

Paul Elam has made attempts at a respectable mainstream image, organizing the movement's first in-person conference. But he also has a history of advocating violence, writing that women who go clubbing are "begging" to be raped, and that

> there are a lot of women who get pummeled and pumped because they are stupid (and often arrogant) enough to walk [through] life with the equivalent of a I'M A STUPID, CONNIVING BITCH—PLEASE RAPE ME neon sign glowing above their empty little narcissistic heads.[27]

Another site Elam launched, Register-her.com, allowed men to post personal information for women they claim made false accusations (or otherwise outraged the movement) in order to target them for harassment. In 2011, feminist writer Jessica Valenti fled her house under a barrage of threats after her information appeared on this site.

Other strains of online male supremacism include pick-up artists (PUAs), who advocate male sexual entitlement and give sexist advice on seducing women; the Red Pill, a community named for a *Matrix* reference that seeks to awaken men to the "reality" of dominant "feminist culture";[28] Men Going Their Own Way, which advocates cutting ties with women; and Jack Donovan's "gang masculinity," which calls on men to form warrior gangs to escape domestication by women.[29] Deviating from the online movement's predominantly secular nature are Christian masculinists, who, as Dianna Anderson writes at *Rewire*, "have fused manosphere rhetoric with what they see as 'biblical' gender roles to envision a hierarchical, patriarchal ideal world."[30] These varied communities share adherents, though there is also conflict among their competing perspectives.

The virulent misogyny promoted by male supremacists, often couched as antifeminism and accompanied by racism and nativism, has serious repercussions that play out on a global stage. In 1989, the Montreal mass shooter killed 14 women at an engineering school under the guise of "fighting feminism."[31] In 2009, the Collier Township gym shooter killed three women and then himself

8 Alex DiBranco

at a fitness class in Pennsylvania, leaving behind a website that complained about being rejected by women (and leading PUAs to coin the term "going Sodini").[32] The Norway attacker murdered 77 adults and children in Norway in 2011, leaving behind a manifesto attacking "the radical feminist agenda," Islam, political correctness, and "Cultural Marxism" (see David Neiwart's article in this issue).[33] And in May 2014, the Santa Barbara perpetrator set out to "slaughter every single spoiled, stuck-up blonde slut" at the "hottest" sorority at the University of California, Santa Barbara, writing, "I don't know why you girls aren't attracted to me, but I will punish you for it."[34] He ultimately killed six people and himself, though he failed to make it inside the sorority.

The Southern Poverty Law Center's *Intelligence Report* editor-in-chief, Mark Potok, wrote,

> Men's rights activists did not tell [the Santa Barbara perpetrator] to kill—but in their writings, it seems like many of them wouldn't mind doing some killing of their own. [The Santa Barbara perpetrator] said as much in his manifesto, writing that PUAHate "confirmed many of the theories I had about how wicked and degenerate women really are" and showed him "how bleak and cruel the world is due to the evilness of women."[35]

The Santa Barbara perpetrator's story has parallels with that of the White supremacist Charleston church shooter, convicted in 2016 of murdering nine Black congregants at a Charleston church.[36] Though the media typically portrays such acts of right-wing violence as perpetrated by mentally disturbed individuals[37]—so-called Lone Wolves—as PRA contributor Naomi Braine writes, "a decision to act alone does not mean acting outside of social movement frameworks, philosophies, and networks."[38] Both young men encountered inaccurate and hateful rhetoric online that inflamed existing dissatisfactions by depicting them as victims.[39] Thus, Lone Wolf violence emerges from a right-wing context "systematically erased" by media misrepresentation of these as isolated and irrational actors.

Some members of the male supremacist online movement hailed the Santa Barbara perpetrator as a hero on PUAHate.com messaging boards or Facebook fan pages.[40] Others distanced themselves while defending their own misogynist content, much as the Council of Conservative Citizens, the White nationalist group the Charleston church shooter cited in his manifesto, claimed to condemn the Charleston church shooter's violence while blaming society for ignoring White people's "legitimate grievances."[41] Daryush Valizadeh ("Roosh V"), a professional PUA and founder of the site *Return of Kings*, argued, "Until you give men like [the Santa Barbara perpetrator] a way to have sex, either by encouraging them to learn game, seek out a Thai wife, or engage in legalized prostitution... it's inevitable for another massacre to occur."[42]

Meanwhile, equity feminists stepped up to whitewash a clearly misogynist attack. IWF senior editor Charlotte Hays wrote that calling the Santa Barbara perpetrator's violence a "product of sexism" was a "bizarre response" by feminists.[43]

Video Games, Misogyny, and the Alt Right

Video games might not seem like a vital social justice battleground. However, as sociologist and gaming critic Katherine Cross has pointed out, the virulence of online White male reactions to increasing gender and racial diversity in game players and creators, and to critiques of the industry's sexism, indicates a problem with dismissing this as a trivial issue.[44] Only a few months after the Santa Barbara perpetrator's fatal 2014 attack, an incident dubbed "Gamergate," ostensibly about gaming industry ethics and media corruption, resulted in the Federal Bureau of Investigation (FBI) looking into the barrage of violent rape and death threats against women who criticized video games' sexist portrayals of women and lack of diversity.[45] Anita Sarkeesian, one of the primary targets, canceled a talk at Utah State University after the school received a threat to repeat the Montreal mass shooter's massacre and demonstrate "what feminist lies and poison have done to the men of America."[46] While circles of progressive female journalists took the movement behind Gamergate seriously, their voices were largely ignored by the mainstream media.[47]

Through Gamergate, vocal misogynist personalities such as Mike Cernovich, associated with the pick-up artist community, and Milo Yiannopoulos, a *Breitbart* writer, expanded their online following to be leveraged in future attacks on feminism and women. Yiannopoulos had over 300,000 Twitter followers at the time the social media platform finally banned him for offensive content in 2016; at the time of this writing, he has more than 1.9 million Facebook likes and 568,000 subscribers on YouTube, in addition to his platform at *Breitbart*, where he has bragged about writing headlines such as "Would You Rather Your Child Had Feminism or Cancer?"[48] In "An Establishment Conservative's Guide to the Alt-Right," Yiannopoulos and co-author Allum Bokhari write, "The so-called online 'manosphere,' the nemeses of left-wing feminism, quickly became one of the alt-right's most distinctive constituencies."

The New Yorker's Andrew Marantz writes that Cernovich "developed a theory of white-male identity politics: men were oppressed by feminism, and political correctness prevented the discussion of obvious truths, such as the criminal proclivities of certain ethnic groups."[49] In 2016, in tweets that received more than 100 million views, Cernovich focused on supporting "unapologetically masculine" Trump and attacking Hillary Clinton with conspiracy theories regarding her failing health and emails.

Following Trump's election, mainstream and progressive media outlets worried that using the movement's chosen name, the Alt Right, helped euphemize and normalize old-fashioned bigotry. As *Think Progress'* editors wrote, "[Alt Right Leader Richard] Spencer and his ilk are essentially standard-issue white supremacists who discovered a clever way to make themselves appear more innocuous— even a little hip"; their publication, they declared, wouldn't do "racists' public relations work for them."[50]

But nowhere in this statement from a major progressive news outlet exists a single reference to sexism or misogyny—a glaring omission given its significance

10 Alex DiBranco

to the Alt Right's mobilization to defeat the first woman to receive a major party nomination for president.[51] Some respected outlets and organizations, including the Associated Press and SPLC, described the movement's misogyny, but their recommended definitions referenced White nationalism, neglecting to acknowledge male supremacy as a core component.[52] While some Alt Right leaders, such as former *Breitbart* executive (now Trump administration chief strategist) Stephen Bannon, hail from more racist corners of the umbrella movement, others, like Yiannopoulos and Cernovich, rose to prominence primarily on their misogynist rhetoric.

These omissions aren't surprising. In a 2008 study, "The Absence of a Gender Justice Framework in Social Justice Organizing," activist and consultant Linda Burnham wrote, "All too many organizers and activists affirm a commitment to women's human rights or gender justice while having no clear idea of sexism as a systemic phenomenon with tangled historical, social, economic and cultural roots and multiple manifestations." In her interviews of activists, Burnham found "the subordination of sexism as a legitimate concern among 'competing isms,'" antipathy to the feminist movement (which is perceived as White), a feeling that "there's already a level of equity and there's no need to struggle over it anymore," and a lack of tools for structural analysis.[53] (Groups with a better intersectional approach, Burnham footnoted, included reproductive justice organizations like SisterSong.[54])

Matthew N. Lyons, co-author of *Right-Wing Populism in America*, further argues that this heightened misogyny distinguishes the Alt Right from other White supremacist and neonazi mobilizations, which have practiced a "quasi-feminism" that viewed women as holding distinct but complementary gender roles important to the movement. Especially since the 1980s, Lyons writes, neonazi groups have increasingly lauded White women as "race warriors."[55]

Some early Alt Right writers did encourage their compatriots to do more to attract women and root out sexual harassment.[56] Now even that has disappeared. Today the movement is better characterized by dismissive ideology like that of White male supremacist Matt Forney, who asserts in a 2012 "anti-feminist classic" post on *Alternative Right* that women are "herd creatures" who are "unimportant" to the men who will make history. "Attempting to convince such flighty creatures to join the alt-right with logical arguments is like begging escaped inmates to please pretty please come back to the insane asylum."[57] Forney also argues, "Every feminist, deep down, wants nothing more than a rapist's baby in her belly."[58] Lyons writes,

> Alt-rightists tell us that it's natural for men to rule over women and that women want and need this, that "giving women freedom [was] one of mankind's greatest mistakes," that women should "never be allowed to make foreign policy [because] their vindictiveness knows no bounds," that feminism is defined by mental illness and has turned women into "caricatures of irrationality and hysteria."[59]

Richard Spencer, the now-infamous White nationalist leader credited with coining the term "Alt Right," promotes male supremacist rhetoric that includes yet goes beyond traditional arguments for women belonging in the home. Along with his position on women's "vindictiveness" (quoted by Lyons above), Spencer defended Trump against sexual assault accusations with the argument, "At some part of every woman's soul, they want to be taken by a strong man."[60]

Cas Mudde, a Dutch political scientist who studies right-wing movements, describes the Alt Right's assertion of women's inferiority as "a sexist interpretation of xenophobia. It's the same view they have of immigrants and minorities, that they're threatening their way of life. A life where men are dominant. A life where they have privilege in virtually every domain."[61]

Vox writer Aja Romano argues that misogyny is not only a significant part of the Alt Right; it's the "gateway drug" for the recruitment of disaffected White men into racist communities. David Futrelle, a journalist who watches the men's rights and other online misogynist movements, told *Vox* that it's "close to impossible to overstate the role of Gamergate in the process of [alt-right] radicalization. ... Gamergate was based on the same sense of aggrieved entitlement that drives the alt-right—and many Trump voters." Within this narrative, Futrelle said, they saw their harassment of women as defending "an imperiled culture," moving into other online enclaves populated by neonazis and White supremacists that recruited them for "fighting against 'white genocide.'"[62]

2016 Election: Where Has This Misogyny Led Us?

In 2006, IWF managing director Carrie L. Lukas wrote,

> In the past, victims of rape were made to feel that the crime was their fault. Many women around the world still suffer this bias. Today in the United States, the pendulum has swung too far in the other direction. A man accused of rape often is convicted in the court of public opinion without evidence.[63]

Yet in Trump's campaign, that was far from the case. Multiple accusations of sexual assault and harassment against the Republican candidate were ignored throughout the campaign; when audio recordings exposing him admitting to sexual assault finally brought widespread attention to his treatment of women, he defended his comments as "locker-room talk." And those comments did not ultimately cost him the election.

While IWF and equity feminism, like other libertarian ideologies, tend toward the conservative side of the political spectrum, there is more diversity there than among women in anti-feminist movements and the Christian Right. This allows the ideological tent to include Democrats like Christina Hoff Sommers, independents like former IWF president Michelle Bernard, and Republican women who might criticize aspects of their party's gender dynamics. After applauding

Sarah Palin for breaking free of sexist attempts to control her image as the 2008 Republican vice-presidential nominee, in 2009, Bernard spoke of bright prospects ahead for Hillary Clinton: "She is incredibly smart, brilliant, an excellent campaigner, and I think her time will come."[64]

However, misogynist and anti-feminist Rightist ideologies have taken a toll beyond leaders' control. Though during the primaries IWF gave favorable attention to Carly Fiorina, the only female Republican candidate, a poll showed Trump leading the Republican pack among female voters. Historian Catherine Rymph explained that the exodus of feminism and women's rights advocacy from the GOP means that, among those left, "voters, including women, who don't like Democratic feminism or so-called 'political correctness' in general may very well find refreshing Trump's delight in using language about women that many find offensive."[65] When then-*Fox News* anchor Megyn Kelly criticized Trump's misogyny while moderating a 2015 primary debate, Trump responded, to audience cheers, that "the big problem this country has is being politically correct"— code for resistance to misogyny, racism, xenophobia, and homophobia. Trump went on to call Kelly a "bimbo" and imply she was menstruating. After Trump's continued attacks on Twitter rallied online misogynists to further harassment, Kelly received death threats.[66]

For some equity feminists, it's gone too far. IWF senior editor Charlotte Hays argues that Trump's history of misogynist statements goes beyond "bucking political correctness." In March 2016, Hays worried, "If Trump is the nominee, the [Leftist claims of a] 'war on women' will be back with a vengeance. And this time there will be a degree of fairness in the charge."[67] Sommers referred to Trump as an example of "amoral masculinity" that "preys on women."[68] She joined conservative female media pundits in calling for Trump to fire his original campaign manager, Corey Lewandowski, after *Breitbart News* reporter Michelle Fields charged him with physically assaulting her.[69] Trump denied Lewandowski's culpability, only firing him three months later after apparently unrelated problems.[70] And when former *Fox News* anchor Gretchen Carlson filed suit against CEO Roger Ailes for sexual harassment—which Kelly also reported experiencing—Trump asserted that Carlson's accusations against his informal advisor were "[t]otally unfounded."[71]

Fields resigned from *Breitbart*, which former executive and Trump senior strategist Stephen Bannon proudly called "the platform for the alt-right,"[72] over the outlet's inadequate response.[73] Commenting on the successive Alt Right online harassment of Fields, Kelly said, "This woman hasn't done anything wrong, anything, other than find herself on the wrong end of these folks, for whom she used to work."[74]

Some equity feminists, like Sommers, may have expected their own elite conservative colleagues to be taken seriously, not realizing that the damage done in disparaging other women would find its way back to them. In response to Sommers' criticism of Trump, Mike Cernovich disdainfully pointed out that she had previously "mocked women who played the damsel in distress."[75]

On the other hand, the appreciation for Hillary Clinton's political merits seems to have disappeared under IWF's new leadership, which got on board with Trump after his nomination. Trump hired IWF board member Kellyanne Conway to replace Lewandowski as his new campaign manager, which followed the organization's efforts to peddle palatable sexism under a female face. IWF's campaign affiliate, Independent Women's Voice (IWV), supported Trump's campaign, with CEO Heather Higgins coming around to offer her full-throated support in the general election.[76]

The men's rights movement lacked these internal divisions over Trump's outright misogyny. Early in the primary season, members of online male supremacist communities touted Trump as an example of an "alpha" male given how "he insults and dominates women, preys on their insecurities and refuses to ever apologize for it."[77] And as though he was directly channeling men's rights talking points, at a campaign rally in May 2016 Trump declared,

> All of the men, we're petrified to speak to women anymore. …You know what? The women get it better than we do, folks. They get it better than we do. If [Hillary Clinton] didn't play [the woman] card, she has nothing.[78]

While Trump's rhetoric reflects MRA vitriol, it is the long fight against feminism by groups embraced in the mainstream, like equity feminists and Republican women, that legitimized the candidacy—and election—of an overt misogynist who has bragged about sexual assault.

Defending Gender Justice Post-Election

Trump's rhetoric shares more in common with equity feminist and men's rights ideologies than with "family values" framing—and with the reality of Christian Right misogyny, such as the vitriol of clinic protesters and the anti-feminism of the late Phyllis Schlafly, a staunch Trump supporter.

It will be important to track the growing connections between these secular and religious movements, bridged by underlying misogyny, racism, and nativism, especially as individuals aligned with the Alt Right, like Bannon, and equity feminism, like Conway, gain influence. The seeds are already there. The libertarian Koch brothers, infamous major donors to libertarian and conservative causes, fund both IWF and CWA. Alt Right figures like blogger Matt Forney oppose reproductive rights, writing that pro-choice women have "evil" in their souls and that "[g]irls who kill their own children despise life itself and will do their best to destroy yours."[79] Pick-up artist communities advise members to seek submissive wives who can easily be controlled and oppose abortion and contraception as a means of weighing them down with children.[80] And, extending "father's rights" arguments within the men's rights movement, a Missouri lawmaker proposed in 2014 a bill requiring paternal consent to an abortion.[81]

14 Alex DiBranco

The influence of ideology on the broader population, outside of active movement participants, bears particular importance with a president who uses his platform to broadcast virulent misogyny, racism, nativism, and Islamophobia.[82] In tracking reported bias-related incidents since Election Day, the Southern Poverty Law Center found that perpetrators were most likely to explicitly reference Trump in anti-woman attacks—82% of the 45 reported incidents, more than double the next-highest rate.[83] In multiple incidents of harassment of women, assailants from middle school boys to groups of adult men parroted Trump's boast that he can "[g]rab [women] by the pussy."[84]

Sen. Jeff Sessions (R–AL) originally claimed it was a "stretch" to "characterize [Trump's comment] as sexual assault" (later backpedaling under questioning during his confirmation hearing for U.S. attorney general).[85] Before Trump was even sworn in as president, his administration's threat to reproductive rights, protections addressing violence against women and campus rape, and other women's equality programs had already been made alarmingly clear.[86] Under the Trump-Pence administration, threats will come from the Christian Right, conservative secular and libertarian groups, empowered White supremacist figures, and, of course, a president who has shown his comfort with overt displays of racism, nativism, and misogyny. This disturbing combination may now jeopardize a wider expanse of policies reducing structural oppression that had seemed settled.

But the fact of this combined threat may also bring more dissenters into a more holistic response. Loretta Ross, a longtime reproductive justice and women's human rights leader, is optimistic about the power vested in intersectional feminist organizing. "Now with the Women's March on Washington using the 'Women's Rights Are Human Rights' call for mobilizations in <u>616 simultaneous marches</u> worldwide," she wrote at *Rewire*,

> I believe feminists in the United States have finally caught up to the rest of the global women's movement. I feel like celebrating our inevitable progress toward victory for equality, dignity, and justice, despite the reasons we are marching in the first place: to unite to challenge the immoral and probably illegitimate presidency of Donald Trump.[87]

Notes

1 David S. Cohen, "Trump's Assassination Dog Whistle Was Even Scarier Than You Think," *Rolling Stone*, August 9, 2016, http://www.rollingstone.com/politics/features/trumps-assassination-dog-whistle-was-scarier-than-you-think-w433615.

2 Alex DiBranco and Chip Berlet, "The Ideological Roots of the Republican Party and Its Shift to the Right in the 2016 Election," working draft, http://www.progressive-movements.us/now/site-guide/research-resources/#ideological.

3 Matthew N. Lyons, "Notes on Women and Right-Wing Movements – Part Two," *ThreeWayFight* (blog), October 1, 2005, http://threewayfight.blogspot.com/2005/10/notes-on-women-and-right-wing.html.

4 Pam Chamberlain and Jean Hardisty, "Reproducing Patriarchy: Reproductive Rights Under Siege," *Political Research Associates*, April 1, 2000, https://www.politicalresearch. org/2000/04/01/reproductive-patriarchy-reproductive-rights-under-siege.

5 Political Research Associates, *Defending Reproductive Justice: An Activist Resource Kit* (Somerville: Political Research Associates, 2013), https://www.politicalresearch.org/ sites/default/files/2018-10/Defending-Reproductive-Justice-ARK-Final.pdf.

6 Political Research Associates, *Defending Reproductive Justice.*

7 Liz Welch, "6 Women on Their Terrifying, Infuriating Encounters with Abortion Clinic Protesters," *Cosmopolitan*, February 21, 2014, http://www.cosmopolitan.com/ politics/news/a5669/abortion-clinic-protesters/.

8 Caryl Rivers and Rosalind C. Barnett, *The New Soft War on Women: How the Myth of Female Ascendance Is Hurting Women, Men—and Our Economy* (New York: Tarcher/ Penguin, 2013), 85.

9 Alex DiBranco, "Profiles on the Right: Americans United For Life," *Political Research Associates*, April 7, 2014, https://www.politicalresearch.org/2014/04/07/profiles-on-the-right-americans-united-for-life/#sthash.Zz04Fcm6.epvFr2db.dpbs.

10 Kevin Cirilli, "Trump Reverses on Abortion Ban, Saying Doctors, Not Women, Would Be Punished," *Bloomberg Politics*, March 30, 2016, http://www.bloomberg.com/politics/articles/2016-03-30/trump-says-abortion-ban-should-carry-punishment-for-women.

11 Sarah Havard, "8 Worst Things Phyllis Schlafly Ever Said about Women's Rights," *Identities.Mic*, September 6, 2016, https://mic.com/articles/153506/8-worst-things-phyllis-schlafly-ever-said-about-women-s-rights#.4Wxyh3b3x.

12 Josh Israel, "Women from Koch-Funded Conservative Groups Lambaste Equal Pay Measure," *Think Progress*, April 9, 2014, https://thinkprogress.org/women-from-koch-funded-conservative-groups-lambaste-equal-pay-measure-d8eb0ea3edb7#. lj3d1onh2.

13 Lisa Graves, "Confirmation: The Not-So Independent Women's Forum Was Born in Defense of Clarence Thomas and the Far Right," *Center for Media and Democracy*, April 21, 2016, http://www.prwatch.org/news/2016/04/13091/confirmation-how-not-so-independent-womens-forum-was-launched-aid-clarence.

14 Alex DiBranco, "Who Speaks for Conservative Women?," *Political Research Associates*, June 9, 2015, https://www.politicalresearch.org/2015/06/09/who-speaks-for-conservative-women/.

15 Andrew Belonsky, "Michelle Bernard: 'The Republican Party Needs to Find Its Soul,'" *Independent Women's Forum*, April 9, 2009, http://www.iwf.org/news/2435006/ Michelle-Bernard:-'The-Republican-Party-Needs-to-Find-Its-Soul'.

16 As my 2015 article, "Who Speaks for Conservative Women?" explains, neoliberal feminism shares significant ideological similarities with equity feminism in denying the impact of structural forces and arguing that women can get ahead through individual actions.

17 Joan Walsh, "Meet the 'Feminists' Doing the Koch Brothers' Dirty Work," *The Nation*, August 18, 2016, https://www.thenation.com/article/archive/meet-the-feminists-doing-the-koch-brothers-dirty-work/.

18 Megan Rosenfeld, "Feminist Fatales," *The Washington Post*, November 30, 1995, https://www.washingtonpost.com/archive/lifestyle/1995/11/30/feminist-fatales/ cfd56f87-296b-4580-9d76-fcfba15c6296/?utm_term=.93e2dd0b66d0.

19 Mariah Blake, "Mad Men: Inside the Men's Rights Movement—And the Army of Misogynists and Trolls It Spawned," *Mother Jones*, January/February 2015,

16 Alex DiBranco

http://www.motherjones.com/politics/2015/01/warren-farrell-mens-rights-movement-feminism-misogyny-trolls.

20 Rivers and Barnett, *The New Soft War on Women*, 7.

21 Danielle Paquette, "The Alt-Right Isn't Only about White Supremacy. It's about White Male Supremacy," *The Washington Post*, November 25, 2016, https://www.washingtonpost.com/news/wonk/wp/2016/11/25/the-alt-right-isnt-just-about-white-supremacy-its-about-white-male-supremacy/?utm_term=.25af1245eb6b.

22 Blake, "Mad Men."

23 Tom McKay, "College President's Horrifying Rape Comments Are Basically Conservative Dogma," *The Daily Banter*, November 12, 2014, http://thedailybanter.com/2014/11/college-presidents-horrible-remarks-campus-rape-basically-conservative-dogma/.

24 Taylor Malmsheimer, "Conservatives Are Obsessed with Debunking the 1-in-5 Rape Statistic. They're Wrong, Too," *New Republic*, June 27, 2014, https://newrepublic.com/article/118430/independent-womens-forum-challenges-one-five-statistic.

25 Nicole Grether, "Men's Right Activist: Feminists Have Used Rape 'as a Scam,'" *Aljazeera America*, June 6, 2014, http://america.aljazeera.com/watch/shows/america-tonight/articles/2014/6/6/mena-s-rights-activistfeministshaveusedrapeaasascama.html; Roni Caryn Rabin, "Nearly 1 in 5 Women in U.S. Survey Say They Have Been Sexually Assaulted," *The New York Times*, December 14, 2011, http://www.nytimes.com/2011/12/15/health/nearly-1-in-5-women-in-us-survey-report-sexual-assault.html?_r=0.

26 Charlotte Hays, "Portrait of a Modern Feminist: Helen Smith," *Independent Women's Forum*, September 19, 2012, http://iwf.org/modern-feminist/2789205/Portrait-of-a-Modern-Feminist:-Helen-Smith.

27 Alex DiBranco, "Men's Rights Conference Host Says Women Who Drink & Dance Are 'Begging' for Rape," *Political Research Associates*, July 2, 2014, https://www.politicalresearch.org/2014/07/02/mens-rights-conference-host-says-women-who-drink-dance-are-begging-for-rape; Adam Serwer and Katie J.M. Baker, "How Men's Rights Leader Paul Elam Turned Being a Deadbeat Dad into a Moneymaking Movement," *Buzzfeed News*, February 6, 2015, https://www.buzzfeed.com/adamserwer/how-mens-rights-leader-paul-elam-turned-being-a-deadbeat-dad?utm_term=.bvY2OY9yl#.ukPZzDNx6.

28 Comment on TheRedPill, an "Official Subreddit of TRP.RED," *Reddit* (blog), https://www.reddit.com/r/TheRedPill/comments/12v1hf/almost_a_hundred_subscribers_welcome_newcomers/.

29 Matthew N. Lyons, "Jack Donovan on Men: A Masculine Tribalism for the Far Right," *Three Way Fight*, November 23, 2015, http://threewayfight.blogspot.com/2015/11/jack-donovan-on-men-masculine-tribalism.html.

30 Dianna Anderson, "MRAs for Jesus: A Look Inside the Christian 'Manosphere,'" *Rewire*, September 30, 2014, https://rewire.news/article/2014/09/30/mras-jesus-look-inside-christian-manosphere/.

31 Arthur Goldwag, "Leader's Suicide Brings Attention to the Men's Rights Movement," *Southern Poverty Law Center Intelligence Report*, March 1, 2012, https://www.splcenter.org/fighting-hate/intelligence-report/2012/leader%E2%80%99s-suicide-brings-attention-men%E2%80%99s-rights-movement.

32 Nicky Woolf, "'PUAhate' and 'ForeverAlone': Inside Elliot Rodger's Online Life," *The Guardian*, May 20, 2014, https://www.theguardian.com/world/2014/may/30/elliot-rodger-puahate-forever-alone-reddit-forums.

33 Blake, "Mad Men."

Mobilizing Misogyny **17**

34 Mark Potok, "War on Women," *Southern Poverty Law Center Intelligence Report*, August 20, 2014, https://www.splcenter.org/fighting-hate/intelligence-report/2014/war-women.

35 Potok, "War on Women."

36 Rebecca Hersher, "Jury Finds Dylann Roof Guilty in S.C. Church Shooting," *NPR*, December 15, 2016, http://www.npr.org/sections/thetwo-way/2016/12/15/505723552/jury-finds-dylann-roof-guilty-in-s-c-church-shooting.

37 Mark Berman, "Prosecutors Say Dylann Roof 'Self-Radicalized' Online, Wrote Another Manifesto in Jail," *The Washington Post*, August 22, 2016, https://www.washingtonpost.com/news/post-nation/wp/2016/08/22/prosecutors-say-accused-charleston-church-gunman-self-radicalized-online/?utm_term=.0afcab8108f7.

38 Naomi Braine, "Terror Network or Lone Wolf? Disparate Legal Treatment of Muslims and the Radical Right," *Political Research Associates*, June 19, 2015, https://www.politicalresearch.org/2015/06/19/terror-network-or-lone-wolf/.

39 Mark Berman, op cit.

40 Adi Kochavi, "The Sad Heroification of Elliot Rodger," *Vocativ*, May 25, 2014, http://www.vocativ.com/underworld/crime/sad-heroification-elliot-rodger/.

41 Earl Holt III, "Media Interviews with the CofCC," June 21, 2015, https://web.archive.org/web/20150622033926/http://conservative-headlines.com/2015/06/media-interviews-with-the-cofcc/.

42 Roosh Valizadeh, "No One Would Have Died if PUAHate Killer Elliot Rodger Learned Game," *Return of Kings*, May 25, 2014, http://www.returnofkings.com/36135/no-one-would-have-died-if-pua-hate-killer-elliot-rodger-learned-game.

43 Charlotte Hays, "'Toxic Feminism:' Cathy Young Dissects the Bizarre Response to a Mass Murder," *Independent Women's Forum*, May 30, 2014, http://www.iwf.org/blog/2794091/%22Toxic-Feminism:%22-Cathy-Young-Dissects-the-Bizarre-Response-to-a-Mass-Murder.

44 Katherine Cross, "What 'GamerGate' Reveals about the Silencing of Women," *Rewire*, September 9, 2014, https://rewire.news/article/2014/09/09/gamergate-reveals-silencing-women/.

45 Caitlin Dewey, "The Only Guide to Gamergate You Will Ever Need to Read," *The Washington Post*, October 14, 2014, https://www.washingtonpost.com/news/the-intersect/wp/2014/10/14/the-only-guide-to-gamergate-you-will-ever-need-to-read/?utm_term=.d3cb125407d0.

46 Nadine Santoro, "USU Shooting Threat: This Isn't a Game," *Disrupting Dinner Parties*, November 10, 2014, https://disruptingdinnerparties.com/2014/11/10/usu-shooting-threat-this-isnt-a-game/#more-29965.

47 Jaclyn Friedman, "A Look Inside the 'Men's Rights' Movement That Helped Fuel California Alleged Killer Elliot Rodger," *The American Prospect*, October 24, 2013, http://prospect.org/article/look-inside-mens-rights-movement-helped-fuel-california-alleged-killer-elliot-rodger; Amanda Hess, "Why Women Aren't Welcome on the Internet," *Pacific Standard Magazine*, January 6, 2014, https://psmag.com/why-women-aren-t-welcome-on-the-internet-aa21fdbc8d6#.mdzlvrvd4.

48 Abby Ohlheiser, "Just How Offensive Did Milo Yiannopoulos Have to Be to Get Banned from Twitter?," *The Washington Post*, July 21, 2016, https://www.washingtonpost.com/news/the-intersect/wp/2016/07/21/what-it-takes-to-get-banned-from-twitter/?utm_term=.69e3e83044cc.

49 Andrew Marantz, "Trolls for Trump," *The New Yorker Magazine*, October 31, 2016, http://www.newyorker.com/magazine/2016/10/31/trolls-for-trump.

50 Editorial Staff, "ThinkProgress Will No Longer Describe Racists as 'Alt-Right,'" *Think Progress*, November 22, 2016, https://thinkprogress.org/thinkprogress-alt-right-policy-b04fd141d8d4#.av5b2ftsm.

51 Susan Faludi, "How Hillary Clinton Met Satan," *The New York Times*, October 29, 2016, http://www.nytimes.com/2016/10/30/opinion/sunday/how-hillary-clinton-met-satan.html?_r=4.

52 John Daniszewski, "Writing about the 'Alt-Right,'" Associated Press, November 18, 2016, https://blog.ap.org/behind-the-news/writing-about-the-alt-right; Josh Harkinson, "We Talked to Experts about What Terms to Use for Which Group of Racists," *Mother Jones*, December 8, 2016, http://www.motherjones.com/politics/2016/12/definition-alt-right-white-supremacist-white-nationalist.

53 Linda Burnham, "The Absence of a Gender Justice Framework in Social Justice Organizing," *Center for the Education of Women: University of Michigan*, July 2008, http://www.cew.umich.edu/sites/default/files/BurnhamFinalProject.pdf.

54 While the women of color-led "reproductive justice" framework advocated by organizations like SisterSong provides an example for incorporating analysis of race, gender, class, and other intersectional issues, it should not be expected to substitute for a gender justice and women's human rights frame in social justice organizing. Though intended to include economic issues and gender-based rape and violence, which leaders like Loretta Ross had backgrounds working on, the "reproductive" label maintains a particular focus. "Gender justice" (Burnham also uses the term "social justice feminism") shifts the emphasis to meet the challenges of a broader misogynist movement—with religious and secular expressions—that poses threats in terms of reproductive control, sexual harassment and assault, violence against women, workplace sexism and wage discrimination, and other gender-based oppressions.

55 Matthew N. Lyons, "Alt-right: More Misogynistic than Many Neonazis," *ThreeWayFight*, December 3, 2016, http://threewayfight.blogspot.com/2016/12/alt-right-more-misogynistic-than-many.html.

56 Matthew N. Lyons, "Ctrl-Alt-Delete: The Origins and Ideology of the Alternative Right," *Political Research Associates*, January 20, 2017, https://www.politicalresearch.org/2017/01/20/ctrl-alt-delete-report-on-the-alternative-right/.

57 Matt Forney, "Who Cares What Women Think," *Alternative Right* (blog), January 29, 2015, http://alternative-right.blogspot.com/2015/01/who-cares-what-women-think.html.

58 Matt Forney, "Why Feminists Want Men to Rape Them," *Matt Forney.com*, February 26, 2016, http://mattforney.com/feminists-want-men-rape/.

59 Matthew N. Lyons, "Alt-Right: More Misogynistic Than Many Neonazis," *ThreeWayFight*, December 3, 2016, http://threewayfight.blogspot.com/2016/12/alt-right-more-misogynistic-than-many.html.

60 Sarah Posner, "Meet the Alt-Right 'Spokesman' Who's Thrilled with Trump's Rise," *Rolling Stone Magazine*, October 18, 2016, http://www.rollingstone.com/politics/features/meet-the-alt-right-spokesman-thrilled-by-trumps-rise-w443902.

61 Danielle Paquette, "The Alt-Right Isn't Only about White Supremacy. It's about White Male Supremacy," *The Washington Post*, November 25, 2016, https://www.washingtonpost.com/news/wonk/wp/2016/11/25/the-alt-right-isnt-just-about-white-supremacy-its-about-white-male-supremacy/?utm_term=.25af1245eb6b.

62 Aja Romano, "How the Alt-Right's Sexism Lures Men into White Supremacy," *Vox*, December 14, 2016, http://www.vox.com/culture/2016/12/14/13576192/alt-right-sexism-recruitment.

63 Carrie L. Lucas, "One in Four? Rape Myths Do Injustice, Too," *Independent Women's Forum*, April 27, 2006, http://www.iwf.org/news/2432517/One-in-Four-Rape-myths-do-injustice-too#sthash.EOyWF55L.dpuf.

64 Andrew Belonsky, "Michelle Bernard."

65 Nia-Malika Henderson, "Donald Trump's Nonexistent Problem with GOP Women," *CNN*, September 11, 2015, http://www.cnn.com/2015/09/10/politics/donald-trump-women/.

66 Rich Hampson, "Exclusive: Fox Anchor Megyn Kelly Describes Scary, Bullying 'Year of Trump,'" *USA Today*, November 15, 2016, http://www.usatoday.com/story/news/politics/elections/2016/11/15/megyn-kelly-memoir-donald-trump-roger-ailes-president-fox-news/93813154/.

67 Charlotte Hays, "Donald Trump Breathes New Life into Left's War on Women," *Independent Women's Forum*, March 18, 2016, http://www.iwf.org/news/2799633/Donald-Trump-Breathes-New-Life-into-Left%E2%80%99s-War-on-Women.

68 Christina Hoff Sommers, "'Amoral Masculinity': A Theory for Understanding Trump from Feminist Contrarian Christina Hoff Sommers," *American Enterprise Institute*, November 2, 2016, https://www.aei.org/publication/amoral-masculinity-a-theory-for-understanding-trump-from-feminist-contrarian-christina-hoff-sommers/.

69 Dylan Byers, "Conservative Female Pundits Want Donald Trump to Fire His Campaign Manager," *CNN Money*, March 30, 2016, http://money.cnn.com/2016/03/30/media/female-conservatives-fire-corey-lewandowski/.

70 Maggie Haberman, Alexander Burns, and Ashley Parker, "Donald Trump Fires Corey Lewandowski, His Campaign Manager," *The New York Times*, June 20, 2016, http://www.nytimes.com/2016/06/21/us/politics/corey-lewandowski-donald-trump.html.

71 Eddie Scarry, "Trump Defends Roger Ailes from Sexual Harassment Accusations," *The Washington Examiner*, July 14, 2016, http://www.washingtonexaminer.com/article/2596510.

72 Sarah Posner, "How Stephen Bannon Created an Online Haven for White Nationalists," *Mother Jones*, August 2, 2016, http://www.theinvestigativefund.org/investigations/politicsandgovernment/2265/how_stephen_bannon_created_an_online_haven_for_white_nationalists/.

73 Cassandra Vinograd, "Breitbart's Michelle Fields and Three Others Resign over Trump Incident," *NBC News*, March 14, 2016, http://www.nbcnews.com/news/us-news/breitbart-s-michelle-fields-ben-shapiro-resign-over-trump-incident-n537711.

74 Brendan Karet, "Right-Wing Civil War: Megyn Kelly Trades Barbs with Breitbart Editor-at-Large over Dangers of Empowering 'Alt-Right,'" *Media Matters for America*, December 7, 2016, https://mediamatters.org/blog/2016/12/07/right-wing-civil-war-megyn-kelly-trades-barbs-breitbart-editor-chief-over-dangers-empowering-alt/214754.

75 Mike Cernovich, "16 Feminists Who Have Taken over 'Conservative' Media," *Danger & Play*, March 30, 2016, https://www.dangerandplay.com/2016/03/30/16-feminists-who-have-taken-over-conservative-media/.

76 ExposedByCMDEditors, "'Independent' Women's Group Backing Trump Skirts Law to Influence Election," *Center For Media and Democracy*, November 1, 2016, http://www.exposedbycmd.org/2016/10/25/independent-womens-group-backing-trump-skirts-law-influence-elections/.

77 Tracy Clark-Flory and Leigh Cuen, "Donald Trump Has the Pickup Artist Vote in the Bag," *Vocativ*, August 24, 2015, http://www.vocativ.com/224810/donald-trump-anti-feminist-pickup-artists/.

78 Tim Hains, "Trump: Men Today 'Are Petrified to Speak to Women Anymore,' 'Women Get It Better Than We Do, Folks,'" *Real Clear Politics*, May 8, 2016, http://www.realclearpolitics.com/video/2016/05/08/trump_remember_this_when_you_see_hillarys_phony_paid-for-by-wall_street_ads.html.

79 Matt Forney, "Why You Should Shun Girls Who Support Abortion," *Return of Kings*, August 18, 2016, http://archive.is/zQwx4#selection-769.269-769.363.

80 Hesse Kassel, "5 Lines That Potential Wives Cannot Cross," *Return of Kings*, November 11, 2014, http://www.returnofkings.com/47540/5-lines-that-potential-wives-cannot-cross.

81 Amanda Marcotte, "Missouri Lawmaker Uses 'Men's Rights' Talking Points to Justify Abortion Restriction," *Raw Story*, December 17, 2014, http://www.rawstory.com/2014/12/missouri-lawmaker-uses-mens-rights-talking-points-to-justify-abortion-restriction/.

82 Melissa Jeltsen, "Trump's Election Raises Fears of Increased Violence against Women," *The Huffington Post*, November 15, 2016, http://www.huffingtonpost.com/entry/trump-women-rights-violence-fears_us_582a0f63e4b02d21bbc9f186.

83 Hatewatch Staff, "Update: 1,094 Bias-Related Incidents in the Month Following the Election," *Southern Poverty Law Center Hatewatch*, December 16, 2016, https://www.splcenter.org/hatewatch/2016/12/16/update-1094-bias-related-incidents-month-following-election.

84 Cassie Miller and Alexandra Werner-Winslow, "Ten Days After: Harassment and Intimidation in the Aftermath of the Election," *Southern Poverty Law Center*, November 29, 2016, https://www.splcenter.org/20161129/ten-days-after-harassment-and-intimidation-aftermath-election; Ben Mathis-Lilley, "Trump Was Recorded in 2005 Bragging about Grabbing Women 'by the Pussy,'" *Slate*, October 7, 2016, http://www.slate.com/blogs/the_slatest/2016/10/07/donald_trump_2005_tape_i_grab_women_by_the_pussy.html.

85 Ryan J. Reilly, "Jeff Sessions Now Admits Grabbing a Woman by the Genitals Is Sexual Assault," *The Huffington Post*, January 10, 2017, http://www.huffingtonpost.com/entry/jeff-sessions-trump-sexual-assault_us_58753f08e4b043ad97e64369; Scott Glover, "Colleague, Transcripts Offer Closer Look at Old Allegations of Racism against Sen. Jeff Sessions," *CNN*, January 10, 2017, http://www.cnn.com/2016/11/18/politics/jeff-sessions-racism-allegations/.

86 Alex Brandon, "Trump Says His Supreme Court Nominees Will Be Ready to Take on Abortion Ruling," *The Columbus Dispatch*, November 27, 2016, http://www.dispatch.com/content/stories/insight/2016/11/27/1-trump-says...; Katie Van Syckle, "Here's What a Trump Administration Could Mean for Campus Sexual Assault," *New York Magazine*, January 18, 2017, http://nymag.com/thecut/2017/01/what-a-trump-administration-means-for-campus-sexual-assault.html; Mark Landler, "Transition Team's Request on Gender Equality Rattles State Dept.," *The New York Times*, December 22, 2016, https://www.nytimes.com/2016/12/22/us/politics/state-department-gender-equality-trump-transition.html; Sophia Tesfaye, "Donald Trump Will Adopt Heritage Foundation's 'Skinny Budget': Arts, Violence against Women Funding to Be Cut," *Salon*, January 19, 2017, http://www.salon.com/2017/01/19/donald-trump-will-adopt-heritage-founda....

87 Loretta Ross, "Women's Rights Are Human Rights and the Women's March on Washington," *Rewire*, January 19, 2017, https://rewire.news/article/2017/01/19/womens-rights-human-rights-womens-march-washington/.

2

THE INVERSIVE SEXISM SCALE

Endorsement of the Belief That Women Are Privileged

Emily K. Carian

Several contemporary male supremacist groups share the same foundational belief: feminism has privileged women and disadvantaged men. This worldview runs counter to the consensus among social scientists that women are structurally oppressed on account of their gender. By justifying resistance to feminist change efforts, this worldview serves to maintain patriarchy. Drawing on primary source data from a men's rights forum, this chapter develops an original scale to measure inversive sexism or the belief that society provides women with more opportunities, rights, power, and status than men because of feminism. This chapter uses survey data to measure Americans' endorsement of inversive sexism, identify its demographic predictors, and describe its predictive utility across a host of behaviors relevant to gender inequality. Despite its association with extreme male supremacist groups, Americans endorse inversive sexism at the same level as other forms of sexism. Younger people and lower-middle-class people are more likely to endorse inversive sexism. Compared to other forms of sexism, inversive sexism is the best predictor of political behaviors and the belief that women lie about sexual assault, indicating that this male supremacist worldview is particularly relevant to the current political and cultural moment.

> As a man in the western world I have never ever ever experienced preferential treatment for my gender, nor have I ever experienced the strawman that is the patriarchy. But I have seen, talked to, and heard the feminists. I have seen girls getting special treatment because of their gender.
>
> —*Man, men's rights forum*[1]

> I didn't see much of the misogyny that feminists kept talking about. I just saw men toiling by the side of the road, men walking on eggshells, men treating me with respect, men struggling to deal with their emotions, men pandering

DOI: 10.4324/9781003164722-3

22 Emily K. Carian

> to women. I saw privileged, bitchy women everywhere, ordering men about, complaining about their husbands and partners, saying negative derogatory things about men in general, and getting shit bought for them and done for them over and over again.
>
> —*Woman, men's rights forum*

Since its emergence in the 1970s,[2] the men's rights movement has grown considerably. At the time of this writing, r/MensRights, a popular men's rights forum on the website Reddit, had over 300,000 subscribers. The movement has also influenced other groups, like Men Going Their Own Way, pickup artists, and involuntary celibates (incels). While these communities are distinct from one another, they all advance a male supremacist agenda, which they justify through a shared ideology: feminism has privileged women at men's expense. I term this ideology "inversive sexism" for the way it inverts the gender order empirically documented by social scientists; within this worldview, women hold a dominant position in the gender hierarchy compared to men. According to inversive sexism, men are disadvantaged because feminism has made women into a privileged class. The two previous quotes are exemplary of the logic of inversive sexism.

While secular male supremacist groups, like the men's rights movement, are sometimes dismissed as extremist or fringe, their ideology appears to be popular in the broader culture. Inversive sexism is reflected in many contemporary social concerns: that inclusive employment practices result in the hiring of less qualified women,[3] that legislating women's proportional representation in college sports comes at the cost of male sports teams,[4] and that adjudicating sexual assault allegations through university processes constitutes discrimination against men students.[5] Inversive sexism permeates popular understanding of these issues despite decades of social science research that documents the continued disadvantage women face in nearly every arena.[6] As sociologists Emily Carian and Amy Johnson show in their study of how individual-level explanations for gender inequality limit endorsement of radical, structural solutions for gender inequality, sense-making about whether and why men and women are unequal shapes the popular imagination around what should be done about gender inequality.[7] Applied to these examples, the inversive sexism ideology upholds real gender inequality by suggesting that any efforts to reduce it would discriminate against men. Inversive sexism imagines the status quo as discriminatory against men when it is in fact discriminatory against women. Its rejection of efforts to reduce women's disadvantage maintains hiring practices that favor men, disinvestment from women's sports, justice denied for sexual assault survivors, and so on. More generally, in creating the false narrative that feminism harms men, inversive sexism justifies both anti-feminism and men's continued dominance.

While these examples are suggestive, much is still unknown about inversive sexism, including whether it is widely endorsed and whether it predicts other attitudes and behaviors relevant to gender inequality. In this chapter, I devise a reliable scale for measuring the inversive sexism ideology. In the first part,

I compare the endorsement and demographic predictors of inversive sexism to that of three other, well-studied forms of sexism. In the second part, I determine whether inversive sexism is predictive of an array of policy preferences and attitudes. I find that inversive sexism is unique in terms of the population that endorses it (younger, lower-class men *and* women) and the attitudes and behaviors it predicts (responses to threats to the gender status hierarchy, like beliefs about sexual assault accusations and voting preferences) while still reaching the level of endorsement of other forms of sexism. I show that inversive sexism, while perhaps best known for characterizing rhetoric in extremist male supremacist communities, is a mainstream discourse deserving of further study.

Contemporary Sexism

I use three well-studied forms of sexism as points of comparison to inversive sexism: hostile, benevolent,[8] and modern[9] sexism (see Table 2.1). The present study is primarily concerned with inversive sexism. I chose the other three as comparisons because they are ideologically unique, have reliable scales for measurement, and likely lead to different attitudes and behaviors relevant to gender inequality.

Hostile and Benevolent Sexism

Psychologists Peter Glick and Susan Fiske[10] describe sexism as having an ambivalent character consisting of both positive and negative feelings toward women, which they term benevolent and hostile sexism, respectively. Hostile sexism involves negative stereotypes of women that justify excluding them from high-status roles. An example of hostile sexism is not recommending a woman for a promotion based on the belief that women are generally less competent than men. Benevolent sexism, on the other hand, consists of feelings that are subjectively positive and encourage prosocial behaviors toward women but nevertheless are derived from traditional stereotypes that restrict women to low-status roles. One example of benevolent sexism is not promoting a woman to a more demanding position out of concern that women (but not men) care about having ample time with their children. Hostile and benevolent sexism are complementary because they both maintain that men and women have fundamentally unequal abilities and personality traits. They also target different subgroups of women: hostile sexism is directed toward women who threaten men's status (e.g., female managers), and benevolent sexism is directed toward women who fulfill traditional roles (e.g., stay-at-home mothers). The ambivalent nature of sexism serves as both carrot and stick for maintaining women's subordinate status.

In cross-national studies, Glick and Fiske have shown that hostile and benevolent sexism are widespread.[11] Men's average scores for hostile sexism and both genders' average scores for benevolent sexism are negatively associated with national measures of gender equality. For example, in countries where men and women's hostile sexism scores and men and women's benevolent sexism scores

24 Emily K. Carian

TABLE 2.1 Differences among four types of sexism

	Logic	Valence of Feelings toward Women	Target
Hostile	Women are less qualified for high-status roles than men	Negative	Women who challenge men's status (e.g., feminists)
Benevolent	Women are more suited to low-status roles than men	Positive	Women who do not challenge men's status (e.g., housewives)
Modern	Women and men have equal opportunities	Ambivalent	Not specified by theory
Inversive	Women have more opportunities than men	Negative	All women, who are seen as having successfully challenged men's status

Sources: Glick and Fiske (1996); Swim et al. (1995).

are higher, women's participation in the economy and political system are lower. Other studies have shown the linkage between these two sexisms and attitudes at the individual level. For instance, individuals' hostile and benevolent sexism scores are positively associated with their endorsement of the sexual double standard or their negative evaluation of women and positive evaluation of men for engaging in similar sexual behaviors.[12]

Modern Sexism

Psychologists Janet Swim, Kathryn Aikin, Wayne Hall, and Barbara Hunter developed the concept of modern sexism, which entails the denial of continued discrimination against women, lack of sympathy for women's demands, and resentment about concern for women.[13] It maintains that society provides men and women with equal opportunities and resources. The items Swim and colleagues use to measure modern sexism reflect this. For example, they measure endorsement of the statements, "Discrimination against women is no longer a problem in the United States," and "It is rare to see women treated in a sexist manner on television." In effect, modern sexism disadvantages women by ignoring the unevenness of the playing field.

Modern sexism has been linked to attitudes about homosexuality and anti-gay behavior,[14] rape myth acceptance,[15] and more. Exposure to modern sexism is also associated with anxiety in women.[16]

Inversive Sexism

Inversive sexism is the idea that feminism has created a gender order in which women hold the dominant position and men hold the subordinate position.

The Inversive Sexism Scale **25**

Thus, inversive sexism goes a step further than modern sexism by claiming that women have *more* opportunities than men. Inversive sexism entails a zero-sum perspective[17] in which men and women compete for finite resources—power, jobs, favors, even empathy—and men are losing. Unlike hostile and benevolent sexism, inversive sexism does not target a specific subgroup of women. Rather, it holds that women as a group are the recipients of unwarranted special treatment.

A society's cultural narratives about inequality reflect both its historical trajectory and its current conditions.[18] I argue that inversive sexism is a new form of sexism that justifies patriarchy in light of recent, though limited, changes to women's status and power within the gender order. The current political moment in the United States is one characterized by demonstrations of women's greater empowerment: Hillary Rodham Clinton became the first woman presidential nominee for a major political party;[19] women across diverse industries publicly accused powerful men of sexual harassment, assault, and abuse as part of the #MeToo movement;[20] a record number of women ran for public office in 2018;[21] and Kamala Harris became the first Black and Indian woman to be elected vice president in 2020.[22] These displays of empowerment have activated male supremacist responses. In regard to the #MeToo movement, for example, numerous commentators have accused whistleblowers of lying to damage men's careers.[23] Individuals who hold inversive sexist beliefs perceive symbolic events, like the #MeToo movement and Hillary Rodham Clinton's historic campaign for presidency, as challenges to the gender status hierarchy.[24] They engage in inversive sexism as a way to maintain this hierarchy. As a result, individuals who are more vigilant about status threat[25]—low-status individuals, like those who are lower class—may be more likely to endorse the inversive sexism ideology. This also means that women may endorse inversive sexism since literature on system justification shows that they are also susceptible to the social psychological processes that motivate us to justify the status quo.[26] Additionally, inversive sexism should predict behaviors that minimize perceived threat to the gender status hierarchy, like those posed by women who publicly accuse men of sexual assault and women who run for political office.

Developing an Inversive Sexism Scale

I first developed a reliable scale to measure inversive sexist attitudes using posts from one men's rights forum as source material.[27] In order to protect posters' privacy, I have chosen not to name the forum. Data used are primary posts, rather than comments to posts, and come from a single thread on the forum in which posters describe why they first joined the men's rights movement. This thread is particularly suited for analyzing cultural narratives about gender inequality, as posters describe their understandings of the groups "men," "women," and the relationship between them. Posts were scraped from the Web using Python. Of the 159 total posts dating from December 2012 (when the thread was created) to January 2015 (when data was collected), 20 were excluded from analysis because

26 Emily K. Carian

they were truncated, linked only to outside content (e.g., a personal video blog) or were written by feminist opponents to the forum. I coded the remaining 139 posts using modified grounded theory,[28] letting themes emerge organically in a first round of coding and then using a refined coding scheme in the second round. Using this analysis, I developed 35 statements characteristic of inversive sexism. Next, a research assistant and I independently reanalyzed the forum posts to document the frequency with which these 35 statements appeared in the sample (coders matched 87% of the time, with a Cohen's κ of 0.46). I discarded those statements that were present in fewer than one-tenth of the forum posts as determined in our coding, retaining 24 items.

To validate the scale with a general population, I recruited 251 participants (131 men, 120 women) living in the United States through Amazon Mechanical Turk. Amazon Mechanical Turk is a crowdsourcing website commonly used in social psychological studies and produces similar results as other population-based and convenience samples.[29] Fourteen (5.6%) participants were dropped from the sample due to missing data, leaving 237 total participants (124 men, 113 women). Participants were asked to indicate their agreement with the 24 inversive sexism items on a five-point scale from disagree strongly (1) to agree strongly (5). Items were randomized. I performed iterated principal components analysis on this data to reduce the number of items further. Principal components analysis is an exploratory process. In this context, it allowed me to examine the dimensionality of the data (i.e., whether multiple underlying processes govern a person's inversive sexism score) and reduce the number of scale items while retaining sufficient variation in the data. The eigenvalue for the first component was 14.04, and all others had eigenvalues less than 1, suggesting a one-component (or one dimension) solution. After retaining one component and using varimax rotation (available upon request), I selected the 11 items with the highest factor loadings to construct the final inversive sexism scale, as listed in Table 2.2. I limited the scale to 11 items for consistency with the indexes for hostile and benevolent sexism.

TABLE 2.2 Inversive sexism scale items

These days, women have more power than men.
Women receive undeserved special treatment because of their gender.
Today, prejudice against men is more common than prejudice against women.
Women today do not have more privileges than men.[a]
Men are not hurt by the focus on women's issues today.[a]
No one cares about men's issues today.
Feminism makes it so women do not have to take responsibility for themselves.
Feminists have too much political influence.
Feminists treat men fairly.[a]
Feminism is responsible for many of men's problems today.
Feminists have succeeded in getting preferential treatment for women.

a Item is reverse-scored.

The scale constructed by averaging these 11 items is reliable ($\alpha = 0.96$) and highly correlated with the average of all 24 items ($r = 0.98$, $p < 0.001$). As another check of reliability that is commonly used in the creation of scales measuring sexism,[30] I found that men had significantly higher scores on the 11-item scale than women (men = 2.76, women = 2.06, $t = 5.22$, $p < 0.001$). As a final step, I rephrased three of these items to be reverse-scored (i.e., for higher scores to indicate lower, rather than higher, levels of sexism) to mitigate acquiescence response bias or the tendency to agree with statements regardless of their content.[31]

Endorsement and Sociodemographic Predictors of Inversive Sexism

Method and Sample

In this section, I compare the level of endorsement and demographic predictors of inversive sexism to hostile, benevolent, and modern sexism (Table 2.3). Five hundred twenty-four participants (248 males, 276 females) living in the United States were recruited through Amazon Mechanical Turk to complete the survey. Thirteen (2.5%) participants were excluded from analysis due to missing data, resulting in a final sample of 512 individuals (243 males, 269 females).

Table 2.3 summarizes the demographic characteristics of the respondents in this sample, which I refer to as sample 1. As with most Amazon Mechanical Turk samples, this one is not fully representative of adults living in the United States. In general, the sample is slightly younger,[32] more female, more educated,[33] and more employed[34] than the general population. The sample also underrepresents Blacks and non-religious individuals and overrepresents Asians.

Participants were asked to indicate their agreement on a five-point scale with randomized statements characteristic of inversive, hostile, benevolent, and modern sexism and answer demographic questions. Statements characteristic of hostile and benevolent sexism were taken from the Ambivalent Sexism Index,[35] and those characteristic of modern sexism were drawn from work by Swim, Aikin, Hall, and Hunter.[36] Although the Ambivalent Sexism Index is typically measured with respect to a six-point scale, I use a five-point scale from disagree strongly (1) to agree strongly (5) for all survey items for consistency. The modern sexism scale was developed using a five-point scale, and research has demonstrated that individuals who choose a middle neutral category do not answer the question in the same way as other respondents when forced to choose sides.[37] Scales with an odd number of categories are, therefore, more reliable than scales without a middle category.

Each participant's scores across the items for inversive, hostile, benevolent, and modern sexism were averaged to calculate the individual's overall score for each sexism. Indexes created for each type of sexism were highly reliable (inversive $\alpha = 0.92$, hostile $\alpha = 0.93$, benevolent $\alpha = 0.91$, modern $\alpha = 0.91$). Importantly, the scale for inversive sexism was as reliable as the other three.

28 Emily K. Carian

TABLE 2.3 Demographic characteristics of sample 1

	Mean or %		*Mean or %*
Female	52.54	Employment status	
Age (in years)	36.81	Full time	54.10
Race		Part time	19.14
White	76.95	Temporarily not working	0.59
Black	7.62	Unemployed	8.20
Asian	9.18	Disabled	1.56
Hispanic	4.49	Keeping house	8.59
Other	1.76	Student	3.91
Marital status		Retired	2.34
Single	46.68	Other	1.56
Married	36.91	Personal income	
Partnered	8.79	<$10,000	23.24
Separated	0.78	$10,000–$19,999	17.38
Divorced	5.47	$20,000–$29,999	19.92
Widowed	1.37	$30,000–$39,999	12.70
Respondent's education		$40,000–$49,999	8.20
Less than high school	0.59	$50,000–$59,999	7.03
High school	10.94	$60,000–$69,999	3.12
Trade	1.37	$70,000–$79,999	2.93
Some college	25.78	$80,000–$89,999	1.56
AA	13.09	$90,000–$99,999	1.37
BA	36.72	$100,000+	2.54
Postgraduate	11.52	Religion	
Father's education		Buddhist	3.32
Less than high school	10.16	Hindu	0.98
High school	32.42	Jewish	1.76
Trade	4.30	Catholic	15.43
Some college	12.50	Mormon	1.37
AA	8.20	Protestant—Evangelical	7.62
BA	20.70	Protestant—Mainline	9.77
Postgraduate	11.72	Protestant—Other	0.39
Mother's education		Christian—Other	7.81
Less than high school	7.62	Other religion	2.73
High school	32.23	None	26.37
Trade	4.10	Atheist	22.46
Some college	16.02	Religiosity	2.71
AA	9.77	Region	
BA	20.90	Northeast	17.78
Postgraduate	9.38	Midwest	19.92
Political ideology		South	36.33
General	3.42	West	26.17
Social issues	3.10		
Economic issues	3.70		
Self-identified class			
Working	28.12		

(Continued)

TABLE 2.3 (Continued)

	Mean or %	Mean or %
Lower middle	26.17	
Middle	40.43	
Upper middle	5.27	

Note: n = 512. All political ideology scales are measured on a seven-point scale from extremely liberal (1) to extremely conservative (7). Religiosity is measured on a seven-point scale from not at all religious (1) to extremely religious (7).

First, I compare average scores for each sexism to determine whether inversive sexism is, in fact, a fringe discourse or whether its endorsement reaches the same level as other types of sexism. Then, I use ordinary least squares regression analysis to predict individuals' inversive sexism scores using sociodemographic characteristics and compare these results with those of the other three types. I use Wald tests to compare the coefficients across each type of sexism to see if certain sociodemographic factors differentially predict inversive sexism.

Results

Endorsement of Inversive Sexism

Is inversive sexism a fringe cultural narrative, or is its level of endorsement similar to that of other types of sexism? Figure 2.1 compares the means of the four types of sexism. Respondents' mean score for inversive sexism (2.32; SD = 0.87) was similar to that of hostile sexism (2.36; SD = 0.96) and modern sexism (2.38; SD = 0.95). Respondents scored markedly higher on the benevolent sexism scale (mean = 2.64; SD = 0.91) than the other three. It is important to note that the mean for each type of sexism is below 3, which corresponds to an answer of "neither agree nor disagree." This suggests that outright endorsement of each of these types of sexism is low. In fact, only about a quarter of people score above the neutral midpoint for inversive (22.07%), hostile (27.34%), and modern (24.41%) sexism, and about a third do for benevolent sexism (35.35%). Low endorsements are not surprising given that the sample is slightly more female and that many of these statements are publicly considered sexist, so social desirability may have affected responses.[38]

Figure 2.1 shows that the level of endorsement of inversive sexism is statistically indistinguishable from that of hostile and modern sexism (p > 0.050). It indicates that inversive sexism should not be considered less mainstream than these two types of sexism. Figure 2.1 also demonstrates that benevolent sexism is distinct in its level of endorsement. The mean benevolent sexism score was significantly higher than the other three (all p values < 0.050). This is, perhaps, unsurprising, given benevolent sexism entails positive affect toward women and appears less blatantly sexist.

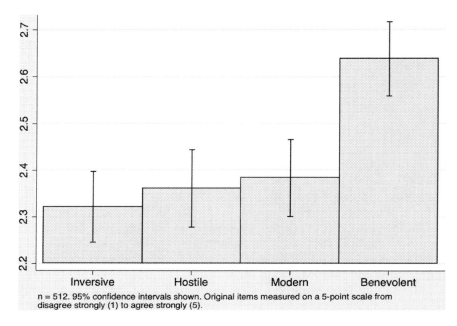

FIGURE 2.1 Average sexism scores.

Examining the distributions for each type of sexism provides more evidence that inversive sexism is not a fringe ideology. For instance, there was not a significant number of outliers that scored drastically higher on inversive sexism than the rest of the sample, which would be the case if inversive sexism were a discourse relegated to fringe groups. Additionally, Figure 2.2 illustrates that the distribution of scores for inversive sexism is not markedly different from that of the others in terms of its minimum, maximum, and 25th and 75th percentile scores.

Sociodemographic Predictors of Inversive Sexism

Do sociodemographic characteristics differentially predict inversive sexism scores? I used ordinary least squares regression analysis to model each type of sexism. I first created full models of each type of sexism including all sociodemographic variables (available by request). I constructed more parsimonious models by excluding variables that were not significant for any type of sexism in the full models, followed by those that did not improve the model fit for inversive sexism as determined by F-tests. The first column of Table 2.4 reports the regression

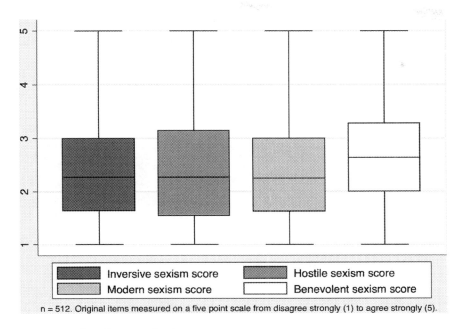

FIGURE 2.2 Distribution of sexism scores.

predicting inversive sexism. Individuals who identify as female[39] are predicted to have an inversive sexism score 0.29 lower than those who identify as male, and this difference is statistically significant. Each additional year of age is significantly associated with a 0.02 reduction in one's inversive sexism score. Each one-point increase in social conservatism on a seven-point scale is expected to increase an individual's inversive sexism score by 0.24. Individuals who identify as lower middle class are predicted to have an inversive sexism score 0.20 greater than those who identify as middle class. The results for the other class categories are not significant.

To explore whether inversive sexism is distinct from the other three sexisms in terms of their predictors, Table 2.5 reports the results of Wald tests comparing the coefficients from the parsimonious regression models (Table 2.4) across the four types of sexism. For a particular predictor, a Wald test determines whether the coefficient for one sexism is significantly different from the coefficient for another. I focus on the differences between inversive sexism and hostile and modern sexism since most of the coefficients for benevolent sexism were not

32 Emily K. Carian

TABLE 2.4 Ordinary least squares (OLS) regressions of inversive, hostile, modern, and benevolent sexism on select sociodemographic factors

	Inversive	Hostile	Modern	Benevolent
Female	−0.29***	−0.37***	−0.34***	−0.03
	(0.07)	(0.07)	(0.07)	(0.07)
Age (in years)	−0.02***	−0.01***	−0.01**	−0.004
	(0.002)	(0.003)	(0.003)	(0.003)
Political ideology (social	0.24***	0.25***	0.26***	0.22***
issues)	(0.02)	(0.02)	(0.02)	(0.02)
Self-identified class (excluded = middle)				
Working	−0.02	0.01	−0.02	0.05
	(0.08)	(0.09)	(0.09)	(0.09)
Lower middle	0.20*	0.20*	0.18+	0.02
	(0.08)	(0.09)	(0.09)	(0.09)
Upper middle	−0.11	−0.09	0.17	0.12
	(0.15)	(0.17)	(0.17)	(0.17)
Constant	2.27***	2.20***	2.02***	2.10***
	(0.13)	(0.14)	(0.14)	(0.14)
Adjusted R-squared	0.2794	0.2532	0.2681	0.1633
F-statistic (comparing this model with null model)	34.03***	29.87***	32.19***	17.62***

Note: n = 512. $^+p < 0.100$, $^*p < 0.050$, $^{**}p < 0.010$, $^{***}p < 0.001$. Political ideology is measured on a seven-point scale from extremely liberal (1) to extremely conservative (7).

TABLE 2.5 Results of Wald tests comparing the OLS regression analysis coefficients for inversive sexism to the other sexisms

	Inversive–Hostile	Inversive–Modern	Inversive–Benevolent
Female	+		**
Age (in years)	+	**	**
Political ideology (social issues)			
Class (excluded = middle)			+
Working			
Lower middle			
Upper middle			

Note: n = 512. $^+p < 0.100$, $^*p < 0.050$, $^{**}p < 0.010$, $^{***}p < 0.001$. Coefficients are from models listed in Table 2.4. Each column shows results of Walt tests comparing the coefficients for two types of sexism. Test for class indicates results for the accumulated Wald tests.

significant in Table 2.4, and other analyses indicate that benevolent sexism is quite unique. The relationship between age and inversive sexism is significantly different from that of modern sexism (p < 0.010) and marginally different from that of hostile sexism (p < 0.100). This means that one's inversive sexism score is expected to decrease more with every additional year of age as compared to one's hostile or modern sexism score, as shown in Figure 2.2. In other words, inversive sexism is more concentrated among the young than hostile and modern sexism. Likewise, inversive sexism's relationship with sex is marginally different than that for hostile sexism (p < 0.100), meaning inversive sexism may be more evenly distributed by sex than hostile sexism.

While the coefficients for the lower middle class for hostile, modern, and inversive sexism are not statistically different from one another, including class predictors in the regression model significantly improves model fit for inversive sexism only (F(3, 504) = 2.91, p = 0.03). This means that class explains more variation in inversive sexism than it does in hostile or modern sexism.

Conclusion

I find that inversive sexism reaches the same level of endorsement as hostile and modern sexism and is not concentrated among a few extremists. I also find that inversive sexism is more concentrated among the young, more equally endorsed by males and females, and better explained by social class. Because inversive sexism is particularly endorsed by low-status individuals who are more vigilant about status threat[40]—those who are lower class—I also find evidence that inversive sexism is a response to perceived threats to the gender status hierarchy. Next, I investigate whether inversive sexism is more predictive of attitudes and behaviors challenging symbolic threats to the gender status hierarchy.

Identifying the Predictive Utility of Inversive Sexism

Method and Sample

In this section, I compare the predictive utility of inversive sexism with that of hostile, modern, and benevolent sexism. I test whether inversive sexism is, in fact, more predictive of attitudes and behaviors that are responses to symbolic challenges to the gender status hierarchy, as I have argued should be the case. Two hundred fifty-two participants living in the United States were recruited through Amazon Mechanical Turk to complete the survey. One (4.0%) participant was excluded from analysis for failing an attention check, resulting in a final sample of 251 individuals (142 males, 106 females, 3 others). Demographic characteristics for the sample, which I refer to as sample 2, are listed in Table 2.6. As in study 1, the sample is not representative of adults living in the United States. This sample is younger and more male than the general population and overrepresents Asians.[41]

TABLE 2.6 Demographic characteristics of sample 2

	Mean or %
Female	42.23
Age (in years)	33.41
Race	
White	72.11
Black	11.55
Asian	9.16
Hispanic	5.58
Other	1.59
Political ideology on social issues	3.17
Class	
Working	22.71
Lower middle	23.11
Middle	47.41
Upper middle	6.37
Upper	0.40

Note: n = 251. Political ideology on social issues measured on a seven-point scale from extremely liberal (1) to extremely conservative (7).

The survey was similar to that used in the previous section. Participants first completed the indexes for inversive, hostile, benevolent, and modern sexism on a scale from 1 (strongly disagree) to 5 (strongly agree). These items were randomized. Then, participants were asked to indicate their thoughts on 18 attitudes and policy preferences related to gender inequality, which served as dependent variables for this analysis. Finally, participants answered demographic questions. Participants' scores for each type of sexism were found by averaging their scores for those items. Indexes were highly reliable (inversive $\alpha = 0.93$, hostile $\alpha = 0.94$, benevolent $\alpha = 0.89$, modern $\alpha = 0.92$). Once again, the scale for inversive sexism was as reliable as the other three.

In choosing the dependent variables, I deliberately selected a diverse set of attitudes, policy preferences, and behaviors related to gender and gender inequality that are of interest to a wide range of researchers. In addition to those that I created, five questions related to corporate and government policies were adapted from the General Social Survey[42] and the American National Election Studies (ANES).[43] Three questions about voting behavior and feelings toward 2016 presidential candidates were also adapted from the ANES. Seven questions measuring agreement with rape myths were drawn from the short form Illinois Rape Myth Acceptance (IRMA) Scale.[44] These items were averaged to produce a single variable measuring agreement with myths about sexual assault ($\alpha = 0.89$). I included this wide range of dependent variables because, as yet, there is no theory guiding researchers in their selection of sexism scales as predictors for a multitude of dependent variables of interest.

To compare the predictive utility of inversive sexism to the other three sexisms, I used ordinary least squares analyses for continuous dependent variables and logistic regression analyses for binary dependent variables. I constructed two models for each dependent variable. The first model (referred to as model A) includes inversive sexism and the demographic characteristics measured in this survey. If inversive sexism predicts the dependent variable beyond sex, age, social conservatism, and class, its coefficient will be significant in model A. Inversive sexism will be a particularly good predictor of a dependent variable if it totally explains its relationship with sex, which is often used to explain differences in policy preferences and behaviors related to gender inequality.[45] The next model (referred to as model B) adds hostile, modern, and benevolent sexism as predictors of the dependent variable. If inversive sexism is a better predictor of the dependent variable than the other three sexisms, its coefficients will also be significant in model B and larger in absolute size than that of the other three sexisms (if they, too, are significant).

Results

Tables 2.7 through 2.9 show the results of the analyses determining the predictive utility of inversive sexism. Table 2.7 shows regressions for support for corporate and government policies; Table 2.8 shows regressions for beliefs related to rape and attitudes toward feminism; Table 2.9 shows regressions for political preferences and behaviors. Model A for each dependent variable listed in Tables 2.7 through 2.9 shows that inversive sexism significantly predicts these policy preferences and attitudes (with the exception of believing that women should be able to obtain an abortion for any reason) net of demographic characteristics.

For some of the dependent variables, the coefficient for inversive sexism does not remain significant when hostile, modern, and benevolent sexism are added as predictors in model B. These attitudes and behaviors are better predicted by one or more of the other three types of sexism than by inversive sexism. Some dependent variables are best predicted by inversive sexism, including the percent (from 0 to 100) of sexual assault accusations the respondent indicated they believed might be false, as shown in models 8A and 8B in Table 2.8. In model 8A, controlling for demographic characteristics, a one-point increase in an individual's inversive sexism score is significantly associated with a 10.91-point increase in the percent of sexual assault accusations the respondent believes are false. This represents more than half of a standard deviation and is practically large, considering research estimates the percent of accusations that are false to be between 2 and 10.[46] Model 8B adds the respondents' hostile, modern, and benevolent sexism scores as predictors. Inversive sexism remains significant, although the coefficient is reduced to 5.37, indicating that some of the effect measured in model 8A is explained by these other sexism scores. The coefficient (7.45) for hostile sexism is also significant. The difference in size between these two coefficients is not statistically significant ($F(1, 239) = 0.24$, $p = 0.63$), indicating that inversive and

TABLE 2.7 Regressions of inversive sexism on agreement with corporate and government policies related to gender

	Employers Should Hire/ Promote Women		Employers Should Be Required to Pay Men and Women the Same		Government Should Increase Business Opportunities for Women		Government Should Reduce Gender Inequality		Women Should Be Able to Obtain Abortion for Any Reason	
	Model 1A	Model 1B	Model 2A	Model 2B	Model 3A	Model 3B	Model 4A	Model 4B	Model 5A	Model 5B
Inversive	−0.59★★★	−0.28	−0.43★★★	0.05	−0.66★★★	−0.13	−0.69★★★	−0.16	−0.26	−0.40
	(0.09)	(0.19)	(0.07)	(0.16)	(0.08)	(0.17)	(0.09)	(0.19)	(0.26)	(0.60)
Hostile		−0.01		−0.28★		−0.09		−0.11		0.24
		(0.15)		(0.13)		(0.14)		(0.16)		(0.52)
Modern		−0.44★★★		−0.29★★		−0.65★★★		−0.59★★★		−0.19
		(0.10)		(0.09)		(0.09)		(0.11)		(0.32)
Benevolent		0.26★★		0.05		0.29★★★		0.18★		−0.65★
		(0.08)		(0.07)		(0.07)		(0.08)		(0.30)
Female	0.33★	0.22	0.07	0.04	0.27†	0.13	0.33★	0.22	0.11	0.16
	(0.14)	(0.14)	(0.12)	(0.12)	(0.14)	(0.12)	(0.15)	(0.14)	(0.49)	(0.51)
Age	0.01	0.01	0.01	0.01	−0.003	−0.004	−0.01	−0.01	−0.05★	−0.05★
	(0.01)	(0.01)	(0.01)	(0.01)	(0.01)	(0.01)	(0.01)	(0.01)	(0.02)	(0.02)
Political ideology on social issues	−0.16★★	−0.14★★	−0.05	−0.01	−0.13★★	−0.09★	−0.09†	−0.04	−0.87★★★	−0.77★★★
	(0.05)	(0.05)	(0.04)	(0.04)	(0.05)	(0.05)	(0.05)	(0.05)	(0.18)	(0.19)
Class (excluded = middle)										
Working	−0.07	−0.01	−0.13	−0.09	−0.06	0.01	−0.12	−0.07	0.10	−0.13
	(0.18)	(0.17)	(0.15)	(0.15)	(0.17)	(0.15)	(0.18)	(0.17)	(0.56)	(0.58)
Lower middle	0.04	0.04	0.01	−0.00	−0.03	−0.04	−0.13	−0.15	0.06	−0.08
	(0.17)	(0.16)	(0.15)	(0.14)	(0.17)	(0.15)	(0.18)	(0.17)	(0.60)	(0.61)

Upper middle	−0.35	−0.23	0.10	0.05	−0.46†	−0.34	−0.22	−0.15	−0.06	−0.29
	(0.28)	(0.27)	(0.24)	(0.24)	(0.27)	(0.25)	(0.29)	(0.27)	(0.96)	(0.96)
Upper	−0.04	−0.20	−1.11	−1.12	−0.44	−0.64	−0.59	−0.75		
	(1.08)	(1.01)	(0.90)	(0.88)	(1.03)	(0.92)	(1.10)	(1.02)		
Constant	4.81***	4.50***	5.19***	5.25***	5.65***	5.37***	5.77***	5.68***	7.08***	8.85***
	(0.31)	(0.33)	(0.26)	(0.29)	(0.30)	(0.30)	(0.32)	(0.34)	(1.09)	(1.54)
Model fit	0.3554	0.4265	0.2163	0.2524	0.3876	0.5224	0.3456	0.4321	70.72***	75.62***
Model A v. model B	11.00***		4.90**		23.77***		13.29***		4.58	
N	251		251		251		251		229	

Note: †$p < 0.010$, *$p < 0.050$, **$p < 0.010$, ***$p < 0.001$. Models 1A through 4B show OLS regression coefficients, with dependent variables measured on a scale from 1 (disagree strongly) to 5 (agree strongly); models 5A and 5B show log-odds coefficients from logistic regression and are measured as 0 (no) or 1 (yes; analysis excludes respondents who selected "Don't know"). "Model fit" row shows adjusted $R2$ for OLS regressions and likelihood ratio test (comparing model with null model) for logistic regressions. "Model A v. model B" row shows F-test for OLS regressions and chi^2 test for logistic regressions, both comparing model A to model B.

TABLE 2.8 Regressions of inversive sexism on beliefs related to gender

	Identifies as a Feminist		Identifies as an Anti-Feminist		Percent of Sexual Assault Accusations Respondent Believes Is False		Agreement with Rape Myths	
	Model 6A	Model 6B	Model 7A	Model 7B	Model 8A	Model 8B	Model 9A	Model 9B
Inversive	−1.46★★★	−0.16	2.42★★	1.31	10.91★★★	5.37★	0.83★★★	0.14
	(0.30)	(0.66)	(0.74)	(1.00)	(1.11)	(2.47)	(0.07)	(0.15)
Hostile		−0.31		1.69†		7.45★★★		0.62★★★
		(0.51)		(0.97)		(2.04)		(0.12)
Modern		−1.32★★		−0.41		−2.54†		0.12
		(0.44)		(0.67)		(1.39)		(0.08)
Benevolent		−0.24		−0.10		1.78†		0.10
		(0.24)		(0.72)		(1.08)		(0.06)
Female	0.83★	0.92★	−0.13	−0.05	1.69	0.49	−0.09	−0.13
	(0.39)	(0.42)	(1.09)	(1.23)	(1.88)	(1.82)	(0.11)	(0.11)
Age	0.01	0.01	0.04	0.06	−0.19★	−0.17†	−0.01★	−0.01★
	(0.02)	(0.02)	(0.04)	(0.04)	(0.09)	(0.09)	(0.01)	(0.01)
Political ideology on social issues	−0.90★★★	−0.80★★★	0.18	0.29	0.90	0.83	0.002	−0.04
	(0.18)	(0.19)	(0.25)	(0.29)	(0.66)	(0.67)	(0.04)	(0.04)
Class (excluded = middle)								
Working	−0.04	−0.30	−1.01	−1.11	0.06	−0.15	0.25†	0.22†
	(0.49)	(0.53)	(1.10)	(1.20)	(2.31)	(2.23)	(0.14)	(0.13)
Lower middle	−0.10	−0.34	−2.73†	−3.02†	0.20	0.25	−0.15	−0.13
	(0.47)	(0.50)	(1.52)	(1.63)	(2.26)	(2.18)	(0.14)	(0.13)

Upper middle	−1.13	−1.48			3.66	6.71[†]	−0.11	0.10
	(0.91)	(1.03)			(3.71)	(3.61)	(0.22)	(0.21)
Upper					1.42	−1.77	−0.62	−0.79
					(14.02)	(13.45)	(0.85)	(0.80)
Constant	3.84***	4.82***	−12.93***	−14.52**	−2.03	−5.33	0.63*	0.31
	(1.05)	(1.21)	(3.19)	(4.21)	(4.09)	(4.44)	(0.25)	(0.26)
Model fit	121.77***	133.68***	38.94***	42.15***	0.4037	0.4523	0.5006	0.5575
Model A v. model B	10.00*		3.02		8.16***		11.37***	
N	250		234		251		251	

Note: [†]$p < 0.010$, *$p < 0.050$, **$p < 0.010$, ***$p < 0.001$. Models 6A through 7B show log-odds coefficients from logistic regression. Models 8A through 9B show OLS regression coefficients. Identifies as a feminist and identifies as an anti-feminist are measured as 0 (no) or 1 (yes). Agreement with rape myths is a composite of seven items from the IRMA Scale, originally measured on a scale from 1 (disagree strongly) to 7 (agree strongly). "Model fit" row shows adjusted R^2 for OLS regressions and likelihood ratio test (comparing model with null model) for logistic regressions. "Model A v. model B" row shows F-test for OLS regressions and chi^2 test for logistic regressions, both comparing model A to model B.

TABLE 2.9 Regressions of inversive sexism on political attitudes and behaviors

	Feelings toward Hillary Clinton		Vote for Hillary Clinton (versus All Other Candidates)		Feelings toward Donald Trump		Vote for Donald Trump (versus All Other Candidates)	
	Model 10A	Model 10B	Model 11A	Model 11B	Model 12A	Model 12B	Model 13A	Model 13B
Inversive	−8.94★★★	−12.62★★	−1.36★★★	1.70★	9.70★★★	−0.30	1.41★★★	1.47†
	(2.04)	(4.72)	(0.30)	(0.70)	(1.80)	(4.13)	(0.35)	(0.80)
Hostile		5.01		0.59		6.02†		−0.13
		(3.89)		(0.53)		(3.41)		(0.62)
Modern		−2.01		−0.34		5.66★		0.29
		(2.65)		(0.33)		(2.32)		(0.38)
Benevolent		2.73		−0.34		0.16		0.77†
		(2.05)		(0.28)		(1.80)		(0.42)
Female	9.59★★	8.41★	0.61	0.54	−2.61	−2.31	0.01	−0.08
	(3.45)	(3.47)	(0.45)	(0.46)	(3.04)	(3.04)	(0.55)	(0.57)
Age	−0.22	−0.21	−0.07★★	−0.07★★	0.55★★★	0.58★★★	0.10★★	0.10★★
	(0.17)	(0.17)	(0.02)	(0.02)	(0.15)	(0.15)	(0.03)	(0.03)
Political ideology on social issues	−6.01★★★	−6.23★★★	−0.67★★★	−0.58★★	9.25★★★	8.47★★★	0.98★★★	0.85★★★
	(1.21)	(1.28)	(0.17)	(0.18)	(1.07)	(1.12)	(0.22)	(0.22)
Class (excluded = middle)								
Working	−9.66★	−9.50★	−0.28	−0.39	1.79	1.22	−0.27	−0.06
	(4.24)	(4.25)	(0.58)	(0.59)	(3.74)	(3.72)	(0.66)	(0.68)
Lower middle	−6.51	−6.29	−0.92	−0.92	3.67	4.10	−0.80	−0.79
	(4.16)	(4.15)	(0.56)	(0.57)	(3.66)	(3.63)	(0.94)	(0.93)

Upper middle	−0.44	2.03	−0.20	0.20	6.47	7.80	0.80	1.01
	(6.81)	(6.89)	(1.04)	(1.09)	(6.00)	(6.03)	(1.17)	(1.23)
Upper	6.70	4.13			18.66	18.30		
	(25.76)	(25.67)			(22.70)	(22.45)		
Constant	89.31***	84.37***	8.38***	9.23***	−46.38***	−49.57***	−11.56***	−13.94***
	(7.52)	(8.48)	(1.42)	(1.62)	(6.62)	(7.42)	(1.94)	(2.56)
Model fit	0.3162	0.3228	106.63***	110.07***	0.5087	0.5204	124.37***	128.22***
Model A v. model B	1.78		3.31		2.97*		3.47	
N	251	251	192	192	251	251	192	192

Note: †p < 0.010, *p < 0.050, **p < 0.010, ***p < 0.001. Models for feeling thermometers show OLS regression coefficients. Models for voting behavior show log-odds coefficients from logistic regression. Feelings outcomes are measured from 0 (cold) to 100 (warm). "Model fit" row shows adjusted R^2 for OLS regressions and likelihood ratio test (comparing model with null model) for logistic regressions. "Model A v. model B" row shows F-test for OLS regressions and χ^2 test for logistic regressions, both comparing model A to model B.

42 Emily K. Carian

hostile sexism are equally good predictors for the belief that women lie about sexual assault.

Model 9B in Table 2.8 shows that hostile sexism is a superior predictor for agreement with rape myths: hostile sexism is significantly and positively correlated with agreement with rape myths, whereas inversive sexism is not statistically significant. The dependent variable for this model is an average of items from the short form of the IRMA Scale, which consists of seven questions, each corresponding to a different dimension of rape myths.[47] Of these seven dimensions, the category Payne and colleagues refer to as "She lied" is most similar in sentiment to belief about the prevalence of false sexual assault accusations. When analysis is done only on the measure representing the "She lied" dimension (i.e., agreement with the statement, "Rape accusations are often used as a way of getting back at men"), the same pattern of results emerges: both inversive and hostile sexism are significant ($p < 0.05$) and are statistically indistinguishable from one another ($F(1, 239) = 0.46$, $p = 0.50$; analyses available upon request). Importantly, inversive sexism is only predictive of the "She lied" measure; it is not significant for any other individual measure in the short form IRMA Scale when hostile, modern, and benevolent sexism are included in the regression. This pattern suggests that inversive sexism is not related to beliefs about rape generally but only to the particular belief that women lie about sexual assault and that this relationship is independent of hostile sexism. Given the other results shown in Tables 2.7 and 2.8, I conclude that the ideology of inversive sexism is less relevant to policy preferences and ideas about formal equality. Rather, it seems to be particularly related to the idea that women are distrustful and that the challenges they pose to men's moral goodness should not be believed. This reflects the use of inversive sexist discourse in male supremacist spaces. For instance, men's rights activists claim that feminists' demands that universities and law enforcement take women's accounts of sexual assault seriously amount to infringement on men's due process rights. Within the inversive sexist worldview, trusting women serves to disadvantage men rather than equalize the playing field.

Table 2.9 shows regressions for dependent variables related to political attitudes and behaviors, and here, the predictive utility of inversive sexism is even more evident. Inversive sexism predicts feelings toward and voting behaviors for Hillary Rodham Clinton (referred to as "Hillary Clinton" in the survey) and Donald Trump net of demographic characteristics, as shown in model A for each dependent variable in Table 2.9. When hostile, modern, and benevolent sexism are added to these regressions, inversive sexism still significantly predicts feelings toward Rodham Clinton, and the coefficient actually increases in magnitude: a 1-point increase in an individual's inversive sexism score is associated with a 12.62-point decrease in feelings of warmth toward Hillary Rodham Clinton (on a scale from 0 to 100) net of demographic characteristics and other sexism measures. Inversive sexism is the only sexism scale that has a significant relationship with this dependent variable, indicating that it is the best predictor. Modern sexism, on the other hand, is the best predictor of feelings toward Trump.

A similar pattern emerges when comparing predictors of voting behavior. While inversive sexism significantly predicts voting for Hillary Rodham Clinton (model 11A) and Donald Trump (model 13A) net of demographic characteristics, the coefficient for inversive sexism only remains significant when predicting voting for Rodham Clinton after the other sexism scales are added to the regressions. Model 11B shows that inversive sexism is the best predictor for voting for Rodham Clinton.

Conclusion

The data supports that inversive sexism is particularly related to beliefs and preferences that neutralize perceived threats to the gender status hierarchy: inversive sexism is predictive of beliefs about false rape accusations and feelings and voting for Rodham Clinton. When women accuse men of sexual assault, they challenge the assumption that men deserve access to the power and resources their identity prescribes. As the first woman to compete for the highest political office in the United States with a major party's support,[48] Hillary Rodham Clinton posed an enormous threat to the gender status hierarchy. Those high in inversive sexism were more likely to reject these challenges to the gender status hierarchy: they believe a greater percentage of sexual assault accusations are false, have colder feelings toward Rodham Clinton, and were more likely to have rejected Rodham Clinton at the polls. Importantly, inversive sexism is not the best predictor of preferences for policies geared toward achieving formal equality. These analyses suggest the need for a more nuanced understanding of the varied cultural ideologies that legitimize the many facets of gender inequality.

Discussion

The data indicate that inversive sexism is not merely an ideology of a radical fringe group, like the men's rights movement. Instead, inversive sexism reaches a level of endorsement that is statistically indistinguishable from that of hostile and modern sexism, two well-documented and recognized forms of sexism. The analyses also show that inversive sexism is endorsed by a unique population as compared to hostile, benevolent, and modern sexism: it is more concentrated among the young and lower middle class and more evenly distributed by sex. This fits with the presumed demographics of secular male supremacist groups, which are often described as young, working-class men (and some women). Finally, I find that inversive sexism is particularly predictive of attitudes and behaviors that defend the gender status hierarchy from symbolic threats, including accusations of sexual assault and feelings and voting for Hillary Rodham Clinton. These results demonstrate that inversive sexism is not a new take on an old cultural narrative but a

44 Emily K. Carian

unique ideology with distinct sociodemographic predictors, specifically aimed at undermining threats to the gender status hierarchy.

This is a critical moment for studying sexism, particularly the brand represented in the inversive sexism discourse. Inversive sexism is the through line for many conversations around gender inequality today: the assertion that there is a "war on men,"[49] the claim that the gender wage gap does not exist and more attention is spent on women's pay than is warranted,[50] and the concern that trust in (social) science is diminishing and that many deny the empirical realities of gender inequality.[51] The men's rights movement—a social movement founded upon inversive sexism—has gained supporters in powerful quarters, such as mainstream politics[52] and Silicon Valley.[53] The backlash against Hillary Rodham Clinton played an important role in her loss in the 2016 presidential election,[54] and backlash to the #MeToo movement is ongoing.[55] Measuring inversive sexism can help us understand how cultural narratives around gender inequality evolve to maintain male dominance in light of new threats to the gender order. If research is to pinpoint the mechanisms of persistent gender inequality, developing and testing tools for measuring this form of sexism is an important first step.

Notes

1 I have anonymized the men's rights forum to afford a greater degree of privacy for posters. Posters' genders were self-identified.
2 Michael A. Messner, *Politics of Masculinities: Men in Movements* (Lanham, MD: AltaMira Press, 1997), 41.
3 Meir Shemla and Anja Kreienberg, "Gender Quotas in Hiring Drive Away Both Women and Men," *Forbes*, October 16, 2014, http://www.forbes.com/sites/datafreaks/ 2014/10/16/gender-quotas-in-hiring-drive-away-both-women-and-men/.
4 Christina Hoff Sommers, "Title IX: How a Good Law Went Terribly Wrong," *Time*, June 23, 2014, http://time.com/2912420/titleix-anniversary/.
5 Jake New, "More Students Punished over Sexual Assault Are Winning Lawsuits against Colleges," *Inside Higher Ed*, November 5, 2015, https://www.insidehighered. com/news/2015/11/05/more-students-punished-over-sexual-assault-are-winning-lawsuits-against-colleges.
6 Paula England, "The Gender Revolution: Uneven and Stalled," *Gender & Society* 24, no. 2 (2010): 150.
7 Emily K. Carian and Amy L. Johnson, "The Agency Myth: Persistence in Individual Explanations for Gender Inequality," *Social Problems* Advance article, (2020): 15, https://doi.org/10.1093/socpro/spaa072.
8 Peter Glick and Susan T. Fiske, "The Ambivalent Sexism Inventory: Differentiating Hostile and Benevolent Sexism," *Journal of Personality and Social Psychology* 70, no. 3 (1996): 491.
9 Janet K. Swim et al., "Sexism and Racism: Old-Fashioned and Modern Prejudices," *Journal of Personality and Social Psychology* 68, no. 2 (1995): 199.
10 Glick and Fiske, "The Ambivalent Sexism Inventory," 491.
11 Peter Glick and Susan T. Fiske, "An Ambivalent Alliance. Hostile and Benevolent Sexism as Complementary Justifications for Gender Inequality," *The American Psychologist* 56, no. 2 (February 2001): 111–12.

12 Yuliana Zaikman and Michael J. Marks, "Ambivalent Sexism and the Sexual Double Standard," *Sex Roles* 71, no. 9–10 (2014): 333.

13 Swim et al., "Sexism and Racism," 199–200.

14 Bernard E. Whitley, "Gender-Role Variables and Attitudes toward Homosexuality," *Sex Roles* 45, no. 11–12 (2001): 691.

15 Allison C. Aosved and Patricia J. Long, "Co-occurrence of Rape Myth Acceptance, Sexism, Racism, Homophobia, Ageism, Classism, and Religious Intolerance," *Sex Roles* 55, no. 7–8 (2006): 481.

16 Manuela Barreto and Naomi Ellemers, "The Perils of Political Correctness: Men's and Women's Responses to Old-Fashioned and Modern Sexist Views," *Social Psychology Quarterly* 68, no. 1 (2005): 75.

17 Joelle C. Ruthig et al., "When Women's Gains Equal Men's Losses: Predicting a Zero-Sum Perspective of Gender Status," *Sex Roles* 76, no. 1–2 (2017): 17.

18 Ralph H. Turner, "Sponsored and Contest Mobility and the School System," *American Sociological Review* 25, no. 6 (1960): 856–57.

19 Amita Kelly, "Hillary Clinton Becomes First Woman to Top Major-Party Ticket," *NPR*, June 6, 2016, https://www.npr.org/2016/04/27/475765145/clintons-road-to-the-nomination-was-paved-by-other-women-who-ran.

20 Sophie Gilbert, "The Movement of #MeToo," *The Atlantic*, October 16, 2017, https://www.theatlantic.com/entertainment/archive/2017/10/the-movement-of-metoo/542979/.

21 Chelsea Hill, "Data Point: 2018, A Year of the Woman Like 1992?" (Center for American Women and Politics, Rutgers University, January 23, 2018), http://www.cawp.rutgers.edu/sites/default/files/resources/data-point-compare-1992-2018.pdf.

22 Lisa Lerer and Sydney Ember, "Kamala Harris Makes History as First Woman and Woman of Color as Vice President," *The New York Times*, November 7, 2020, https://www.nytimes.com/2020/11/07/us/politics/kamala-harris.html.

23 Greg Price, "Women in #MeToo Can 'Ruin a Man's Career' without Due Process, Morning Joe's Mika Brzezinski Says," *Newsweek*, December 19, 2017, https://www.newsweek.com/women-ruin-men-career-metoo-morning-joe-752386.

24 Laurie A. Rudman et al., "Status Incongruity and Backlash Effects: Defending the Gender Hierarchy Motivates Prejudice against Female Leaders," *Journal of Experimental Social Psychology* 48, no. 1 (2012): 165–67.

25 Michael W. Kraus et al., "Social Class Rank, Threat Vigilance, and Hostile Reactivity," *Personality & Social Psychology Bulletin* 37, no. 10 (October 2011): 1376.

26 John T. Jost, Mahzarin R. Banaji, and Brian A. Nosek, "A Decade of System Justification Theory: Accumulated Evidence of Conscious and Unconscious Bolstering of the Status Quo," *Political Psychology* 25, no. 6 (2004): 891.

27 Emily K. Carian, "'We're All in This Together': Leveraging a Personal Action Frame in Two Men's Rights Forums," Mobilization, forthcoming.

28 Kathy Charmaz, "Constructionism and the Grounded Theory Method," in *Handbook of Constructionist Research*, 397; modified grounded theory is an inductive method of analysis that extracts themes directly from the data. Unlike grounded theory, it allows the researcher to use previous literature to formulate initial coding categories.

29 Jill Weinberg, Jeremy Freese, and David McElhattan, "Comparing Data Characteristics and Results of an Online Factorial Survey between a Population-Based and a Crowdsource-Recruited Sample," *Sociological Science* 1 (2014): 292.

30 Bernadette Campbell, E. Glenn Schellenberg, and Charlene Y. Senn, "Evaluating Measures of Contemporary Sexism," *Psychology of Women Quarterly* 21, no. 1 (1997): 95.

46 Emily K. Carian

31 Philip M. Podsakoff et al., "Common Method Biases in Behavioral Research: A Critical Review of the Literature and Recommended Remedies," *The Journal of Applied Psychology* 88, no. 5 (2003): 884.
32 "The World Factbook: North America: United States," Central Intelligence Agency, 2017, https://www.cia.gov/library/publications/resources/the-world-factbook/geos/us.html.
33 Camille L. Ryan and Julie Siebens, "Educational Attainment in the United States: 2009," US Census Bureau, 2012: 4.
34 "Table A-1. Employment Status of the Civilian Population by Sex and Age," Bureau of Labor Statistics, January 6, 2017, https://www.bls.gov/news.release/empsit.t01.htm.
35 Glick and Fiske, "The Ambivalent Sexism Inventory," 500.
36 Swim et al., "Sexism and Racism," 212.
37 George F. Bishop, "Experiments with the Middle Response Alternative in Survey Questions," *Public Opinion Quarterly* 51, no. 2 (1987): 220.
38 Podsakoff et al., "Common Method Biases in Behavioral Research," 881.
39 I use the terms "female" and "male" throughout this chapter (rather than "women" and "men") because they correspond to the answer categories with which respondents could self-identify their sex.
40 Kraus et al., "Social Class Rank, Threat Vigilance, and Hostile Reactivity," 1376.
41 "The World Factbook: North America: United States," Central Intelligence Agency, accessed January 9, 2017, https://www.cia.gov/library/publications/resources/the-world-factbook/geos/us.html.
42 Tom W. Smith et al., "General Social Surveys, 1972–2016," *NORC at the University of Chicago*, 2018, http://gssdataexplorer.norc.org/.
43 "The American National Election Studies, 2016 Time Series Study," *Stanford University and the University of Michigan*, December 2017, http://www.electionstudies.org/studypages/anes_timeseries_2016/anes_timeseries_2016.htm.
44 Diana L. Payne, Kimberly A. Lonsway, and Louise F. Fitzgerald, "Rape Myth Acceptance: Exploration of Its Structure and Its Measurement Using the Illinois Rape Myth Acceptance Scale," *Journal of Research in Personality* 33 (1999): 49–50.
45 Campbell, Schellenberg, and Senn, "Evaluating Measures of Contemporary Sexism," 95.
46 "False Reporting," National Sexual Violence Resource Center, 2012, https://www.nsvrc.org/sites/default/files/Publications_NSVRC_Overview_False-Reporting.pdf.
47 Payne, Lonsway, and Fitzgerald, "Rape Myth Acceptance," 49–50.
48 Kelly, "Hillary Clinton Becomes First Woman to Top Major-Party Ticket."
49 Suzanne Venker, "The War on Men," *Fox News*, November 26, 2012, http://www.foxnews.com/opinion/2012/11/24/war-on-men.html.
50 Danielle Kurtzleben, "In Wage Gap Debate, a Fight Over 77 Cents," *US News & World Report*, June 10, 2013, http://www.usnews.com/news/articles/2013/06/10/in-wage-gap-debate-a-fight-over-77-cents.
51 Deborah L. Rhode, *Speaking of Sex: The Denial of Gender Inequality* (Cambridge: Harvard University Press, 1997), 2.
52 Erin Dooley, Janet Weinstein, and Meridith McGraw, "DeVos' Meetings with 'Men's Rights' Groups over Campus Sex Assault Spark Controversy," *ABC News*, July 14, 2017, http://abcnews.go.com/Politics/betsy-devos-meetings-mens-rights-groups-sex-assault/story?id=48611688.
53 Nellie Bowles, "Push for Gender Equality in Tech? Some Men Say It's Gone Too Far," *The New York Times*, September 23, 2017, https://www.nytimes.com/2017/09/23/technology/silicon-valley-men-backlash-gender-scandals.html.

54 Peter Beinart, "Fear of a Female President," *The Atlantic*, September 8, 2016, http://www.theatlantic.com/magazine/archive/2016/10/fear-of-a-female-president/497564/; Susan Faludi, "How Hillary Clinton Met Satan," *The New York Times*, October 29, 2016, http://www.nytimes.com/2016/10/30/opinion/sunday/how-hillary-clinton-met-satan.html.
55 Nicole Hemmer, "The Pre-emptive #MeToo Backlash," January 16, 2018, https://www.usnews.com/opinion/thomas-jefferson-street/articles/2018-01-16/aziz-ansari-and-the-pre-emptive-metoo-backlash.

3

THE U.S. FAR RIGHT'S POLITICS OF GENDER

Matthew N. Lyons

> The following is an excerpted version of a chapter on gender and sexuality that originally appeared in Matthew Lyons's 2018 *Insurgent Supremacists: The U.S. Far Right's Challenge to State and Empire* (PM Press). The author is grateful to Kersplebedeb Publishing for permission to reuse the material.

Issues of gender and sexuality tend to get short shrift in discussions of the U.S. far right. The far right is often defined as synonymous with the white nationalist movement, for whom race is the overriding issue, while the Christian right and other currents that emphasize gender and sexuality are treated as separate. Discussions of neonazis and other white nationalists don't necessarily address the ways that gender and sexuality permeate and help define racial politics. In addition, when gender and sexuality are discussed, the treatment does not usually explore complexities, contradictions, or debates within the movement or the ways that far-right positions on these issues have evolved over time.

For the past hundred years, far-right movements in both Europe and North America have promoted politics of gender and sexuality based on some synthesis—or contradictory mixture—of four ideological themes:

Patriarchal traditionalism: Often formulated in religious terms, this theme promotes rigid gender roles based on a romanticized image of the past. Women are confined to domestic roles as wife, mother, caregiver, plus at most a few (under) paid jobs that extend these roles into the wage economy. Women are to obey men, especially fathers and husbands, who are supposed to provide them security and protection (especially, in racist versions, protection against sexually aggressive men of other ethnicities). Traditionalism emphasizes the family as the main framework for male control over women. Homosexuality and gender nonconformity are strictly taboo and treated as immoral, sick, or part of

DOI: 10.4324/9781003164722-4

The U.S. Far Right's Politics of Gender   **49**

a deliberate effort to undermine the family and the social order. This is the most conservative current of far-right gender politics, although the "traditions" being defended are arbitrary, selective, and often made up.

Demographic nationalism: This theme embodies fears that the nation or race is not reproducing fast enough. A variant says that the quality of the national "stock" is declining because of cultural degeneration or racial mixing, and therefore eugenics programs are needed to control human breeding. Demographic nationalism says women's main duty to the nation or race is to have lots of babies (and, in the eugenics variant, the right kind of babies). This doctrine rejects homosexuality as a betrayal of the duty to reproduce but also sometimes clashes with patriarchal traditionalism—for example, in the Nazis' program to encourage out-of-wedlock births among "racially pure" Germans. Demographic nationalism (especially eugenicist versions) also tends to centralize male control over women through the state, which weakens patriarchal authority within the family.

Male bonding through warfare: This theme (which is also referred to as male tribalism) emphasizes warfare (hardship, risk of death, shared acts of violence, and killing) as the basis for deep emotional and spiritual ties between men. It is often implicitly homoerotic and sometimes celebrates male homosexuality (especially masculine gay men) and is frequently at odds with "bourgeois" family life. In the resulting cult of male comradeship, women may be targets of violent contempt or simply sidelined as irrelevant and unimportant. In Europe during and after World War I, this current flourished as an ideology that spoke to the camaraderie of the trenches and later street-fighting organizations.

Quasi-feminism: This theme advocates specific rights for women (or at least women of the privileged nation or race), such as educational opportunities, equal pay for equal work, and the right to vote, and encourages such women to engage in political activism, develop self-confidence and professional skills, and take on leadership roles. Quasi-feminism may criticize sexist dynamics within the movement or in society more broadly. At the same time, quasi-feminism accepts men's overall dominance, embraces gender roles as natural and immutable, advocates only specific rights for women rather than comprehensive equality, and often promotes intensified oppression for poor or working-class women or women who are targeted on ethnoreligious grounds.

Far-right movements have related to these four themes in different ways. Some far-right currents have mainly stuck to one theme, while others have combined two or more, depending on their ideology and constituency and on the pressures and opportunities of a given historical moment. In the United States for the past several decades, far-right politics have responded to the feminist and LGBT movements, as well as societal changes in family structures, employment, the legal system, and popular culture. While all of these responses have bolstered male dominance, some have been harshly and explicitly patriarchal, while others have borrowed feminist ideas and language in distorted form; some have tried to

50 Matthew N. Lyons

mobilize women by offering them specific benefits, while others have ignored or excluded them. Similarly, while all far-right currents have promoted heterosexism and gender conformity, some have offered limited space for certain forms of male homosexuality while others have not.

Using Feminist Language to Strengthen the Patriarchy

The modern Christian right, which first emerged on a mass scale in the 1970s, put gender and sexual politics at the center of its program. The movement largely represented a reaction to the 1960s upsurge of movements for women's liberation and gay liberation and promoted patriarchal traditionalism through initiatives against the Equal Rights Amendment, abortion rights, and LGBT rights. Christian rightists attacked both feminism and homosexuality as immoral, antifamily, elitist, and part of a secular-humanist conspiracy to weaken and ultimately enslave America.

The Christian right recruited large numbers of women with a contradictory blend of messages. On the one hand, the movement promoted a system of gender roles that offered many women a sense of security and meaning and, in Andrea Dworkin's words, "promise[d] to put enforceable restraints on male aggression."[1] Women were told that if they agreed to be obedient housewives and mothers, their husbands would reward them with protection, economic support, and love. Feminism was denounced as unnatural, man-hating, and a dangerous rejection of the safety that the traditional family supposedly offered women.

Within this overall framework, however, Christian rightists often framed their arguments in terms borrowed from feminism—for example, arguing that abortion "exploits women" or that federal support for childcare is wrong because it supposedly limits women's choices.[2] To varying degrees, some Christian right groups encouraged many women to become more self-confident and assertive, speak publicly, take on leadership roles, and get graduate training—as long as they did so in the service of the movement's patriarchal agenda.[3] In 1976, Christian right leaders Timothy and Beverly LaHaye published a bestselling sex manual, titled *The Act of Marriage*, which declared that (married, heterosexual) women have a right to sexual pleasure, endorsed birth control, and encouraged women to be active in lovemaking.[4]

In 1979, Beverly LaHaye founded Concerned Women for America (CWA), which today claims over half a million members and calls itself "the nation's largest public policy women's organization." CWA vilifies feminism as a threat to the traditional family and healthy moral values, but it also seeks to appeal to a mass audience of women who don't necessarily reject all feminist positions. For example, CWA's president, Penny Nance, has argued that it's a violation of religious liberty to require health insurers to pay for contraception, but the organization doesn't officially oppose contraception itself, claiming its members "hold a variety of views on the subject."[5]

The U.S. Far Right's Politics of Gender   **51**

CWA has often used feminist-sounding language about letting women think for themselves and make their own decisions. An article rejecting calls for wage equality between women and men concludes,

> Women's career plans come in all different shapes and sizes. They have different needs.... Stop trying to force ill-conceived policies on women that will ultimately hurt them in the workforce! In the rare instances of sex-based wage discrimination, there are already laws on the books which address it. *That* is something which all women should applaud.[6]

An article opposing federal funding for birth control accuses feminists of believing that "[w]omen are irresponsible. Women cannot make informed choices. / Without the government bailing them out or telling them what to do, women just wander hither and yon like helpless kittens."[7] In such ways, Christian rightists have used the language of women's empowerment to bolster their patriarchal agenda.

But like the rest of the Christian right, CWA has been unambiguous in rejecting LGBT experiences. CWA claims that "homosexual sex is dangerous and destructive to the human body" and has denounced same-sex marriage as an "abomination to God," harmful to children, and "as wrong as giving a man a license to marry his mother or daughter or sister or a group."[8] CWA has also declared that "transgenderism is a form of broken sexuality" at odds with the immutable, physical sex categories that God created.[9]

Calling Your Husband "Lord"

Over the past three decades, Christian Reconstructionists (a key part of the Christian right's hard-line theocratic wing) have spearheaded a shift away from the quasi-feminism exemplified by CWA to a much harsher ideology of male dominance. In 2008, when the Republican Party nominated Christian conservative Sarah Palin as its vice-presidential candidate, Reconstructionist Doug Phillips commented,

> Today, our friend Janice Crouse of Concerned Women for America offered a press release in which she declared: "Here is a woman of accomplishment who brings a fresh face to traditional values and models the type of woman most girls want to become." ... I respectfully disagree with part of that statement. I am confident that Mrs. Palin is a delightful, sincere, thoughtful, and capable woman with many commendable virtues. But in fairness, there is nothing "traditional" about mothers of young children becoming career moms, chief magistrates, and leading nations of three hundred million, nor is this pattern the Biblical ideal to which young women should aspire.[10]

Christian Reconstructionists have led the rise of the biblical patriarchy movement (which emphasizes that a woman's number one religious duty is "submission" to

52 Matthew N. Lyons

her husband) and its branch known as Quiverfull (which calls for couples to have as many babies as possible). Kathryn Joyce summarizes these doctrines:

> The "biblical" woman ... checks in with her husband as she moves through her day to see if she is fulfilling his priorities for her. When he comes home, she is a submissive wife who bolsters him in his role as spiritual and earthly leader of the family. She understands it's her job to keep him sexually satisfied at all times and that it's her calling as a woman to let those relations result in as many children as God wants to bless her with. She raises families of eight, ten, and twelve children, and she teaches her daughters to do the same. She's not the throwback to the fifties summoned in media-stoked "mommy wars"; she is a return to something far older.[11]

This "something far older," in Joyce's view, is Reconstructionism's idealized version of 17th-century Puritan society: "a collection of autonomous patriarchal households under the authority of the local church. America before democracy." Or to put it in slightly different terms, "it would be a form of Christian feudalism." In keeping with this vision, biblical patriarchy advocates oppose women's suffrage, arguing that it's the husband's role to be the political voice for his family.[12]

A slightly watered-down version of biblical patriarchy known as complementarianism (as in, men's and women's God-given roles are different but complementary) has a much wider reach among Protestant evangelicals.[13]

Biblical patriarchy's vision of godly husbands and fathers benevolently ruling over their families offers obvious privilege benefits to men. And as Cheryl Seelhoff, an ex-Quiverfull woman turned feminist, observes,

> many otherwise ordinary men with ordinary jobs who didn't command high levels of respect, societally, found a way to obtain respect in the Quiverfull community by being the leader of a devout, large family—the husband of a submissive wife, raising sons who would be future leaders in the church and daughters who would bear large families and care for them at home, and so on.[14]

What biblical patriarchy offers to women is more complex but also important. Unlike white nationalism, which aims to remove or exterminate those defined as Other, biblical patriarchy (like most male supremacist doctrines) keeps the subordinate Other within the home on terms of intimate interdependence. As a result, biblical patriarchy requires constant indoctrination of women and girls to get them to accept and, if possible, embrace their subordinate position. Many of the authors and bloggers who promote and articulate this ideology are themselves women. Biblical patriarchy praises women who fulfill their appointed roles as wives, homemakers, and mothers of large families and tells them that "feminism" (which it falsely equates with capitalist mass culture) treats these roles with

The U.S. Far Right's Politics of Gender **53**

contempt. It tells them that slavery to God is the only true freedom: freedom from sin and freedom from burdens that women were never meant to bear, such as having to make decisions for themselves or their families.[15]

Biblical patriarchy tells women and girls that feminism is their original sin— Eve's sin of disobedience to godly authority. It teaches them that their body belongs to their husband, not to them. It teaches them to trust men and not themselves.[16]

Biblical patriarchy and Quiverfull represent the most extreme version of patriarchal traditionalism, but Quiverfull, specifically, also incorporates a strong secondary element of demographic nationalism. If having big families is primarily about avoiding sin, to Quiverfull advocates, it is also a way to expand the population of faithful Christians and eventually overpower unbelievers through sheer numbers. In addition, Quiverfull advocates (most of whom are in the United States) have made common cause with other Christian rightists in warning Europeans against the threat of "demographic winter." This campaign exploits fears that declining birthrates among white Europeans, coupled with rising numbers of darker-skinned and Muslim immigrants, will destroy Europe's cultural and racial identity. To ward off this fate, Quiverfull advocates urge Europeans to reject the evils of abortion, contraception, and feminism; reaffirm the patriarchal family; and accept their reproductive responsibility. Here, as elsewhere, theocratic ideology incorporates an implicit white nationalism.[17]

All Believers Called to Be Priests

The New Apostolic Reformation (NAR) movement is much more racially diverse and inclusive than Christian Reconstructionism, and it promotes a strikingly different model of women's social and political roles as well. Like Reconstructionism, NAR is a theocratic movement that wants to impose a deeply repressive moral code across all spheres of society, but this vision, unlike biblical patriarchy, allows significant room for women's agency and voice. New Apostolic Reformers declare that God created men and women differently and with different roles, yet in NAR, a number of women not only serve as ministers but hold high international leadership roles in the movement as prophets and apostles—something that would be inconceivable in Reconstructionism.[18]

Cindy Jacobs, co-leader of Generals International and one of the top-ranking women in NAR, has provided a forum for a number of other female NAR ministers to speak out on gender issues. Diane Lake of Christian International Ministries found biblical support for women's leadership, noting that Deborah served as a judge in ancient Israel and women worked with Paul in apostolic ministry.[19] Lonnie Crowe argued that viewing Eve as the conduit through which sin entered Creation was the result of "faulty Biblical exegesis."[20] Pastor Tisha Sledd declared that women were "fighting to be freed from" a "system of patriarchal beliefs."[21]

In an article on her own ministry's website entitled "How Patriarchy Is Killing the American Church," Sledd stated that she was a "suffragist" but not a "feminist" because feminism was rooted in "selfishness and anger" and had

54 Matthew N. Lyons

been "hijacked by women who hate men." In contrast, a suffragist believed that women were "equal to men in every way" and "deserve the right to vote in every facet of society."[22]

Given the patriarchal Christendom that Sledd has described, it's unlikely that the average NAR congregation is supportive of women challenging male control. Yet NAR's quasi-feminist tendencies are important both because they force us to rethink standard assumptions about the Christian far right and because they highlight the far right's capacity to appropriate progressive, egalitarian politics for its own repressive, anti-egalitarian, and anti-humanist goals.

Both Warriors and Bearers of the Race

For neonazis, racial ideology is the overarching framework that shapes their gender politics. In general, neonazis promote subordination for all women but in different ways depending on racial identity. For example, White Aryan Resistance and other neonazi groups have opposed abortion for white women but supported it for women of color.[23] Drawing on old themes prominent in both U.S. white supremacy and European fascism, many neonazis emphasize a need to control non-Jewish white women's bodies so as to maintain the purity of the race. In propaganda works such as William Pierce's *The Turner Diaries*, combating interracial sex is a major concern, particularly the victimization of innocent white women by black rapists and Jewish pimps, as well as racial treason by white women who willingly have sex with men of color.

In a 1982 article, Pierce offered an overview of sexual rules based on racial ideology:

> [T]he primary purpose of sexual activity is the upbreeding of the race. The strongest taboo, then, must be against any sexual activity which tends to degrade the race. ... Next in order of sinfulness is an act of symbolic degradation. The act of a man and woman intended to engender a healthy, white child should be viewed as a sacramental act. Even when a sex act is not specifically sacramental—i.e., not intended to produce children—it ought not to be of a nature which clashes with sacramental sex or which tends to undermine or distort the basic view of sexual activity. Thus bestiality and homosexuality are beyond the pale, just as interracial sex with a sterile partner (or involving contraception) is.[24]

Although white supremacist rightists have fixated on interracial sex for much of U.S. history, they have focused on homosexuality only since the 1970s, in response to the rise of gay and lesbian activism. Since then, neonazis have been implicated in a number of violent anti-LGBT attacks, such as the 1987 murder of three men at a gay bookstore in Shelby, North Carolina (for which two former members of the White Patriot Party were indicted but not convicted), and Eric Rudolph's 1997 bombing of an Atlanta lesbian bar, which injured five people.

The U.S. Far Right's Politics of Gender **55**

(Rudolph also bombed two women's health clinics to protest abortion.)[25] Starting in the 1980s, neonazis exploited anti-gay fears associated with the AIDS crisis in an effort to win popular support. Harold Covington argued in his 1987 book *The March Upcountry* that AIDS represented a strategic opportunity for the movement:

> At long last, using AIDS as an excuse, White people could really say what they felt about faggots! And from saying and openly admitting what they really feel about queers, it is only a short step to saying what they really feel about those other major AIDS carriers, the blacks. ... And who knows? Once Whites get really used to speaking their mind, maybe Yehudi [the Jew] himself might come in for a mention or two.[26]

To some extent, neonazis call for implementing sexual rules through patriarchal traditionalism—centered on controlling white women within the family. But many neonazis also emphasize demographic nationalism and—in sharp contrast with Christian rightists—advocate eugenicist policies to improve the white race's fitness and purity. The current American Nazi Party (not to be confused with the 1960s organization of the same name), for example, has declared that "Aryan men and Aryan women have distinctive but complementary social roles to play, and that just as the man is the natural breadwinner and warrior, so the woman is the natural homemaker." But the party has also called for the state to impose "positive eugenic measures" to promote "propagation of the highest racial elements," as well as steps "to halt the spread of hereditary defects and racially impure blood within the gene pool of the racial community."[27] The National Socialist Movement has called for reestablishing "the nuclear family in which the father works while the mother stays at home and takes care of the children if they so choose." It also advocates "a structured system of pay raises for those that give birth to healthy babies" and prohibiting "abortion and euthanasia, except in cases of rape, incest, race-mixing, or mental retardation."[28]

On the broader questions of women's roles in the movement and in society, neonazis range from hard-line misogyny to quasi-feminism. In the 1980s and '90s, Aryan Nations and National Alliance tended to oppose paid employment and any public political role for women.[29] Aryan Nations declared, "[F]eminism is the means to weaken Aryan masculinity, promoted by the international Jew."[30] More recently, the Vanguard News Network (VNN) has continued this line of thought. VNN founder Alex Linder claimed, for example, that

> [w]omen are repeaters. It is not in them to originate or create anything but a baby except in the most unusual case. ... Plenty of women are smart, but only in a mechanical sense. ... Smart women are just able to access the answer authority wants to hear quicker than others—but they can't truly think about anything. It really is true, what Schopenhauer (said)—men are what is referred to when we speak of humans. Women are just ways of getting new men.[31]

VNN has also attacked women's supposed political power. One VNN post, entitled "The Female Vote: A Terrible Idea Since 1920," declared,

> And it isn't just female *voting* that's a problem, it's female power in general: women have much more power today than they did in 1970. They control big businesses. They often hold positions of legislative power, and they often control households as well. That's **not** a good thing. White men built Western culture and only White men can manage it properly. One big consequence of more female power is the incredible growth of the federal government. Women, like liberals, are big believers in federal power.[32]

However, quasi-feminism has also been represented in the neonazi movement. For example, in the 1980s and '90s, Molly Gill of St. Petersburg, Florida, edited a neonazi newsletter under a series of titles: *Independent Woman*, *The Radical Feminist*, and *The Rational Feminist*. Gill wrote that she had been involved in the women's movement since 1977 and served on the board of directors of the First Tampa Bay Women's Rape Crisis Center. In the spring 1991 issue, she explained, "We use the term 'radical feminist' to indicate that we agree in general with the principles in the book, *The Sexual Liberals and the Attack on Feminism*" (an anthology of anti-pornography feminist writings published in 1990). "We oppose the exploitation of women in any form, to a greater degree than other feminist factions such as NOW, anarchist feminists, etc."[33] A regular feature of Gill's publication was the "Feminist Counseling Column," which for example argued that "over-controlling, domineering daddies" were often to blame for young women "running with men of other races." "So don't ride herd too hard," Gill cautioned white fathers, "or she's likely to slip in a little miscegenation."[34]

Tom Metzger's White Aryan Resistance (WAR), too, has long promoted a racist quasi-feminism. In the 1980s, WAR sponsored an affiliate called the Aryan Women's League, which declared that white women had important roles to play both as mothers and nurturers on the one hand and as "women warriors fighting to save our noble Aryan race" through direct political activism.[35]

Sociologist Kathleen Blee conducted a study of women who were active in "Ku Klux Klan, neo-Nazi, Christian Identity, white-power, skinhead, and other white-supremacist groups" in the mid-1990s.[36] She noted widespread conflict within such groups over women's roles—for example, in white supremacist skinhead groups: "Many skin groups are intensely male-dominated and violently misogynist ..." yet "skinhead women are often the racist movements' most physically aggressive women, and at least some prominent skinhead women publicly confront the sexism of male skinhead culture."[37]

Blee also found that female activists' experiences were often much more negative than the propaganda image of Aryan women warriors. While some white supremacist women she spoke with felt empowered by racist activism, many others spoke of "having made great sacrifices to be in a movement that has given

The U.S. Far Right's Politics of Gender   **57**

them little in return." To some extent, this reflected the specific demands that white supremacist groups placed on female members, especially the intense focus on biological reproduction, "ensuring the purity of racial bloodlines … and increasing white birthrates." But many of the frustrations that these women activists experienced reflected sexist dynamics common to other social movements, including liberal and leftist ones: women were "expected to perform material and wifely roles," relegated to "middle-level and informal leadership positions," and frustrated with their organizations' failure to address their needs.[38]

Without Women Getting in the Way

In recent years, the alt-right has revitalized far-right politics in the United States with skillful online activism and a dynamic relationship with Donald Trump's political candidacy. Alt-right ideology centers on white nationalism but also draws on other political currents, some of which focus on reasserting male dominance more than on racial issues. Although alt-rightists largely echo neonazi positions on gender and sexuality, there are some notable differences. Alt-rightists have generally repudiated quasi-feminism and thus are, if anything, even more harshly misogynistic than many neonazis of recent decades. At the same time, in sharp contrast to U.S. neonazism, alt-rightists do not necessarily reject homosexuality. A few openly homosexual men have been important participants in alt-right forums, and alt-rightists have actively debated the place of homosexuality in the movement and in the white race's history and future.

Harassment and vilification of women and girls have been central to the alt-right's political activism. Such tactics reflect an intense misogyny that runs through the movement. Most of the alt-right declares that women are intellectually and morally inferior to men and should be stripped of any political role.

Alt-rightists have claimed that it's natural for men to rule over women and that women want and need this, that "giving women freedom [was] one of mankind's greatest mistakes," that women should "never be allowed to make foreign policy [because] their vindictiveness knows no bounds," and that feminism is defined by mental illness and has turned women into "caricatures of irrationality and hysteria."[39] And while alt-rightists give lip service to the traditionalist idea that women have important, dignified roles to play as mothers and homemakers, the overwhelming message is that women as a group are contemptible, pathetic creatures not worthy of respect.

On some issues, notably abortion, alt-rightists combine race and gender positions in ways that closely parallel the neonazi movement. While some alt-rightists have argued that abortion should simply be banned as immoral, others counter that it plays a useful role as a form of eugenics. They claim that legal abortion is disproportionately used by black and Latina women and potentially could be a way to weed out "defective" white babies as well. Dismissing the idea that women have a right to control their own bodies, *Counter-Currents* editor Greg Johnson commented, "in a White Nationalist society … some abortions should be forbidden, others should be mandatory, but under no circumstances should they simply be a matter of a woman's choice."[40]

The anti-feminist online subculture known as the manosphere overlaps with the alt-right and has had a significant influence on alt-right ideology and tactics. While some manospherians claim that they simply want equality between the sexes, others advocate patriarchy openly. Some manospherians are family-centered traditionalists while others celebrate a more predatory sexuality.

Daryush Valizadeh (Roosh V) embodies this tension. His 8,000-word "What Is Neomasculinity?" argues that male and female identities are genetically determined at birth; traditional sex roles are products of human evolution; gender equality is a myth with no scientific basis; patriarchy is the best social system for individual fulfillment and civilization as a whole; the nuclear family with one father and one mother in the same home is the healthiest unit for raising children; socialism is damaging because it makes women dependent on the government and discourages them from using their "feminine gifts" to "land a husband." Yet the staunch traditionalism of this document contrasts starkly with Valizadeh's role as a pick-up artist. He has written ten how-to books for male sex tourists with titles such as *Bang Ukraine* and *Bang Iceland*. The blurb for *Bang Colombia* says that the book is "for guys who want to go to Colombia mostly to fuck women. It contains tons of moves, lines, and tips learned after six months of full-time research in the city of Medellin, where I dedicated my existence to cracking the code of Colombian women." Valizadeh doesn't dwell on his own glaring inconsistency, but does suggest in "What Is Neomasculinity?" that the dismantling of patriarchal rules has forced men to pursue "game" as a defensive strategy "to hopefully land some semblance of a normal relationship." (Since this was written, Valizadwh has embraced Orthodox Christianity and renounced casual sex.)[41]

Manospherians tend to promote homophobia and transphobia, consistent with their efforts to reimpose rigid gender roles and identities. At *Return of Kings*, Valizadeh has denounced the legalization of same-sex marriage as "one phase of a degenerate march to persecute heterosexuals, both legally and socially, while acclimating young children to the homosexual lifestyle."[42] On the same website, Matt Forney warned that trans women who have sex with cis men might be guilty of "rape by fraud."[43] At the same time, some manosphere sites have sought to reach out to gay men. *A Voice for Men* published a series of articles by Matthew Lye that were later collected into the e-book *The New Gay Liberation: Escaping the Fag End of Feminism*, which Paul Elam described as "a scorching indictment of feminist hatred of all things male."[44]

Jack Donovan, who was an active and influential participant in the alt-right from 2010 to 2017, has contributed to some manosphere publications but offers his own distinctive male tribalist ideology. Donovan's "Way of the Gang" is a vision of male supremacy based on the shared loyalty of men prepared to fight and die together. This is the ideology of male bonding through warfare in pure form. Donovan rejects any compromises with feminism, ignores demographic nationalism, and clashes head-on with patriarchal traditionalism, as can be seen by comparing his ideas with biblical patriarchy doctrine.

The U.S. Far Right's Politics of Gender **59**

Like biblical patriarchy, Donovan's ideology calls for reasserting "traditional" gender roles, confining women to the domestic sphere, and excluding them from any say in running society or the state. But in other ways, the two doctrines are miles apart. A former Satanist, Donovan anchors his ideas in evolutionary psychology, not the Bible—an approach that's probably meaningless, if not satanic, to Adam and Eve creationists. And while even the most hard-core biblical patriarchs aim to recruit women, as well as men (claiming their path offers women security and respect, not to mention salvation through Jesus), Donovan does not write for women at all. His audience, his community, his hope for the future, is entirely male.

In Donovan's ideal society, which he calls "The Brotherhood," women's main roles would be to birth and raise children and to help preserve the memory of the ancestors because "young men should grow up knowing what their great-grandfathers and great-great-grandfathers did, and who they were, and what they believed." To some extent, this sounds consistent with biblical patriarchy, but there's a difference. To biblical patriarchy advocates, the family is the basic economic and political unit of society. To Donovan,

> The family is a means for the continuation of The Brotherhood, and gives a sacred role to women in The Brotherhood. The ideal woman is Queen Gorgo of Sparta ... boasting that only women of her tribe give birth to worthy men.[45]

This is a reversal of the idea that men become hunters and warriors to protect and provide for their families. As Jef Costello noted on the white nationalist website *Counter-Currents*, Donovan is saying that women exist in order to bring men into the world, and the family exists because it makes idealized male gang life possible.[46]

Donovan's open homosexuality and advocacy of sexual relationships between masculine men are his most dramatic disagreement with biblical patriarchy.[47] He does not call himself gay, rejects gay culture as effeminate, and justifies homophobia as a defense of masculinity rooted in the male gang's collective survival needs.[48] In Donovan's ideology, "androphilia" is a consummation of the priority that manly men place on each other. As he has commented, "When you get right down to it, when it comes to sex, homos are just men without women getting in the way."[49]

Unlike Christian rightists, who argue that feminism misleads women into betraying their true interests, Donovan sees feminism as an expression of women's basic nature, which is "to calm men down and enlist their help at home, raising children, and fixing up the grass hut." Today, feminists' supposed alliance with globalist elites reflects this: "Women are better suited to and better served by the globalism and consumerism of modern democracies that promote security, no-strings attached sex and shopping." It's not that women are evil, Donovan claims. "Women are humans who are slightly different from men, and given the opportunity they will serve their slightly different interests and follow their own

60 Matthew N. Lyons

slightly different way." But that slightly different way inevitably clashes with men's interests and therefore needs to be firmly controlled, if not suppressed.[50]

White nationalist alt-rightists place ideas about gender and sexuality within the framework of race, as neonazis have done for decades, but to varying degrees, they are also influenced by writers such as Donovan and Valizadeh, for whom race is secondary. In "The Woman Question in White Nationalism," Greg Johnson of *Counter-Currents Publishing* declared, "Preserving our race's biological integrity... requires the defeat of feminism and emasculation (male infantilization) and the restoration of sexual roles that are not just traditional but also biological: men as protectors and providers, women as nurturers." In parts of this essay, Johnson sounds like a manospherian: "[E]very man knows another man who has been emotionally and financially savaged by the punitive feminist biases now codified in laws governing marriage, divorce, and child custody." Yet he also implicitly rejected the pick-up artist and "men going their own way" lifestyles celebrated by many manospherians:

> In a White Nationalist society, men will no longer be allowed to prolong their adolescence into their thirties and forties. They will be expected, encouraged, and enabled to take on adult responsibilities as soon as they are able. They will become husbands and fathers, providers and protectors for their families.[51]

In the alt-right's early years quasi-feminism had a foothold, as when National-Anarchist Andrew Yeoman criticized the "constant litany of abuse and frequent courtship invitations from unwanted suitors" that women faced from men in the movement. Yeoman argued that "We need women's help, now more than ever," yet "nothing says 'you are not important to us' [more] than sexualizing women in the movement."[52] A year later, Greg Johnson also acknowledged that "a sizable and vocal enough minority" of white nationalists were "genuine woman haters," but unlike Yeoman, he argued that they should be given free rein and that women activists should simply be "tolerant and understanding" of such misogyny, "as a personal sacrifice to the greater good."[53] More recently, alt-rightists have tended to dismiss or trivialize the issue entirely, as when the Traditionalist Youth Network (TYN) declared that women were underrepresented in the movement because by nature they are "neither designed nor inclined to develop or encourage politically aggressive subcultures."[54] *The Daily Stormer* instituted a policy against publishing anything written by women and called for limiting women's involvement in the movement—in the face of criticism from women on the more old school neonazi discussion site *Stormfront*. Manospherian-turned-alt-rightist Matt Forney declared, "Trying to 'appeal' to women is an exercise in pointlessness. ... [I]t's not that women should be unwelcome [in the alt-right], it's that they're unimportant."[55] The few women who have identified themselves with the alt-right have embraced a subordinate role.[56]

TYN has claimed that "women's biological drives are contrary to the best interests of civilization and ... the past century or so of women's enfranchisement and liberation has been detrimental to societal stability." But the group

The U.S. Far Right's Politics of Gender **61**

framed this position as relatively moderate because, unlike some manospherians, they didn't believe "that women are central to the destruction of Western Civilization"—they are simply being manipulated by the Jews.

> While there's an organic (and not entirely degenerate) thread of indigenous feminist interest in expanding female power and influence in our society, the nature and scope of feminism in the contemporary West is almost entirely Jewish in origin and character.

TYN conceded that "western women" "can and should be trusted in a variety of leadership and leading roles in a healthy Western society," although they shouldn't be allowed to vote "in matters relating to foreign policy or immigration policy" because "feminine nurturing impulses" cloud their judgment.[57]

True to its name, the Traditionalist Youth Network/Traditionalist Worker Party takes a patriarchal-traditionalist position with regard to homosexuality, declaring, "In Western pagan and Christian civilization, homosexual behavior has always been looked upon as being a degenerate behavior," and "homosexuality in the 21st century has become the vehicle for a demonically [i.e., Jewish] inspired attack upon our civilization and our culture."[58]

Many alt-rightists share TYN's utter rejection of homosexuality—but a significant number of them don't. Writing in 2010, Greg Johnson agreed that "leftist gays really are repulsive" but urged white nationalists to welcome white gays who shared their politics. "Quite a number of homosexual men do not fit the effeminate stereotype. They are masculine, and appreciate masculine things like facts, logic, and forthright action. And even effeminate gay men can make a real contribution." Directly contradicting TYN's positions, Johnson claimed that "homosexual behavior was not only tolerated by ancient Aryan peoples, it was considered normal, in some cases even ideal," and that homophobia—not homosexuality—had been promoted by Jews to divide and weaken the white race. Fear of homosexuality "has chilled same-sex friendships and male bonding, and it is the bonded male group, the *Männerbund*, that is the foundation of all higher forms of civilization, particularly Aryan civilizations."[59]

Johnson's comments here resonate with Jack Donovan's work and also with the writings of white nationalist and alt-rightist James O'Meara, a homosexual man who, like Donovan, rejects the label "gay." O'Meara has called homosexual men "the natural elite of the Aryan peoples" and argued that

> The origin of the handing down (tradition) of culture, at least in the Aryan world, lies not in the family ... but in those who have broken from it and established their own groups for these purposes: the various *Männerbunde* of warriors, priests, scholars, vigilantes, etc.[60]

O'Meara has no interest in combating homophobia ("taking pity on some sniveling queen in a closet demanding 'my rights!'") but, unlike Donovan, his vision of male brotherhood has ample room for effeminate, as well as masculine members.[61]

Conclusion

Many far-right ideas about gender and sexuality have deep historical roots, but the rise of the feminist and LGBT movements since the 1960s has made these issues more prominent and politically volatile than they were before. Far rightists have responded to these movements in different ways, offering various versions or combinations of patriarchal traditionalism, demographic nationalism, quasi-feminism, and the cult of male comradeship. Some New Apostolic Reformers have celebrated women's empowerment and challenged male dominance in ways that belie standard assumptions, and even some neonazis have done the same. But in recent years, there has also been a strong trend toward increasingly harsh and explicit male supremacist doctrines, ranging from Christian Reconstructionist–inspired biblical patriarchy to the male warrior culture of Jack Donovan and others. At the same time, some alt-rightists have contested the far right's traditional blanket rejection of homosexuality, either because they want to drive a wedge between LGBT people and liberal/left politics or as a pure expression of male bonding "without women getting in the way." All of this adds up to a complex, conflicted, and dynamic political landscape that cannot be fought with dismissive stereotypes.

Notes

1 Andrea Dworkin, *Right-Wing Women* (New York: Coward-McCann, 1983), 21.
2 Sara Diamond, *Spiritual Warfare: The Politics of the Christian Right* (Boston, MA: South End Press, 1989), 104–106.
3 Susan Faludi, *Backlash: The Undeclared War against American Women* (New York: Anchor Books, Doubleday, 1991), 250–252.
4 Tim LaHaye and Beverly LaHaye, *The Act of Marriage: The Beauty of Sexual Love* (Grand Rapids, MI: Zondervan Publishing House, 1976).
5 "About Us," *Concerned Women for America* (website), n.d.; Penny Young Nance, "There Is No War on Women," *Politico*, October 4, 2013.
6 Crystal Goodremote, "Award Winning Display of Ignorance," *Concerned Women for America* (website), February 23, 2015.
7 CWALAC Staff, "Make Love Not War (on Women)," *Concerned Women for America* (website), October 7, 2013.
8 Janice Shaw Crouse, "Five Myths about Same Sex Marriage," Townhall.com, March 9, 2010; "Church's Decision to Endorse the Sin of Homosexuality Is an Act of Apostasy," *Christian Today*, n.d.; CWALAC Staff, "Why Homosexual 'Marriage' Is Wrong," *Concerned Women for America* (website), September 16, 2003.
9 CWALAC Staff, "Christ Restoring a Male/Female Identity in a Sexually Confused World," *Concerned Women for America* (website), May 13, 2016.
10 Quoted in Julie J. Ingersoll, *Building God's Kingdom: Inside the World of Christian Reconstruction* (New York: Oxford University Press, 2015), 165.
11 Kathryn Joyce, *Quiverfull: Inside the Christian Patriarchy Movement* (Boston, MA: Beacon Press, 2009), ix.
12 Ibid., 27, 101.
13 Ibid., x, 13–16.
14 Ibid., 206.

The U.S. Far Right's Politics of Gender **63**

15 Ibid., 17, 50, 93–94, 98–99, 102.

16 Ibid., 81, 96–97, 135, 208.

17 Ibid., 184, 189–192.

18 Rick Joyner, "The High Calling of Womanhood," *MorningStar Ministries* (website), 2003; Rachel Tabachnick, "Resource Directory for the New Apostolic Reformation," *Talk to Action* (website), January 20, 2010.

19 Diane Lake, "A Great Company of Women," *Generals International* (website), May 9, 2016.

20 Lonnie Crowe, "Redeeming Eve," *Generals International* (website), May 23, 2016.

21 Tisha Sledd, "Return to Eden: Equality for Women in God's Kingdom," *Generals International* (website), May 16, 2016.

22 Tisha Sledd, "How Patriarchy Is Killing the American Church," *Tisha Sledd Ministries* (website), April 4, 2016.

23 Barbara Perry, "'White Genocide': White Supremacists and the Politics of Reproduction," in *Home-Grown Hate: Gender and Organized Racism*, ed. Abby L. Ferber (New York: Routledge, 2004), 85–86.

24 Quoted in Mab Segrest and Leonard Zeskind, *Quarantines and Death: The Far Right's Homophobic Agenda* (pamphlet) (Atlanta, GA: Center for Democratic Renewal, 1989), 25.

25 Segrest and Zeskind, *Quarantines and Death*, 7; Leonard Zeskind, *Blood and Politics: The History of the White Nationalist Movement from the Margins to the Mainstream* (New York: Farrar Straus Giroux, 2009), 132, 460–462; Crystal Bonvillian, "Serial Bomber Eric Rudolph Targeted Olympics, Gay Club, Abortion Clinics," *Atlanta Journal-Constitution*, March 19, 2018.

26 Quoted in Segrest and Zeskind, *Quarantines and Death*, 13.

27 "What We Stand For," *American Nazi Party* (website), 2012.

28 "25 Points of American National Socialism," *National Socialist Movement* (website), n.d.

29 Martin Durham, *White Rage: The Extreme Right and American Politics* (New York: Routledge, 2007), 88–89.

30 Quoted in Kathleen M. Blee, "Women and Organized Racism," in *Home-Grown Hate*, ed. Ferber (New York: Routledge, 2004), 66.

31 Alex Linder, "Alex Linder on Women vs. Men," *Vanguard News Network* (website), September 21, 2009.

32 Alex Linder, "The Female Vote: A Terrible Idea Since 1920," *Vanguard News Network*, February 9, 2016.

33 Molly Gill, *The Radical Feminist*, vol. 5, no. 2 (Spring 1991).

34 Gill, *The Rational Feminist*, 6.

35 Durham, *White Rage*, 95.

36 Blee, "Women and Organized Racism," 49.

37 Ibid., 68, 69.

38 Ibid., 73.

39 Northman, "Women Should Hate Freedom," *The Right Stuff* (website), December 2, 2013; Danielle Paquette, "The Alt-Right Isn't Only about White Supremacy. It's about White Male Supremacy," *Chicago Tribune*, November 25, 2016; Gregory Hood, "A Cat Lady Culture," *Radix Journal*, June 2, 2015.

40 Greg Johnson, "Abortion & White Nationalism," *Counter-Currents Publishing* (website), April 2016; see also Aylmer Fisher, "The Pro-Life Temptation," *Radix Journal*, April 8, 2016; Brad Griffin [Hunter Wallace], "The Pro-Choice Temptation," *Occidental Dissent* (blog), April 12, 2016; T.M. Goddard, "Unintended Consequences," *Radix Journal*, April 13, 2016.

41 Roosh V [Daryush Valizadeh], "What Is Neomasculinity?" *Roosh V* (website), May 6, 2015; "Travel Books," *Roosh V Store* (website), n.d.; Emily Shugarman and Will Sommer, "Noxious Pickup Artist Roosh Say He Has Found God," *Daily Beast*, May 23, 2019.

42 Roosh V [Daryush Valizadeh], "Why Homosexual Marriage Matters for Straight Men," *Return of Kings* (website), October 12, 2015.

43 Matt Forney, "Are Transsexuals Who Sleep with Straight Men Guilty of Rape?" *Return of Kings* (website), December 8, 2014.

44 Paul Elam, "Andy Bob Exposes Feminist Hatred of Gay Men in New Book," *A Voice for Men* (website), January 7, 2016.

45 Jack Donovan, *A Sky without Eagles: Selected Essays and Speeches 2010–2014* (Milwaukie, OR: Dissonant Hum, 2014), 160, 158.

46 Jef Costello, "Jack Donovan's *A Sky without Eagles*" [review], *Counter-Currents Publishing* (website), July 2014.

47 Chip Smith, "The First Rule of Androphilia: An Interview with Jack Malebranche," *The Hoover Hog* (website), January 2009.

48 Jack Donovan, *The Way of Men* (Milwaukie, OR: Dissonant Hum, 2012), 60–62.

49 Jack Donovan, comment on "Jack Donovan" discussion thread, *Roosh V Forum* (website), November 16, 2012.

50 Donovan, *The Way of Men*, 137, 148, 150.

51 Greg Johnson, "The Woman Question in White Nationalism." *Counter-Currents Publishing*, May 25, 2011.

52 Andrew Yeoman, "We Will Lose," AlternativeRight.com, June 9, 2010, reposted in *Radix Journal*.

53 Johnson, "Woman Question in White Nationalism."

54 Matt Parrott, "Where the White Women At?" *Traditionalist Worker Party* (website), April 13, 2015.

55 "White Supremacists Feud over the Racist Gender Gap," *Anti-Defamation League* (blog), April 26, 2016; Paquette, "Alt-Right Isn't Only about White Supremacy."

56 E.W., "Women and the Alt-Right," *The Economist*, February 1, 2017; Flavia Dzodan, "Alt-Feminism and the White Nationalist Women Who Love It," *This Political Woman* (website), March 7, 2017.

57 Matt Parrott, "Jews Destroy Women: A Response to 'Women Destroy Nations,'" *Traditionalist Worker Party* (website), February 18, 2016.

58 Matthew Heimbach, "The Homosexual Lobby," *Traditionalist Worker Party* (website), June 19, 2013.

59 Greg Johnson, "Homosexuality & White Nationalism," *Counter-Currents Publishing*, October 4, 2010 [originally published on *Vanguard News Network*, June 28, 2002, under the pseudonym F.C.I. Clarke].

60 Quoted in Ann Sterzinger, "Fashy Homos & Green Nazis in Space" [review of *Green Nazis in Space! New Essays on Literature, Art, and Culture* by James J. O'Meara], *Counter-Currents Publishing*, May 20, 2016.

61 Andy Nowicki, "The Homo and the Negro: An Interview with James O'Meara," *Alternative Right* (alternative-right.blogspot.com), April 6, 2014 [originally Published December 10, 2012].

PART II
Patriarchal Traditionalism

4

"I WANT TO THANK MY HUSBAND FRED FOR LETTING ME COME HERE," OR PHYLLIS SCHLAFLY'S OPPORTUNISTIC DEFENSE OF GENDER HIERARCHY

Amélie Ribieras

> We have the immense good fortune to live in a civilization which respects the family as the basic unit of society. This respect is part and parcel of our laws and our customs. (…) The fact that women, not men, have babies is not the fault of selfish and domineering men, or of the establishment, or of any clique of conspirators who want to oppress women. It's simply the way God made us.[1]

Conservative Roman Catholic activist Phyllis Schlafly (1924–2016) asserted that men and women had fundamentally different biological natures, which assigned them specific societal roles. Rooted in a religious, biologically essentialist view of men and women, her discourse on sexual differences and gender complementarity countered that of second-wave feminism in the 1970s and upheld patriarchal precepts such as heterosexual marriage and traditional gender roles. Women on the Right like Schlafly fought emancipatory movements that aimed to change the rules of the patriarchal society, in which men dominated virtually all areas of political and social life and maintained women in a state of subordination, adhering to the ideology of gender hierarchy and male supremacism. While a variety of historical and sociological studies have demonstrated conservative women's significant involvement in right-wing groups, this case is of interest because of Schlafly's key role in opposing a major movement for women's equality.[2]

In 1972, the Equal Rights Amendment (ERA), which would have finally inscribed equality between the sexes into the U.S. Constitution, passed in Congress and went to the states for ratification. Supporters of the amendment had a seven-year deadline to convince three-quarters of state legislatures to vote in favor of the amendment, the first section of which made a simple claim: "Equality of rights under the law shall not be denied or abridged by the United States or by any State on account of sex." At first, ratification appeared to be sailing through,

DOI: 10.4324/9781003164722-6

68 Amélie Ribieras

but an edition of a newsletter written by Phyllis Schlafly inspired conservative women to turn the tide. In "What's Wrong with 'Equal Rights' for Women," published in February 1972 in her newsletter *The Phyllis Schlafly Report*, Schlafly vilified this feminist initiative that, she argued, would deprive women of the protection of marriage and, more precisely, a husband's support. According to her, legal equality entailed a loss for women: "Why should we lower ourselves to 'equal rights' when we already have the status of special privilege?" (This claim regarding women's so-called privileges also became a recurrent argument used in the men's rights movement; in their case, it was used to complain about inequality of treatment toward men.) Schlafly was at the center of an antifeminist countermovement that rallied against the ERA, rejecting sex equality as demeaning the position of mother and housewife.

Phyllis Schlafly's Influence and Mobilizing Capacity

When Schlafly launched her movement in 1972, she could count on her political expertise, civic experience, and personal network to mobilize conservative women against the ERA. She had been involved in numerous philanthropic and social organizations, in the anticommunist movement, and the women's branch of the Republican Party in the 1950s, and her reputation grew tremendously in 1964 when she ostensibly supported conservative presidential candidate Barry Goldwater. As the conservative movement started to rally more supporters and had become a "resolutely militant force" after World War II[3]—although in the background of more prominent progressive movements—she took advantage of the momentum created by Goldwater's candidacy to write a manifesto in his favor, selling more than three million copies of *A Choice Not an Echo* (1964), which catapulted her to the foreground of the Republican Right.[4]

From this vantage point, Schlafly had access to a vast audience of women, especially through groups like the National Federation of Republican Women, the Daughters of the American Revolution, and the Goldwater campaign.[5] She succeeded in getting their attention and raising their awareness of sociocultural issues by focusing on the ERA. First with the STOP ERA campaign (1972) and then her organization Eagle Forum (1975), Schlafly gathered traditional women around their powerful collective identity as endangered housewives and around the model of the nuclear family, which also upheld men's ascendancy over women.[6] Many conservative women, who valued a traditional lifestyle framed by cultural and religious traditions, did not seek more opportunities in the workplace, better access to abortion, or the freedom to live one's sexuality, as feminists advocated for. They claimed that they derived a superior position from their roles as wives, mothers, and homemakers and that liberation was therefore superfluous. As a result, they saw feminism as a dangerous societal project that would hurt marriage, family, children, and also men. In that context, Schlafly launched the beginning of a countermovement to defend the traditional values that seemed to benefit conservative women.[7] The STOP ERA campaign and later her organization Eagle Forum[8] were at the forefront of antifeminist resistance, eventually leading to the failure of the ERA.

A Study of Women's Contribution to Maintaining Patriarchy: Data and Method

In his famous 1998 study of men's domination, entitled *La domination masculine*, Pierre Bourdieu argues that "symbolic power cannot be exercised without the contribution of those who undergo it."[9] In the case of Phyllis Schlafly's Eagle Forum, conservative women participated in preserving, and even strengthening, the traditional gender roles that were foundational to gender hierarchy. This chapter looks at their compliance to patriarchy, which, *a priori*, constrained them, although Schlafly argued that it afforded them "special privileges." The discrepancy between conservative women's perceived power through patriarchy and their abiding by a hierarchical order is of interest. In that regard, Gerda Lerner's definition of patriarchy acknowledges that women are not deprived of all their rights in this system:

> Patriarchy in its wider definition means the manifestation and institutionalization of male dominance over women and children in the family and the extension of male dominance over women in the family and the extension of male dominance over women in society in general. It implies that men hold power in all the important institutions of society and that women are deprived of access to such power. It does *not* imply that women are either totally powerless or totally deprived of rights, influence, and resources.[10]

Herein lies the paradox for right-wing women who defended the patriarchal family. They institutionalized the same conventional gender roles that limited them while awarding themselves a moral influence to compensate for their lack of opportunities. Eagle Forum women expanded their reach beyond the boundaries of the home—albeit directed toward the protection of "family values" and traditional gender attributions—thus infringing on men's assigned gender roles. Throughout this journey inside the microcosm of Eagle Forum, this chapter will delineate the outline of antifeminism and the efficiency of this movement in quietly defending cis men's supremacy under the guise of protecting housewives.

This study is based on an analysis of archival documents related to Schlafly's organization, found in different U.S. archives, as well as on oral history interviews conducted with Schlafly, her relatives, and some of the Eagle Forum state chapters' presidents. In addition to the opposition to the ERA, this study examines Schlafly and Eagle Forum's involvement in later sociocultural debates—regarding femininity, sexual harassment, and the workplace, among others. This examination of a conservative women's group explores the structuring features of a countermovement that conditioned the fate of the U.S. feminist movement at the end of the 20th century.[11] This chapter investigates how Schlafly's activism can be

70 Amélie Ribieras

situated in both women's history and that of the U.S. conservative movement by analyzing the discourse and the social movement practices of its members, using both framing analysis and the cultural approach to social movements developed in sociology. This chapter echoes the growing field of research that studies gender on the Right, and it hopefully contributes to better characterizing the roots of male supremacist ideologies and their link to the antifeminist movement.[12] By reflecting on conservative women's role in the maintenance of gender hierarchy in the 1970s, 1980s, and 1990s, this chapter sheds light on the reasons why sex equality is still not inscribed in the U.S. Constitution to this day.[13]

The Feminist Myth of an Oppressive Patriarchy

Women on the Right disagreed with the feminist denunciation of the patriarchal system that evolved in the 1960s, reaffirming the primacy of patriarchal unions and reinforcing traditional gender roles for men and women.[14] This section looks at three frames Schlafly used to defend the status quo for her class: extolling patriarchal marriage, glorifying motherhood, and presenting a counter-image of a powerful woman.

Extolling the Benefits of Patriarchal Marriage

Phyllis Schlafly demonstrated that the patriarchal system was in fact beneficial to women, especially when they were married, erecting patriarchal marriage and "nuclear family" as the crucible of gender relations. Functionalist views of the married couple attracted new attention in the 1950s, as the country revitalized the concept of the American dream after the trauma of World War II and in the context of the Cold War. The family was presented as a haven to retreat to. Sociologists like Talcott Parsons promoted the family unit, centered around a husband and a wife and their offspring, as the best vector for children's socialization, controlled sexuality, and economic viability. The "nuclear family" imposed strict gender roles onto the partners: men assumed the role of the breadwinner, providing financially for the family, while women took on the role of homemaker, taking care of the home and the well-being of the children. In the postwar era, characterized by "domestic containment," this normative ideal surfaced as the most desirable familial arrangement.[15] The "nuclear family"—portrayed as the epitome of the American identity and as a means to ensure the preservation of middle and upper classes—favored the constitutive elements of patriarchy, namely heterosexuality, marriage, and traditional gender roles.

As the idealized nuclear family model came under threat from the feminist and gay rights movements of the 1970s, Phyllis Schlafly defended traditional marriage as beneficial to (heterosexual) women. In her opening salvo against the ERA in February 1972, Schlafly argued for a view of men and women as complementary rather than equal:

Our Judeo-Christian civilization has developed the law and custom that, since women must bear the physical consequences of the sex act, men must be required to bear the *other* consequences and pay in other ways.[16]

The laws and customs of "Judeo-Christian civilization," to which Schlafly refers, stem from provisions in English common law adopted by the American colonies and later the United States, which guaranteed women social protection within marriage in exchange for their sexual and procreative contribution. Under the social framework called *coverture*, a bride's material and financial possessions were transferred along with the fruits of her labor to her husband, and in return, he was liable for her financial maintenance.[17] A bond of mutual responsibilities thus insured the economic survival of the spouses and their family.[18] As this marital bargain was inscribed in the laws of the States, it endured as a foundational feature of marriage.[19]

Schlafly promoted the idea that women enjoyed certain benefits thanks to this tradition. Patriarchal marriage and the reproductive mission associated with it constituted crucial elements of a lifestyle that traditional women were supposed to desire. According to Schlafly, they would benefit from this social framework: "Of all the classes of people who ever lived, the American woman is the most privileged. We have the most rights and rewards, and the fewest duties."[20] For example, the wife was not required to work and would not have to relinquish her children in case of divorce. Additionally, her sex prevented her from being subjected to the military draft. In this vision, mutual obligations ensured that women would be financially protected but established men's socioeconomic superiority and control.

Schlafly's framing furthermore represented a "gendered class interest."[21] She sought to preserve the economically and culturally "dominant class" to which she belonged through the defense of the nuclear family and stay-at-home wife.[22] Many of her arguments clearly spoke to the wealthier, such as referring in her manifesto to men's purchase of diamond rings, fur pieces, houses, and life insurance policies for their wives.[23] This economic ideal was hardly attainable for all Americans. The preservation of traditional gender roles thus represented the bedrock of economic status and functioned as a marker of belonging to an elite whose members positioned themselves as guardians of conservative sociocultural values. In particular, conservative women made claims to responsibility for cultural and moral power. The defense of motherhood offered women a way to counterbalance men's authority with an aura of their own, perpetuating a long tradition that erected mothers as respected cultural figures.

The Prestige of Motherhood

Patriarchal ideology operates on discourses that value women solely for their role in the family, praising their social and moral contribution to society and stressing motherhood over other opportunities for fulfillment. Feminists fought for better access to higher education and to salaried work, sexual liberation, and the end of marriage and heterosexuality as prescriptive standards. But for conservative women, traditional gender roles were seen as the safeguard of a woman's place within the sacrosanct family. Schlafly appropriated and reframed the moral authority associated with mothers in the face of alternative models of womanhood put forward by feminists, drawing from both religious and civic discourses.

Though Catholicism was not fully embraced by Protestant Christians in the United States in the 1970s, the devoutly Roman Catholic Schlafly developed an interfaith Christian alliance and drew on her own religious background for a symbol of esteemed motherhood. Drawing on Christian tradition, Schlafly wrote in her attack on the ERA,

> [W]e are the beneficiaries of a tradition of special respect for women which dates from the Christian Age of Chivalry. The honor and respect paid to Mary, the Mother of Christ, resulted in all women, in effect, being put on a pedestal.[24]

Schlafly spoke to her audience in religious language, explaining a women's role was governed by religious precepts and, in particular, by their resemblance to Mary, mother of Jesus Christ. Mary is a more significant figure in the Catholic tradition than in other Christian faiths, but invoking Mary enabled Schlafly to bestow upon women a cultural authority imbued with the ideas of purity, devotion, and self-sacrifice. Her discursive choice to appeal to religion resonated: faith was a major dimension of the sociocultural profile of women who joined Eagle Forum. Analysis of 389 applications to become president of an Eagle Forum state chapter in the 1970s–1980s revealed that most of the candidates were Christians: in the sample, 52% were Protestants, 23% were Mormons, and 21% were Catholics (total 96%).[25]

The prestige of motherhood was not only heavily associated with Christian precepts; it also borrowed from another sociocultural ideal dating back to the postrevolutionary period. In the 18th century, reflections on the place for women's political contributions to the new nation led to the elaboration of a gendered discourse known as "Republican Motherhood."[26] Women's participation in society only counted through their virtuous status as mothers and their task of nurturing the next generation of citizens.[27] Both religious and civic discourses surrounding motherhood concealed women's submission to offer instead a rhetoric of fulfillment. These discourses helped to disguise women's participation in the patriarchal system and to dismiss feminist calls to put an end to the male supremacist system, in part supported by the traditional construction of marriage and family. The alleged protection and power that women derived from patriarchy were incorporated into Schlafly's recipe of compliance to the gender status quo: the philosophy of positive womanhood.

The "Positive Woman": A Rhetoric of Female Power

To convince conservative women not to reject gender norms, Schlafly provided a rationale that explained how to comply with patriarchy, which, contrary to what feminists claimed, was not detrimental to women. In light of the greater benefits women supposedly enjoyed, Schlafly blamed the feminist movement for making women unhappy by teaching them "to see themselves as victims of an oppressive patriarchy," as she reflected in her 2014 book *Who Killed the American Family?*[28] She exonerated men from accusations of male supremacism and instead suggested women themselves must be the problem, demonstrating the "himpathy" that scholar Kate Manne describes as the excess of sympathy toward men (particularly those who perpetrate violence against women).[29] Feminism, not patriarchy, was accused of being responsible for women's misery. Schlafly continued, "If you believe you can never succeed because you are a helpless victim of mean men, you are probably correct."[30] This type of ridicule and misconstruing of feminist denunciations of men's domination appeared often in her publications.[31] Her newsletter and her books were punctuated by mocking expressions, such as the "clique of conspirators who want to oppress women" or the "conspiracy of male chauvinist pigs," aiming to delegitimize feminist discourse.[32] Presenting the feminist fight as a pitiful lamentation of discontented women disappointed by marriage and family, Schlafly shamed their subversive criticism and reframed it as bitterness to her readers, dismissing the movement as a way for women to achieve true fulfillment.

Offering an alternative to feminist identity for conservative women to coalesce around, Schlafly created the model of the "positive woman," described in her 1977 book *The Power of the Positive Woman*.[33] This guidance book provided a code of conduct for conservative women to follow if they wanted to be truly fulfilled and a collective identity for them to form around. Not an object but a subject, the positive woman "understands that men and women are different, and that those very differences provide the key to her success as a person and fulfillment as a woman."[34] Comforting women in their traditional roles as housewives and mothers, Schlafly recommended abnegation, spirituality, and pride to regain power. As Mother Nature and God had supposedly designed men and women with innate differences, women were supposed to celebrate their procreative mission. Schlafly further reassured the "positive woman" of her agency and unsuspected power over her husband through sexual control. Contending that men had a stronger sexual drive than women, Schlafly claimed that a wife exercised influence over her husband through sexual consent: she can "inspire him, encourage him, teach him, restrain him, reward him."[35]

The creation of the figure of the "positive woman," conveying the ideas of moral influence and self-sacrifice, was indicative of Schlafly's intention to provide a counternarrative to the feminist discourse. Inside social movements, narratives are used to foster a sense of belonging through a common reading of events; leaders develop storytelling practices to ensure adherence to the movement's message

74 Amélie Ribieras

and community.[36] Narratives eventually form part of the culture of a movement. At Eagle Forum, the story of the "positive woman" stands as an interesting feature of the antifeminist stratosphere, as it insidiously maintained women's subservience to traditional gender roles. This rhetoric of women's power somehow attenuated the constraints of men's domination.

The Cost of Feminism for the Social Fabric: Manhood and Womanhood in Crisis

The depreciation of feminism, which lay at the core of the antifeminist ideology, went hand in hand with the construction of another argument about the disappearance of essentialized gender identities. Both womanhood and manhood as categories were endangered by the feminist critique of gender hierarchy, according to Schlafly. As feminism—and especially the women's liberation movement—was portrayed as radical, revolutionary, and subversive, it was denounced as the ultimate threat to the ordering of U.S. society.

Gender Essentialism against the "Unisex Society"[37]

To Schlafly and her followers, the essence of gender roles was threatened by feminist ideology and notably by the reflections developed in the wake of Simone de Beauvoir's attempt to deconstruct those roles. In her groundbreaking book *The Second Sex* (1949), de Beauvoir contended, "One is not born, but rather becomes, woman." Anti-essentialist feminists attempted to identify the social mechanisms through which sexes and genders were framed and sought to ease the weight of normative models—namely, the "female woman" and the "male man." Feminists were divided on this issue; as William H. Chafe recounts,

> [T]here had always been a division between those who believed fundamentally that women were *individuals* and should be treated exactly the same as men and those who believed women were different, biologically and psychologically, and should be allowed to act *collectively* to implement their distinctive mission.[38]

In that regard, the ERA was put forward to erase sex as a category to differentiate between men and women in the eyes of the law.

This enraged conservative women, whose gendered behavioral culture was ruled by biology. The inescapable character of nature lay at the heart of Schlafly's rhetoric. Schlafly premised her argument on the "countless physical differences between men and women."[39] As Pierre Bourdieu writes, once biological differences between the sexes are ascertained, especially in terms of anatomy, they can stand as a natural justification for the socially constructed differences between the genders.[40] Schlafly mentioned the amount of body water and fat tissues, the tendency toward color blindness, life expectancy, physical endurance, psychology, and a person's emotional state, as evidence of two separate—although complementary—human natures. Promoting this framework, a sticker from her group STOP ERA reads, "You Can't Fool Mother Nature."[41] The differences between men and women, inscribed in their bodies, were presented as inevitable because they had been enacted by an all-powerful Mother Nature.

Schlafly warned women against transgressing the boundaries of their sex. She asserted that the emancipation of women from their "natural" destiny, as encouraged by feminism, would provoke chaos, and she warned against "neuterizing society."[42] In particular, she saw a major threat in feminist influence toward adopting gender-neutral language. Commenting on a report issued by the textbook company Macmillan in her book *The Power of the Positive Woman*, Schlafly ridiculed the new spelling rules adopted by the collection:

> [Y]ou may not say *mankind*, it should be *humanity*. You may not say *brotherhood*, it should be *amity*. *Manpower* must be replaced by *human energy*; *forefathers* should give way to *precursors*. *Chairman* and *salesman* are out; and "in" words are *chairperson* and *salesperson*.[43]

For Schlafly, these linguistic changes meant the destruction of a traditional vision of the genders.[44] She argued that it would hurt femininity and masculinity and that it would lead to disastrous consequences. The "excision" of the words *gentleman*, *masculine*, and *manly* from day-to-day vocabulary proved that feminists were waging a war on men and their right to be masculine.[45] Schlafly's defense of an authentic masculinity, as embodied by a Gary Cooper or a John Wayne—famous actors often alluded to in her writings—appears as a discourse on the "crisis of masculinity." For scholar Francis Dupuis-Déri, the motif of the disappearance of the "real male" is a crucial component of the antifeminist discourse that arises when women start questioning patriarchal norms. Feminism was presented by its opponents as imposing a considerable identity challenge onto men, detrimental to their gender responsibilities.[46] Schlafly saw virility, encompassing both ruggedness and the ability to provide for a family, as threatened by the feminists and their subversive discourse on women's emancipation.

In conservative women's minds, there was a concern about emasculating men or, even worse, feminizing them as a result of years of feminism. Castration and gender reversal, used to connote homosexuality, were also employed to characterize the feminist enterprise.[47] A misreading of feminism as lesbianism and the refusal to allow lesbian and gay couples to adopt children or teach in schools regularly fueled Schlafly's arguments for the preservation of traditional gender roles. Thus, protecting the rights of masculine men amounted to protecting the social structure as a whole. Schlafly tirelessly attempted to halt every reform that would erase differences between traditional couples and what she called "alternative lifestyles"—homosexual, single-parent, or dual-income families, for example.

If the ERA could hurt men, it would also potentially liberate them, at the expense of homemakers. Schlafly feared the liberation of men from their marital

76 Amélie Ribieras

duties and she sometimes referred to the ERA as "a men's lib amendment."[48] Elaborating on George Gilder's famous book *Sexual Suicide* (1973), in which he argued that the family had civilized the man, Schlafly explained that the attachment to this social unit had tamed him: "If he is deprived of his role, he tends to drop out of the family and revert to the primitive masculine role of hunter and fighter."[49] The structure of the family was seen by Schlafly as the best insurance against the desertion of men and their return to a state of nature, and therefore the guarantee of social stability. According to radical feminist Andrea Dworkin, this right-wing discourse urged women to accept their state of subordination to men, precisely because it was presented as the only way to control their aggression.[50] Conservative women who engaged on Schlafly's side in the battle against sex equality seemed to have prioritized the defense of their status, even though it required the preservation of men's ascendancy over them. In order to avoid social chaos and the disruption of traditional male and female categories, they undertook to reassert the power of the husband-breadwinner, whom they saw as threatened by feminism.

Protecting the Integrity of the Husband-Breadwinner

Men's interests appeared to be endangered by the feminist alleged attempt to "neuterize" society. Schlafly's antifeminist movement envisioned men's roles through the prism of strict gender roles, roles that would contribute to coercing them into participating in and supporting the family.[51] In conservative women's worldview, the husband-breadwinner was in need of protection too.

In the 1970s, Schlafly started to warn against men being targeted as the enemy by creating the stereotype of the "man-hating feminist." For her, their project of an ERA would obliterate "the husband's rights"—namely, establishing the location of his home, having his children carry his last name, and providing for his family.[52] But the most devastating impact of the ERA was about men as family support. Men "have lost their ambition to work hard and achieve success to build a life to support home, wife, and children. Feminists have kicked men out of their family provider role."[53] Schlafly claimed that men were persecuted and that their role in the family would decline because of feminism.

This rhetoric about preserving the gender status quo went beyond the ERA and targeted any attempt at changing the traditional gender balance. In 1979, Schlafly focused her attention on a project of the U.S. Department of Health, Education, and Welfare aiming at transforming Social Security and adapting it to the increasing number of working women, especially married ones. In the 1970s, a married woman was still eligible to receive Social Security benefits based on her husband's earnings, whether or not she had been employed. The system in place since the New Deal implemented a differentiation between the "male citizen-husband-provider" and the "female citizen-mother-dependent."[54] Commenting on a report produced by the Department of Health,

"Social Security and the Changing Roles of Men and Women" (1979), Schlafly excoriated the "homemaker tax," which would count the domestic contribution of the housewife as effective hours of work and require Social Security contributions accordingly (paid out of the husband's earnings). This feminist initiative, she said, degraded the tasks performed by housewives inside the home and threatened the financial survival of the traditional family who lived on the so-called "family wage" earned by the breadwinner.[55]

Moreover, Schlafly contended that the feminist push in favor of women's emancipation impacted men directly in the workplace because women were stealing their jobs. The 1970s debate around "comparable worth" is an illustrative example of Schlafly's discourse on the "war of the sexes" in the job market. Despite the Equal Pay Act of 1963, which attempted to bridge the gap between women's and men's salaries, wage inequalities persisted. In sectors dominated by women—service jobs, office work, and care, among others—they continued to suffer wage discrimination while men earned the "family wage."[56] As feminists became preoccupied with the lot of these working women (often white members of the middle and upper class since other women had always worked to contribute to their family's economic survival), they proposed to reexamine the "value" of women's work. In an effort to enhance women's professional careers and to alleviate pay inequalities, the theory of "comparable worth" meant to offer equal monetary compensation to men and women in occupations that required comparable qualifications and efforts. Schlafly criticized this strategy as unjust "affirmative action" and "reverse discrimination" against men, claiming that it would create unfair competition with women.[57] Trying to stir resentment from working- and middle-class men, Schlafly insisted, "The comparable worth advocates are trying to freeze the wages of blue-collar men while forcing employers to raise the wages of some white- and pink-collar women above marketplace rates."[58] "Comparable worth" was firmly rejected by Schlafly, who seized this opportunity to fuel the flame of sex and class conflicts. The confrontation of the sexes in the workplace worked as a powerful argument in Schlafly's discourse, as she protested the implementation of "reverse discrimination" at the expense of men.[59]

This was also an argument developed by activists in the men's rights movement, in parallel to the rise of second-wave feminism. Dissatisfied with traditional gender roles and standards of masculinity deemed toxic, men—mostly straight white ones—had started to join feminists in their social critique and formed a "men's liberation movement."[60] As scholar Michael Messner shows, conservative and moderate men broke away from the movement and created a men's rights movement and groups that coopted the language of victimhood, claiming that gender conflicts were exacerbated by feminism. The collective struggle against rape, violence, and sexual harassment alarmed these men, and they put forward an argument about the existence of gender discrimination against men.[61] For them, as for Phyllis Schlafly, feminism had created new inequalities between men and women.

78 Amélie Ribieras

Throughout her career, Schlafly continued to vilify feminism and show that it had severely damaged men's *raison d'être* within the family. Three decades after the ERA struggle, she wrote about what feminism had allegedly cost men:

> Feminists have rigged the social system, the educational system, and the workforce against men (...). They write articles and books filled with phrases such as "the end of men," "females are the breadwinners," and "men are not necessary," and women want a seat at the table—at the head of the table.[62]

Schlafly asserted that men were the collateral victims of a social project that had destroyed the family unit by offering women equal life opportunities. Feminism, Schlafly continued, had been devastating for the social fabric and the cultural appreciation of manhood, despite her effort at reasserting their social roles. Although Schlafly considered in reflection that her movement had in large part failed to preserve the prerogatives of husbands, it appears that she was more successful at crafting a powerful image of conservative womanhood that reaffirmed women in their femininity.

In Favor of Feminine Women

As discussed earlier, Schlafly's position was informed by essentialized versions of manhood and womanhood. Her discourse on sexual differences and the prestige of motherhood, along with her narrative of positive womanhood, converged toward her praising of traditional femininity. Her use of conventional ideas about women's proper behavior served a double purpose: providing a contrast with both the "masculine man" and the "radical feminist."

For Schlafly and the conservative women in her movement, standing out as feminine was a crucial part of their activism, used to underline their mission and to appear less threatening than the feminists. The annual Eagle Forum conference, called Eagle Council, emerged as a privileged training ground to learn a variety of gender performances. At the first gathering in 1975, in Springfield, Illinois, Schlafly insisted on traits like affability and dignity, proposing a workshop on the art of smiling.[63] For conservative women, it became crucial to demonstrate their conformity to traditional womanhood and their discipline. Emotional restraint and sober beauty were key features of the feminine model promoted by Eagle Forum. Women were not supposed to be overweight, had to keep their manners in check, and were to avoid wearing high heels and garish colors.[64] Everything was supervised: from the style of their manicures to the color of their eye shadow. The guiding principle of conservative women's political activism was propriety, epitomized by the modest and discreet lady.[65]

This code of conduct, transmitted in Schlafly's organization, aimed to reinforce a collective identity of housewives, but it also entailed the rejection of a counter-model of womanhood that violated traditional norms. Schlafly derided feminists since they appeared to contest traditional femininity. Some radical activists had demonstrated as early as 1968 when protesting the Miss America Pageant, their rejection of what they described as the feminine instruments of their oppression. They famously threw objects like hair curlers, girdles and bras into a "freedom trash can" to protest beauty standards imposed on women.[66] This event marked the emergence of the distorted figure of the "bra-burning feminist"—although nothing was actually burned—a stereotype weaponized by their opponents to exaggerate the subversive undertones of feminism.[67] Later, in the context of the ERA struggle, other feminists, from the state of Illinois, organized an illegal raid in the halls of the Illinois Congress by spreading pig blood on the floor to protest the resistance to a change of their lawmakers, and Schlafly featured a photograph of the scene in her newsletter.[68] This type of event was used by Phyllis Schlafly to construct an antagonism between the ladylike homemakers of Eagle Forum and the aggressive feminist activists. She shamed feminists for what she considered to be inappropriate behavior. In the March 1978 and April 1983 issues of *The Phyllis Schlafly Report*, Schlafly circulated photographs of handcuffed feminists arrested by the police and vilified their violent and disruptive tactics.[69] Often portrayed as virulent, loud, and bitter, she presented feminists as deviating from gender norms. They were described by Schlafly as women who were "unhappy with their gender [and who] want[ed] to be treated like men," and this discourse fed her argument about the sexual denaturation of feminists. Their manly attitude, as described by Schlafly, represented the strongest threat to the gendered status quo. In that regard, Christine Bard contends that the concerns around the possibility of differentiating between the sexes are nothing less than the "engine of history" and are typical of conservative resistance to women's emancipation.[70]

Conservative women claimed essentialized womanhood as a powerful tool in their social movement practices and erected conventional gender behavior as a trademark of antifeminist mobilizations. As their gender and that of their partners were considered as a force, we are led to question the purpose of the antifeminist movement regarding the maintenance of a male supremacist system. It is relevant to investigate whether it eventually served men's or women's interests.

The Antifeminist Cause and the Negotiation of Boundaries

Conservative women fought the ERA and other progressive reforms under the leadership of Phyllis Schlafly to maintain the socioeconomic status quo from which they believed they benefited and derived cultural power. At the same time, they seemed to have clearly defended the interests of their male counterparts. What was the ultimate goal of the antifeminist cause? Did conservative women opposing progressive gender reforms operate for themselves or for their men? The following section will try to determine whether antifeminism contributed to maintaining men's authority over women and/or if it provided women with a way to "bargain with patriarchy."[71]

A Women's Forum Supported by Husbands

The Eagle Forum was initially conceived as a women's community, to be led and nurtured by women. At its beginning, the organization was composed of primarily women members and focused on women's issues.[72] In an online testimonial, activist Shirley Curry mentioned that the expression "woman power" had been considered as a name for the organization, but it was eventually dismissed because of its feminist connotation.[73] Several archival documents reveal the existence of a "Women's Forum" also led by Schlafly, possibly an earlier name for the organization.[74] The name Eagle Forum was nevertheless eventually adopted to encompass other dimensions of the conservative movement's fight for traditional values.[75]

Within this structure, activists developed a network that can be characterized as a "social movement community," consisting of strong links between the members and in mechanisms of solidarity aimed at sustaining the cohesion of the group.[76] Schlafly encouraged Eagle Forum women to be in contact with and to write to one another to provide an emotional safety net during the hard times. She exhorted adherents to send letters of support, like in 1979, when an activist lost her son in a car accident.[77] She endeavored to strengthen a sense of belonging through collective rituals, such as with the annual conferences of the organization or the galas celebrating the defeat of the ERA.[78] Scholars of social movements argue that these strategies foster "affective commitment or loyalties" and thus nurture a group.[79] Emotions are viewed as a core element of social movements' mobilization and they reinforce their sustainability. At Eagle Forum, these processes resulted in a strong women's team spirit, probably comparable to the sisterhood developed by the feminists.

To maintain the conservative gender order even in the women-led Eagle Forum, Schlafly made sure to recognize the husbands' contributions, as with her regular statement at events of her gratitude to Fred Schlafly for giving her permission to be there. This approach has lasted the entire history of the organization. In a 2013 interview with the author, Schlafly reflected, "[T]he basic part was that these women were mostly full-time homemakers who had supportive husband who encouraged them, the same as my husband encouraged me."[80] Husbands were sometimes credited with putting their wives on the path of anti-ERA activism. South Dakota Eagle Forum chapter president, Kitty Werthmann, said in an interview, "When we heard on the radio about the Equal Rights Amendment so my husband said: 'alright, it's starting here, you better go up to the capital and tell those legislators "do not vote for that bill, it's bad."'"[81] Moreover, the wealthiest of the men contributed their money and expertise in specific situations. For example, Phyllis Schlafly's husband engaged his own law firm in the fight against the ERA, and in 1976, he initiated a lawsuit against the feminist national conference scheduled for the following year.[82] He went as far as using his own business for the benefit of his wife's cause. These examples show that men might have been more than mere observers in this sociocultural battle. Though some of the men occupied a more prominent place in Schlafly's organization as, over time, a handful of chapters were led by men, they generally assumed a discreet role.

Although their socioeconomic interests as head of the family were clearly at stake too, cis men's remaining in the background could be explained by the nature of the movement's cause. Open antifeminist activism by men was rarely visible at that point of history and, as Schlafly put it herself in the title of one of her books, there are things that "conservative women know—and men can't say."[83] In order to appear more acceptable, the fight to sustain patriarchy needed to be endorsed by women. Some organizations led by men thus welcomed Schlafly's unabashed defense of their interests. Archival documents indicate that Schlafly was in contact with at least one of them: the Men's Rights Association (now known as the Men's Defense Association). Founded in 1972, as the ERA was being passed by Congress, and headed by Richard F. Doyle, a former member of the air force and author of *The Rape of the Male* (1976), the group expressed its gratitude to Schlafly regarding a topic that had alienated men's rights activists.[84] In a letter from 1981, Doyle congratulated Schlafly upon her testimony to the Senate on sexual harassment in the workplace.[85] She asserted that no additional legislation was needed to protect women at work because sexual harassment did not impact "virtuous" women:

> Non-criminal sexual harassment on the job is not a problem for the virtuous woman except in the rarest of cases. When a woman walks across the room, she speaks with a universal body language that most men intuitively understand. Men hardly ever ask sexual favors of women from whom the certain answer is "no."[86]

Pitting so-called virtuous women against less virtuous ones, Schlafly implied that the moral qualities of a woman determined her worthiness and her ability to avoid sexual predators. Her statement was abundantly criticized by feminists and mentioned in national newspapers.[87] She was blamed for dismissing the victims' traumatic experiences and for exonerating men from taking responsibility. Ultimately, her intervention helped maintain a traditional patriarchal order in which white men held most of the power.

Shoring up patriarchy and creating alliances with men, Schlafly's Eagle Forum endeavored to give them a special place in her movement. The organization inaugurated in 2017 the "Fred Schlafly Award," named after Phyllis Schlafly's late husband, to recognize men's contribution to the antifeminist movement. The award was meant to revere the men who supported their wives.[88] That first year, the prize went to the husband of Gayle Ruzicka, the president of the Eagle Forum chapter in Utah and a close friend of Schlafly's. Beyond their personal accomplishments (among which were 12 children), the Ruzickas were distinguished for the strength of their partnership and complementary gender roles. Gayle Ruzicka confessed the sacrifices that her activism entailed:

> Phyllis asked me to be the president of Eagle Forum in Utah, and that was 29 years ago, yeah, it was life changing. Our whole family worked on it together, and we all sacrificed, in order to do the things that I needed to do to be the president of Eagle Forum. Because not only does it take up

all of my time, it's 100% volunteer, [...], the hours it takes up is more than what a full-time job would be. But it's all volunteer. (...) We sacrificed our finances drastically, we sacrificed our personal time. But I always made sure that I kept my family involved with me. I'm certainly not ever going to sacrifice my family. So I was doing this, we're a family organization, we protect the family, and I'm not going to go out and neglect my family. We always fight for the family. So my children and my husband have always been involved with me.[89]

Despite Ruzicka's framing of her activism and leadership from a "pro-family" lens, this testimony highlights a gap between conservative women's ideals about gender roles and their family practices. The familial arrangement was undeniably rearranged by conservative women's leadership. As devoted activists, Eagle Forum women did not personify the full-time homemaker figure their group promoted. In this regard, the awards attributed to homemakers and breadwinners seemed to have worked as a cover as these women activists remodeled their own housewife status.[90]

Schlafly's Model of the Housewife-Activist

There was an emancipatory dimension to STOP ERA activism, at least for Phyllis Schlafly. The Eagle Forum derived from the story of a woman who liberated herself from patriarchal constraints while maintaining, in appearance, a traditional lifestyle. Schlafly's career consisted of two interwoven narratives: that of the busy political activist and that of the perfect wife and mother.

On the one hand, she and her husband appeared to conform to the period's ideal of the "nuclear family" in a suburban setting, as her biographer explains:

> Phyllis Schlafly realized the postwar American dream—a handsome, devoted, successful and prominent husband; a small but attractive home (with a white picket fence); a healthy family that would grow to six children (four boys and two girls), summer vacations at the Schlafly family summer house in Harbor Point, Michigan; and entrance into the small and unpretentious but wealthy social circle in the small Illinois river town.[91]

Phyllis Schlafly respected traditional gender roles in that she never had a paid job during her marriage and let her husband be the breadwinner. She raised a large family and boasted in her newsletter of having been an exemplary mother, having both breastfed her six children and taught them how to read—as if these were the ultimate proofs of good mothering. She always claimed to be a qualified homemaker; for instance, in an interview with historian Mark DePue, she details the healthy breakfasts she gave her children.[92] Embodying the perfect wife and mother was important for Schlafly's reputation.

On the other hand, Phyllis Schlafly multiplied social and political engagements outside of her private sphere.[93] She devoted time to charity work, to women's groups and political organizations, and even to political campaigns in which she tried to run as the "average housewife." Despite this strategic move, these occupations reveal Schlafly as an ambitious woman who transgressed conventional gender roles. She did not abide by the rules of "separate spheres" for men and women, even though she acknowledged this concept as the touchstone of the traditional family.[94] The juxtaposition of her traditional gendered tasks and her political commitment was a lifelong leitmotif that exposed a double standard in her discourse.

To alleviate her controversial posture of housewife-activist, Schlafly developed a marketing strategy. She regularly staged gender hierarchy in a series of gendered performances. In a 1978 issue of the *Alton Telegraph*, a local Illinois newspaper, she appeared with her husband in her prototypical role. The Schlaflys are featured in their kitchen, with Fred in the foreground, reading a newspaper, and Phyllis Schlafly in the background, taking baked apples out of the oven. Yet, the journalist was not deceived by this mise-en-scène. He wrote, "[L]ike an eager actress, she is concerned that the light be adequate for photographers and that she is always wearing an affable smile."[95] Earlier the same year, she and her husband had been invited to the set of *Good Morning America* to talk about their marriage. They had both guaranteed the audience that Phyllis was very "submissive" and that Fred was "the boss of the family."[96] This roleplay was necessary to maintain Phyllis Schlafly's reputation and to ensure she would not appear as a domineering wife, imbued with too much ambition. But, even if she often started her public meetings with the famous sentence "I want to thank my husband Fred for letting me come here," she evidently was an independent woman, and he remained in the shadows.[97] She even sometimes impinged on his turf, such as when she enrolled in law school in 1975, triggering an angry response from her husband. She reported that her son John criticized her for belittling his father: "Mother, you have everything else in the world and now you're trying to take his law practice away from him."[98]

As Phyllis Schlafly carved a large space for herself as a celebrity, it had crucial implications in terms of her representation. The ambiguity of her position was decried by numerous feminists who reproached her for betraying women while living an independent lifestyle. The same duality was present in her organization, as Schlafly encouraged homemakers to get involved in politics, invading an area where cis white men usually reigned supreme. Does this constitute the limit to antifeminism's connection to male supremacism?

Emancipation in Subjugation?

Despite her conservative discourse, Schlafly paradoxically offered a degree of freedom to her peers by extending the traditional reach women enjoyed. Being involved at Eagle Forum meant that women activists were able to participate in political activities, albeit as homemakers.

Schlafly's organization was simultaneously a vector of oppression and emancipation for women, as she spread opposite messages. Schlafly refused to let women be reduced to what Catherine Rymph called the "housework of government" while proposing, as discussed earlier, a format of activism adapted to their gender.[99] Women learned new skills, such as talking in front of the media, testifying at public hearings, and lobbying legislators while being told to prioritize a "female" approach to politics embedded in normative gendered practices. These contradictory trends are illustrated by the different prizes that Eagle Forum awarded. The "Fulltime Homemaker Award," delivered to worthy housewives, existed alongside the "Eagle Award," which recognized the dedication of the most efficient leaders.[100] It seems that Schlafly wanted her peers to become real "policymakers" while instrumentalizing their gender.[101]

This paradoxical combination indicates that Schlafly's position regarding women's emancipation was very ambiguous. In this regard, an author interview with an Eagle Forum leader, a middle-aged man recruited in the 2010s (as the leadership became less women-dominated) brings attention to this paradox, suggesting that "maybe the real feminists are the Eagle Forum women." He continued, "A lot of these women are getting a little older now, but they're as strong as any man I've ever known. And you don't tell them, you know, what to do. They ... these are strong women. ... So they're not going to be dominated by a man."[102] This is perhaps a surprising comparison, given Schlafly's investment in distinguishing her conservative women as feminine and attacking feminists as being too much like men. But Eagle Forum women activists empowered themselves with a voice, elaborating a status encompassing marriage and motherhood, along with activism and politics. For political scientist Ronnee Schreiber, "conservative women tend to be gender-conscious political actors who may organize as, and speak for, women, but shun feminism."[103] Therefore, this gender-conscious activism has encouraged the continuation of conservative social structures while giving traditional women an opportunity to break free from them.

This approach to the empowerment of conservative women had ambivalent outcomes. Eagle Forum members undoubtedly contributed to slowing down the ratification process of the ERA in the 1970s–1980s. They participated in U.S. democracy beyond the boundaries of their home and family, signaling a disruption of their original mission as homemakers. This suggests power and influence, at least for those elite middle- and upper-middle-class white women involved with the Eagle Forum. In a 2011 interview, historian Mark DePue asked Schlafly about gender factionalism within the Republican Party and in the conservative movement, wondering if she had been herself the victim of sexism. Dismissing any allegation that the men did not welcome her properly, she responded, "I was friends with all the powerful people in the conservative movement and the Republican Party. I never heard anybody who voted for or against me because I was a woman."[104] She indeed managed to collaborate with conservative politicians like Henry Hyde and Jesse Helms.[105]

Yet the historical record indicates limitations to the level of influence and power Schlafly and women like her could achieve. Despite the tremendous help she provided to the presidential campaigns of Barry Goldwater and Ronald Reagan, after his election, Reagan did not reward Schlafly with a presidential appointment. The only political position won by Schlafly was Illinois delegate to the Republican National Conventions—undoubtedly a meager consolation for such an ambitious woman.[106] Schlafly was not the only Eagle Forum member to seek greater political power. Like Schlafly had tried to do in 1952 and 1970, Janine Hansen, who joined the anti-ERA initiative in Nevada in the 1970s, campaigned unsuccessfully for a seat in the Nevada state senate (2016) and in the U.S. House of Representatives (2020). Their failure to achieve greater goals in the political sphere may testify to the difficulty for a woman to gain access to this domain, and it illustrates the limits of conservative women's gendered vision and activism.

Conclusion

In response to the rise of feminism in the 1960s, conservative women mobilized to halt its progress and, more specifically, the feminists' symbolic project to include sex equality in the U.S. Constitution. Under the leadership of Phyllis Schlafly, women who were involved in a constellation of causes in the growing conservative movement mobilized to oppose the ERA passed by Congress in 1972. Arguing in favor of the preservation of normative gender roles within marriage, Schlafly insisted that the ERA would hurt the lifestyle of traditional men and women. She also argued that feminism would threaten their innate nature, as the behavior of feminists allegedly showed. In fact, she defended a gendered class interest that contributed to maintaining the ideal of the nuclear family as the most valuable sociocultural norm. Right-wing women wished to protect their role in this framework because it gave them social prestige and economic protection. They turned a blind eye to the preservation of the gendered hierarchy that their position entailed, however. They coupled subjugation and protection and invented a new social role for the housewife. In spite of upholding traditional gender norms, Phyllis Schlafly also promoted their involvement in the political realm. Her organization Eagle Forum became a crucible of political training for numerous right-leaning women who—paradoxically—opposed women's emancipation. Presented as an extension of their natural mothering duty, their activism nevertheless provided an escape from the boundaries set for their gender. These negotiations appear nonetheless limited and the scope of the homemakers' power restricted. Conservative women moved from being simple housewives to housewife-activists, breaching the codes of the very system they defended and putting them in an impossible position to maintain. Antifeminism was therefore an insidious struggle for conservative women: it offered the possibility of a relative emancipation, which was, in reality, constrained by the very nature of their

86 Amélie Ribieras

fight—namely, the preservation of patriarchal structures and ideals and therefore of a male supremacist system.

Moreover, if antifeminism, as exemplified at Eagle Forum, contributed to reasserting men and women's specific attributions and duties, it did not always function as a stepping-stone for the men's rights movement, which also developed in reaction to feminism. Men benefited from the mobilization of their female allies in organizations such as Phyllis Schlafly's but also combated some of the ideas promoted by antifeminists. As the men's rights movement insisted on defending the interests of a specific sex, which the antifeminist movement did not openly do, it seems that these two movements were destined to be circumstantial bedfellows.

Notes

1 Phyllis Schlafly, "What's Wrong with Equal Rights for Women?" *The Phyllis Schlafly Report*, February 1972, https://eagleforum.org/publications/psr/feb1972.html.

2 Scholars have worked on women's engagement in racist movements (Kathleen Blee, *Women of the Klan: Racism and Gender in the 1920s.* Berkeley: University of California Press, 1991; Elizabeth G. McRae, *Mothers of Massive Resistance: White Women and the Politics of White Supremacy.* New York: Oxford University Press, 2018); in antisuffragism (Susan Marshall, *Splintered Sisterhood: Gender and Class in the Campaign against Woman Suffrage.* Madison: University of Wisconsin Press, 1997); in anti-abortion groups (Kristin Luker, *Abortion and the Politics of Motherhood.* Berkeley, Los Angeles and London: University of California Press, 1984; Karissa Haugeberg, *Women against Abortion: Inside the Largest Moral Reform Movement of the Twentieth Century.* Urbana: University of Illinois Press, 2017); in the Republican Party (Catherine E. Rymph, *Republican Women: Feminism and Conservatism from Suffrage through the Rise of the New Right.* Chapel Hill: The University of North Carolina Press, 2006); in the New Right (Pamela Conover and Virginia Gray, *Feminism and the New Right: Conflict over the American Family.* New York: Praeger, 1983; Rebecca Klatch, *Women of the New Right.* Philadelphia, PA: Temple University Press, 1987), in the conservative movement (Michelle Nickerson, *Mothers of Conservatism: Women and the Postwar Right.* Princeton, NJ: Princeton University Press, 2012); and also in antifeminist countermovements and organizations (Ronnee Schreiber, *Righting Feminism: Conservative Women and American Politics.* Oxford and New York: Oxford University Press, 2008; Marjorie Spruill, *Divided We Stand: The Battle over Women's Rights and Family Values That Polarized American Politics.* London and New York: Bloomsbury, 2017).

3 George H. Nash, *The Conservative Intellectual Movement in America since 1945* (Wilmington, DE: ISI Books, 2006 [1976]), xiii. Scholars Donald Critchlow and Nancy MacLean, for instance, explain that the conservative movement gathered speed thanks to the anticommunist fight, embodied by Senator Joseph McCarthy, and the renewal of a conservative intellectual movement (Donald Critchlow and Nancy MacLean, *Debating the American Conservative Movement: 1945 to the Present.* Lanham, MD: Rowman & Littlefield Publishers, 2009, 10).

4 Donald Critchlow, *Phyllis Schlafly and Grassroots Conservatism: A Woman's Crusade* (Princeton, NJ and Oxford: Princeton University Press, 2005), 109

5 Founded in 1890, the Daughters of the American Revolution is a patriotic organization dedicated to the promotion of U.S. history and, more precisely, of the American

Revolution. Its members must be connected to the event through a member of their family.

6 For more details on the construction of this collective identity, see the author's PhD dissertation, "The Sociocultural Discourse and the Social Movement Practices of Conservative Women in the United States. The Example of Phyllis Schlafly and Eagle Forum," defended at La Sorbonne Nouvelle, France, on November 29, 2019, and supervised by Hélène Le Dantec-Lowry.

7 The reality of people's approval of traditional gender roles during the period is complex. Rita Simon and Jean Landis, who studied men's and women's support of gender roles, marriage and the family between 1972 and 1984, found that Americans increasingly approved of women's work outside the home. Yet, traditional arrangements persisted: even at the peak of the feminist movement, around 1977, respondents seem to have preferred marriage over any other type of union, and men and women generally agreed that a woman's place was in the home (Rita J. Simon and Jean M. Landis, "A Report: Women's and Men's Attitudes about a Woman's Place and Role," *The Public Opinion Quarterly* 53, no. 2 (Summer 1989): 265–76).

8 Phyllis Schlafly created Eagle Forum in 1975 so that she could concentrate her effort against the ERA and gather conservative women in an official organization. Its initial mission was to oppose feminism and, more particularly, the ratification of the Equal Rights Amendment. Yet, it also focused on other sociocultural issues such as abortion rights or the preservation of traditional values. Eagle Forum settled in the U.S. states where the ERA was being more acrimoniously debated and in areas of the country where Phyllis Schlafly was particularly influential (such as California or Illinois).

9 Pierre Bourdieu, *La Domination Masculine* (Paris: Éditions du Seuil, 1998), 62.

10 Gerda Lerner, *The Creation of Patriarchy* (New York and Oxford: Oxford University Press, 1986), 239.

11 Sociologist Tahi L. Mottl defines a countermovement as "a particular kind of protest movement which is a response to the social change advocated by an initial movement" (Tahi L. Mottl, "The Analysis of Countermovements," *Social Problems* 27, no. 5 (June 1980): 620–35). See also David S. Meyer and Suzanne Staggenborg, "Movements, Countermovements, and the Structure of Political Opportunity," *American Journal of Sociology* 101, no. 6 (May 1996): 1628–60.

12 See, among others, Hank Johnston, ed., *Culture, Social Movements, and Protest* (Farnham and Burlington: Ashgate, 2009). On framing analysis, see Robert D. Benford and David A. Snow, "Framing Processes and Social Movements: An Overview and Assessment," *Annual Review of Sociology* 26, no. 1 (August 2000): 611–39.

13 First proposed in 1923 by the feminists of the National Woman's Party led by Alice Paul, the ERA did not pass Congress until 1972. It was then sent to the States for ratification, with a deadline established in 1979 (then extended to 1982). Due to the movement triggered by Phyllis Schlafly, however, it was never adopted. The debate on the ERA was recently revived as Virginia ratified the ERA in January 2020. It has now been approved by the necessary three-quarters of the States to become an amendment to the U.S. Constitution.

14 For example, Betty Friedan had debunked the postwar middle-class ideal of the homemaker in her 1963 essay *The Feminine Mystique*. In it, Friedan criticized a pervasive female ideal centered around domesticity, in which the housewife and her husband formed a familial unit perceived as the best site for emotional and economic stability, as well as an expression of the American way of life. Her seminal study was based on a survey of her classmates at Smith College (mostly white middle-class women).

88 Amélie Ribieras

15 Elaine Tyler May, *Homeward Bound: American Families in the Cold War Era* (New York: Basic Books, 2008 [1988]), 2. Other scholars have also argued that the rise of the nuclear family in the postwar years signaled the advent of the familial structure as a vector of consumption, whereby the housewife was seen as the primary consumer and would emerge as a primary target for advertising. Becoming a homeowner in a suburb and buying goods such as home appliances or cars were expressions of the American way of life, as well as markers of the middle class (Lizabeth Cohen, *A Consumers' Republic: The Politics of Mass Consumption in Postwar America.* New York: Vintage Books, 2004). For a detailed examination of conservative women's rationale on the benefits of the traditional family, see also my article "'Stop Taking Our Privileges:' Phyllis Schlafly's Traditional Womanhood and the Fight for Sociocultural Hegemony in the 1970–1980s," *USAbroad-Journal of American History and Politics* 4, March 2021, https://usabroad.unibo.it/article/view/11614/12363.
16 Schlafly, "What's Wrong."
17 Nancy Cott, *Public Vows: A History of Marriage and the Nation* (Cambridge, MA and London: Harvard University Press, 2000), 11–12.
18 Ibid., 50–53.
19 However, in the 1830s, 1840s, and 1850s, most States enacted laws that allowed a woman to retain and manage her property. Later, married women gained further independence with the earnings acts of the 1870s and 1880s, which gave them control over their labor performed outside the home, but it did nothing to the labor contract within marriage. For more details, see Sara L. Zeigler, "Wifely Duties: Marriage, Labor, and the Common Law in Nineteenth-Century America," *Social Science History* 20, no. 1 (Spring 1996): 63–96.
20 Schlafly, "What's Wrong."
21 Susan Marshall, *Splintered Sisterhood: Gender and Class in the Campaign against Woman Suffrage* (Madison: University of Wisconsin Press, 1997).
22 Eric Agrikoliansky and Annie Collovald, "Mobilisations conservatrices: comment les dominants contestent?" *Politix* 106, no. 2 (2014): 7–29.
23 Schlafly, "What's Wrong."
24 Schlafly, "What's Wrong."
25 I examined 389 applications sent to Phyllis Schlafly to become state chapter president between 1974 and 1982. On the form, applicants mentioned their state of origin, their occupation, their religion, their experience in a social movement, their personal motivations, and two references known to the organization (Eagle Forum, "State chapters president applications," Eagle Forum Archives, Collection Eagle Forum, Series Organization, Box 11, File 4, 5, 6, 7, 8; Box 12, File 1, 2). With regards to Schlafly's use of the term "Judeo-Christian," no Jewish women were found in the sample.
26 Linda Kerber, "The Republican Mother: Women and the Enlightenment—An American Perspective," *American Quarterly* 28, no. 2 (Summer 1976): 187–205.
27 Ruth H. Bloch, "American Feminine Ideals in Transition: The Rise of the Moral Mother, 1785–1815," *Feminist Studies* 4, no. 2 (June 1978): 100–126.
28 Phyllis Schlafly, *Who Killed the American Family?* (Washington, D.C.: WorldNetDaily, 2014), 216.
29 Kate Manne, *Down Girl: The Logic of Misogyny* (New York: Oxford University Press, 2018), 197.
30 Schlafly, *Who Killed the American Family?*, 216. According to sociologist Alex DiBranco, Schlafly's patriarchal reasoning, and especially her rejection of the victimhood trope, could have laid the ground for later reflections on women's equality.

She mentions the brand of "equity feminism" (as opposed to "gender feminism") described by conservative author Christina Hoff Sommers. In her provocative book *Who Stole Feminism? How Women Have Betrayed Women* (New York: Touchstone/Simon & Schuster, 1994), Sommers rejected the victimhood ideology (Alex DiBranco, "Mobilizing Misogyny," *The Public Eye*, Winter 2017, https://www.politicalresearch.org/2017/03/08/mobilizing-misogyny).

31 Although some feminists decried men's behavior towards women, particularly in cases of violence or sexual assault, others focused on the systemic oppression of women. Places like the workplace and the family were identified as primary locations for gender struggles, like in the 1970 book of Kate Millett, *Sexual Politics*.

32 Schlafly, "What's Wrong"; Phyllis Schlafly, *The Power of the Positive Woman* (New Rochelle, NY: Arlington House Publishers, 1977), 11.

33 Schlafly's book may have hinted at the work of Norman Vincent Peale, a popular American minister and lecturer. In 1952, he wrote *The Power of Positive Thinking*, in which he praised faithfulness to God and self-discipline as crucial components of a happy life.

34 Schlafly, *The Power of the Positive Woman*, 11.

35 Ibid., 17.

36 See, for example, Francesca Polletta, "'It Was like a Fever...:' Narrative and Identity in Social Protest," *Social Protest* 45, no. 2 (May 1998): 137–59.

37 Schlafly, *The Power of the Positive Woman*, 27.

38 William H. Chafe *in* Cott, *No Small Courage: A History of Women in the United States*, 554–55.

39 Schlafly, *The Power of the Positive Woman*, 15.

40 Bourdieu, *La domination masculine*, 24–25.

41 STOP ERA, "You Can't Fool Mother Nature" (Archives of the Schlesinger Library, Collection Memorabilia, Box 23 O'Reilly).

42 Schlafly, *The Power of the Positive Woman*, 25.

43 Ibid., 26.

44 Acting as a watchdog for language, she later attacked Ruth Bader Ginsburg's project on discrimination in the English language, explained in her report *Sex Bias in the U.S. Code* (1977). Schlafly vehemently criticized her recommendations to use "spouse" instead of "husband" and "wife" or "parent" for "father" and "mother" for instance (Schlafly, *Who Killed the American Family?*, 219).

45 Phyllis Schlafly, *Feminist Fantasies* (Dallas: Spence, 2003), 39. She does use the word "excised."

46 Francis Dupuis-Deri, "Le discours de la 'crise de la masculinité' Comme Refus de l'Égalité Entre les Sexes: Histoire d'une Rhétorique Antiféministe," *Cahiers du Genre* 52, no. 1 (2012): 119–43.

47 During the Cold War, the conservatives' obsession with communists also translated into a sexual paranoia that led the State to lay off civil servants suspected of being homosexual (Elaine Tyler May, *Homeward Bound*, 92). The anticommunist witch hunt was then linked to a climate of suspicion called the Lavender Scare. It has persisted in conservative discourse up until today.

48 Schlafly, *The Power of the Positive Woman*, 95.

49 Ibid., 95–96. Schlafly's idea of a woman's taming abilities could derive from an ideological framework described by Louise M. Newman. At the turn of the 20th century, elite white women assumed a self-assigned "civilizing mission" and participated in temperance movements, domestic and foreign missionary movements, charity work

90 Amélie Ribieras

or even international peace movements, on the basis of their supposedly superior racial position (Louise M. Newman, *White Women's Rights: The Racial Origins of Feminism in the United States.* New York: Oxford University Press, 1999).

50 Andrea Dworkin, *Right-Wing Women: The Politics of Domesticated Females* (London: The Women's Press, 1983), 21.

51 In light of Michal Messner's argument that the men's rights movement rejected "sex roles," or gender roles, conservative women's insistence on the figure of the husband-breadwinner might have also contributed to exacerbate men's resistance toward their responsibilities within the traditional family.

52 Schlafly, *The Power of the Positive Woman*, 92–93.

53 Schlafly, *Who Killed the American Family?*, 217.

54 Cott, *Public Vows*, 176.

55 Phyllis Schlafly, "Changing Social Security to Hurt the Homemaker," *The Phyllis Schlafly Report* (June 1979) (Archives of the Schlesinger Library, Collection Phyllis Schlafly Report, Book 2: 1978–79). Feminists debated on the issue of women's work inside the home in order to take into account the experience of "displaced homemakers"—namely, widows or divorced women—who often found themselves in a dire financial situation. Having left the job market to take care of their children, they struggled to provide for their family without their husband's income. A brochure of the national women's conference organized in 1977 shows that feminist activists supported measures at the state level to alleviate their difficulties and notably an Equal Opportunity for Displaced Homemakers Act (National Commission on the Observance of International Women's Year, "Legal Status of Homemakers: A Workshop Guide," March 1977, Eagle Forum Archives, Collection Phyllis Schlafly, Series ERA, Series IWY, Box 1, File 6).

56 Roslyn L. Feldberg, "Comparable Worth: Toward Theory and Practice in the United States," *Signs* 10, no. 2 (Winter 1984): 311–28.

57 Schlafly, *The Power of the Positive Woman*, 23.

58 Phyllis Schlafly, "Statement by Phyllis Schlafly to the Compensation & Employee Benefits Subcommittee of House Post Office and Civil Service Committee" (May 1985) (Archives of the Library of Congress, Collection Winn Newman, Box 406, File 8).

59 Schlafly, *The Power of the Positive Woman*, 23.

60 Bethany M. Coston and Michael Kimmel, "White Men as the New Victims: Reverse Discrimination Cases and the Men's Rights Movement," *Nevada Law Journal* 13, no. 2, art. 5 (2013).

61 Michael Messner, "Forks in the Road of Men's Gender Politics: Men's Rights vs Feminist Allies," *International Journal for Crime, Justice and Social Democracy* 5, no. 2 (2016): 6–20.

62 Schlafly, *Who Killed the American Family?*, 217.

63 "Smile, You're on Candid Camera, Training Session for Radio and TV" (STOP ERA, Participation Form to the Annual Conference, June 25–26, 1975, Springfield, Illinois, Archives of the Schlesinger Library, Collection Carabillo, Box. 15.10).

64 DVD 1129, "How to Communicate Eagle Forum's Message: Appearance, Makeup and Dress," September 8, 2000, Eagle Forum Archives, Collection DVD.

65 The feminine ideal of the lady was derived from the gendered model of the southern lady in vogue in the Antebellum South. This mythical representation of womanhood was characterized by sophistication, purity, and devotion to the home. Only white women of the elite could aspire to embody this social type.

I Want to Thank my Husband Fred **91**

66 For example, in their manifesto, they rejected the prototypes of the "Degrading Mindless-Boob-Girlie Symbol," "the Unbeatable Madonna-Whore Combination," or "Military Death Mascot" (New York Radical Women, "No More Miss America!," 1968, https://www.redstockings.org/index.php/no-more-miss-america).

67 Debra Baker Beck, "The 'F' Word: How the Media Frame Feminism," *NWSA Journal* 10, no. 1 (Spring 1998): 139–53.

68 Phyllis Schlafly, "Ten Years of ERA Is Enough!," *The Phyllis Schlafly Report*, April 1983 (Archives of the Schlesinger Library, Collection Phyllis Schlafly Report, Book 4: 82–84).

69 Idem.; Phyllis Schlafly, "E.R.A. Suffers 1978 Defeats," *The Phyllis Schlafly Report*, March 1978 (Archives of the Schlesinger Library, Collection Phyllis Schlafly Report, Book 1: 75–78).

70 Christine Bard, ed., *Un siècle d'antiféminisme* (Paris: Fayard, 1999), 27.

71 I borrow this expression to Deniz Kandiyoti (see her article "Bargaining with Patriarchy," *Gender and Society* 2, no. 3 (September 1988): 274–90).

72 A few men later headed Eagle Forum state chapters. Such was the case of Schlafly's cousin, Ned Pfeifer, in Pennsylvania, from 2009 onwards.

73 Shirley Curry, "Shirley Curry," Project Voices of Truth, 2016, http://eagleforum-truth.com/voices-of-truth/.

74 For example, I found a flier of the organization Women's Forum indicating that Phyllis Schlafly was its president (Archives of the Schlesinger Library, Collection Women's Forum).

75 The eagle was chosen in 1782 to be the emblem of the United States of America as it embodies liberty and authority. Phyllis Schlafly chose this animal for its patriotic symbolism but also because it is mentioned in a verse of the Bible. Isaiah 40:31 reads, "They that wait upon the Lord shall renew their strength; they shall mount up with wings as eagles, they shall run, and not be weary; and they shall walk and not faint."

76 Steven Buechler, *Women's Movements in the United States: Woman Suffrage, Equal Rights, and Beyond* (New Brunswick, NJ: Rutgers University Press, 1990), 41–84; Suzanne Staggenborg, "Social Movement Communities and Cycles of Protest: The Emergence and Maintenance of a Local Women's Movement," *Social Problems* 45, no. 2 (May 1998): 180–204.

77 Phyllis Schlafly, Letter to STOP ERA Leaders, August 16, 1979 (Eagle Forum Archives, Collection Phyllis Schlafly, Series ERA, miscellaneous, Box 2, File 2).

78 Schlafly organized two parties to celebrate the failure of the ERA, in 1979 and in 1982, as the amendment obtained a new deadline for its ratification.

79 James Jasper, "Emotions and Social Movements: Twenty Years of Theory and Research," *Annual Review of Sociology* 37 (2011): 285–303.

80 Phyllis Schlafly, Interview with the author, St. Louis, August 26, 2013.

81 Kitty Werthmann, Interview with the author, St. Louis, August 31, 2016.

82 Schlafly, Godfrey & Fitzgerald, "Lawsuit Filed against Commission on International Women's Year," April 9, 1976 (Archives of the Library of Congress, Collection League of Women Voters, Box 133, File opposition anti-ERA literature 75–77). As 1975 had been declared the "International Women's Year" by the United Nations, U.S. feminists had decided to organize a national conference. Women delegates from every state convened in Houston, Texas, on November 18–21, 1977, to discuss the reforms they wanted to see implemented by public authorities.

83 One of Schlafly's books is entitled *The Flipside of Feminism: What Conservative Women Know—and Men Can't Say* (Washington, D.C.: WND Books, 2011).

92 Amélie Ribieras

84 National Coalition for Men, "Richard F. Doyle, MRA," https://ncfm.org/advisor-board/richard-f-doyle/.
85 Richard Doyle, Letter to Phyllis Schlafly, May 8, 1981 (Eagle Forum Archives, Collection Phyllis Schlafly, Series ERA, Subjects, B. 4, D. 7).
86 Phyllis Schlafly, "Testimony to the Senate Labor and Human Resources Committee," April 21, 1981 (Archives of the Schlesinger Library, Collection Carabillo, Box 15.9).
87 In its edition of April 22, 1981, *The Washington Post*, for example, featured an article by Spencer Rich entitled "Schlafly: Sex Harassment on Job No Problem for Virtuous Women."
88 Field Observation Notes, Eagle Council, Washington D.C., September 14–17, 2017.
89 Gayle Ruzicka, Interview with the author, phone, November 16, 2017.
90 Several of the very active members received it, like current Eagle Forum president Eunie Smith.
91 Critchlow, *Phyllis Schlafly and Grassroots Conservatism*, 32–33.
92 Mark DePue, Interview with Phyllis Schlafly, Abraham Lincoln Presidential Library, Oral History Program, "ERA fight in Illinois" Series, Clayton, Missouri, January 5–6, January 15, February 21–22, March 29–30, 2011, 160.
93 Schlafly's biographers disagree on that point. Donald Critchlow argues that "home remained the primary focus of Phyllis Schlafly's life," whereas Carol Felsenthal contends that "Schlafly, obviously, has never been 'just your average housewife'" (Critchlow, *Phyllis Schlafly and Grassroots Conservatism*, 33; Carol Felsenthal, *The Sweetheart of the Silent Majority: The Biography of Phyllis Schlafly*. Garden City, NY: Doubleday, 1981, 121).
94 Linda Kerber, "Separate Spheres, Female Worlds, Woman's Place: The Rhetoric of Women's History," *The Journal of American History* 75, no. 1 (June 1988): 9–39.
95 Walt Sharp, "At Home with the Schlaflys," *Alton Telegraph*, February 18, 1978 (Eagle Forum Archives, Collection Phyllis Schlafly, Series ERA, subjects, Box 26, File 8).
96 DVD 261, "Phyllis and Fred on Good Morning America," January 1, 1978 (Eagle Forum Archives, Collection DVD). The video can be watched at https://www.youtube.com/watch?v=dd0E72ZU5oM.
97 For instance, Carol Felsenthal reveals that he was an invaluable partner, "giving her her messages like a secretary" (Felsenthal, *The Sweetheart of the Silent Majority*, 111–12).
98 Quoted by Phyllis Schlafly in her interview with historian Mark DePue.
99 Catherine E. Rymph, *Republican Women: Feminism and Conservatism from Suffrage through the Rise of the New Right* (Chapel Hill: The University of North Carolina Press, 2006), 4.
100 For more details see https://eagleforum.org/projects/homemaker-awards.html and https://eagleforum.org/projects/eagle-awards.html. Some women who received the "Fulltime Homemaker Award" hardly fit the definition, as shown by their numerous activities listed in their biographies on the website.
101 DVD 291, "PS Speech for Families in Crisis Seminar: Homemakers as Policy Makers," May 8, 1981 (Eagle Forum Archives, Collection DVD).
102 Interviewee X, Interview with the author, phone, November 22, 2017.
103 Ronnee Schreiber, "Is There a Conservative Feminism? An Empirical Account," *Politics & Gender* 14 (2018): 56–79.
104 DePue, Interview with Phyllis Schlafly.
105 Jesse Helms was senator for North Carolina from 1973 to 2003 and a recognized leader of the conservative movement. Henry Hyde was representative for Illinois from 1975 to 2007.

I Want to Thank my Husband Fred **93**

106 She was elected delegate in 1956, 1964, 1968, 1984, 1988, 1992, 1996, 2004, 2012, and 2016, and alternate delegate in 1960, 1980, 2000 and 2008 (Phyllis Schlafly Eagles, "The Life and Legacy of Phyllis Schlafly," https://www.phyllisschlafly.com/phyllis/). Ronald Reagan did make a gesture in 1985 and appointed her to the Commission on the Bicentennial of the United States Constitution (1983–1991), which was in charge of putting together commemorative activities related to the celebration of the signature of this founding text.

5

CREATED EQUAL, BUT EQUAL IN NO OTHER RESPECT

Opposing Abortion to Protect Men

Carol Mason

At the University of Kentucky, signs on the campus lawn alert pedestrians that they are about to encounter something upsetting. Further along this path, they see gory signs and, finally, a large digital screen in the center of the quad, roped off but visible and visually dominating the space. The digital centerpiece is a jumbotron, usually used as a scoreboard at sporting events. This technology has been borrowed from the highly masculinist rituals of sports entertainment to create another sphere of masculinist ritual: scaring and enraging passersby on college campuses. Although the jumbotron is said to show footage of "a baby being dismembered," the moving images are moving only because they are animated by probing instruments and fingers.[1] The digital screen shows a video of rubber-gloved fingers fondling bloody fetal parts. One particularly cringe-inducing moment occurs when a gloved hand rolls what appears to be a fetal eyeball.

Often, passersby readily recognize that the images are not accurate depictions of terminating a pregnancy, but the validity of the images is less the issue. Those who consider that the bloody flesh shown on the jumbotron is no longer part of a woman—or never was part of a woman, as it is a "preborn" being—can find this display enraging because it represents to them dismemberment. And those who see it differently can also be enraged because it might represent the need for abortion as a consequence of unwanted sexual activity that resulted in pregnancy. The issue of consent is literally at hand. Whose flesh is the jumbotron exposing, and who has the right to look at it and touch it? Who has given consent to obtain and film the uterine flesh? Whose flesh is it? Who owns it? Who owns the person it came from? Who gets to see, who gets to show, who gets to touch—and who is being victimized—are issues that override questions of whether or not the projected images are true.

This article examines the anti-abortion movement to advance discussions about what it means for white men to promote themselves as victims. As previous

DOI: 10.4324/9781003164722-7

Created Equal, but Equal in No Other Respect **95**

scholarship attests, opposing abortion as a matter of protecting women has been the norm—a transnational strategy since the 1990s.[2] In such pro-woman rhetoric, women are depicted, much as are "unborn babies," as victims of a depraved abortion industry. Scholars have also recognized that the anti-abortion movement often racializes "the unborn" to symbolize an imperiled white future and the end of Christian civilization.[3] This symbolic depiction of the white minority-in-the-making has encouraged white men to see themselves as Christian warriors who are fending off a presumed apocalyptic future in which they are demographically and culturally subordinated. What comes into focus now at a time of heightened right-wing militancy across the globe is an escalation in the use of "the unborn" to fuel racist, populist beliefs that white *men*, as well as women, are facing not only a precarious future but also an embattled present. Representations of "the unborn" currently are used as an occasion in real time and space to invite conflict and to provoke actual physical altercations in which white men do not prevail but are shown, instead, as victimized.

This analysis focuses on the Ohio-based anti-abortion group Created Equal (CE) to demonstrate the current tactic of depicting white men as victims in need of protection. As a Christian anti-abortion organization, CE emerged in conjunction with earlier groups, including a male-dominated and male-centered men's ministry that sought to restore power to men as heads of the family and the state. Key to this restoration was, according to CE and its predecessor, contextualizing abortion in histories of racial and religious persecution. I will elaborate on the group's historical development in relation to its racial and religious rhetoric before turning to an examination of four digital film projects produced contemporaneously by or about the group. I chose these four film projects because they demonstrate the variety of aesthetic and rhetorical techniques used to depict white men as victims.

The first filmic example is a collection of digital video accounts of encounters between CE personnel and passersby in the public sphere and on college campuses. These edited videos adhere to formal conventions of conservative "documentaries," which aim to show an even playing field and rational debate. Second, I explain how a CE-created "exposé" of the supposed satanic ritualization of abortion, called *Abortion: Doctrine of Demons*, conforms to generic conventions of the gothic, which shapes CE's presence in public spaces. I analyze a third film shot and edited by student news media not connected to CE to look at how the group's tactics play out on college campuses. "Anti-Abortion Protest on UK Campus" demonstrates that CE's visual politics become less about the validity of images and more about the issue of access. Who gets to see, who gets to show, and who gets to touch are issues that override questions of whether or not displayed and projected images are true and accurate depictions. Indeed, CE's campus activities set up scary contests of consent, touching, and free speech, corresponding both with the weaponization of anti-abortion lawsuits inaugurated in the 1990s and with more recent tactics by the alt-right that provoke physical altercations on campus. Fourth, I examine footage disseminated as news reportage on conservative television and YouTube with the headline "Caught on Cam: Pro-life activists confronted, attacked by woman." This news clip is designed to demonstrate that women are hostile perpetrators of violence against men.

I analyze all four visual representations of or by CE intersectionally to recognize the interplay among issues of race, class, nation, gender, religion, and sexuality. In the 1980s and 1990s, Kimberlé Crenshaw proposed the analytical framework of *intersectionality* in her groundbreaking legal analyses; Angela Davis critiqued the white complexion of the pro-choice movement; Dorothy Roberts elucidated how the histories of reproductive and racial politics are inextricable; Loretta Ross explored how white supremacy is at the root of right-wing movements that affect reproductive policies.[4] Since that time, many scholars have produced important studies of race and reproduction by shining an intersectional light on how people of color have been persecuted and prosecuted as potential or current mothers and fathers. Inspiring such scholarship is the activist movement for *reproductive justice*, which also emerged in the 1990s to connect reproductive *rights* with social *justice*, vastly expanding older perspectives.[5] My writing adds to this body of work, and this article examines how the four visual representations of or by CE reveal that opposing abortion is paramount to protecting white men and their supposedly God-given domain. True to its Christian tenets as well as its ideological commitments to male supremacism, CE's foundational belief in patriarchal traditionalism operates in opposition to a presumed "testosterone deficiency," an "epidemic of fatherlessness," and the sin of nonprocreative sexuality, of which abortion is an indication. This examination of CE ultimately suggests that to protect the so-called unborn is to protect embattled white men who feel under attack.

CE in Historical, Religious, and Racial Contexts

An important context for CE is the men's movement called the Promise Keepers. The Promise Keepers (PK) formed in 1990 "to disciple men through vibrant men's ministries to become godly influences in their world."[6] PK encouraged revival and spiritual awakening because "men across the country had abdicated their responsibilities to their families and their church."[7] Men were encouraged to compassionately but firmly retake their rightful place as head of family and society, where women had been given too much responsibility and too many decisions to make. PK emerged, therefore, as part of what Susan Faludi then labeled a cultural backlash against feminist gains in policy and the popular imagination.[8] The premise of PK complemented sentiments by contemporary anti-abortionists such as Michael Bray, who laid out a rationale for stopping abortion with lethal force and in 1994 argued that men were suffering from a "testosterone deficiency."[9]

Around the same time—the mid-1990—Klansmen contributed to this idea of men being oppressed by women by picketing a Florida abortion clinic with signs protesting "Big Sister Federal Tyranny."[10] This phrase encapsulated an anti-government sentiment that was suffusing paramilitary culture with both "patriot" and anti-abortion iterations. Riffing on the Orwellian idea of big brother, such militants felt threatened by a purported omnipresent "big sister" of federal overreach, surveillance, and subjection, a tyrannical power that worked on behalf of women to the detriment of men. Militants such as Bray and the anti-abortion klan argued in the 1990s that men needed to take measures—including killing physicians to stop abortions—to end such emasculation. With this mindset, anti-abortion militants of the 1990s saw the Supreme Court decision of *Roe v. Wade* as an assault on men's right to make decisions about their own families. Prominent female cabinet members, such as Attorney General Janet Reno, became symbols to these anti-statist men who felt under siege by a female-controlled federal government.

This siege mentality blended well with two movements of the 1990s: the bourgeoning militia movement and the church-based efforts to convince youth that they are "survivors" of abortion. The militia movement dovetailed both with the white power movement and with the anti-abortion movement, which became more militant in practice and more apocalyptic in tone, resulting in domestic terrorism in the form of clinic bombings, sniper shootings, and threats of chemical warfare targeting physicians and clinic personnel.[11] Seven physicians and clinic workers were murdered throughout the 1990s: Leanne Nichols, Shannon Lowney, James Barrett, Robert Sanderson, John Bayard Britton, Michael Griffin, and Barnett Slepian. Anti-abortion homicide returned in 2009 when George Tiller was murdered while attending his church. Since the 1990s, Tiller's murderer had been associated with both anti-abortion organizations and anti-government militia.[12]

A distinguishing feature of most of the attacks on reproductive health care professionals in the name of stopping abortion was antisemitism in the form of Holocaust denial and appropriation. At the turn of the millennium, perpetrators justified the homicide of physicians and clinic workers by claiming abortion was a holocaust. Simultaneously, thousands of American youth were being taught the same lesson: abortion is a holocaust, and they, as living people, should consider themselves "survivors" of that Holocaust.[13] In this way, the siege mentality that motivated militia groups, anti-abortion killers, and paramilitary white supremacists was also systemically introduced to the mildest members of the American right: kids of Christian conservatives. These youths were taught to believe they were targets of state-sanctioned genocidal efforts. The false equivalency of (1) individual women choosing to terminate individual pregnancies with (2) state officials planning and executing mass murder of imprisoned citizens or slaves was perpetuated by homicidal abortion foes *and* churchgoers at Sunday schools. It was also the basis of the Genocide Awareness Project (GAP).

The GAP illustrated this false equivalency by juxtaposing magnified images of stillbirths and extracted fetal/uterine flesh with historical pictures of lynching of Blacks in the U.S. South and genocide of Jews in Nazi Germany. As I argue elsewhere, the analogy of abortion as slavery and the Holocaust is not merely a

98 Carol Mason

comparison. It purports a timeline of human atrocities in which abortion appears as the most heinous culmination of End Times evil.[14] It effectively relegates racial and religious persecutions against people of color and Jews to the past, displacing them with concern for the "unborn," which is most often depicted as white babies. In this way, racism and antisemitism "read as manifestations of historical prejudice that have been resolved."[15] In addition to conveying this apocalyptic temporality, the images promote an urgent sense of horror, deploying gothic themes of gore, injury, and dismemberment displayed as super-sized vinyl banners. Individual fetuses are innocent victims in this rendering, imbued with the same collective identities and societal connections that characterize entire cultures. Existing scholarship examines such representations as matters of racial appropriation, historical cooptation, visual misrepresentation, and medical misinformation.[16] More to my current point, in claiming fetuses as victims of violence perpetrated amid a so-called testosterone deficiency, the GAP reflected the particularly male supremacist siege mentality of the anti-abortion, militia, and men's movements in the 1990s. Indeed, GAP debuted at a PK assembly in the late 1990s in Washington, D.C.; its acronym was intended to correspond with the assembly's biblical theme of "stand in the gap."[17]

Prior to 2003, an Ohio State University alum who majored in marketing named Mark Harrington oversaw the Midwest circulation of the GAP as director of the regional hub of the Center for Bio-Ethical Reform (CBR), a pseudoscientific "pro-life" organization devoted to arguing that abortion is categorically genocide.[18] In 2011, Harrington moved from CBR to found the group Created Equal. He continued the racial and religious assumptions of GAP, overtly appropriating civil rights rhetoric. According to Michelle Kelsey Kearl, CE taps "into American public memory" of Martin Luther King Jr. and the 20th-century civil rights movement (CRM), investing "their own connotative meaning" onto them. "This appropriation or coopting of the rhetorical legacy of MLK and CRM," argues Kearl, "allows Created Equal to repurpose the past towards contemporary political ends incongruous with King and the movement."[19] Co-opting the framing of African American campaigns for civil rights was an explicit and conscious decision for Harrington: "Needing a model to give direction to the vision," according to the CE website, "Mark turned to stories from the Freedom Rides of the 1960s,"[20] which challenged Jim Crow prohibitions on interstate travel by racially integrated parties. Kearl carefully delineates how CE's Justice Rides "appropriate a specific anti-racist strategy and repurpose it in form only."[21] The result is a jarring juxtaposition of civil rights activists who withstood ambush, arson, beatings, murders, and state-sanctioned violence with "white teenagers braving public conversations about abortion."[22] CE personnel participating in anti-abortion Justice Rides "are not putting their lives in danger and are rarely, if ever, harmed in any way." Moreover, as Kearl avers, CE manages to "stake out an anti-racist position without being anti-racist."[23] Under Harrington's leadership, CE has continued to depict opposing abortion as activism on par with fighting

Created Equal, but Equal in No Other Respect **99**

against segregation and for equality, even while opposing anti-racist organizations and appearing antagonistic to people of color.

Examples of comparing abortion foes to civil rights activists abound in videos documenting CE in the public sphere. Says one CE spokesperson, "I think back on the civil rights movement, and I think, you know, if I were living in that time I would have been on those marches, I would have been breaking segregation laws with people and just challenging that."[24] The spokesman goes on to say that people will look back on this time and ask why others didn't fight abortion. Evident here is not only an appropriation of Black history but also a usurpation of the moral high ground that the CRM represents in national memory. As Daniel Martinez HoSang and Joseph E. Lowndes explain, some right-wing articulations of African American struggle produce "a redemptive subjectivity, in which Blackness becomes represented as the ethical embodiment of a distinctly American national identity and exceptionalism."[25] CE's embrace of Martin Luther King Jr. exemplifies how "longstanding narratives of Black uplift" and "the moral perseverance of the civil rights movement are repurposed to defend and naturalize" structural inequalities and neoliberal policies that keep the majority of Black people down.[26] CE personnel who challenge passersby with an admonishing claim of righteousness by comparing their anti-abortion stance with civil rights are perversely redefining reproductive control as a pursuit of American equality.

Students of conservatism know that such perverse redefinitions are hardly new. In particular, redefining what it means to be created equal can be traced back to Barry Goldwater's 1960 *The Conscience of a Conservative*. This immensely popular book elucidated a logic in which conservatives recognize that all men are created equal by their creator, as the Declaration of Independence claims. Of course, the exclusivity of the phrase "all men" already limits the purview of the declaration to males. But Goldwater, or more precisely his ghostwriter L. Brent Bozell Jr., made explicit additional limitations implicit in that Declaration. Americans are, according to the conservative conscience, "all equal in the eyes of God but we are equal *in no other respect*."[27] Understanding this statement as an underlying logic helps illuminate why, without a sense of hypocrisy, conservatives can uphold the idea of being created equal while assiduously opposing the goal of an egalitarian society, which according to Goldwater "does violence both to the charter of the Republic and to the Laws of Nature."[28] Harrington's adoption of the phrase "created equal" as a name for the group is likely not a conscious reference to *Conscience of a Conservative* but rather is taken from a quotation from Martin Luther King Jr., whose recorded speech on the Washington mall is used as a voice-over in several of CE's videos. Nevertheless, the same Christian conservative logic articulated in 1960 helps explain why CE does not consider it hypocritical to appropriate Black history while denying racial equality. We are, according to this logic, all equally loved by God because we are all created by him—but any sexual, gender, class, or racial divisions remain as his laws of nature.

We see this logic operating in podcasts of *Activist Radio: The Mark Harrington Show*. On his 2021 New Year's Eve broadcast, one of Harrington's guests cites this concept in discussing "the racial tensions" on campuses that teach critical theory.[29] "Whereas we believe that all people have a common shared humanity and that we're all image bearers of God," the guest contends, critical theory ostensibly prescribes—rather than describes—different classes in society and analyzes the power relations among them. As Harrington and his guest go on to discuss the Black Lives Matter movement (BLM), they say that blaming "social ills" instead of taking "personal responsibility" is not commensurate with the Christian worldview. The BLM movement is, therefore, anti-Christian, they say. The emphasis on personal responsibility redefines "neoliberalism as a form of antiracist freedom,"[30] while the idea that we are all image bearers of God underscores the religious foundation of being created equal. Both views allow for a complete and disdainful dismissal of the movement for Black lives.

In a different broadcast that delineates why Christians should not participate in or sympathize with the BLM movement, the concept of "created equal" emerges again.[31] Harrington's guest for the November 2020 show was Ryan Bomberger, an employee of the Virginia-based Radiance Foundation, which launched a mass media campaign in 2010 that purported abortion is Black genocide.[32] The campaign was, according to some analysts, an attempt to sow division among African American voters during the midterm elections of Barack Obama's first term.[33] Building on this established history of channeling resentment over the oppression of Black people into the anti-abortion cause, Bomberger directly relies on the religious idea of being created equal to situate the issue of Black lives in a Christian conservative view. He opines, "Of course we believe that Black lives matter. Why? Because we are all created in the image of God. And we're all loved equally by God." Then Bomberger, an African American man, delineates objections to BLM, including the oft-repeated ideas that there is more Black-on-Black violence than interracial violence and that police kill more white people than Black in any given year. He ignores the fact "that police kill Black men and women at disproportionate rates, ranging from 2.5–3 times more often than white Americans, according to numerous reports."[34] Sidestepping this information, Bomberger claims that "the abortion industry" killed more Black people than did cops and blames an "epidemic of fatherlessness" for all violence.

The "epidemic of fatherlessness" he cites is a familiar conservative narrative used to explain Black poverty as the result of a lack of male leadership in families and communities,[35] and it reinforces the overall presumption that men are dispossessed of their rightful role in society. The podcast implies that to protect men from continued dispossession and degradation, they need to oppose abortion as a means of restoring the natural order of life according to a Christian belief that we all—men, women, unborn, Black, white, Jew, gentile, young, and old—are equally created by God.[36]

But, as these broadcast conversations illustrate, this belief in being created equal by God demands recognizing one's place in this supposed natural order.

CE's patriarchal traditionalism sees that natural order as men serving as leaders and women serving as reproducers. Abortion, in their view, offends this natural order, so opposing abortion protects men's rightful place. Moreover, we have seen that in their co-optation of the heritage of the CRM and the valorized figure of Martin Luther King Jr., as an exemplar of personal responsibility, American exceptionalism, and moral perseverance, CE consistently depicts opposing abortion as a matter of national and racial pride. Let us now look at how CE's videos defend this highly religious and racialized stance against interlocutors who recognize that the racial pride that CE promotes is not synonymous with racial justice or equality for people of color.

Videos of CE in the Public Sphere

CE's videos exemplify how conservatives make art that they market as documentary films. The CE website is an archive of videos that show how they use public spaces to proselytize an anti-abortion faith, even as they eschew religious rhetoric. The videos are designed to show a seeming dialogue in which anti-abortionists, whose faces viewers often don't see because the camera is attached to their bodies, convince passersby that abortion is wrong. Each video aims to present an evenhanded dialogue in which the anti-abortionist appears to win fair and square, intellectually, and dispassionately. Opposition to the anti-abortionist side is presented as hostile, irrational, or feeble. Documentary filmmaking has always appealed to objective truth-telling, despite the fact that it is an art form with formal aspects that are intentionally designed. Especially in their capacity to document what appears to be a political debate, the videos produced by CE follow filmmaking techniques and adopt a rhetorical style that characterizes other conservative documentaries.

In particular, the CE videos are similar to recent documentary films produced by conservatives in which the "formal appearance of political debate" is deployed "for a contradictory end: to deny outright an encounter with political difference and thereby to refuse any serious consideration of the issues, ideas, or arguments expressed by a political opponent" (Krzych, 80). These videos simulate dialogue "in a manner that maintains a fundamental barrier against any significant exchange between self and (an antagonistic) other."[37] This is especially clear when interlocutors raise the question of the conditions under which people become pregnant as something that CE personnel are not taking into account. In several videos, stopped passersby try to steer the conversation toward the socio-economic situations that may contextualize an unwanted pregnancy. The passersby raise questions about structural inequalities that shape people's ability to meet the needs of a pregnancy or parenthood. But this recognition of people's conscientiousness in weighing the complexities involved in deciding their own capacity to take on such responsibilities is paradoxically inverted as a lack of morality. If conception is a life, then ending conception is killing: as explored more fully later in this chapter, this bottom-line thinking is a "simplification of

102 Carol Mason

complex subject matter into moralistic binaries [that] is an all too common feature of contemporary political discourse."[38]

For example, one video, in particular, demonstrates how CE avoids analyses of structural inequalities and provides a "simulacrum of debate intent on the denial of political difference."[39] When a young Black woman approaches CE personnel, she points out that the person seeking to terminate a pregnancy may have been raped. Rape is an issue of male dominance that is historically intertwined with gendered and racialized violence. At the word "rape," the white male CE personnel responds with a fluid and measured contention that the resultant baby may be unloved, but that does not justify killing because it is not right to kill the unloved or the unlovable, using teenage girls and the homeless as examples of others who are unloved but not killed.[40] Moreover, as Kearl notes, "[T]he visual representation of white men, who [as CE personnel] believe themselves to be part of an oppressed group, engaged in prescribing behaviors and beliefs to black women about abortion and/or their reproductive objections should cause some alarm."[41] This particular video does not include the Black woman's response. Instead, at the close of the specious chain of equivalences delivered by the CE personnel, a white woman approaches to shake his hand, and she says, "[W]e need people like you." In this way, the Black woman's reasonable intervention is overwhelmed by a steady stream of paternalistic condescension, which a white woman then complements in a de facto act of racial solidarity.

The exchanges in this CE video exemplify the tendency of conservative films to "revel in the accumulation of facts, details, and qualifications that distract from, but do not fundamental[ly] respond to, material appearances of political difference."[42] The "material appearances" of race appear only as inconsequential in this video. Any racial differences are absolutely ignored on the scene and in the discussion. CE personnel do not respond to the larger implications of the Black woman's point, to the fact of her race, to her perspective as a woman of color, or to any lived experience she has to bring to bear on this issue. She is shut down. But the filmmaking—the formal aspects of the video—suggests that this has been an equitable exchange of opinions in which the apparent victor has played fairly and honorably.

These videos put the viewer in the shoes of CE personnel. The camera often situates the video viewer as the anti-abortionist, whose voice emerges as the individual spectator's. The voice also functions as the seemingly omnipotent speech effect known as the "voice of God" in documentary filmmaking, which is fitting because the actual argument made is essentially a religious appeal to the idea of conception as a "life" and as "human." This religious argument assumes life is created by God and therefore cannot be tampered with without spurning the gift of God. This religious argument sidesteps the fact that since 1965 the American College of Obstetricians and Gynecologists has defined pregnancy as a fertilized egg implanted in the uterine lining.[43] We never see a person counter with the fact that an ovum can be fertilized but washed away with the sloughing off of the uterine lining during menstruation. According to the videos, once you concede conception is life; you must also say that ending conception is killing and that therefore anyone who ends conception is a killer. The basis of this equation goes back to that religious belief that life is God's dominion, and you are a sinner if you spurn his gift of life. CE personnel avoid stating any such underlying religious assumption in favor of humanistic inferences. The belief in pregnancy as God's sacred gift is delivered in a secular frame of human rights and equal rights that obscures this fundamental religious ideology.

Doctrine of Demons

Devoted to Christian views, CE uses films to translate that religious perspective into secular frameworks. The gothic genre is instrumental in this regard. *Abortion: A Doctrine of Demons* is a CE production that uses generic conventions of the gothic to convince viewers that abortion is fundamentally a demonic enterprise, rather than one of the most common and safe medical procedures done in the United States and around the world.[44] Moreover, the film has an apocalyptic tone and argumentative structure that reduce the issues down to a diametrical opposition between good and evil. The good people are Christians who oppose abortion: no surprise there. The bad people "have a religious dogmatism of their own" but in an inverse way: they are "religiously secularist" in their quest for "autonomy," and "the greatest representative of pursuing autonomy is Satan." A voice-over provides a caveat, claiming that "mocking Christianity does not prove a doctrinal connection between killing preborn babies and Satanism, but those who love death are often quick to embrace its tenets." This manufactured moral divide is the bedrock of the apocalyptic narrative that reads abortion in the United States as a sign of the End Times of American decency, white civilization, and the Christian nation.[45] The film goes on to interview Zachary King, a "satanic high wizard," who claims to have used blood obtained by abortions for demonic worship. The film includes many references to Satan, apparently gleaned from heated exchanges when facing off with counter-protesters and from more elaborate street theater and performance art. In their original presentations and venues, these references to Satan likely were meant to indict and ridicule the use of gore, depravity, and demons by abortion foes. In *Doctrine of Demons*, any such ironic images are stripped of their original context and represented as sober evidence of mocking Christ and supporting the supposed satanic blood sacrifice that is, they claim, abortion.

The idea that abortion is an anti-Christian and even satanic practice is a very old idea rooted in the ancient antisemitic myth of blood libel.[46] Anti-abortion materials have since the 1970s purported to uncover the hidden truth that physicians performing abortions are Jews who kill children as a sacrificial rite.[47] They imply and sometimes outright claim that abortion providers constitute a satanic, Jewish-run cabal. This portrayal blends with the related antisemitic myth that asserts that a Jewish cabal is conspiratorially and secretly controlling the government and the media. Most recently, we can see this kind of conspiracism reflected

104 Carol Mason

in Trump supporters who followed Q, the supposed government insider who ostensibly provided clues about how democrats and Hollywood elite would be exposed for their sex trafficking of very young children, some of whom were sacrificed in weird rituals.[48] Like QAnon conspiracists, abortion foes pit a satanic cabal craving baby flesh against humble heroes who supposedly can see what less enlightened people cannot. In its regular depiction of clinic workers and reproductive health care professionals as characterized by depravity and blood-lust, abortion foes primed the American imagination for QAnon conspiracism. But there is an even more commonplace precursor, one that situates the belief that abortion is intrinsically bloody, injurious, and depraved firmly in the secular register. The gothic is used to create the more secular, less overtly antisemitic version of abortion as a satanic practice.

As literary scholar Karyn Valerius has shown, the gothic genre has been deployed to vilify abortion for more than a century. Valerius demonstrates how, since the 1800s, gothic conventions have served to portray "abortionists as depraved villains who prey on female victims in vice-ridden urban spaces."[49] Her example of this portrayal from the 20th century is *The Silent Scream*, a highly controversial 1984 film featuring anti-abortion physician Bernard Nathanson. Valerius analyzes the film as a disingenuous depiction of abortion built on conventions of the gothic. She writes:

> *The Silent Scream* falsely claims to present empirical evidence that abortion causes fetuses to suffer, but the video's moral authority depends on this faulty evidence and on the emotional force of Nathanson's decidedly gothic narration. This gothic narrative transforms a routine medical procedure into a violent spectacle as it encourages audiences to identify with a fetal protagonist said to experience emotions and physical sensations.[50]

Similarly, the gothic narrative of *Doctrine of Demons* also is transformative. It renders abortion a depraved spectacle and invites spectators to immerse themselves in the generic pleasures and powers of horror.

In addition to the content that sets up an apocalyptic dyad between Christian religion and "religious secularists" aligned with Satan, *Doctrine of Demons* is marketed as a forbidden and "banned video" with graphic depictions and exposés of debaucherous scenes and criminal activities. Ominous music, slow motion, dark hues, and other editing features add to the foreboding tone. It is a creepy film used to disgust and delight those already predisposed to see abortion as an evil enterprise instead of a safe and common medical procedure. Like *The Silent Scream*, it

> resembles gothic fiction in both form and content: it promises to frighten and appall readers; it uncovers the 'hideous truth' about secret crimes; it uses lurid description to simultaneously express moral outrage and excite fascination with the illicit activity it depicts; and it refuses to name the unmentionable topic it nonetheless discusses in colorful detail.[51]

In *Doctrine of Demons*, the unmentionable topic is the presumption that Jews, acting in concert with or as Satanists, are responsible for abortion. *Doctrine of Demons* approaches this unspeakable topic when it examines "child sacrifice" that goes back to "antiquity." It then asserts that this ancient practice is as current as 2016 Jewish presidential candidate and Vermont Senator Bernie Sanders, whose "pro-choice" answer to a debate question is evidence that, as the voice-over claims, "many still call for child sacrifice." *Doctrine of Demons* never explicitly equates Jews with Satanists; it only implies this supposedly most horrific of secrets and thereby conforms to all of the generic conventions of the gothic. These gothic conventions enact the powers of horror that make abortion a lurid and forbidden practice and its proponents a spectacularly depraved bunch. Putting abortion in a gothic light secularizes the more religiously based narrative that abortion is a sign of the End Times, evidence of culminating events that are part of a cataclysmic conflict between satanic and Christian forces. CE straddles and merges both narratives of abortion: abortion becomes a sign of impending apocalypse, and abortion becomes a matter of gothic horror. We can see this merger also reflected in their campus activities.

Anti-abortion Protest on Campus

CE's campus activities enjoy amicable communication, if not professional collaboration, with law enforcement that seems to privilege the protection of private property over the right of women to express themselves and to be free from unwanted touch. CE's access to campus, like its access to uterine flesh—a.k.a., fetal parts—seems greater than women's access to abortion and other reproductive health care.[52] In the midst of the Me-Too movement and debates about how Title IX should be implemented to combat sexual assault on campus, CE redirects big questions about unwanted touching away from what women say to what CE's opponents do. *Implicit* questions of ownership and consent become *explicit* questions of ownership and consent when passersby are provoked into action and knock down or flip over any of the signs or equipment. The opponents of CE are then accused of destruction of private property, theft, or vandalism. It is not, therefore, only a politics of abjection or gothic horror operating in the spectacle of the enlarged, medically misleading, gory images. It is also a politics of touching, consent, and property. CE's politics of touching successfully *decenter* and deflect women's experiences of nonconsensual touching and sexual assault that may lead to unwanted pregnancy.

Returning to the scene of the jumbotron, a video produced by the *Kentucky Kernal*, a student newspaper at the University of Kentucky, demonstrates this confluence of issues during a visit by CE.[53] In October 2017, CE met spirited opposition from students on the Lexington campus. In one scene, a student, Adrienne Rogers, is shown to have been angered by CE's display, which she considered hate speech rather than free speech. She flipped over one of the large lawn signs sporting a gory image. Campus police then pursued her. The video shows

106 Carol Mason

police following Rogers through the crowd, grabbing at her shoulder and her backpack. When she stops, U.K. police captain Bill Webb confronts her, calmly admonishing her for knocking over one sign. He explains that CE has permission to be on campus: "It's their right to be here." Rogers responds, "It's also my right to push that over. I didn't touch anybody. It is in a public space." As she continues to detail her rights, Webb cuts her off: "I'm not going to argue with you. Please don't touch their property." Immediately another female student interjects: "Please don't touch *her*." Rogers repeats, "Yeah, please don't touch *me*." Before Webb can think about what to say, the other student emphasizes, "Don't touch my girlfriend." At this point, Webb seems confused. He stammers. He closes his eyes. Webb is momentarily rendered speechless.

The women have not only made a demand; they also have made a comparative inquiry. Why does his entitlement to pursue and touch her without consent trump her right to topple over an inanimate object, even if that object belongs to someone else? Why is she less protected than a lawn sign? Why does she have fewer rights than a piece of plastic and board? Rogers was not charged with any criminal misconduct. In this instance, the woman's right not to be touched commanded the center of attention. And the declaration that one woman was the other's girlfriend nodded to a whole different economy of consent and touching, in the face of which patriarchal law appeared momentarily dumbfounded.

CE may suggest that their occupation of the public sphere is a level playing field in which, Harrington says, you should "bring your point of view in the marketplace."[54] But the "marketplace" is not a neutral space or a level playing field. To rebel against the disparity of access and financial means that CE represents to individuals is to risk being sued, which could add to the organization's revenue and fuel the fire of CE's male persecution complex.[55] Anti-abortionists' attempts not only to propagandize a siege mentality but also to profit from it have proliferated. This proliferation is an expansion of the tactic that Mark Crutcher of Life Dynamics started in the 1990s when he launched a campaign called ABMAL, short for "abortion malpractice." Like ambulance chasers from law firms hoping to profit from accidents, the ABMAL campaign sought to convince people that they may be "victims" of abortion. Life Dynamics offered legal advice and support for anyone who would come forward. The ABMAL campaign came under scrutiny when it was discovered that Crutcher had paid an "eyewitness" to testify with lies about the "abortion industry" in 2000.[56] Since then, the tactic of weaponizing lawsuits against abortion providers or advocates has shifted from clinics to campuses.

GAP, CE, and "pro-life" student groups began in the 2010s to make legal claims regarding their right to free speech on campus. Various lawsuits emerged, capitalizing on offended and outraged opposition that GAP provoked in onlookers. In 2013, for example, a pro-life student organization sued Oklahoma State University citing First Amendment rights when they were denied space on campus.[57] In 2014, a University of California, Santa Barbara professor was sued for assault after taking a sign of a teenage anti-abortion demonstrator.[58] In 2015,

Boise State University paid a "pro-life" student group $20,000 to settle a free speech lawsuit, only $100 of which went to the group; the remainder covered fees for legal services by the Alliance Defending Freedom, a right-wing organization.[59] In 2017, students aided by the Alliance Defending Freedom sued Miami University in Ohio.[60] That same year, Cal State University San Marcos was sued by Students for Life represented by Alliance Defending Freedom; eventually, the university paid $240,000.[61]

In each of these examples, the issue of free speech emerged in the same way that it did for the alt-right. In 2017, the free speech issue erupted as the "Battle of Berkeley" pitted the alt-right against the University of California. When university officials denied conservative celebrity speakers Milo Yiannopoulos and Ann Coulter the right to speak on campus, the alt-right staged protests that resulted in street fighting between progressive and far-right demonstrators.[62] Far-right strategist Richard Spencer saw the conflict on Berkeley's campus as a good indication that more campus demonstrations could unleash street fighting and force people to pick sides, so he and other organizers set out to reproduce the melee several months later on the University of Virginia campus in a campaign to Unite the Right in Charlottesville.[63] What the alt-right did on campuses in 2017 on a large scale was what anti-abortionists had been doing for decades on campuses nationwide. The tactic of provocation deployed by both has particular objectives. It seeks to make opponents appear as the hostile, irrational, and reckless instigators of physical altercation. Documented or livestreamed, the fight can ostensibly accomplish at least two goals: (1) to create a basis for a profitable lawsuit and (2) to prove that white Christian men are under attack.

Caught on Cam

CE produces and distributes short video clips to news media to promote and popularize the idea that men are victims of violence perpetrated by women. Inverting understandings of domestic violence and sexual assault as crimes of power exerted by men over women, this idea that women attack men is as old as the caricature of the hen-pecked or cuckolded husband. The particular news clip I analyze next corresponds, intentionally or not, with how online communities—known as the manosphere—characterize women as exerting too much power over men. Men, disgruntled with women's sexual power, including incels—who claim to be involuntarily celibate because women ignore them as potential sexual partners—and pick-up artists—whose disdain for women leads them to serial fornication as a matter of subjection—populate the manosphere. Their fear and loathing of women's presumed sexual power is the flipside of the fear and loathing of women's power to terminate pregnancy that results from sexual activity and that abortion opponents try to stop. In both cases, men are seeing in women a sexuality and power that men cannot control, which they see as the problem. It is a problem because men, according to this view, are the victims of out-of-control women who attack them.

108 Carol Mason

As if to prove this idea, CE distributes news media clips that can end up as features on local television, as was the case with "Caught on Cam: Pro-life Activists Confronted, Attacked by Woman."[64] This news spot aired on a local Columbus, Ohio, channel and then was subsequently posted by pro-life websites and featured on the nationally syndicated program *Fox and Friends*. In this news clip, a young woman is shown profanely yelling at an apparently younger man identified as a summer intern. We hear nothing about what he may have said prior to the news clip, but she is heard contesting the validity of the images depicting products of an aborted pregnancy.

The clip mirrors the basic assumption that women must be stopped from dominating men. In particular, it resembles scenarios from the manosphere. In the manosphere, a particular type of victim, the nerd or geek, is subject to attacks from "normies" and "basic bitches" (read: unintelligent women) who infiltrate their digital space. The news clip resembles this situation by interspersing points of view from a handheld camera and from a body cam. The result is comical or cringeworthy, depending on your sense of the politics of the situation. The view from the body cam provides a sense of being aggressively pushed by the woman's larger, bulkier body, and the angle of the camera provides a full view of her chest. The view from the handheld camera shows an aggressive face-off, with the woman yelling profanity at the teenager, often with her index finger pointing at him as he stands his ground silently. These actions appear to be uncalled for, and the woman comes off as not reacting to the arguments or materials in particular but as a volatile, irrational bully who is out of control with unwarranted anger. The cameras focus on and exacerbate her corpulence, presenting a cartoonish caricature of an out-of-control woman. One need not condone her actions to recognize that the editing of the encounter results in a clip that provides us with the stereotype of the angry feminist. The cultural work that this clip performs is not only to laugh at or disdain the woman but also to feel sorry for and defensive *of the teenager*. He is depicted as the victim. CE's creation and distribution of this depiction fit precisely in its overall view that men are under attack and that opposing abortion is an honorable way for men to stand their ground against the onslaught of women's rights and abusive feminists.

A reporter later follows up with the woman to get her point of view. By asserting that she "assaulted" the CE crew, the reporter puts the woman on the defensive. She defends herself by questioning whether knocking down signage and shoving a cameraman who had no consent to film her constitutes assault. Ultimately, a judge ordered the woman to pay $80 for the two signs she knocked down, and the prosecutor dropped charges of assault and criminal damage.[65]

In interviews about the situation, Harrington predictably invoked the legacy of Martin Luther King Jr. and expressed pride in his staff and Christian concern for the woman. As we saw in the video from the University of Kentucky, the contest of consent over touching property overrode the issue of whether or not the images in the signs she knocked down were medically, biologically accurate, and truthful depictions of abortion. Moreover, on *Fox and Friends*, the CE

Created Equal, but Equal in No Other Respect **109**

director of summer programs, Seth Drayer, reports that their impetus is to de-escalate violence; he also indicates that recording action to be used in court is the ultimate goal. "When people respond that way we don't try to win the debate or challenge their claims, we just want to try to diffuse the anger while still again documenting so that later our rights and the law will be upheld," resulting in a public opinion or legal win.[66] This quotation suggests that going to court is the goal of these encounters in the public sphere. Not fighting back and not engaging in honest debate to address political differences is part of the plan.

Caught on Cam is a clear example of how CE visualizes opposing abortion as a call for protections for men, as well as for women and "the unborn." Opposing abortion helps protect white men from purported federal tyranny orchestrated to dismantle men's privileges and exalt women's sexual and political dominance. Opposing abortion helps protect white men from accusations of rape by delegitimizing and decentering women's experiential knowledge in campus contests of consent. Opposing abortion helps protect white men from succumbing to a demographic decline, the supposed end of the white race. Opposing abortion helps protect Christian men from accusations of antisemitism because if abortion is a holocaust, they are fighting the premier signifier of antisemitism. Perhaps most clearly, opposing abortion helps protect white men from accusations of racism by wresting the moral high ground from the CRM and the movement for Black lives.

Conclusion: Implications for Studying the Right and Male Supremacism

All of these representations of CE—the films and videos they produce, as well as those made about them—bear witness to a broader trend among right-wing movements to vilify women and position men as underdogs. It is important to note this trend because it is one of the unifying aspects of right-wing movements and ideologies worldwide. Opposing abortion by positioning men as victims to be protected fits and fuels larger populist campaigns. This is especially true for far-right populists who depict white people as under siege by people of color who threaten to overpower them demographically with high birth rates. This fear of demographic and cultural demise has for years manifested as opposition to abortion for white people. The fear of being a minority has been promoted alongside the satanic panic purporting that anti-Christian demons are ritualizing abortion as part of an ongoing (or in a lead-up to) apocalyptic battle. CE's materials and practices reflect all of these fears, apparently stoking them for profit. As such, they exemplify how some scholars of right-wing studies are theorizing victimhood.

According to such scholars, in many far-right and conservative communities, the idea of being a victim is not about who has sustained injury or endured suffering but, instead, who occupies the lowest stratification of social hierarchy.[67] In this way, victimhood is imagined to be both reversible and reciprocal. In other words, white people who have occupied the privileged position atop social hierarchy

110 Carol Mason

imagine that any change to that status will surely result in total and violent subjugation. I contend that the anti-abortion movement has supplied images of injury and violence that have contributed to these fears of white Christians being victimized. The anti-abortion movement has visualized and encouraged others to visualize the dissolution of the white race with gothic fetal imagery. Christian white people have been taught to see themselves as survivors of abortion and to identify with "the unborn," bloody images of which signify the dismemberment, torture, and debasement that would befall them if what they perceive as the natural order erodes. For some white Christian men, abortion signifies no longer an *impending* apocalyptic battle between Christian and anti-Christian forces but an apocalypse *in progress*. Images of white men as victims of women's abuse confirm their sense of this conflict. Therefore, it should come as no surprise that groups such as CE are investing in visual narratives of men withstanding verbal and physical attacks. The fact that they create spaces and opportunities in which such altercations are bound to occur indicates, therefore, not only a profitable weaponizing of lawsuits but also a psychological wage of confirming their dystopic worldview that the "natural order"—patriarchal traditionalism—is imperiled and that men must be protected.

Notes

1 Kentucky Kernal, "Anti Abortion Protest on UK Campus," Video posted with editorial, "No Matter What you Say, Free Speech Belongs to Everyone," October 19, 2017, http://www.kykernel.com/opinion/editorial-no-matter-what-you-say-free-speech-belongs-to-everyone/article_28c7b132-b51a-11e7-a54a-df29910c49f6.html
2 Carol Mason, "Opposing Abortion to Protect Women: Transnational Strategy since the 1990s," *Signs: Journal of Women in Culture and Society* 44, no. 3 (2019): 665–92.
3 Alex DiBranco, "The Long History of the Anti-abortion Movement's Links to White Supremacists," *The Nation*, February 3, 2020, https://www.thenation.com/article/politics/anti-abortion-white-supremacy/; Carol Mason, "Chapter Nine. Minority Unborn," in *Fetal Subjects, Feminist Positions*, eds. Lynn M. Morgan and Meredith Wilson Michaels (Philadelphia: University of Pennsylvania Press, 2016), 159–74; Mason, "Opposing Abortion."
4 Kimberlé Crenshaw, "Mapping the Margins: Intersectionality, Identity Politics, and Violence against Women of Color," *Stanford Law Review* 43, no. 6 (1991): 1241–99; Angela Y. Davis, *Women, Race and Class* (New York: Random House, 1983); Dorothy Roberts, *Killing the Black Body: Race, Reproduction and the Meaning of Liberty* (New York: Vintage Books, 1998); Loretta Ross, "White Supremacy in the 1990s," in *Eyes Right! Challenging the Right-wing Backlash*, ed. Chip Berlet, 166-181 (Boston, MA: South End Press, 1995).
5 For a comprehensive history of the movement, see Loretta J. Ross and Rickie Solinger, *Reproductive Justice: An Introduction* (Berkeley: University of California Press, 2017).
6 American Bible Society, *Stand in the Gap: A Sacred Assembly of Men. Commemorative Edition New Testament. Contemporary English Version* (Nashville, TN: Thomas Nelson Publishers, 1997).
7 American Bible Society, *Stand in the Gap.*

Created Equal, but Equal in No Other Respect **111**

8 Susan Faludi, *The Undeclared War against American Women* (New York: Crown Publishing, 1991).

9 Michael Bray, *A Time to Kill* (Portland, OR: Advocates for Life, 1994), 156.

10 Carol Mason, *Killing for Life: The Apocalyptic Narrative of Pro-life Politics* (Ithaca, NY: Cornell University Press, 2002), 35.

11 Mason, *Killing for Life*; Patricia Baird-Windle and Eleanor J. Bader, *Targets of Hatred: Anti-abortion Terrorism* (New York: Palgrave, 2001); Jennifer Jefferis, *Armed for Life: The Army of God and Anti-abortion Terror in the United States* (Santa Barbara, CA: Praeger, 2011).

12 Nicholas Riccardi, "Suspect in George Tiller's Slaying Reportedly Belonged to Anti-government Militia," *Los Angeles Times*, June 2, 2009, https://www.latimes.com/archives/la-xpm-2009-jun-02-na-tiller-suspect2-story.html

13 Jennifer L. Holland, *Tiny You: A Western History of the Anti-abortion Movement* (Berkeley: University of California Press, 2020).

14 Mason, *Killing for Life*, 117.

15 Michelle Kelsey Kearl, "'WWMLKD': Coopting the Rhetorical Legacy of Martin Luther King, Jr. and the Civil Rights Movement," *Journal of Contemporary Rhetoric* 8, no. 3 (2018): 193. Kearl makes this argument in relation to racism and sexism as she analyzes the Created Equal brochure.

16 Kearl, "WWMLKD"; Shyrissa Dobbins-Harris, "The Myth of Abortion as Black Genocide: Reclaiming Our Reproductive Cycle," *National Black Law Journal* 26, no. 1, 86-127 (2017); Kathryn Joyce, "Abortion as Black Genocide," *Public Eye*, April 29, 2010, https://www.politicalresearch.org/2010/04/29/abortion-as-black-geno-cide-an-old-scare-tactic-re-emerges; Celeste Condit, *Decoding Abortion Rhetoric* (Urbana and Chicago, IL: University of Illinois Press, 1994); Karen Newman, *Fetal Positions: Individualism, Science, Visuality* (Stanford, CA: Stanford University Press, 1996); Rosalind Petchesky, *Abortion and Woman's Choice* (Boston, MA: Northeastern University Press, 1984); Mason, *Killing for Life*, 38–45.

17 Mason, *Killing for Life*, 43.

18 For refutations and examinations of this claim that abortion is genocide, see Kearl, "WWMLKD"; Mason, *Killing for Life*, 38–45 and 114–29; Jessica Woolford and Andrew Woolford, "Abortion and Genocide: The Unbridgeable Gap," *Social Politics: International Studies in Gender, State and Society* 14, no. 1 (2007), 126–53. For refutations of the claim that abortion is black genocide, see Dobbins-Harris, "The Myth"; Ross and Solinger, *Reproductive Justice*; and the five-part video series *Abortion Conspiracy* by Stuart TV, the first installment of which analyzes the billboard campaign claiming Black babies are an "endangered species" due to abortion, YouTube video, posted November 8, 2010, https://www.youtube.com/watch?v=HndqGMNnqDg&t=25s.

19 Kearl, "WWMLKD," 184.

20 Created Equal, "Our Story," https://www.createdequal.org/our_story/.

21 Kearl, "WWMLKD," 196–99.

22 Ibid., 197.

23 Ibid., 197.

24 Created Equal, "One Question Stumps College Student," https://www.createdequal.org/outreach/.

25 Daniel Martinez HoSang and Joseph E. Lowndes, *Producers, Parasites, Patriots: Race and the New Right-Wing Politics of Precarity* (Minneapolis: University of Minnesota Press, 2019), 15.

26 Ibid.

112 Carol Mason

27 Barry Goldwater, *Conscience of a Conservative* (Shepherdsville, KY: Victor Publishing, 1960), 38.

28 Ibid.

29 Mark Harrington, "Social Justice Critical Theory and Christianity," *Radio Activist: The Mark Harrington Show*, December 31, 2020, https://createdequal.podbean.com/e/social-justice-critical-theory-and-christianity-are-they-compatible-the-mark-harrington-show-12-31-2020/.

30 Hosang and Lowndes, *Producers*, 15.

31 Mark Harrington, "Top Ten Reasons to Not Support the #BlackLivesMatter Movement," *Activist Radio: The Mark Harrington Show*, podcast, November 5, 2002, https://markharrington.org/live/top-ten-reasons-to-not-support-the-blacklives-matter-movement-the-mark-harrington-show-11-05-2020/.

32 For relevant critiques: Zakiya Luna, "'Black Children Are an Endangered Species': Examining Racial Framing in Social Movements," *Sociological Focus* 51, no. 3 (2018), 238–51. In addition to the Atlanta billboards, similar billboards emerged around the same time in New York and Chicago. See Akiba Soloman, "Another Day, Another Race-Baiting Abortion Billboard," *Colorlines*, March 29, 2011, https://www.colorlines.com/articles/another-day-another-race-baiting-abortion-billboard; Michelle Goldberg, "Obama Billboard Shows Anti-abortion Focus on African-Americans," *Daily Beast*, March 30, 2011, https://www.thedailybeast.com/obama-billboard-shows-anti-abortion-focus-on-african-americans; Sujatha Jesudason, "The Latest Case of Reproductive Carrots and Sticks: Race, Abortion and Sex Selection," *The Scholar and Feminist Online* 9.1–9.2 (Fall 2010/Spring 2011), http://sfonline.barnard.edu/reprotech/jesudason_01.htm.

33 Kathryn Joyce, "Abortion as Black Genocide," *Public Eye*, April 29, 2010, https://www.politicalresearch.org/2010/04/29/abortion-as-black-genocide-an-old-scare-tactic-re-emerges.

34 Malaika Jabali, "White People Are Killed by Cops Too. But That Doesn't Undermine Black Lives Matter," *The Guardian*, July 16, 2020, https://www.theguardian.com/commentisfree/2020/jul/16/trump-police-abolition-black-americans.

35 Daniel Geary, *Beyond Civil Rights: The Moynihan Report and Its Legacy* (Philadelphia: University of Pennsylvania Press, 2015).

36 Kearl, "WWMLKD," 192–96. A comprehensive take down of CE's claims that abortion is ageism can be found in Kearl's analysis of a CE brochure.

37 Scott Krzych, "The Price of Knowledge: Hysterical Discourse in Anti-Michael Moore Documentaries." *The Comparatist* 39 (2015): 81.

38 Ibid., 90.

39 Ibid., 81.

40 CreatedEqualFilms, *JumboTron College Campus Debut*, YouTube, Video, https://www.youtube.com/watch?v=7Nbp6ewiLPU&feature=emb_logo.

41 Kearl, "WWMLKD," 197.

42 Krzych, "The Price," 96.

43 Grace S. Chung, Ryan E. Lawrence, Kenneth A. Rasinski, et al. "Obstetrician-Gynecologists' Beliefs about When Pregnancy Begins," *American Journal of Obstetrics and Gynecology* 206, no. 2 (2012): 132.e1–7, https://www.ajog.org/article/S0002-9378(11)02223-X/fulltext.

44 Created Equal, *Abortion: Doctrine of Demons*, video, https://www.createdequal.org/doctrine-of-demons/, https://www.youtube.com/watch?v=KI-BfncsYSw.

45 Mason, *Killing for Life*.

Created Equal, but Equal in No Other Respect **113**

46 Nazis used the idea of blood libel, a false allegation that Jews ritualistically use the blood of children, to promote antisemitism. United States Holocaust Memorial Museum, "Blood libel," *Holocaust Encyclopedia*, https://encyclopedia.ushmm.org/content/en/article/blood-libel.

47 Mason, *Killing for Life*, 171–79.

48 Jessica Winter, "The Link between the Capitol Riot and Anti-abortion Extremism," *The New Yorker*, March 11, 2021, https://www.newyorker.com/news/daily-comment/the-link-between-the-capitol-riot-and-anti-abortion-extremism.

49 Karen Valerius, "A Not-So-Silent Scream: Gothic and the US Abortion Debate," *Frontiers* 34, no. 3 (2013): 28.

50 Ibid., 28.

51 Ibid., 27.

52 American College of Obstetricians and Gynecologists, "Increasing Access to Abortion," https://www.acog.org/clinical/clinical-guidance/committee-opinion/articles/2020/12/increasing-access-to-abortion. Nearly 89% of counties in the United States have no clinic that provides abortions.

53 Kernal, "Anti Abortion Protest."

54 Ibid.

55 According to the 2018 form 990 they submitted to the IRS, Created Equal reported revenue of more than a million dollars, and Harrington's salary was listed as $99,250. Reform America, Form 990 for fiscal year ending in 2018, obtained from https://projects.propublica.org/nonprofits/organizations/331097372.

56 Mason, *Killing for Life*, 174.

57 Silas Allen, "Anti-abortion group sues Oklahoma State University," *The Oklahoman*, January 29, 2013, https://oklahoman.com/article/3749938/anti-abortion-group-sues-oklahoma-state-university?page=1.

58 Loree Lewis, "Court Rules on Miller-Young Case," *Daily Nexus*, August 27, 2014, https://dailynexus.com/2014-08-27/court-rules-on-miller-young-case/.

59 Bill Roberts, "BSU, Anti-abortion Group Settle Free Speech Lawsuit," *Idaho Statesman*, June 3, 2015. https://www.idahostatesman.com/news/local/education/boise-state-university/article40861854.html

60 Kate Murphy, "Students Sue Miami University," *Cincinnati Inquirer*, December 1, 2017, https://www.cincinnati.com/story/news/2017/11/30/students-sue-miami-university-over-anti-abortion-protest/908549001/.

61 Rick Seltzer, "Cal State to Pay $240,000 to Settle Anti-abortion Speaker Lawsuit," *Inside Higher Ed*, February 6, 2020, https://www.insidehighered.com/quicktakes/2020/02/06/cal-state-pay-240000-settle-anti-abortion-speaker-lawsuit.

62 Ryan Lenz, "The Battle for Berkeley," *Southern Poverty Law Center*, May 1, 2017, https://www.splcenter.org/hatewatch/2017/05/01/battle-berkeley-name-freedom-speech-radical-right-circling-ivory-tower-ensure-voice-alt.

63 Richard Fausset and Allan Feuer, "Far Right Groups Surge into National View in Charlottesville," *New York Times*, August 13, 2017, https://www.nytimes.com/2017/08/13/us/far-right-groups-blaze-into-national-view-in-charlottesville.html

64 WSYX (Sinclair), "Caught on Cam: Pro-life Activists Confronted, Attacked by Woman," *16 KMTR*, 10 July 2014, https://nbc16.com/news/nation-world/caught-on-cam-pro-life-activists-confronted-attacked-by-woman.

65 Lisa Bourne, "Ohio Woman Must Pay," *LifeSite News*, August 26, 2014, https://www.lifesitenews.com/news/ohio-woman-must-pay-80-after-attack-on-pro-lifers-assault-charge-dropped.

66 "Pro-life Activists Confronted, Attacked on Camera," *Fox News*, July 11, 2014, https://video.foxnews.com/v/3669804665001#sp=show-clips.

67 "Fear, Fantasy and Feelings on the Far-Right" panel of the 2021 Joint Conference on Right-Wing Studies and Research on Male Supremacism, May 10, 2021, featured Sophie Bjork-James and Josefine Landberg, whose research and conversation inspired this insight.

PART III
Secular Male Supremacism

6

OF VICTIMS, MASS MURDER, AND "REAL MEN"

The Masculinities of the "Manosphere"

Ann-Kathrin Rothermel, Megan Kelly and Greta Jasser[1]

Over the last few decades, a network of misogynist blogs, websites, wikis, and forums has developed, where users share their bigoted, sexist, and toxic views of society in general and masculinity and femininity in particular.[2] This male supremacist online network has come to be collectively known as the manosphere. While there had initially been only marginal interest in academia, mostly by feminist scholars,[3] more recently misogyny has been taken more seriously as a driving force by both terrorism studies[4] and social movement studies scholars.[5] Another strand of research subsumes the manosphere under a broad umbrella of digital hate culture, addressing the toxic environment these and white supremacist communities produce online.[6] However, studies have tended to focus on subgroups of the manosphere without assessing the manosphere as a whole,[7] consider the online community as a more or less homogeneous[8] arena, rely on concepts that no longer fit the full extent and diversity of male supremacist groups,[9] or even misattribute separate groups[10] or individuals.[11] While this has helped to draw attention to the relevance of misogyny for mobilization into violent acts, it arguably often leads to a limited understanding of the broader space of the manosphere, the pathways of mobilization, and the types of action and discourse it brings about.[12] The groups of the male supremacist network do not espouse a unitary vision of society and their position in it. Instead, they vary in their understanding of gender relations in society and their corresponding repertoire of both violent and nonviolent responses. In this chapter, we argue that these differences become visible in the different ways the groups of the manosphere construct and perform masculinity, which is at the core of their gendered construction of society. We pull apart and disaggregate the manosphere by providing an analysis that dissects the different masculinities embraced and performed by its various groups and shows how they are related to the differences in the groups' strategies

DOI: 10.4324/9781003164722-9

and ideologies. Our analysis of the manosphere provides a needed intervention, correcting past mischaracterizations of the manosphere.

We conduct an in-depth analysis of online content from the five secular male supremacist groups most prominent in the manosphere[13]: men's rights activists (MRAs), pick-up artists (PUAs), the red pill (TRP), men going their own way (MGTOW), and misogynist involuntary celibates[14] (incels). The analysis is informed by feminist literature on masculinity, in particular Raewyn Connell's and Demetrakis Demetriou's sociocultural conceptualizations of hegemonic and hybrid masculinity. Connell defines hegemonic masculinity as a normatively encoded way of "being a man," which requires other masculinities to "position themselves in relation to it."[15] In this way, masculinities should be considered as "performed" rather than as an inherent quality of their members. This conceptualization allows us to expose how the relationship between hegemonic masculinity, nonhegemonic[16] masculinities, and femininity is a pattern that legitimizes unequal gender relations,[17] and encourages male supremacist violence. Additionally, we use the concept of hybrid masculinity by Demetriou, according to which hegemonic masculinity can borrow elements or characteristics produced by other nonhegemonic masculinities to continue to ensure hegemony in a changing landscape.[18] These concepts help us to uncover how each of the groups of the manosphere "repudiates and reifies elements of hegemonic masculinity."[19]

The results of the analysis show that while all groups in essence are misogynist and antifeminist, the masculinities advocated by the various subgroups of the manosphere differ in nature. We find that masculinity is performed in a dialectical reproduction of (1) the diagnosis of the current situation of society and (2) the resulting strategies/reactions chosen and enacted by the group. Focusing on these dialectics provides important insights into the ways in which hybridization in the manosphere works to reproduce male supremacist ideology. We argue that a better understanding of how the groups of the manosphere conceptualize their masculinities can help to disentangle the web of the manosphere's radicalizing discourses. The analysis aims to expose the different ways in which the masculinities of the manosphere establish gender hierarchies and reinforce patriarchal norms. We argue that this is a prerequisite to understanding the pathways of radicalization into male supremacist beliefs, as well as the resulting reactions of those who are radicalized, ranging from political activism to sexual harassment and on- and offline violence.

The chapter is structured as follows: We first outline the conceptual framework of hegemonic and hybrid masculinity. We then provide a brief overview of the historical development of the manosphere and its various configurations and present our analysis of the masculinities performed by the five groups of the manosphere. The final part summarizes the results of the analysis and relates them to the growing discussions on male supremacist violence.

Hybrid and Hegemonic Masculinities

The concept of hegemonic masculinity was articulated by Connell and colleagues in the 1980s as "the pattern of practice (i.e., things done, not just a set of role expectations or an identity) that allowed men's dominance over women to continue."[20] This pattern of practice defines the "most honored" way of being a man and establishes hierarchies with other types of (nonhegemonic) masculinities. What is defined as hegemonic is thereby open to change both across time and place. Moreover, hegemonic masculinity is not a trait of individual men. Its different elements can be adopted and discarded situationally through discursive practices.[21] Similarly, nonhegemonic masculinities cannot be defined per se but only in relation to historically specific hegemonic masculinities. For instance, in the 1960s, a very specific romanticized vision of idealized masculinity in the form of "boy culture" took hold in some contexts. This was established by juxtaposing "real masculinity" as opposed to "visibly feminized" soft men of the new left ("a new lumpen leisure-class of assorted hippies, homosexuals, artistic poseurs, and 'malevolent blacks'").[22] This highlights that the relationship between hegemonic and other masculinities is based on a complex web between performed femininities and masculinities and that idealized masculinities are both temporally and spatially specific.

Demetriou[23] argues that masculinities should be read in a dialectical way because, as Connell and Messerschmidt write, "[H]egemonic masculinity appropriates from other masculinities whatever appears to be pragmatically useful for continued domination."[24] Drawing on Bhabha's notion of hybridity, he explains that hegemonic masculinity is "a hybrid bloc that unites practices from diverse masculinities in order to ensure the reproduction of patriarchy."[25] Demetriou identifies two forms of hegemony: domination over women/femininity (external) and domination over other men/masculinities (internal). Both forms of hegemony must be read as fluid and in conjunction with one another. In other words, in order to deconstruct hegemonic masculinity and its effect on the subordination of women, one has to understand how different masculinities (and femininities) work together in discourse and practice and adjust to fit particular political and historical situations.

Developing the theoretical approach further, in 2010, Messerschmidt concluded that masculinity is "fluid and flexible" at regional and global levels.[26] Relatedly, Bridges and Pascoe found that hybrid masculinities specifically have "attained ideological power and influence on a global stage."[27] They argue that the process of hybridization, in which hegemonic masculinities appropriate aspects of nonhegemonic masculinities, obscures gender inequalities through three mechanisms: (1) creating symbolic distance between men and hegemonic masculinity; (2) positioning the masculinities of "young, White, heterosexual men as somehow less meaningful than the masculinities associated with various marginalized and subordinated Others"; and (3) reinforcing existing social and symbolic boundaries, which then work "to conceal systems of power and inequality in historically new ways."[28]

While all these mechanisms serve to establish hybrid masculinities as non-hegemonic and separate from a patriarchal order, a careful look at the process and effect of hybridization exposes how they do work to uphold the patriarchal gender order on a global level. For example, studies of hybrid masculinity have centered on "new ways of performing heterosexuality while engaging in 'gay' styles, practices, and sex."[29] While the adoption of traits of nonhegemonic, subordinated masculinities might at first seem subversive, rather than challenging a patriarchal gender order, the adoption of hybrid masculinities can instead work to obscure systems of power and inequality.

Ging attributes the increasing globalization of hybrid masculinities to the rise of the internet, which has allowed hybrid masculinities to transverse local and regional boundaries and evade containment.[30] Similarly, both Massanari and Salter identify the internet and various online platforms as vehicles for further hybridization.[31] One particular example of this is "geek masculinity." In her work on the online platform Reddit and targeted harassment, Massanari explores geek masculinity as a form of hybrid masculinity, which both "repudiates and reifies elements of hegemonic masculinity." She points to geek masculinity's embrace of "facets of hypermasculinity by valorizing intellect over social or emotional intelligence" but points out that simultaneously individuals who perform geek masculinity might "demonstrate awkwardness regarding sexual/romantic relationships" and "reject other hypermasculine traits"[32] like showing interest in sports or athletics.

In recent years, the manosphere has become more prominently known as an online space where the construction and reproduction of hybrid and hegemonic masculinities (internal domination) and, in turn, patriarchal subordination of women (external domination) occurs. However, extant analyses have tended to conceptualize the manosphere as a (more or less coherent) whole.[33] For example, in their analysis of MRAs, Schmitz and Kayzak[34] subsume MGTOW and PUA forums as men's rights groups or "men's rights affiliated." While they pick up on some of the nuances and divergences of these groups, they fail to acknowledge the distinct groups in the network by placing them all under the men's rights label. Others have focused on deconstructing the performance of masculinity prevalent in one of its various groups of misogynist "involuntary celibates" (incels),[35] MRAs,[36] MGTOWs,[37] TRP,[38] and PUAs.[39] Moreover, with increasing interest in the manosphere among terrorist studies scholars, there has been a rise in misattributions of (often violent) misogynist reactions to individual groups, mostly misogynist incels.[40]

In this chapter, we draw on this work but provide a deeper engagement with the differences and overlaps between the masculinities of the various groups of the manosphere. Our analysis provides a reorientation from the conflation, common to previous work, of the groups of the manosphere and the masculinities therein, as well as from the mischaracterization of one prominent group, like

Of Victims, Mass Murder, and "Real Men" **121**

misogynist incels, as emblematic of the network as a whole. We borrow analytical concepts from Oliver and Johnston's work on movement ideologies and their conceptualization of movement's "diagnosis (how things got to be how they are), prognosis (what should be done and what the consequences will be), and rationale (who should do it and why)."[41] We employ these concepts to analyze how the groups' social theory and their proposed reactions and solutions serve their construction of masculinity and vice versa, as well as how these constructions of masculinity interact with hegemonic masculinity.

This analysis also challenges the misconception that these groups solely represent nonhegemonic masculinities. In particular, Nagle (2017) portrays the growing antifeminism online as a backlash to "evermore radical liberal gender politics and increasingly common anti-male rhetoric that went from obscure feminist online spaces to the mainstream."[42] Nagle characterizes the masculinities advocated for in the manosphere as nonhegemonic or "beta" masculinities that are defensive in nature and therefore do not uphold hegemonic masculinity.[43] This portrayal buys into a narrative endorsed in the manosphere and other antifeminist movements: that there is "too much feminism," that gender equality somehow "got out of hand," and that whoever is a feminist now must simply hate men, conveniently manufacturing a men-hating society.[44] However, as Bridges and Pascoe posit, while "discursive distance" between men and hegemonic masculinity can be created in hybrid masculinities through self-representation as subordinated, this distancing can also, subtly, allow men to align themselves further with hegemonic masculinity.[45] Building on this, the analysis shows the specific ways in which marginalized and subordinated masculinities can, and through their hybridity do, contribute to reproducing hegemonic masculinities.

A Brief History of the Manosphere

Prior to the advent of the manosphere, an online iteration of male supremacist mobilizations, both Men's Rights Activists (MRAs) and Pick-up artists (PUAs) developed as offline movements in the 1970s. MRAs have long organized around issues such as "father's rights" and to oppose legal protections against sexual harassment and violence.[46] MRAs have repeatedly attacked feminist groups and spaces, which they blame for a decline in men's rights. This has led to a general consent among (feminist) scholars that, despite their framing around "men's rights" as a reversed mirror of women's rights activism, the men's rights movement (MRM) is "defined as much *against* feminism as it is *for* men's rights."[47] Scholars have shown that they remain caught up in "an endless polarizing reproduction of anger and outrage that has become [their] signature online."[48] They engage in "indignation mobilization mechanisms," providing a "mix of highly biased opinion pieces, disinformation, and accurate information in order to provoke indignation and mobilize their readers."[49] In contrast, PUAs tend to consider themselves as less political and more associated with popular culture and relationship advice. In the 1970s, the term "pick-up artist" was coined to describe men who used manipulation and "seduction"

122 Ann-Kathrin Rothermel et al.

strategies to try and "pick up" women. (In the mid-2000s, PUAs became part of the pop culture mainstream, largely due to a best-selling book *The Game* and the VH1 Reality show *The Pick-Up Artist*. This pop culture spotlight led to new growth in existing PUA forums and content.[50])

In the 1990s and early 2000s, both MRAs and PUAs increasingly moved online—inhabiting forums, wikis, and websites to disseminate their content and create spaces for exchange between their followers—and another group, MGTOW (Men Going Their Own Way), emerged. While some scholars have categorized MGTOWs as an MRA group,[51] MGTOWs are a distinct group that emerged from existing men's rights activist and antifeminist spaces of the late 1990s and early 2000s. In their initial form, MGTOWs were "almost uniformly libertarian, and their distaste for 'big government' led to a schism with the men's human rights movement."[52] Today, MGTOWs advocate for men to abstain from (legal)[53] relationships with women.[54]

In the early 2010s, the online space of these various groups became more and more consolidated, and the manosphere emerged as an umbrella term.[55] At the same time, the groups associated with the manosphere experienced several shifts in content and following. In 2012, on the social media board Reddit, the subreddit r/TheRedPill was created anonymously by former Republican New Hampshire State Representative Robert Fisher.[56] For the manosphere, "taking the red pill" describes "becoming enlightened to life's ugly truths. TRP philosophy purports to awaken men to feminism's misandry and brainwashing."[57] Members of "The Red Pill" groups center around this shared narrative of awakening. In 2016, TRP leadership took a political stance and rallied behind Trump's campaign, especially in light of sexual assault allegations made against him.[58] While members explicitly distance themselves from MRAs and PUAs, the forum contains material from both groups. The two most active sections on the forum are "Red Pill Strategy" and "Men's Rights," highlighting the interconnectivity of the different groups of the manosphere.

Throughout the 2010s, the manosphere also gained attention in the media due to its connection to both sexual[59] and mass violence.[60] Some men who had come to believe PUA strategies were a scam began to congregate on the now-defunct website PUAhate.[61] Many of the members of this site were not only angry at PUAs but also women for (still) rejecting their sexual advances. PUAhate made headlines after a member of the site named it in his manifesto before murdering six people and injuring 14 others in Isla Vista, California, in 2014. In his manifesto and online postings, the perpetrator stated that he wanted to punish all women, whom he blamed for his "lonely, celibate life."[62] In the years since this attack, multiple new online misogynist incel (involuntary celibate) communities have formed, grown, and been connected to more recent acts of violence.[63] Analysis has shown that there has been a considerable shift of followers from MRA and PUA forums to misogynist incel and MGTOW forums.[64]

The network of the manosphere emerged organically from separate antifeminist and male supremacist spaces and groups, which have found a home in an ever-growing online conglomeration of blogs, websites, and forums. While the space can broadly be divided into these five groupings (MRAs, PUAs, MGTOWs, TRP, and misogynist incels), their content and membership within the manosphere have shifted over time. All these groups have shown that they are able to generate a following around gender and masculinity, which has resulted in both on- and offline violence.[65]

Analyzing the Manosphere

The manosphere is centered around masculinities. The emphasis of our analysis lies in the ways in which the different groups construct and perform their concept of masculinity. We focus in particular on the role of masculinity in the respective group's (1) social theory, i.e., their *diagnosis* of society, and (2) their *reactions* to this diagnosis. The social theory of a group is a belief "that explain[s] how social arrangements came to be and how they might be changed or strengthened."[66] This social theory—or the diagnosis of society, which determines where "society went wrong" or what ought to be changed in the current social fabric—is vital to understanding what unites the groups of the manosphere, as well as their differences. It sets up their worldview. Second, we analyze the reactions the groups formulate to these diagnoses and society as they perceive it. The diagnoses and reactions of the groups connote the way the respective group performs masculinity. It encompasses both the options the group members consider as societal and individual "solutions" or "strategies."

As data, we selected one forum per group. Forums, compared to more static websites, enable individuals to form a virtual community around interests and issues and afford a space for exchange.[67] We analyzed r/MensRights, MPUAForum. com, mgtow.com, r/TheRedPill, and incels.co.[68] MPUAForum.com, mgtow. com, and incels.co are stand-alone sites, while r/MensRights and r/TheRedPill are subreddits and therefore hosted on Reddit. In choosing these forums, we aimed for information-rich cases that best show the nature of each of these communities. To achieve this, we purposefully selected the ten threads that created the highest engagement from users (as measured by the number of comments/replies) and those ten threads that were deemed essential or popular (as measured by most views or indexed as "must-read" or "most popular" by the forum moderators) from each forum. The five most popular threads from each forum—i.e., those that appeared on both the top-ten comments/replies list and the most read/viewed/ popular list—were then selected for analysis. To keep the data to a size fit for a qualitative analysis, we extracted the first 50 comments. Overall, we analyzed 250 comments for each group and a total of 1,250 comments overall.

Additionally, we analyzed homepages, FAQs, or wikis that were directly linked to by each of these forums (for full data see Table 6.1). The resulting data were subjected to a qualitative content analysis with a focus on hegemonic and hybrid masculinity, as well as social theories (diagnosis) and (re)actions of the groups. In a collaborative and iterative process, we inductively added and compared codes to account for themes across the threads and groups. The results in

124 Ann-Kathrin Rothermel et al.

TABLE 6.1 Selected text corpus divided by groups of the manosphere

Group	Forums Analyzed
MRA[69]	r/MensRights/, Wiki4Men.com, avoiceformen.com
PUA	MPUAForum.com
MGTOW	mgtow.com
The Red Pill[70]	/r/TheRedPill
Misogynist Incels	incels.co,[71] incel.wiki

Table 6.1 show the different ways the groups position themselves (and their masculinity) in relation to other masculinities and how these result in reproducing or challenging hegemonic masculinity.

MRAs

Diagnosis

MRAs perceive their respective societies as inherently stacked against men. These societies are seen as feminist, "gynocentric," and/or favoring women over men. As one post read, "Well, men are disposable to today's society, so of course only women are counted [in homelessness statistics]." While most issues MRAs invoke are societal issues that need addressing, they fail to identify the broader, underlying structures causing them and focus their analysis on the fate of men and the unfairness they face (compared to women). Their main grievances surround family courts, which they make out to treat men unfairly, sexual violence against men, male suicide rates, and rape allegations against men, which they consider false. All of these issues are presented, not as broader social issues but rather as gender issues whereby men are disproportionately affected and disadvantaged. To emphasize this assessment, MRAs often adopt terms and language from the civil rights movement, as well as feminist movements. For example, they juxtapose the "glass ceiling" women face when striving for higher positions usually held by men with a "glass cellar," as one post stated, "MR [Men's Rights] is about the vast number of people at the bottom—the glass cellar—including the homeless, unemployed, divorced, victims of violence, depressed/suicidal, etc. These are also predominantly men."

Reaction

As the name of the movement indicates, MRAs navigate the framework of human and civil rights. They position themselves as activists. A large proportion of their forums and websites is dedicated to recruiting new members and/or convincing readers that MRAs' causes are worthwhile. They provide material for school projects, as well as answers to questions that are likely to come up when being challenged on MRA views. They largely claim not to be antifeminist or anti-woman. However, they often attribute their grievances to a feminist society. Besides identifying grievances, online MRA communities focus on activism. Following this positioning, the outward-facing MRA web pages are oriented toward changing laws and policies and often call for signing petitions. In an introductory page on the MRA wiki, they situate themselves alongside other movements as "working toward equality":

> The MRM want[s] to resolve certain issues facing men and boys and achieve equality of opportunity for all. The MRM opposes the enforcement of traditional gender roles, as well as the perspective to gender relations presented by most forms of feminism.

Masculinity

MRAs emphasize the vulnerability of men and center their masculinity on the status of victimhood in modern societies. Their masculinity is hybrid, as it does not emphasize the classical traits of hegemonic masculinity but centers injustices, grievances, and victimhood status based on their gender. Some strands decidedly reject traditional gender roles, as they are considered harmful to men, in particular vis-à-vis child custody, child support, and alimony. In contrast to other groups of the manosphere, MRAs do not tend to distinguish between different "types" of men and masculinity but present all men as victims of society (with few exceptions). In turn, femininity and all women are presented as the winners under the societal status quo.

While their activism is constructed as geared toward equal rights, their suggestions for change often aim to reclaim lost entitlement. For example, the conception of "fixing" the court system culminates in a reversal of the perceived power dynamics, whereby men have power over the outcome of a divorce, or pregnancy ("my wallet my choice"). MRAs aim to reinstate a (supposedly) lost patriarchal order, which incorporates traits of hegemonic masculinity (power over money, dominance in relationships, and as the head of household) that put them in a position of power and privilege they deem rightfully theirs.

PUAs

Diagnosis

PUAs have no shared diagnosis of society. What unites them is that they strive for individual success to attract women and become involved with them, either aiming at sexual encounters or seeking long-term relationships. To achieve this, PUAs use different "seduction techniques," which they refer to as "Game," and share tips for self-improvement. Aside from temporary obstacles to their sexual success, which are to be solved individually through self-improvement, PUAs are not actively advocating against the society and economy in which they live. Their

126 Ann-Kathrin Rothermel et al.

explicit social diagnosis only seems to concern gender relations, which they tend to frame in the economic language of "investment." One post stated,

> [A]ttraction is triggered any time we invest in something. The harder we work to achieve it, the harder we want it. The key to getting women to want you is to get them to invest in you. Certain characteristics may cause them to invest in you without the need to try hard or even approach. Many people are blessed with a number of these characteristics already, and for the most part, this explains many [of] the success [of] what typical guys get. Increasing the number and quality of these characteristics will have a direct positive effect on our ability with the opposite sex.

Reaction

Generally, PUAs can be described as subscribing to an individualistic, self-help framework. The signatures and profiles of the forum users are filled with inspirational and motivational quotes about believing in oneself. PUAs see their problem as an individual one, thus the strategies to overcome it are developed for individual execution and aimed at individual success. Strategies recommended by (semi-)professional PUAs include "demonstrating high value" and "controlling the frame." In other words, PUAs advise to present oneself as sovereign and dominant in dating situations. Building on the idea of investment, they seek to transfer the tactics and virtues of business negotiations to dating. Detailing strategies for successful phone calls with women, one PUA post notes.

> There's a rule in business that goes something like "Face to face is always better than a phone call, and a phone call is always better than an email." Business and pickup have many of the same rules, and this one is no exception.

While some PUAs' advice is confined to developing self-help, others propose techniques that involve attempts at manipulation. In one pertinent example from one forum thread, "negs" are defined as "backhanded comments that just destabilize a girls [sic] ego, help her lower her 'bitch shield'. They make her think you are not another loser coming up to her in a bar wanting to score." This belief that men must pass "women's defenses" in order to engage in sexual relations encourages sexual harassment and coercion and is rooted in misogyny. In individual instances in the analyzed material, some PUAs question whether manipulative behavior like "negging" is unethical. Most often, however, ethical concerns are quickly brushed aside, and the tactics are characterized in the responses as harmless, funny banter. Other concerns about manipulation are mostly focused on the demoralizing effect of such tactics on the men who use them or the feeling that the tactics are an unfair advantage and constitute "cheating," rather than on the effect of manipulation on women. This exposed the underlying misogyny hiding behind the language of investment and self-improvement.

Masculinity

PUAs approach gender relations in society with the transactional logic of doing business. The advice for seduction thus often relies on the (economic) value of a PUA, which (more than his actual financial situation) is based on his performance of masculinity vis-à-vis women. One forum user posted, "His [successful PUA's] simple thing is that he uses loads of confidence, and he always frames himself as being the MAN!" While PUAs are focused more than the other groups on their individual trajectories rather than broader societal issues, they share a sense of masculinity as capital in today's society, which is necessary to achieve their goal of sexual relationships with women. Much like with other sources of capital, they believe that their individual masculinity can be optimized and "increased," which will allow them an optimal outcome in the "dating market." Their strategies to increase masculine value most often rely on performing traits that are traditionally associated with hegemonic masculinity, like dominance and self-confidence. Women in this equation become the buyer of a product of masculinity, whose ideal value is calculated by its proximity to hegemonic masculinity.

MGTOW

Diagnosis

MGTOWs historicize their group by placing themselves among "great" men of history. They hypothesize that historically significant men (Tesla, Locke, Beethoven, van Gogh, "or even Jesus Christ") were able to achieve their level of success and fulfill their genius precisely because they avoided romantic attachments with women. MGTOWs also firmly believe that men are naturally more likely to be risk-takers, creators, and do-ers than women, which has allowed men to be the "creators of civilization." However, they believe that men have not been given the proper credit or respect that they deserve. Instead, they feel that they are persecuted, that any attempt to acknowledge pro-male sentiment is wrongfully labeled "toxic and misogynistic," and that society is increasingly "gynocentric," i.e. favoring women at the expense of men. At the core of this belief is the idea that women are naturally inferior to men. MGTOWs argue that women's only power is their beauty and that their power diminishes as they age.

MGTOWs are opposed to relationships with women in current society because they believe that women use and manipulate men, and trap them into relationships in order to access their money, status, or sperm. They cite feminism as the reason for this perceived increasingly hostile environment for men, which they believe "was created to destabilize society" and has allowed women to run rampant. They argue that feminism's influence has led to men having little "legal control" in situations like divorce, which they argue is an industry "deliberately designed to transfer his wealth (men's) and freedom to her (women)." MGTOWs position themselves as victims of feminism. Their philosophy to distance themselves from women is framed as a direct reaction to feminism and the ills they believe that feminism has wrought. As an article on the "About" section of the mgtow.com forum explains,

> Men haven't lost their need to find happiness by providing, protecting, sacrifcing [sic] and conquering; we've simply discovered that providing for the modern feminist, working like a dog to protect a family that can be taken away at a moment's notice, or risking our lives to conquer resources for some ungrateful women [sic] who claims she can do it on her own is an empty way to live.

Reaction

The main MGTOW reaction to a perceived gynocentric society is to not engage (legally) with women or with society altogether. This most often takes the form of encouraging men not to marry or have children with women. While some MGTOWs have short-term relationships, other MGTOWs consider even this a risk. MGTOWs suggests that men overall should work to take "women off the pedestal" that the "gynocentric order" has put women on. Another method that MGTOWs employ is to shame women for their sexual activity or looks. One MGTOW thread centers around shaming women who have "hit the wall" and is filled with jubilant MGTOW comments about how women are eventually punished by losing their beauty, and therefore their power, when aging. Within these posts about women "hitting the wall," there is also a sentiment that MGTOWs have experienced a societal expectation to marry a beautiful "trophy wife" as a status symbol. However, they state that taking TRP has unburdened them of this pressure and saved them the trouble of these imagined women one day "hitting the wall." When discussing actresses that were once considered "bombshells" but have since aged, they express pity toward their husbands and gratefulness that they've "taken the red pill ... therefore this scenario will never happen to me. I save face. I save sanity."

Masculinity

MGTOWs frame themselves as independent, self-sufficient, and self-empowered men. Their main proposed strategy for dealing with the "gynocentric society" they believe they live in is to withdraw from that society and instead form an independent and self-sufficient life. They align themselves with some of the stereotypical traits of hegemonic masculinity (risk-taking, dominance, rationality) and with "great" men of history they believe embodied these traits. Further, they advocate for male domination over women, arguing that men as the supposed creators should be able to dictate the rules and norms of "civilization." While MGTOWs claim that they are "going their own way," have been relieved of social pressures to seek out relationships with women, and are carving out independent lives for themselves, much of the discussion on their forums is dedicated to how women have wronged them. They position themselves as victims of women's manipulation and feminism's oppressive nature. Further, in rejecting the role as a "provider" specifically to women and children, they upend stereotypical expectations of hegemonic masculinity. MGTOWs present themselves as rejecting the breadwinner role and in doing so seem to set themselves apart from their perceived expectations of men and challenge hegemonic masculinity. At the same time, they reinforce hegemonic masculinity through this rejection, arguing that men naturally embody greatness, rationality, dominance, and risk-taking, while valuing women only for their beauty and presenting women as an obstacle for men's potential greatness. In doing so, they reassert hegemonic masculinity.

TRP

Diagnosis

TRP members frame feminism as a "sexual strategy" that they believe has allowed women to be in, as the introduction page states, the "best position they can find, to select mates, to determine when they want to switch mates, to locate the best dna [sic] possible, and to garner the most resources they can individually achieve." They then frame the "red pill" as "men's sexual strategy" for a changing world and the "sexual marketplace."[72] They believe the red pill is needed because they perceive society to be feminist and the public discourse to be a "feminist frame." As a result, they believe men have "lost [their] identity because of it [the feminist frame]." TRP members believe they are persecuted for expressing these views. This fear is expressed, for example, through concerns around deplatforming from Reddit. The perpetrator of this persecution is often thought to be an increasingly "politically correct," "cultural marxist [sic]," and feminist culture that does not allow men, specifically TRP members, to speak their minds or to expose how they perceive the world actually operates. One major aspect that is discussed in the forum is the changing nature of the workplace, where a company is described as being forced to "hire enough feminits [sic]/SJWs [Social Justice Warriors] and they will hold [the] company hostage." There is also the sentiment that they as men, especially "straight white males," are suffering the brunt of a "punishment" for "wrongthink," and that groups that purport to be "tolerant" and "open" are hypocritical as they are not open to the opinions of TRP and other views that are "critical."

Reaction

The main strategy that TRP suggests for men to contend with a feminist-centric society is "male sexual strategy." One facet of this proposed strategy is "Game," which they believe helps elevate men's status in the "sexual marketplace." While users of TRP critique existing PUA "Game," they also embrace many aspects of PUA strategies. In their critiques, they claim that in communities like r/ seduction there seems to be an attempt to "feminize the discussion (basically making it sound politically correct if read by a female)." In supposedly "feminizing the discussion," men are just succumbing to women's manipulation and sexual strategy. TRP, therefore, does not frame itself as wanting to help men "become better men," but rather as providing strategies on how to manipulate women in order to have sex. The r/TRP forum is littered with "Game" advice and resources from users. One such resource focuses on men strengthening their "frame," which is later defined as being a "natural leader" and "masculine," in order to seduce women. The author of this resource proposes that women will always go for a man with a stronger "frame" and that women will "test your frame to test your masculinity." The proposed way to pass these "frame tests" is to not take a woman's rejection or "no" for an answer, as these rejections are really just a test to see if the man who approached her is "masculine enough." This is reminiscent of PUA strategies and similarly encourages coercion, sexual violence, and rape:

> She'll act like a bitch. She'll pretend to ignore you. She'll tell you outright to go away. She wants to see if you'll buckle to social pressure, or if your frame will remain calm and consistent regardless of external feedback. She actually WANTS to sleep with you—but she needs to test your strength first.

Masculinity

TRP members present their beliefs as "rational," "scientific," and "natural" or "biological." Thus, they have an essentialist and binary understanding of gender (femininity and masculinity), whereby men are framed as naturally more rational, stronger, dependable, and hardworking than women. Some users claim that women are attracted to men because of a man's performance of masculinity. TRP members claim that feminists are irrational because they are working to change these "natural, biological" differences between men and women, including in the workforce. They, therefore, express strong support for hegemonic masculinity and the resulting hierarchical patriarchal order, which they perceive as being threatened. They also align themselves with ideals associated with hegemonic masculinity, proposing both physical and psychological self-improvement to what they perceive to be nonhegemonic traits and characteristics. TRP members do not perceive themselves as having unchangeable traits of nonhegemonic masculinities. Instead, their victimhood results from a perceived oppression by feminism, which is threatening hegemonic masculinity.

Misogynist Incels

Diagnosis

Many misogynist incels take on a biological determinist and essentialist view that women "naturally select men based on looks rather than personality and that women select men with the best genes." This belief is referred to as the "black-pill." Misogynist incels tend to consider themselves as particularly unattractive and genetically disadvantaged ("subhuman"). They blame women for their existence as involuntary celibates because of "female hypergamy," through which men with a lower "sexual market value" are sidelined in the "sexual market-place." As a result, misogynist incels present themselves as victims because they do not have access to sex with women, which they consider a natural and fundamental part of the human, and especially male, experience. This victimhood is framed in terms of how they perceive they are treated compared to other men, particularly "Chads" (attractive white men). They believe that "Chads" have sexual access to women because of their physical features. In contrast, misogynist incels believe they are genetically unlucky and will continue to be "involuntary celibates" because of their looks.

Even if misogynist incels "ascend" and have sex with a woman, or even have children with them, they still consider themselves victims of their genetics, as they had to work for something that other men were easily given. Additionally, they believe unless a woman is "bound to one man," she will eventually leave for a man with a higher "market value." Women are therefore portrayed by misogynist incels as cruel, stupid, and beholden to their biological impulses. Feminism is particularly egregious to misogynist incels, as they believe that its influence on social and cultural norms has allowed women to be even more hypergamous now than they previously were able to be with stricter patriarchal norms in place. Misogynist incels believe that their numbers will continue to rise as women continue to pursue men with higher "sexual market value," leaving more men competing over the few women with lower standards.

Reaction

Many incels who accept the blackpill express a sense of nihilism and the idea that there is nothing they can personally do to change their perceived suffering. This nihilism results in a variety of "copes" or strategies for how to address a society they believe has wronged them. Most of the strategies suggested are violent or abusive reactions that attempt to assert dominance over women or punish society. Explicit calls for mass violence and sexual violence targeting women specifically are suggested as punishments for women's perceived promiscuity, their rejection of misogynist incels (whether real or imagined), and their hypergamous nature. Some misogynist incels argue that access to sex is and should be recognized as a human right and propose society-wide solutions to achieve dominance over women, which include "socially arranged or enforced monogamy," meaning that the "state-issue[s] girlfriends as a solution to inceldom." Misogynist incels argue that this could work because they believe that women "naturally fantasize about sexual coercion." They acknowledge that it would likely require an "authoritarian state" to enact this as a policy. Other possible solutions include taxing individuals that practice a "promiscuous lifestyle" in order to encourage monogamy, taking away women's right to vote, "reinstalling patriarchy," and lowering the status of women compared to men.

Despite many misogynist incels claiming that there is nothing they can personally do to change their situation, many still aim to have sex with women. They aim to do this either by altering their bodies through working out, steroid usage, and/or plastic surgery. Other solutions include paying for sex at home or abroad or traveling to countries they perceive as "poor" in order to get girlfriends or sexual partners.[73] Some misogynist incels believe that pursuing impoverished women is a possible solution to their inceldom, as having a financial advantage over women means that misogynist incels, as one poster posits, are not "reduce[d] to their looks" alone and have a higher chance of coercing poor women into sex. Additionally, misogynist incels seek to punish women for being the supposed perpetrators of their perceived suffering. Members speak of waiting for the "day of retribution," a reference to the 2014 Santa Barbara attack, during which they believe women will be punished for the suffering of misogynist incels. Finally, "LDARing" (lay down and rot), (mass)-violence, suicide, and "incelicide" (genocide of all incels) are suggested as appropriate coping strategies by misogynist incels who have accepted the blackpill.

Masculinity

While they are more concerned about their own plight, rather than the plight of all men, misogynist incels believe that their suffering and "subhuman" status is a specifically gendered masculine victimhood that cannot be experienced by other genders, least of all women. Misogynist incels demonstrate an interesting case of hybrid masculinity through their merging of (masculine) victimhood and superiority. Misogynist incels construct masculinity in relation to physical embodiment as determined by genetics and a man's access to sexual conquest. They then create a hierarchy where men who meet these criteria of masculinity are superior ("Chads"), while misogynist incels who do not believe they meet these criteria are inferior and denominated "subhuman." Misogynist incels claiming they lack these characteristics might seem to separate themselves from hegemonic masculinity. Yet, the very construction of masculinity around physical embodiment and sexual conquest aligns with hegemonic masculinity, even if they frame themselves as victims through this construction. Further, misogynist incels believe themselves superior both to men who are ignorant of the blackpill and to women. Their aim to assert dominance over or to punish women for their

Of Victims, Mass Murder, and "Real Men" **133**

perceived transgressions speaks to the core construction of hegemonic masculinity. Though misogynist incels might view and present themselves as victims, the strategies they suggest reveal that their goal is dominance and (authoritarian) control over women or complete nihilism until exerting dominance and subordinating women would be installed on a societal level. They thereby demonstrate aggrieved entitlement[74] as an extreme outcome of an ideal hegemonic masculinity, as demonstrated through their suggested "coping strategies," such as enforced monogamy (corresponding with their belief that they are entitled to a woman's body) and sexual and mass violence.

Masculinities of the Manosphere

The results of the analysis show that there are both overlapping characteristics and differences between the ways in which the groups discursively construct and perform their masculinity in relation to women (external), as well as other men (internal). In particular, we observe a repeating dialectical construction between how the groups consider themselves in society (diagnosis) and how they react to it (reaction). All groups use the three mechanisms of hybridization (discursive distancing, strategic borrowing, and fortifying boundaries)[75] by framing themselves as victims of current society in general and feminism (which they construct as a dominant societal discourse) in particular. However, the ways in which they do so through gendered hybridized constructions of femininity and masculinity vary (see Table 6.2).

On one hand, MRAs, MGTOWs, and to a lesser extent TRP members clearly position themselves as part of a superior male gender. They claim a deserved superior status in society as men because they believe men espouse superior traits to women: as "creators of civilization" (MGTOW), "more rational" (MRA), and "scientific" (MRA, TRP). Especially in MRA and MGTOW content, these

TABLE 6.2 Constructions of masculinity in the manosphere

Group	Diagnosis	Reactions	Masculinities[76]
MRAs	Feminism has established a societal and legal system that is stacked against men, in which men's problems are ignored or downplayed.	Recruitment, indignation mobilization, activism, and advocating for policy change.	Focus on injustices, vulnerability, and victimhood of white, heterosexual men. The focus on victimhood symbolically distances men from hegemony, while also aiming to reinstate a (supposedly) lost patriarchal order, which puts men in a position of power and privilege.

(Continued)

134 Ann-Kathrin Rothermel et al.

TABLE 6.2 (Continued)

Group	Diagnosis	Reactions	Masculinities[76]
PUAs	Approach gender relations with transactional logic where seduction relies on the (economic) value of a PUA, which is based on his performance of masculinity.	Self-improvement and manipulation of women as a way for men to seduce women.	Center transformation toward hegemonic masculinity as improvement. Individual (often nonhegemonic) masculinity can be optimized by performing traits that are traditionally associated with hegemonic masculinity, like dominance and self-confidence. Reinforce oppression of other masculinities and femininities as a legitimate gender order accessible and beneficial to every man.
MGTOW	See women (enabled by feminism) as manipulative and dangerous to men's autonomy, including financial autonomy, and society as gynocentric (overly focused on women).	Idealized withdrawal from society and self-reliance, limiting relations with women, especially legally binding ones, and avoiding (all) interactions with women altogether.	Reify hegemonic masculinity as self-sufficient and praise "great" men that deserve recognition and respect for being the "creators of civilization." Hybridization by rejecting certain traits of hegemonic masculinity (breadwinner, caretaker). These (and an imagery of toxic femininity) are portrayed as reasons heterosexual men are victims of a gynocentric gender order. Imagined historical, hegemonic masculinity as the "solution."

Of Victims, Mass Murder, and "Real Men" **135**

TABLE 6.2 (Continued)

Group	Diagnosis	Reactions	Masculinities[76]
TRP	Economize relationships and believe in a sexual marketplace, in which everyone has a certain sexual market value. See feminism as the "sexual strategy" of women to gain higher value males/mates and perceive the "sexual marketplace" as stacked against them as a result.	Manipulation and "Game" to contend in the sexual marketplace, "the red pill" as men's sexual strategy, and an "awakening" to a previously hidden truth.	Detailed ideology of hierarchies between masculinities. Nonhegemonic masculinities produced as victims of both hegemonic masculinity and femininity. At the same time, consider TRP masculinity as superior to other men and women. Aim for a new oppressive hierarchy with TRP masculinity at the top without making hegemonic masculinity itself less oppressive.
Misogynist incels	Believe their looks and feminism to be the reason they are rejected by women. Consider rejection as unjust victimization of their identity and that some part of their humanity is unfulfilled, rendering them "subhuman."	Nihilism that can result in a variety of violent or abusive reactions (e.g., poverty sex-tourism, self-harm, societal insurrection, sexual violence, or mass violence), each asserting dominance over and punishing women.	Detailed hybridization through extensive ideology of masculinity hierarchies. Misogynist incel masculinity is presented as nonhegemonic, powerless, oppressed by "other" masculinities, feminism, and ideals of hegemonic masculinity. Use this (masculine) victimhood to justify sense of superiority over and violence against women and other men.

characteristics are considered justification to dominate women and other, "less masculine" men. In their assessment, MRAs' and MGTOWs' status as victims is therefore not due to their insufficient, nonhegemonic masculinity but rather due to society having unjustly turned against masculine traits. This turn is described as having not been caused by shifts in the ideals of hegemonic masculinity (which would make the groups nonhegemonic), but rather by society's supposed rejection of masculinity and men altogether in favor of a "gynocentric order" ruled by feminism. The groups' reactions are thus to quite literally restore the hegemony of masculinity politically (MRAs) or to create a safe space to perform their understanding of masculinity outside of a feminist society (MGTOWs). In this way, both groups consider themselves to be part of a hegemonic masculinity, a "most honored" way of being a man, and to be victimized through feminism, which they use to justify their misogyny toward individual women, as well as feminist activism.

On the other hand, incels and to a lesser degree PUAs and some TRP members align themselves with nonmasculine aesthetics and personality traits and portray themselves as victims of hegemonic masculinity. They particularly express this victimhood in comparison to other men. However, instead of using this observation to question hegemonic gender expectations and their harm to both men and women, PUA and TRP strategies aim to emulate these very traits. In fact, many of their strategies are even more explicit in their attempts to uphold hegemonic masculinity, advocating for rape, manipulation, and exploitation of women as a way to "prove oneself" as a man. In that sense, the very invocation of nonhegemonic masculinity is used to construct an extreme (toxic) masculinity as the best and only alternative to their own previous performance of nonhegemonic masculinity. They declare this extreme hegemonic masculinity desirable, and all their strategies are geared toward achieving it.

At first glance, misogynist incels appear to reject the enactment of behavior typically associated with hegemonic masculinity (albeit not because it is considered bad but rather because it is deemed unachievable). However, looking through the lens of hybrid masculinity, the discursive distance they create between hegemonic masculinity and their own masculinity is also used to justify extreme strategies of oppression, including stripping women of their lifestyle and relationship choices and their right to vote, own property, or even to live at all. In this way, they navigate hybridity and use nonhegemonic masculinity to ensure continued hegemony.

Conclusion

The aim of this chapter was to analyze the masculinities of the manosphere and how they "repudiat[e] and reif[y]" hegemonic masculinity and male supremacism.[77] The analysis shows that, while all groups overlap in their use of hybridization to create a sense of victimization because of their particular masculine identities, they underline this claim by using and constructing their masculinity as intertwined and juxtaposed with other masculinities and femininity in different ways. Hybridity is essential for their own masculine identity construction; however, the inclusion of nonhegemonic masculine traits does not serve to make them more inclusive toward other men, let alone women. Rather, it justifies their entitlement to oppress women and creates a sense of superiority over other men who are not "redpilled" or "blackpilled" and thus supposedly not aware of the "truth" about gender relations.

Recently, the manosphere has entered more into public discourse after media outlets have linked it to a range of public instances of misogyny and violence.[78] However, existing analyses have tended to homogenize and conflate groups and misattribute individuals. These mischaracterizations have led to problematic descriptions of the radicalization pathways into the manosphere as apolitical[79] and removed from hegemonic masculinity.[80] We have shown that it is essential to keep track of the inner workings of the network. Despite claims of victimization, all groups end up reinforcing rather than challenging hegemonic masculinity and the oppression of women (and other men). Moreover, their hybridization of nonhegemonic and hegemonic masculinities varies according to their social theory. By focusing on the differences in how the groups use hybridization, we show how the groups of the manosphere utilize masculinity to justify their construction of gender relations and identities in society. Online communities like those of the manosphere promote a variety of reactions, ranging from political activism to sexual harassment and violence. Understanding how the masculinities of the manosphere work to produce a network of interweaving, overlapping, and contradictory understandings of masculinity, femininity, and gender relations in society is a prerequisite to understanding the pathways of radicalization into antifeminist activism and violence.

Notes

1 The authors would like to thank Dominik Hammer for his contribution to this chapter, especially the coding and analysis of the PUA data.

2 CONTENT WARNING: In this article, we cite violent misogynist language, which is used in the manosphere. While this language is only employed contextually to illustrate the discursive constructions of the groups, some of the terms and expressions refer to sexual assault, self-harm and suicide, body hatred and fat phobia, and other physical, psychological, and structural types of violence.

3 Molly Dragiewicz, "Patriarchy Reasserted," *Feminist Criminology* 3, no. 2 (2008), https://doi.org/10.1177/1557085108316731; Emma A. Jane, "Your a Ugly, Whorish, Slut," *Feminist Media Studies* 14, no. 4 (2014), https://doi.org/10.1080/14680777.2012.741073; Karla Mantilla, "Gendertrolling: Misogyny Adapts to New Media," *Feminist Studies* 39, no. 2 (2013), http://www.jstor.org/stable/23719068.

4 Chris Wilson, "Nostalgia, Entitlement and Victimhood: The Synergy of White Genocide and Misogyny," *Terrorism and Political Violence* (2020), https://doi.org/10.1080/09546553.2020.1839428.

5 Bailey Poland, *Haters: Harassment, Abuse, and Violence Online*. Lincoln: Potomac Books an imprint of the University of Nebraska Press, 2016. http://search.ebscohost.com/login.aspx?direct=true&scope=site&db=nlebk&AN=1354282; Elizabeth S. Corredor, "Unpacking "Gender Ideology" and the Global Right's Antigender Countermovement." *Signs: Journal of Women in Culture and Society* 44, no. 3 (2019): 613–38. https://doi.org/10.1086/701171.

6 Bharath Ganesh, "The Ungovernability of Digital Hate Culture," *Journal of International Affairs* 71/2 (2018), https://jia.sipa.columbia.edu/ungovernability-digital-hate-culture; Ashley Mattheis, "Understanding Digital Hate Culture," Center for Analysis

of the Radical Right, accessed September 17, 2019, https://www.radicalrightanalysis. com/2019/08/19/understanding-digital-hate-culture/.

7 E.g., Callum Jones, Verity Trott, and Scott Wright, "Sluts and Soyboys: MGTOW and the Production of Misogynistic Online Harassment," *New Media & Society* 200, no. 2 (2019), https://doi.org/10.1177/1461444819887141; Scott Wright, Verity Trott, and Callum Jones, "'The Pussy Ain't Worth It, Bro': Assessing the Discourse and Structure of MGTOW," *Information, Communication & Society* 3, no. 1 (2020), https://doi.org/10.1080/1369118X.2020.1751867.

8 Debbie Ging, "Alphas, Betas, and Incels," *Men and Masculinities* 19 (2017), https://doi.org/10.1177/1097184X17706401.

9 Rachel Schmitz and Emily Kazyak, "Masculinities in Cyberspace: An Analysis of Portrayals of Manhood in Men's Rights Activist Websites," *Social Sciences* 5, no. 2 (2016), https://doi.org/10.3390/socsci5020018.

10 Schmitz and Kazyak, "Masculinities in Cyberspace."

11 Bruce Hoffman, Jacob Ware, and Ezra Shapiro, "Assessing the Threat of Incel Violence," *Studies in Conflict & Terrorism* 43, no. 7 (2020), https://doi.org/10.1080/1057610X.2020.1751459.

12 Greta Jasser, Megan Kelly, and Ann-Kathrin Rothermel, "Male Supremacism and the Hanau Terrorist Attack: Between Online Misogyny and Far-Right Violence," ICCT – International Centre for Counter-Terrorism, accessed December 10, 2020, https://icct.nl/publication/male-supremacism-and-the-hanau-terrorist-attack-between-online-misogyny-and-far-right-violence/.

13 The manosphere is an umbrella term, and at times, there have been other configurations of which groups are counted as part of or identify as belonging to the manosphere. However, these five groups have been frequently analyzed as the core umbrella groups, which means that most groups or communities, which are mentioned in the context of the manosphere, can be grouped into one of them. See, e.g., Filipe N. Ribeiro et al., "The Evolution of the Manosphere Across the Web," 2020, accessed August 25, 2020, https://arxiv.org/abs/2001.07600; Ann-Kathrin Rothermel, "Die Manosphere. Die Rolle Von Digitalen Gemeinschaften Und Regressiven Bewegungsdynamiken Für on- Und Offline Antifeminismus," *Forschungsjournal Soziale Bewegungen* 33, no. 2 (2020), https://doi.org/10.1515/fjsb-2020-0041, https://www.degruyter.com/document/doi/10.1515/fjsb-2020-0041/html.

14 Throughout this article, we refer to "misogynist incel (s)" which, as defined by Kelly et al. (2021), "can be understood linguistically as similar to the construction of the term 'racist skinhead.'" Following Kelly et al. (2021), we use it "to distinguish the male supremacist ideology and movement from personal identification with the term incel." This is not to say that the other groups analyzed are not misogynist, but rather to distinguish the women, men, and non-binary people that have historically and currently identify with the term incel but not the misogynist worldview.

15 R.W. Connell and James W. Messerschmidt, "Hegemonic Masculinity," *Gender & Society* 19, no. 6 (2005): 832, https://doi.org/10.1177/0891243205278639.

16 In reference to nonhegemonic masculinities, some authors distinguish between marginalized and subordinated masculinities, whereby subordinated masculinities include those that profit from hegemonic masculinity and are nonhegemonic but not marginalized. For this chapter, we refer to nonhegemonic masculinities as inclusive of both types of masculinity.

17 Connell and Messerschmidt, "Hegemonic Masculinity"

18 Demetrakis Z. Demetriou, "Connell's Concept of Hegemonic Masculinity: A Critique," *Theory and Society* 30, no. 3 (2001): 349, http://www.jstor.org/stable/657965.

Of Victims, Mass Murder, and "Real Men" **139**

19 Adrienne Massanari, "#Gamergate and the Fappening: How Reddit's Algorithm, Governance, and Culture Support Toxic Technocultures," *New Media & Society* 19, no. 3 (2017): 332, https://doi.org/10.1177/1461444815608807.

20 Connell and Messerschmidt, 832.

21 Ibid., 841.

22 Tim Carrigan, Bob Connell, and John Lee, "Toward a New Sociology of Masculinity," *Theory and Society* 14, no. 5 (1985): 562, http://www.jstor.org/stable/657315.

23 Demetriou, "Connell's Concept of Hegemonic Masculinity."

24 Connell and Messerschmidt, 844.

25 Demetriou, 337.

26 James W. Messerschmidt, *Hegemonic Masculinities and Camouflaged Politics: Unmasking the Bush Dynasty and Its War against Iraq* (Florence: Taylor and Francis, 2010), 161.

27 Tristan Bridges and C.J. Pascoe, "Hybrid Masculinities: New Directions in the Sociology of Men and Masculinities," *Sociology Compass* 8, no. 3 (2014): 251, https://doi.org/10.1111/soc4.12134.

28 Bridges and Pascoe, 246.

29 Ibid., 249.

30 Ging, 16.

31 Michael Salter, "From Geek Masculinity to Gamergate: The Technological Rationality of Online Abuse," *Crime, Media, Culture: An International Journal* 14, no. 2 (2018), https://doi.org/10.1177/1741659017690893.

32 Massanari, 332.

33 Lise Gotell and Emily Dutton, "Sexual Violence in the 'Manosphere': Antifeminist Men's Rights Discourses on Rape," *International Journal for Crime, Justice and Social Democracy* 5, no. 2 (2016), https://doi.org/10.5204/ijcjsd.v5i2.310; Mary Lilly, "'The World Is Not a Safe Place for Men': The Representational Politics of the Manosphere," Université D'Ottawa / University Of Ottawa, 2016; Donna Zuckerberg, *Not All Dead White Men: Classics and Misogyny in the Digital Age* (Cambridge, MA and London: Harvard University Press, 2018).

34 Schmitz and Kayzak.

35 Jan Blommaert, "Online-Offline Modes of Identity and Community: Elliot Rodger's Twisted World of Masculine Victimhood," Tilburg Papers in Culture Studie, no. 200 (2017); Stephane J. Baele, Lewys Brace, and Travis G. Coan, "From "Incel" to "Saint": Analyzing the Violent Worldview Behind the 2018 Toronto Attack," *Terrorism and Political Violence* (2019), https://doi.org/10.1080/09546553.2019.1638256; Sylvia Jaki et al., "Online Hatred of Women in the Incels.Me Forum," *Journal of Language Aggression and Conflict* 7, no. 2 (2019), https://doi.org/10.1075/jlac.00026.jak; Christopher Vito, Amanda Admire, and Elizabeth Hughes, "Masculinity, Aggrieved Entitlement, and Violence: Considering the Isla Vista Mass Shooting," *NORMA* 13, no. 2 (2018), https://doi.org/10.1080/18902138.2017.1390658.

36 Srimati Basu, "Looking through Misogyny: Indian Men's Rights Activists, Law, and Challenges for Feminism," *Canadian Journal of Women and the Law* 28, no. 1 (2016), https://doi.org/10.3138/cjwl.28.1.45; Carl Bertois and Janice Drakich, "The Fathers' Rights Movement," *Journal of Family Issues* 14, no. 4 (1993), https://doi.org/10.1177/019251393014004007; Michael A. Messner, "Equality with a Vengeance: Men's Rights Groups, Battered Women, and Antifeminist Backlash," *Contemporary Sociology: A Journal of Reviews* 42, no. 3 (2013), https://doi.org/10.1177/00943061134 84702d.

37 Jie L. Lin, "Antifeminism Online: MGTOW (Men Going Their Own Way): Ethnographic Perspectives Across Global Online and Offline Spaces," in *Digital*

Environments: Ethnographic Perspectives Across Global Online and Offline Spaces, eds. Urte U. Frömming, Steffen Köhn, Samantha Fox, and Mike Terry, Media studies 34 (Bielefeld: transcript, 2017); Jones, Trott, and Wright, "Sluts and Soyboys."

38 Pierce A. Dignam and Deana A. Rohlinger, "Misogynistic Men Online: How the Red Pill Helped Elect Trump," *Signs: Journal of Women in Culture and Society* 44, no. 3 (2019), https://doi.org/10.1086/701155; Shawn P. van Valkenburgh, "Digesting the Red Pill: Masculinity and Neoliberalism in the Manosphere," *Men and Masculinities* (2018), https://doi.org/10.1177/1097184X18816118.

39 Ran Almog and Danny Kaplan, "The Nerd and His Discontent," *Men and Masculinities* 20, no. 1 (2017), https://doi.org/10.1177/1097184X15613831; Rachel O'Neill, *Seduction: Men, Masculinity and Mediated Intimacy* (Cambridge, Medford, MA: Polity, 2018).

40 Hoffman, Ware, and Shapiro, "Assessing the Threat of Incel Violence".

41 Pamela E. Oliver and Hank Johnston, "What a Good Idea! Ideologies and Frames in Social Movement Research," *Mobilization: An International Quarterly* 4/1 (2000): 43.

42 Angela Nagle, *Kill All Normies: The Online Culture Wars from Tumblr and 4chan to the Alt-Right and Trump* (Winchester and Washington, D.C.: Zero Books, 2017).

43 Angela Nagle, *Kill All Normies*, 86.

44 Kristin J. Anderson, *Modern Misogyny: Anti-Feminism in a Post-Feminist Era* (Oxford: Oxford University Press, 2014).

45 Bridges and Pascoe, 250.

46 Gotell and Dutton, "Sexual Violence in the 'Manosphere.'"

47 Alice E. Marwick and Robyn Caplan, "Drinking Male Tears: Language, the Manosphere, and Networked Harassment," *Feminist Media Studies* 18, no. 4 (2018), https://doi.org/10.1080/14680777.2018.1450568.

48 Ann-Kathrin Rothermel, "'The Other Side': Assessing the Polarization of Gender Knowledge through a Feminist Analysis of the Affective-Discursive in Anti-feminist Online Communities," *Social Politics: International Studies in Gender, State & Society* (2020), https://doi.org/10.1093/sp/jxaa024.

49 Julia Rone, "Far Right Alternative News Media as 'Indignation Mobilization Mechanisms': How the Far Right Opposed the Global Compact for Migration," *Information, Communication & Society* (2021): 8, https://doi.org/10.1080/13691 18X.2020.1864001.

50 Rebecca Lewis and Alice E. Marwick, "Media Manipulation and Disinformation Online," Data & Society Research Institute, n.d., https://datasociety.net/pubs/oh/DataAndSociety_MediaManipulationAndDisinformationOnline.pdf.

51 Jones, Trott, and Wright, "Sluts and Soyboys;" Wright, Trott, and Jones, "The Pussy Ain't Worth It, Bro.'"

52 Zuckerberg, 19.

53 There are MGTOWs that pursue romantic relationships with women, but the group broadly rejects marriage.

54 Lin, "Antifeminism Online."

55 Emma A. Jane, "Systemic Misogyny Exposed: Translating Rapeglish from the Manosphere with a Random Rape Threat Generator," *International Journal of Cultural Studies* 21, no. 6 (2018), https://doi.org/10.1177/1367877917734042.

56 Bonnie Bacarisse, "The Republican Lawmaker Who Secretly Created Reddit's Women-Hating 'Red Pill'," *Daily Beast*, accessed February 11, 2021, https://www.thedailybeast.com/the-republican-lawmaker-who-secretly-created-reddits-women-hating-red-pill.

Of Victims, Mass Murder, and "Real Men" **141**

57 Ging, 3.
58 Dignam and Rohlinger, "Misogynistic Men Online."
59 Emily Crockett, "Did Roosh V Really Organize "Pro-Rape Rallies"? No, but Here's Why People Are Protesting Him." *Vox*, accessed February 11, 2021, https://www.vox.com/2016/2/6/10926872/roosh-pro-rape-rallies.
60 Alex DiBranco, "Shooting in Tallahassee Illustrates Increasing Misogynist Violence," *Political Research Associates*, accessed February 11, 2021, https://www.politicalresearch.org/2018/11/08/shooting-in-tallahassee-illustrates-increasing-misogynist-violence.
61 Other similar misogynist sites included r/ForeverAlone and love-shy.com.
62 Jack Bratich and Sarah Banet-Weiser, "From Pick-up Artists to Incels: Con(Fidence) Games, Networked Misogyny, and the Failure of Neoliberalism," *International Journal of Communication* 13 (2019): 5003-5027.
63 DiBranco, "'The Incel Rebellion': Movement Misogyny Delivers Another Massacre," *The Public Eye*, Spring 2018, https://politicalresearch.org/2018/05/16/incel-rebellion.
64 Ribeiro et al., "The Evolution of the Manosphere across the Web."
65 Rothermel, "Die Manosphere."
66 Oliver and Johnston, 37–54.
67 Willem de Koster and Dick Houtman, "'Stormfront Is Like a Second Home for Me': On Virtual Community Formation by Right-Wing Extremists," *Information, Communication & Society* 11, no. 8 (2008), https://doi.org/10.1080/13691180802266665.
68 We acknowledge that within these communities, there were other popular forums that have been analyzed in the past. We add to this research by focusing on forums that remained online (i.e., were not taken down due to their harmful content or by the creator). Further, we want to clarify that these forums and groups might not be representative for all strands of each group more broadly.
69 Forums on Reddit have to adhere to Reddit community guidelines. These are often stricter than forums hosted on external web pages. The MRA subreddit remains easily accessible.
70 r/TheRedPill is also on Reddit, and it has been quarantined since September 2018.
71 As of March 2021, after our data collection, incels.co became incels.is.
72 The sexual marketplace is a common trope in the manosphere. It has been used by early MRA and PUA forums and is still heavily used in TRP, incel, and, to a lesser extent, MGTOW terminology and discussions.
73 If a woman enters a relationship with an incel, it is assumed to be only for money or immigration purposes. Some misogynist incels claim that this option is only available to white incels. For more, see Julia DeCook, "Curating the Future: The Sustainability Practices of Online Hate Groups," (dissertation, Michigan State University, 2019).
74 Rachel Kalish and Michael Kimmel, "Suicide by Mass Murder: Masculinity, Aggrieved Entitlement, and Rampage School Shootings," *Health Sociology Review* 19, no. 4 (2010), https://doi.org/10.5172/hesr.2010.19.4.451.
75 Bridges and Pascoe, "Hybrid Masculinities."
76 Rather than reflecting a binary of 'hegemonic' or 'nonhegemonic' masculinities, this column refers to how masculinities are framed (through hybridization) in ways that reproduce hierarchical and oppressive gender relations.
77 Massanari, "#Gamergate and The Fappening."
78 E.g., Baele, Brace, and Coan, "From "Incel" to "Saint.""
79 Hoffman, Ware, and Shapiro, "Assessing the Threat of Incel Violence."
80 Angela Nagle, *Kill All Normies.*

7

MEN'S RIGHTS ACTIVISTS, PERSONAL RESPONSIBILITY, AND THE END OF WELFARE

Alexis de Coning and Chelsea Ebin

The men's rights movement began in the 1960s and developed in earnest in the 1970s alongside second-wave feminism and other civil rights movements.[1] By the 1990s, the movement included a diverse array of communities, from fathers' rights advocates to mythopoetic men.[2] However, these different groups were typically united by the belief that women had achieved social, economic, and legal power and that men were the new victims of gender oppression.[3] During this same period, changes to government-sponsored social welfare programs were accompanied by new paternity reporting requirements and the imposition of more stringent child support enforcement mechanisms that were perceived by some men as targeting fathers. This chapter examines how men's rights activists (MRAs) understood and responded to transformations of the welfare state during the 1990s. In doing so, we inquire into the relationship between the ideology of MRAs and the broader liberal political discourses of "rights," "self-reliance," and "personal responsibility." Focusing specifically on the period between 1994 and 2000, which covers the two years prior to and four years after the introduction of welfare reform legislation, and drawing on a unique dataset of 1,000 posts taken from a Usenet newsgroup archive, this chapter examines how MRAs responded to increasingly stringent paternity and child support requirements imposed by welfare reform.

While we might anticipate finding that the "end of welfare as we know it" would be welcomed by MRAs, as it signaled a conservative embrace of the rhetoric of "personal responsibility" and "self-reliance" alongside a corresponding reduction of the scope of government-sponsored programs, this was not the case. Rather, MRAs perceived the imposition of new child support mandates as a further erosion of their "rights" and an illegitimate act of governmental intrusion into their lives undertaken at the behest of alternately lazy and/or conniving women. This response highlights a fundamental paradox, or illogic, that

DOI: 10.4324/9781003164722-10

characterizes the twin ideologies of "rights" and "self-reliance" as they are inter-preted by MRAs.

Throughout the 1990s, men's rights constituents advocated for the passage of legal reforms that would give men rights equal to those enjoyed by women; how-ever, newsgroup participants had a poor understanding of what legal entitlements would be provided by these rights. As our data show, the concept of rights and its relationship to individual liberty and freedom reflects the uneasy and impos-sibly contradictory subject position that many within the men's rights movement attempt to occupy as radical individualists, supremacists, and victims.

We begin by providing an overview of the men's rights movement and the development and devolution of the social welfare state in the United States. Having established this background context, we then analyze our Usenet news-group archive data. Our analysis advances thematically in three sections and focuses on discourses pertaining to (1) equal and corollary rights, (2) the feminist capture of the state, and (3) parasitical women. We conclude by placing men's rights arguments in the broader historical context of the development of dis-courses of dependency on the one hand and self-reliance, individual liberty, and liberal rights on the other hand.

What Is the Men's Rights Movement?

The men's rights movement is the collective name for a diverse range of groups and individuals who believe the dignity and rights of men and boys are dimin-ished, threatened, or nonexistent.[4] MRAs typically identify feminists in par-ticular (but often women in general) as the cause of their perceived suffering and oppression. As mentioned earlier, this umbrella term encompasses multiple communities that often overlap but are sometimes at odds with each other. Thus, disagreements about key issues and strategies are as likely as coalition-building among different groups.

But what are the "rights" evoked by this expansive movement? Some MRAs campaign for formal legal protections and entitlements. In particular, fathers' and divorce rights activists seek changes to the family court system, particu-larly in matters of child custody and alimony and divorce proceedings. Similarly, anti-circumcision activists (also known as intactivists) aim to criminalize male circumcision. More recently, men's rights organizations[5] collaborated with the U.S. Department of Education under Betsy DeVos's tenure to rewrite Title IX regulations on the grounds that there is a "crisis of false rape allegations against male college students."[6] In these cases, the "rights" of the men's rights movement are quite literal, as they seek to challenge and change legislation they see as dis-criminatory against men.

However, not all MRAs are interested in traditional activism or legal reform. Instead, many MRAs turn to self-help and self-improvement strategies or focus on metapolitical approaches that aim to normalize their views, as opposed to gaining political or institutional power.[7] Here, "rights" play a discursive role.

144 Alexis de Coning and Chelsea Ebin

Drawing on the cultural currency of classical liberal rights discourses lends an air of legitimacy to their claims of disenfranchisement, even as they do not seek legal redress. Some MRAs have even adopted the term men's *human* rights movement, which may seem tautological but indicates a purposeful leveraging of the popularity of contemporary human rights movements and discourses, alongside the implication that men are no longer regarded as human.

It is vital to note, however, that there is no neat separation of the literal and discursive approaches just outlined. Many fathers' rights activists, for instance, are not involved with organizations that campaign for legal change; rather, they may participate in online communities focused on advice and support. This is not surprising, given that all social movements draw on a range of tactics to achieve their goals. With reference to the civil rights movement in the United States, Kimberlé Williams Crenshaw reminds us that African Americans made gains "by using a powerful combination of direct action, mass protest, and individual acts of resistance, along with appeals to public opinion and the courts couched in the language of the prevailing legal consciousness."[8] While the men's rights movement has not mustered enough public support for mass protests or traditional forms of direct action, appeals to both the judicial system and the rhetoric of rights can work in tandem to further its agendas. Thus, our analysis attends to both uses of rights (concerns with legislation/regulation, as well as discursive rights) to parse out the conversations around welfare and personal responsibility in our dataset.

How Has the Social Welfare State Developed in the United States?

The United States was slow to develop a welfare state.[9] It was not until the 1930s, as economic and social inequality cleaved the country, that the nation began to entertain the prospect of the governmental provision of social welfare under Franklin Delano Roosevelt's New Deal program of economic recovery. Despite early resistance from the Supreme Court, Roosevelt succeeded in cajoling the necessary support for the implementation of many New Deal economic recovery programs.[10] The New Deal ushered in what the political scientist Stephen Skowronek has termed a "new political order," whereby the national political consensus shifted in favor of supporting a larger, more robust bureaucracy and a government-sponsored and administered social safety net.[11] It did not, however, usher in a new racial order, and New Deal social welfare programs were informed by white supremacism and reproduced racial inequalities.[12]

The New Deal political consensus was fragile and contested. Moreover, the tentative peace Roosevelt, and those who followed him, brokered was reliant on classist, racist, and misogynistic narratives of dependency.[13] In short, it was built on political quicksand. Accompanied by the rise of a conservative movement termed the "New Right"—which began in the 1960s and solidified at the start of the next decade, and was sped along by recession and stagflation—the New Deal political order began to break down in the 1970s.[14] Furthermore, Reagan's failed 1976 presidential campaign introduced the nation to the trope of the "welfare

Men's Rights Activists **145**

queen," a racialized, hypersexualized, and criminalized caricature drawn from the paranoid recesses of the conservative mind.[15] Loosely basing his "welfare queen" on the figure of Linda Taylor, a skilled con artist in Chicago, Reagan ginned up fears of government largesse for the undeserving. A *New York Times* article from 1976 quoted him saying,

> "There's a woman in Chicago," the Republican candidate said recently to an audience in Gilford, N.H., during his free swinging attack on welfare abuses. "She has 80 names, 30 addresses, 12 Social Security cards and is collecting veterans' benefits on four nonexisting deceased husbands." He added:
> And she's collecting Social Security on her cards. She's got Medicaid, getting food stamps and she is collecting welfare under each of her names. Her tax-free cash income alone is over $150,000.[16]

Elected to the presidency in 1980, Reagan promised to scale back welfare and to slash social safety net spending.[17] Central to Reagan's governing logic was the belief, articulated in his first inaugural address, that "government is not the solution to our problem, government is the problem."[18] It takes time to undo four decades of institutionalized governmental programs, particularly when a nation has come to view many of them as entitlements.[19] Thus, Reagan was not able to end welfare entirely. Nonetheless, he did initiate a new conservative political order premised on the fear of governmental abuse and the valorization of self-reliance.

After 12 years of Republican control of the presidency, Bill Clinton secured the nation's highest office in 1992. Clinton was representative of the "New Democrats," or "those who have shed the welfare-labour coalition of the New Deal in favour of a straightforward deregulated corporate free market agenda."[20] In short, Clinton's domestic policy tended to align with the interests of conservatives and big business. Over the course of two terms, his administration pursued: a policy of criminal justice expansion that was based on increased sentencing, policing, and more prisons; policies to weaken workers' rights and wage protections; and the systematic dismantling of welfare.[21]

The political scientist Howell Williams has noted that Clinton initially paired the conservative rhetoric of personal responsibility with a more New Deal "structural account of poverty."[22] Capitulating to conservative demands and "[i]n response to the Republican congressional takeover of 1994, spearheaded by Newt Gingrich and the 'Contract with America,' and in anticipation of the 1996 presidential election," Williams explains, "Clinton's rhetoric tracked rightward."[23] This rightward movement resulted in a series of reforms to the American welfare system, many of which directly impacted men, particularly in their roles as fathers.

Cast in terms of reducing dependency and fostering "personal responsibility," the signature legislative act of Clinton's domestic agenda was the Personal Responsibility and Work Opportunity Reconciliation Act of 1996 (PRWORA). As Clinton promised, PRWORA effectively was "the end of welfare as we know it." The legislation opened with the assertion, "Promotion of responsible fatherhood and motherhood is integral to successful child rearing and the well-being of children," before detailing the increase in single-parent households across three decades and highlighting the number of single-parent households that receive Aid to Families with Dependent Children (AFDC).[24] At the broadest level, PRWORA replaced this federally administered program with a state-administered program, Temporary Assistance for Needy Families (TANF), and introduced the requirement that welfare recipients work. The legislation mandated welfare "recipients to work 30 hours per week after two years of cash assistance; 10 hours could be spent engaging in job training or education activities that were directly related to employment,"[25] thereby effectively transforming welfare into workfare.

The legislation included several reforms particularly relevant to our analysis. Among these reforms were expanded legal standards to establish paternity. The law mandated voluntary acknowledgments of paternity, affirmed at the time of birth, would become legally binding if not contested within 60 days, and it significantly expanded the use of DNA testing for resolving paternity.[26] Additionally, PRWORA enhanced the existing Child Support Enforcement Program by initiating a mass expansion of the state's ability to coerce child support payments from "delinquent" parents through the creation of a national employment database. Employers were mandated to report all new hires to the database, which would allow their names to be checked against a registry of individuals owing back child support and their wages to be garnished if it were found they were behind on payments. Writing in *Family Law Quarterly*, Paul Legler explains, "The vision for child support enforcement that guided much of the development of the legislation is that the payment of child support should be automatic and inescapable—'like death or taxes.'"[27]

Women were not exempt from the new punitive measures implemented by PRWORA. On the contrary,

> PRWORA intricately links a mother's eligibility for public aid to her compliance with paternity establishment measures. Whereas AFDC regulations required mothers to cooperate with paternity establishment procedures after being determined eligible for aid, TANF requires that mothers prove cooperation *before* qualifying.[28]

Moreover, as compared to AFDC, TANF benefits were no longer guaranteed and, when they were accessible, were often significantly reduced. Finally, PRWORA made no distinction between the household and childcare labor demands experienced by single mothers; like men, women were to work for their welfare benefits.[29]

Data Context, Collection, and Analysis

At the same time that social welfare was being gutted, personal computing technologies were becoming more widespread. And, like many social movements in this era, the men's rights movement was transitioning from print to online media by taking advantage of digital technologies. Usenet resembled a bulletin board system, a popular form of early digital communication that allowed users to share files, send and receive messages, and even play basic text-based games.[30] Usenet offered roughly 100,000 individual newsgroups organized by topic; users would log in using newsreader software and receive a bulk of messages often "threaded" or strung together as conversations developed asynchronously among newsgroup members.[31] In today's terms, Usenet was something between an email chain, a forum, and a social media platform, with users responding to each other's posts, using subject headings to identify thread topics, subscribing to specific topic-based groups, cross-posting among groups, and sometimes sharing or reposting content from websites.

We focus here on a specific men's rights newsgroup, known as alt.mens-rights. The initial "raw" dataset, containing hundreds of thousands of posts from September 1994 to February 2011, was retrieved from the Internet Archive Usenet Historical Collection. This newsgroup is well suited to our analysis because it captures a segment of the men's rights community at a moment when social welfare programs were slashed and neoliberal narratives of personal responsibility and individual rights were deployed by proponents of welfare reform. The alt.mens-rights group was founded by New Zealander and self-published men's rights activist Peter Zohrab to provide a place for "philosophical discussion" and "political activity" in opposition to feminism and as an alternative to the existing newsgroup soc.men, which Zohrab claimed was neither about men's "rights or politics" explicitly (Peter, 1994). Thus, alt.mens-rights was positioned as explicitly for MRAs, in contrast to general men's interest communities on Usenet.

This study uses a unique dataset of 1,000 posts from this newsgroup. To ensure a representative sample, we collected the first 250 posts, in the order they appear, from the beginning of the raw dataset (September 6, 1994). We then collected the first 250 posts that appeared two years later (starting on September 6, 1996), and so on through 2000. The result is 250 posts for each of four years across the Clinton administration (1994, 1996, 1998, and 2000).[32] We did not utilize keyword searches to safeguard against any bias in the selection of the posts. We then read through each of these data segments, taking note of the discursive trends that emerged in each 250-post subset and across the larger 1,000-post dataset.

We identified three interrelated themes: (1) MRA's demands for equal and corollary rights, (2) feminist state capture, and (3) parasitical women. We draw on quotations from across the final dataset in the discussion that follows, as we did not notice any significant change in how these themes and discourses were leveraged over time. All direct quotations appear in their original format, with spelling and grammatical errors as they appear in the data. To maintain the fidelity of the original text, we have not used [sic] to indicate these errors in each quotation where they occur.

Finally, due to the ethical challenges raised by digital archival research,[33] we anonymized our data by giving each user a pseudonym and not citing additional

148 Alexis de Coning and Chelsea Ebin

information (like geographical locations, occupations, etc.) that could make the users of alt.mens-rights easily identifiable. In our direct citations, we have provided the year in which each post was published in parentheses. The only users who have not been anonymized are the group's creator, who has published men's rights content under his name, and public organizations like The National Center for Men and FathersManifesto.net.

Findings

Equal and Corollary Rights

Dotted across our data were frequent discussions of "rights," particularly as applied to sexual activity and reproduction. But we struggled to identify a clear articulation or definition of what was concretely meant by "rights" in any of the archival posts we reviewed. Little distinction was made between the legal ascription of rights and the social status of equality. Rather, participants assumed that attaining "rights" would guarantee equality for men, even as they asserted that the rights granted to women produced unfair privileges. Additionally, while women were construed as having all the rights, they were also characterized as having no responsibilities. On the other hand, men were perceived as being impossibly burdened by legal responsibilities. In short, women were largely viewed as rights-bearing subjects who received cost-free benefits, and men were rights-less subjects, victimized by unfair obligations. The understanding of rights and responsibilities, and the corresponding relationship between the two, expressed in the newsgroup was rife with contradictions. Despite these paradoxes, it was clear that discussion contributors were very much engaged in constructing a discourse that (1) promoted the idea that women have comparatively more rights than men, and (2) men deserve equal and corollary rights, particularly in relation to reproductive decision-making, to those acquired by women.

Posters alleged women had comparatively more power in two broad spheres of life that might be termed the sexual/reproductive and the economic/legal. While explicit discussions of rights centered almost exclusively on sexual activity/reproduction and women's affirmative rights in this sphere, little to no attention was paid to women's economic rights. Instead, discussions of economic/legal issues revolved largely around the perceived disproportionate burden men are forced to assume. Responding to Liam's comment that "[m]en should not get away scott free" if they have drunken intercourse and father an unwanted child, James asked, "Why should men be required to show more responsibility than women?—seems a bit sexist to me" (James, 1994). He followed up the allegation of sexism with an argument about child support and responsibility: "SCOTT FREE? Think again—if she decides to have the baby, he has 19 years of child support payments ahead of him. In california, that's 25% of your take home income. Her choice, your responsibility" (James, 1994). In James's formulation, sharing equal responsibility for the economic cost of raising a child imposes an undue and excessive obligation on the man. Also responding to Liam, Steven continues in the same vein, suggesting women have more rights relating to sexual activity, but they bear less responsibility for their behavior and its reproductive outcomes: "Are you familiar with parental support proceedings? Hey, worst case for a woman is 9 months of inconvience, a man gets 18+ years—and no option for an abortion, either" (Steven, 1994). Implicit in his argument is the basic assertion that women wield their rights as a tool to expressly disadvantage men. Furthermore, we see the belief that women are somehow free of all responsibility made explicit. Steven assumes a woman's "inconvenience" is carrying a pregnancy to term, but he does not recognize that the mother will likely care for her child for the next "18+ years" (regardless of whether or not she receives child support or welfare). The responsibility falls solely on the man.

Nonetheless, the primary "right" women possess, according to alt.mensrights contributors, is access to abortion. Posts frequently express frustration that a woman's right to terminate her pregnancy is not matched by a man's corollary right to suspend his parental responsibility. The 1973 landmark Supreme Court decision *Roe v. Wade*, which legalized access to abortion for women across the United States through the legal recognition of a right to privacy, crops up a number of times, most notably in a post titled "Roe V. Wade for Men." The 1994 post seeks a plaintiff to pursue a legal challenge to "today's restrictive paternity laws." The call, issued by The National Center for Men, explains, "Simply put, we intend to initiate the male Roe v. Wade on the federal level. The basis for our suit is that while women may decline motherhood, men can't decline fatherhood." This call for legal action is predicated on a misrepresentation of the actual right—to privacy—the Roe decision granted to women and men alike.

The lack of clarity concerning how rights are ascribed within the U.S. legal and political system is carried into conversations concerning "Choice for Men" (C4M), a proposal to allow men to disavow their parental responsibilities. As the legal scholar Sally Sheldon succinctly explains, "At the heart of the men's advocates' argument lies the claim that since parenthood is now a choice for women, so too should it be a choice for men."[34] While there is tacit recognition among these commenters that the physiological experience of pregnancy is fundamentally different for the individual carrying the fetus, the proposition that a corollary right to terminate a pregnancy could be granted to men fails to account for this disparate experience in a substantive manner.

C4M is nonetheless promoted as an avenue for men's rights to achieve equal footing. For example, Andrew attempted to dispel what he viewed as pernicious myths surrounding C4M by contributing the following:

> Myth: Choice for men is about men trying to evade parental responsibilities. [Truth]: False and sexist. In the US, choice for men would give men only the rights women have had since Roe v Wade, nothing more. It would not let the man compel the woman to abort.
>
> *(Andrew, 1996)*

150 Alexis de Coning and Chelsea Ebin

Tom (one of C4M's most vocal supporters in the newsgroup) took the opportunity to defend C4M by refuting an argument made by another contributor, Alex. In response to Alex's assertion that men and women can have equal recourse to reproductive rights by utilizing adoption as a tool for opting in/out of parental responsibility, Tom maintained, "Not necessary. She doesn't need his approval to use abortion on demand. He does not need her approval to use C4M. He does exercise C4M and she incubates/ delivers, what she does with her child is her business" (Tom, 1998). Chiming in on the same debate, Xavier argued C4M would give men equality without depriving women of their rights:

> Well, being responsible for a child can put an emotional and financial drain on a man's life as well. Why can't they get the option to opt out, just as she can. THIS is the choice that women have that men should also have, especially since we CAN give it to men as well with a c4m proposal WITHOUT taking away the choice of women.
>
> *(Xavier, 1998)*

Collectively, these posters acknowledge C4M is necessarily different from abortion, even as they articulate it as a demand for the equal and corollary right to "terminate" the parent–child relationship. And yet, how that terminated relationship would be enforced legally or function socially remains relatively unexplored. Would the invocation of C4M be bound to a trimester calendar in the same way abortion access is? Would a father be allowed to disavow paternity following a particularly unpleasant tantrum at his child's second birthday party? It is unclear if C4M would have to be utilized during the early stages of pregnancy when a termination could still be secured by the pregnant woman thereby preserving her choice in the matter or if it could be invoked at any time up to, or even after, the birth of a child. Setting aside unanswered questions about how C4M would be operationalized, defenders of the proposal also fail to address whether children who have been disavowed are entitled to any rights and do not explain how these children should be supported in the absence of paternal support. Moreover, these conversations took place against the backdrop of welfare reform and the replacement of AFDC with TANF and workfare, which drastically reduced the availability of welfare benefits. As conceived here, C4M would create yet another level of vulnerability for children and single mothers that goes unacknowledged and unaddressed by the posters.

However, not all users embraced either abortion rights or C4M wholeheartedly. Some were ambivalent about the morality of abortion, such as Tom, who remarked,

> Wherever the extra, unnatural choice is legal for girls; extra, unnatural choice is a moral right for men and should be legalized. Girls base their right to extra, unnatural choice on the fact that they gestate; men base theirs on the fact that they are sperm donors.
>
> *(Tom, 1998)*

In other words, Tom argued abortion is "an extraordinary, unnatural act," so if women have the right to terminate a pregnancy, "the male has a moral right to extra choice also. Obviously, the only choice C4M takes away from the girl, is the choice to force her mate into subsidizing her decisions" (Tom, 1998). While a number of newsgroup users wrote in support of C4M, they seemingly did so only insofar as it was perceived to be an imperfect and temporary fix to a much bigger problem facing men. This suggests these posters may not have viewed abortion as a woman's right and C4M as its corollary but rather the former as the result of a society corrupted by feminism and the latter as a temporary salve.

While C4M was presented as a mechanism for achieving "equal rights" to those enjoyed by women, the discourse surrounding the rights of men suggests many commentators sought anything but the equality of the sexes. This is seen most clearly in posts concerning the status of men. Professing to speak on behalf of the "conservative" wing of the men's movement, Ray suggests economic equality could extend to men and women alike: "We believe in equal opportunity for all to participate in our capitalist system." Lest anyone gets carried away, he also affirmed that conservative MRAs "believe that their are gender roles that are innate— generally making women good at some things, men at others" (Ray, 1994). Ray further argues the embrace of equal roles for men and women represents "artificial 'equality,' [something] the feminist movement has designed to do so at the expense of men, children and the family" (Ray, 1994). If women stay in their own lane and perform their role as wives and mothers as defined for them by men, they can be regarded as equal to men. In short, "equality" for Ray is fine as long as it is marked by difference. Feminism denies the fundamental differences between men and women. It has not only subverted the natural order of gender difference and hierarchy; it has done so by laying false claim to the very concept of equality.

That men are denied the status to which they feel entitled is reflected in a number of posts, including the aforementioned message thread that aims to dispute common feminist "myths" about C4M. In response to the assertion, "Men (or white males) have it great," Andrew, contends, "On _this_ planet, men are second class citizens in many ways. This is the most cancerous myth of all and those who proselytize it are quite beyond civilized discussion" (Andrew, 1996). Chris further demonstrates this anxiety about the status and recognition afforded to men by society, claiming "there are constant reminders about how inferior they are to women" (Chris, 1996). Read as part of a discursive whole, the conflation of rights and responsibilities concerning sexual agency, the ambiguity over how C4M would function, the vagueness surrounding the morality of abortion, and the underlying antipathy toward the perceived "second-class" status of men reflect ambivalence within the community about the meaning of "rights."

Feminist Capture of the State

Concomitant with men's "second-class" status is the notion that women in general, and feminists in particular, have captured the state. MRAs identify this

152 Alexis de Coning and Chelsea Ebin

"state capture" as one of the reasons for men's lack of equal rights and their unfair treatment in family courts and workplaces. As Miles puts it, "Feminists *have* instituted discrimination as official government and corporate policies" (Miles, 1996). Affirmative action, welfare reform, workplace policies around sexual harassment and diversity, and divorce and custody proceedings are all posited as arenas where women are granted "special privileges" (Miles, 1996) and rights that elevate them over men. In this framework, feminists (and by extension all women) wield immense power over both the public and private sectors, allowing them to conduct a "feminist war on equality" (Fred, 1996). But where does this power come from? The alt.mens-rights users propose two explanations for the pervasiveness of perceived feminist power: unilateral influence over social, political, and legal institutions, and women's inherent ability to manipulate men.

In the first instance, users point to feminists' control of media, policymakers, law, and the police as the means through which they have captured the state. For instance, newsgroup progenitor Peter Zohrab claims that women are

> in a position to be able to provoke domestic violence by whatever means, secure in the knowledge that Feminazi control over the media and police will ensure that she comes out of it with all the kids and half the marital assets.
>
> *(Peter, 1994)*

Similarly, in a discussion about women holding important government positions, Zohrab asserts, "[T]he issue is not so much who holds what job, but what propaganda the Feminist media feeds them, because that is what the decisionmakers and voters base their decisions on" (Peter, 2000). A representative of FathersManifesto.net simply refers to the "feminist media" presenting inaccurate divorce statistics (1998) in his rebuttal of equality between spouses within a marriage.[35] Here, the feminist media apparatus is seen as a mechanism through which women influence other institutions like the police, electoral politics, and family courts. By extension, the law itself is framed as corrupt, untrustworthy, and authoritarian. In a thread about date rape and the apparent ease with which women can make false rape accusations, Steven proclaims, "THE LAW IS WRONG. TWENTY YEARS OF FEMINAXI TYRRANY IN THE LAW SCHOOLS HAS GIVEN THIS TO US" (Steven, 1994). Steven's sentiment echoes conservative fears of a tyrannical "big" government, where feminism has resulted in legal impositions to people's individual rights.

Moreover, for some MRAs, the issue is that feminists supposedly change laws to govern social behavior. In a discussion about sexual harassment in the workplace, Tanay claims,

> If the guidelines were merely suggestions on how to properly respect a MOS,[36] most men would have no problem with them. However, feminists want to put these guidelines in the form of LAW, forbidding men to utter any disrespectful comment to a woman, and this is what troubles the men.

Note that for practical purposes, these guidelines will only affect men, so it is reasonable that they would be the most vocal complainers against a blatant infringement on freedom of speech.

(Tanay, 1994)

It is worth noting here that Tanay collapses sexual harassment, general disrespect, and speech. First, workplace sexual harassment guidelines have clear parameters for what qualifies as harassment, which can be distinguished from disrespect. Second, corporate policies around workplace behavior are not the same as government censorship of one's speech. By subsuming these categories, Tanay positions men as victims and women as all-powerful. In another instance, feminists' immense power is framed in terms of dystopian extremes:

[T]hrough VAWA,[37] rather than the thought police arresting you for your thoughts (as in the Orwellian 1984) you can be arrested FOR SOMEONE ELSE'S THOUGHTS!!! She says she's afraid, go to jail, lose your house, lose your bank account, lose the kids, lose the car, and make montly payments for your child's "emotional" well-being.

(Terrence, 2000)

As with Zohrab's post, Terrence argues here that the police and courts, in collaboration with feminists, ensure women have no trouble taking men's financial assets and children. A similar post claims women have "the power to take away a man's children and assets at the drop of a hat, or a wet hankie moistened with crocodile tears" (Otto, 1998). These examples demonstrate the extent to which MRAs believe women and feminists have control over governmental and legal apparatuses.

Related to the argument that feminists have undue influence because of their capture of social and legal institutions is an argument that women are inherently manipulative and deceitful. As Otto indicated, women's ability to use a "wet hankie" gives feminists the power to seize men's assets. The shrewd woman trope is common.[38] Rodney's post exemplifies this sentiment:

[F]eminists have not yet attempted genocide. They have however, through their rhetoric, their manipulation of chivalry in Congress, etc., managed to isolate a birth group, single out this group with a series of pejorative names (i.e., "witemale"), and held them up for ridicule. [...] The "women's movement" is just that, a "women's movement", it has nothing to do with "equality", it's about power. Women by nature are very good at the manipulation of emotions, far better than most men.

(Rodney, 1996)

Thus, women and feminists are seen as a conspiratorial cabal intent on stripping men of their rights and assets for their own personal gain. It is through their

Parasitical Women

By capturing the state and granting themselves special (and thus unequal) rights, women are also presented as undeserving parasites who leech from both individual men and the state. In a manner that is reminiscent of Reagan's castigation of "welfare queens," women are presented as inherently self-serving. And much like welfare was singled out by its critics for encouraging dependency, the alt.mens-rights users also argue the state itself incentivizes and facilitates this parasitic behavior. By corollary, they frame men's value in terms of their earning potential which, along with the state's complicity, makes men victims of women's greed.

In a thread about men as "objects," for instance, Frank says men are judged by their financial success and no woman wants to marry a man who cannot be a breadwinner. He argues most marriages end due to "money problems" because "*Some* women feel they can get a better provider, if the current one doesn't meet her demands and maintain her security" (Frank, 1994). Similarly, Simon contends men should never legally marry because "when your lover's love for you fades or she finds a new lover it gives her vast opportunity to loot you financially and emotionally" (Simon, 1994). Thus, the "powerful financial rewards" (Gavin, 1996) and ease of no-fault divorce incentivizes women to leave their marriages and strip men of their assets.

Child support is seen as a similar mechanism through which women can parasitize men via the state. As Otto puts it, "Single mothers who steal children and suck out C[hild] S[upport] are witches who should be burned to death at the stake" (Otto, 1998). While this comment may seem extreme in its imagery, the sentiment is echoed by others who claim "most states are passing laws that are mummy support not child support" (Gavin, 1996) and men are simply the "wallet supporter" of their children (Jared, 1998). Within this framework, some MRAs take up the aforementioned notion of C4M. As mentioned earlier, Tom claims C4M does not impede women's reproductive choices, except "the choice to *force their mate to subsidize their decision* to parent/support children" (Tom, 1998, italics added). He also compares child support to slavery, arguing, "Because a girl incubates for a mere 9 months does not entitle her or her child to enslave a male for 18+ years" (Tom, 1998). This leads Tom to conclude, "You girls and your boy supporters are not concerned about responsible decisions, Your concern is about privilege as opposed to equality" (Tom, 1998). While the metaphors differ (from witches to slavery), the message here is that women are able to control men's lives, limit their choices, and impede their individual rights by leeching their financial resources. Women also shirk their individual responsibilities by relying on men and the state to "subsidize" their decisions and enable their behavior.

Men's Rights Activists **155**

In this way, women have both captured the state and become dependents of it. In the aforementioned discussion about date rape, Liam commented that men need to "show more responsibility to their counterparts" (Liam, 1994). Steven responded, "Why? Women aren't as bright? Women need to be protected? Women can't take responsiblity for thier own actions? Women need to be treated as children and protected from their own actions? What?!? DO YOU **REALLY** MEAN TO SAY THAT WOMEN NEED TO BE BABY-SAT BY THE STATE?" (Steven, 1994). Steven uses the discussion as an opportunity to point to women's parasitic relationship with the state, while he simultaneously infantilizes women by reducing them to "children" who need to be "baby-sat." Similarly, in a thread about feminism and "strong women," Edward states the "strong women you say we fear are the women who cannot compete unless they have special programs, special rights, special classes, special privileges and special protections" (Edward, 1996). The implication is often that women need the additional support of the state because they are weaker and lazier than men, while they simultaneously connive to supplement their incomes with welfare, alimony, and child support granted through these "special programs." For instance, Karen claims she would "rather have dug graves with [her] bare hands than take a nickel in alimony from [her] ex" because she is capable, independent, and free (Karen, 1996). By contrast, women who are "depending on someone else to provide everything" for them are not free and thus have no self-respect nor do they deserve respect from others (Karen, 1996). For Karen, the typing skills she learned in high school are "usually enough to at least get a foot in the employment door," and thus others without similar skills should not become parents in the first place. Finally, she reiterates the discourse of independence and self-sufficiency:

> I, too, am sickened by these women who grab, grab, grab all their lives and couldn't support themselves for five minutes if their lives depended on it. I fully expect to get flamed for this, but I see them as modern-day prostitutes—alimony is just a form of prostitution.
>
> *(Karen, 1996)*

Similar to the aforementioned witch and slave-owner metaphors, Karen employs the imagery of "prostitution" to frame "stupid" women as lazy, selfish, and undeserving dependents. What these discussions reveal is an incoherent ideology where women are simultaneously all-powerful manipulators of men and the state *and* weak dependents who parasitize men and the state.

Conclusions

Our analysis sought to draw out the ideological paradoxes that characterize much of the men's rights movement by highlighting its failure to define what is meant by "rights." In the period under examination, MRAs responded to the erosion

156 Alexis de Coning and Chelsea Ebin

of the social welfare state and its replacement with a neoliberal system designed to promote individualism and "personal responsibility" through the maximization of labor force participation. Both the social welfare state and the neoliberal state were denigrated as tools of women. Men's rights discourses during this time simultaneously affirmed the economic primacy and superiority of men even as they decried the imposition of mandated child support and sought to shirk personal responsibility. While the term "dependency" did not crop up in our dataset, the MRA discourses active within the newsgroup can be made sense of through an examination of the concept as it applies to welfare and intersects with race, class, and gender.

In their seminal article "A Genealogy of Dependency: Tracing a Keyword of the U.S. Welfare State," Nancy Fraser and Linda Gordon identify four registers of meaning for dependency in Western Europe: economic, sociolegal, political, and moral/psychological.[39] Fraser and Gordon explain how the meaning of dependency developed and transformed over time from being descriptive of a social relation in pre-feudal and aristocratic society, to being primarily an economic condition during industrialization, to being a moral or psychological failing under the conditions of advanced capitalism.

Fraser and Gordon argue the discursive shift from dependency as structural to characterological "facilitated hostility to public support for the poor" and the comparatively "weak and decentralized" U.S. state "proved fertile soil for the moral/psychological discourse of dependency" in the 19th century.[40] As they illustrate, the moral/psychological discourse of dependency gives rise to a split in how social welfare programs are categorized by the government and understood by the public: the deserving and the undeserving. Programs funded (however fragmentarily) by named payroll taxes, such as Social Security and Medicare, are deserved and, therefore, are entitlements. Those that come out of general government funds, such as the Supplemental Nutrition Assistance Program or the previously mentioned AFDC, are undeserved and, therefore, contestable and subject to retrenchment.

Crucially, Fraser and Gordon also highlight the complex place of women in the lexicon of dependency. During the 19th century, the invention of the housewife shaped social expectations for gendered work and independence:

> [T]he independence of the white workingman presupposed the ideal of the family wage, a wage sufficient to maintain a household and to support a nonemployed wife and children. Thus, for wage labor to create (white male) independence, (white) female economic dependence was required. Women were thus transformed "from partners to parasites."[41]

This discourse is evident in our data, where women are perceived almost exclusively as parasites. While married women are seen as inevitable divorcées-in-waiting, single and divorced mothers are framed as witches, slave drivers, and prostitutes unless they, like Karen, are able to work "16 hours a day at 1 ½ jobs"

Men's Rights Activists **157**

to be independent and free (Karen, 1996). However, there is a critical difference between the discursive framework outlined by Fraser and Gordon and the one we see operating in the alt.mens-rights newsgroup.

As Fraser and Gordon point out, a normative "good" (deserving) dependency was that of wives and children in nuclear households, contrasted with the "bad" (undeserving) dependency of welfare recipients. However, this distinction is not as clear-cut with our newsgroup participants. For instance, while John advises marrying conservative women "who want a decent family" because a "focus on the strong family unit" is the only way to "emerge from the bulk self-victimization" of society (John, 1994), other users clearly resent the role of the breadwinner they see foisted upon them. Furthermore, if we recall Ray's comments about the innate differences between men and women, and feminism's disruption of this gender order "at the expense of men, children and the family" (Ray, 1994), the paradox of dependency becomes clear. Men *should* perform the role of dutiful husband and provider because it is natural and good, but this role also enslaves them to undeserving dependents who will inevitably divorce them and take their wealth. Simultaneously, if women work outside the home to contribute financially and avoid being dependents, they do so at the expense of their families and require the "special programs" that take breadwinning jobs away from men. Within this men's rights paradigm then, a financially and emotionally stable marriage is an impossible contradiction for both men and women.

It is also noteworthy that this paradigm aligns with the discursive racialization of welfare, workfare, and affirmative action of the 1990s. Historically, white women relied heavily on themes of dependency and domesticity to advance their political claims in the post-Reconstruction era.[42] Many suffragists fought for the right to vote on the grounds that their participation in politics would "purify" an otherwise corrupt and foul industry[43]—i.e., the morals of "good" middle-class woman dependents would provide a necessary corrective to the "unwholesomeness" of traditionally masculine politics. Along these lines, domestic virtue became a justification for women's participation in abolition and temperance campaigns. Abolition and temperance women also blurred the lines between domesticity and dependency, arguing that alcoholism made men bad providers and left (good) dependent women destitute, thereby transforming them into bad dependents.[44] In the period following reconstruction, white women demanded an end to coverture[45] (including legislation to entitle wives to their own wages) on the grounds that liberty was defined by the right to contract one's labor; the Thirteenth Amendment had granted that freedom to Black men, and so the time had come for (white) women to also be free.[46]

While labor-based arguments were unsuccessful in the nation's legislatures because white male legislators refused to relinquish their ownership over their wives' household labor, early women's rights advocates found more traction arguing that men's moral turpitude transformed wives from good into bad dependents. State-level legislative reforms resulted in white women gaining rights to their wages for labor done *outside* of the home but a concretization and continuation of

158 Alexis de Coning and Chelsea Ebin

male ownership over labor done *within* the home. For Black women, the situation was altogether different: in a racialized economy that remained dependent on the exploitation of Black labor, they were supposed to contract their labor outside of the home, and a failure to do so represented a personal/moral failure.[47] In other words, should a Black woman in the post-Reconstruction era labor only within the home, thereby performing the kind of dependency that was labeled "good" for her white counterpart, she would be labeled a bad dependent. The result was a discourse that (1) encouraged white women to be good dependents (i.e., to labor in the home), (2) vilified Black women for that same dependency, (3) yet also pathologized Black families for failing to look like white families, (4) cast the failure of any women to perform dependency in the "right" way as a failure to perform their racialized gender, and, finally, (5) pinned the unsustainability and growing collapse of the "family wage" on masculine and underclass failure.

This racial pathologization persisted into the 20th century and undoubtedly informed the tropes of the aforementioned "welfare queen," as well as the Black "matriarch" who causes "poverty, male abandonment, crime, and illegitimacy" with her excessive independence.[48] While the alt.mens–rights participants do not reference these caricatures directly, the historical racialization of welfare, workfare, and affirmative action programs provides further context for the discourses of dependency, parasitization, and "rights" in our dataset. As mentioned earlier, both Andrew and Rodney point to "white males" as the victims of feminist state capture. The implicit corollary here is that Black women are its benefactors. Edward complicates this narrative by arguing that "Ivy League feminists" have taken advantage of diversity programs and affirmative action as "redress against people who have no power and committed no sins" (Edward, 1998). Nonetheless, it is not a stretch to assume the nebulous innocents to whom Edward is referring here are men, and white men in particular.

In this framework, social programs like welfare and affirmative action become a means to "legally and systematically" discriminate against white men and erode their rights (Paul, 1994). Again, we see a paradoxical situation emerge from these discussions. On the one hand, single mothers (often racialized as Black within the larger U.S. discourse) are "bad" dependents for relying on state welfare and moral failures if they do not have the necessary "skills" for paid employment. On the other hand, they are also bad if they work outside the home, which deprives their families of good mothers but also deprives men of their rights and entitlements. The irony, of course, is that neoliberal reforms like "workfare" (i.e., working to earn one's welfare benefits) produced this paradox by putting women in the position of being both "bad" dependent welfare recipients and "bad" mothers competing for men's work and rights. The conversations around C4M and corollary rights contribute further to this conundrum, where single mothers are seen as inherently irresponsible, but men should not be expected to participate in fatherhood or share the financial costs of parenting.

When we began our data analysis, we asked how the conservative and neoliberal retrenchment of welfare, which ostensibly served both to reinvigorate the ideals of self-reliance and small government promoted by many MRAs to check the tyranny of the state, came to be perceived as an attack on men's liberty. However, it became clear that a more accurate way of framing the puzzle required us to acknowledge the specific actions undertaken by the government were immaterial to MRAs' understanding of those actions. While MRA discourses were informed by transformations in the social welfare sphere, neither the actual impacts of welfare reform nor the "personal responsibility" discourse promoted by the Clinton administration seemed to affect the production of MRA beliefs. In other words, although clearly responding to welfare reforms, the discursive malleability of "rights" and "responsibility" allows the newsgroup users to continuously frame men as victims who are denied their rights and women as beneficiaries of the feminist state with no responsibilities, regardless of how welfare policies and legal entitlements actually impacted people. And so, even when the gutting of social welfare caused women economic harm and reforms punished women for failing to be "good" dependents, MRAs persisted in believing women were to blame. This, in part, helps to explain the ideological inconsistencies we found within the newsgroup discourse. While MRAs demanded "rights" and embraced an ideology of personal responsibility, they simultaneously expressed a desire to negate their responsibility (as exemplified by C4M) and demonstrated an understanding of "equal rights" that was deeply circumscribed and constrained by the desire to both castigate women for performing dependence *and* independence the wrong way.

As we suggested previously, these ideological inconsistencies are, at least in part, a function of the state itself. Curran and Abrams argue welfare programs often have "contradictory effects" that both undermine gender hierarchy and "uphold a sexual division of labor by acting as a substitute wage-earning husband" simultaneously.[49] At the same time, this framework often implicitly equates fatherhood with "male wage earning," where the state's role becomes primarily concerned with "extracting male fiscal capital."[50] For marginalized men in particular, the "state frequently acts as a source of 'alien power' and violence."[51] It is thus not altogether surprising the alt.mens-rights users resent the disciplinary mechanisms enacted by the state during the Clinton administration. However, the equally punitive standards placed upon women either remain invisible or are consciously elided by these participants. Instead, women are posited as inherently inferior, lazy, parasitical dependents who are unable to compete with men at the same time that they are manipulative, greedy, wield immense power, have captured the state via feminism, and deny men their rights. While these MRAs' frustrations are grounded in legitimate sociopolitical conditions (e.g., punitive enforcement of paternity and child support or the reduction of fatherhood to financial provider), their ire is directed at the conspiratorial specter of "feminazis" and conniving women.

What is significant about these discourses is that they persist within the men's rights movement today, even after two decades of austerity. At the 2019 International Conference on Men's Issues, for instance, speaker Tommy Sotomayor

160 Alexis de Coning and Chelsea Ebin

echoed the C4M rhetoric, asking why men do not have the option for "financial abortion." He also referred to child support as a "debtors' prison" and berated women (and Black women in particular) for having multiple children with different fathers.[52] Similarly, at a panel discussion titled "How We Are Failing Minority Men and Boys," Brian Martinez suggested the system incentivizes women's bad behavior (i.e., having children out of wedlock and relying on welfare benefits) and that if men could "opt out financially," they might see systemic change.[53] Martinez argued feminists have created a culture in which Black and Hispanic boys grow up with single mothers and are shunted into publicly-funded daycare centers where they are surrounded by women caretakers, essentially depriving them of male role models and healthy masculine behavior.[54] Statements like these suggest the men's rights movement continues to deploy a discourse that damns women for being "good" and "bad" dependents in equal measure. Similarly, the racialization of "bad" women dependents and the continued use of the "welfare queen" trope is an understudied aspect of men's rights ideology. For scholars undertaking research on the contemporary men's rights movement, attention to the themes of equal and corollary rights, feminist state capture, and women-as-parasites could shed light on the longevity of these discourses.

Notes

1 Edward Gambill, *Uneasy Males: The American Men's Movement 1970–2000* (New York: iUniverse, 2005); Judith Newton, *From Panthers to Promise Keepers: Rethinking the Men's Movement* (Lanham, MD: Rowman & Littlefield, 2004). Although pre-cursors to the movement existed prior to this period, most scholars locate the beginning of a formal, organized men's rights movement around this time.

2 Roger Griffin, "From Slime Mold to Rhizome: An Introduction to the Groupuscular Right," *Patterns of Prejudice* 37, no. 1 (2003): 27–50, https://doi.org/10.1080/0031322 022000054321. Although these groups are not commensurate, and while we recognize that others may classify these groups under the umbrella of the "men's movement" or the "manosphere," we include them under the broad banner of the "men's rights movement" because of their "ineliminable" components and characteristics. In other words, these groups coalesce around similar notions that masculinity is threatened in some way. Where mythopoetic men's groups turned to self-help, New Age spirituality, and Jungian psychology to recuperate their masculinity, fathers' rights groups were more active in challenging divorce and custody proceedings they saw as diminishing the roles and rights of fathers. As we unpack below, men's rights activists tended to use both literal and discursive appeals to "rights" to address their perceived victimization at the hands of feminists.

3 Michael A. Messner, *Politics of Masculinities: Men in Movements* (Walnut Creek, CA: Altamira Press, 2000). It is worth noting here that Messner also discusses pro-feminist and feminist-aligned men's groups that existed alongside the anti-feminist communities we explore here.

4 Alexis de Coning, "Men's Rights Movement/Activism," in *The International Encyclopedia of Gender, Media, and Communication*, eds. Karen Ross, Ingrid Bachmann, Valentina Cardo, Sujata Moorti, and Marco Scarcelli, 1. Hoboken, NJ: John Wiley & Sons, Inc, 2020, https://doi.org/10.1002/9781119429128.

Men's Rights Activists **161**

5 Hélène Barthélemy, "How Men's Rights Groups Helped Rewrite Regulations on Campus Rape," *The Nation*, August 14, 2020, https://www.thenation.com/article/politics/betsy-devos-title-ix-mens-rights/. In particular, the National Coalition for Men Carolinas, Families Advocating for Campus Equality, and Stop Abusive and Violent Environments were involved in conference calls and meetings with Department of Education employees, and drafting legislation.

6 Hélène Barthélemy, "How Men's Rights Groups."

7 Alexis de Coning, "Men's Rights Movement/Activism," 4–5.

8 Kimberlé Williams Crenshaw, "Race, Reform, and Retrenchment: Transformation and Legitimation in Antidiscrimination Law," *German Law Journal* 12, no. 1 (January 2011): 280.

9 Considerable diversity exists within and between welfare states, but a baseline definition can be articulated as a state that takes responsibility for and provides some measure of institutional support for meeting its citizens basic needs.

10 Sydney Milkis and Marc Landy, "The Presidency in History: Leading from the Eye of the Storm," in *The Presidency and the Political System*, 11th Edition, ed. Michael Nelson (Thousand Oaks, CA: Sage/CQ Press, 2018), 93-130.

11 Stephen Skowronek, *Presidential Leadership in Political Time: Reprise and Reappraisal*, 2nd Edition (Lawrence: University Press of Kansas, 2011).

12 See, for example, Ira Katznelson, *When Affirmative Action Was White* (New York: W.W. Norton and Co., 2006); Kenneth J. Neubeck and Noel A. Cazenave, *Welfare Racism: Playing the Race Card against America's Poor* (New York: Routledge, 2001); Jill S. Quadagno, *The Color of Welfare* (Oxford and New York: Oxford University Press, 1994).

13 White mothers, for instance, were far more likely to receive aid than African American mothers on the grounds that there was more work available to Black women. For more on the exclusion of Black women from welfare programs during the New Deal era, see Premilla Nadasen, *Rethinking the Welfare Rights Movement* (New York: Routledge, 2012).

14 Margaret Weir, "States, Race, and the Decline of New Deal Liberalism," *Studies in American Political Development* 19, no. 2 (2005): 157-172.

15 Premilla Nadasen, "From Widow to 'Welfare Queen': Welfare and the Politics of Race," *Black Women, Gender Families* 1, no. 2 (2007): 52–77, accessed at: https://www.jstor.org/stable/10.5406/blacwomegendfami.1.2.0052.

16 "'Welfare Queen' Becomes Issue in Reagan's Campaign," *The New York Times*, February 15, 1976, accessed at: https://www.nytimes.com/1976/02/15/archives/welfare-queen-becomes-issue-in-reagan-campaign-hitting-a-nerve-now.html.

17 Ronald Reagan, "Address before a Joint Session of Congress on the Program for Economic Recovery," February 18, 1981, accessed at: "https://www.reaganlibrary.gov/archives/speech/address-joint-session-congress-program-economic-recovery-february-1981.

18 Ronald Reagan, "Inaugural Address," January 20, 1981, accessed at: https://www.reaganfoundation.org/media/128614/inaguration.pdf.

19 Kees Van Kersbergen, "The Politics of Welfare State Reform," *Swiss Political Science Review* 8 (2002), accessed at: https://onlinelibrary.wiley.com/doi/pdf/10.1002/j.1662-6370.2002.tb00392.x.

20 James Petras and Steve Vieux. "From Little Rock to Wall Street: Clinton's Journey beyond Reaganism," *Economic and Political Weekly* 30, no. 5 (1995): 251–53, accessed December 10, 2020, http://www.jstor.org/stable/4402347.

21 Petras and Vieux, "From Little Rock."

22 Howell Williams, "'Personal Responsibility' and the End of Welfare as We Know It," *Political Science and Politics* 50, no. 2 (April 2017): 381.

23 Williams, "Personal Responsibility," 381.

24 Congress.gov, "Text – H.R.3734 - 104th Congress (1995–1996): Personal Responsibility and Work Opportunity Reconciliation Act of 1996," August 22, 1996, https://www.congress.gov/bill/104th-congress/house-bill/3734/text.

25 "A New Paradigm for Welfare Policy: Recommendations to Congress on the Reauthorization of PRWORA," Staff Draft, United States Commission on Civil Rights, July 2002, accessed January 4, 2020, https://www.usccr.gov/pubs/prwora/old.htm.

26 Paul K. Legler, "The Coming Revolution in Child Support Policy: Implications of the 1996 Welfare Act," *Family Law Quarterly* 30, no. 3 (Fall 1996): 519–63.

27 Legler, "The Coming Revolution," 538–41.

28 Laura Curran and Laura S. Abrams, "Making Men into Dads: Fatherhood, the State, and Welfare Reform," *Gender and Society* 14, no. 5 (2000): 666.

29 Dorothy E. Roberts, "Welfare Reform and Economic Freedom: Low-Income Mothers' Decisions about Work at Home and in the Market," *Faculty Scholarship at Penn Law* 44 (2004): 1030, https://scholarship.law.upenn.edu/faculty_scholarship/584.

30 Aaron Delwiche, "Early Social Computing: The Rise and Fall of the BBS scene (1977–1995)," in *The Sage Handbook of Social Media*, eds. Jean Burgess, Alice Marwick, and Thomas Poell (London: SAGE Publications, 2018), https://doi.org/10.4135/9781473984066.n3; Peter Kollock and Marc A. Smith, "Communities in Cyberspace," in *Communities in Cyberspace*, eds. Marc A. Smith and Peter Kollock (New York: Routledge, 1999/2005), 5–6; Barney Warf, "Usenet," in *The Sage Encyclopedia of the Internet*, ed. Barney Warf (Thousand Oaks, CA: SAGE Publications, 2018), https://doi.org/10.4135/9781473960367.n259.

31 Avery Dame-Griff, "Herding the 'Performing Elephants': Using Computational Methods to Study Usenet," *Internet Histories* 3, no. 3–4 (2019), https://doi.org/10.1080/24701475.2019.1652456; Harley Hahn, "Newsgroups and Hierarchies," *Harley Hahn's Usenet Center* (2020), retrieved from http://www.harley.com/usenet/usenet-tutorial/newsgroups-and-hierarchies.html; Kollock and Smith, 5–6.

32 Data from 1993, the first year of Clinton's presidential tenure, is not available.

33 Dame-Griff, "Herding the 'Performing Elephants,'" 224; Ian Milligan, *History in the Age of Abundance? How the Web Is Transforming Historical Research* (Montreal: McGill-Queens University Press, 2019), 16; Kollock and Smith, "Communities in Cyberspace," 211.

34 Sally Sheldon, "Unwilling Fathers and Abortion: Terminating Men's Child Support Obligations?" *The Modern Law Review* 66, no. 2 (2003): 185, 175–94, accessed December 29, 2020, http://www.jstor.org.ezproxy.centre.edu/stable/1097623.

35 FathersManifesto.net is far-right Christian organization with white nationalist overtones and distinct from other fathers' rights activists and groups. A 1999 petition from their website demands that children be returned to their fathers on the grounds that Christianity stipulates that children belong to their fathers and thus their first amendment rights are violated by family courts that award custody to mothers.

36 MOS stands for member of the opposite sex.

37 Terrence is referring to the Violence against Women Act here, which was signed into law by Clinton in 1994. The act strengthened protections for women who were victims of violent crimes.

38 Susan B. Boyd, "Backlash against Feminism: Canadian Custody and Access Reform Debates of the Late Twentieth Century," *Canadian Journal of Woman and the Law* 16 (2004): 282; Emma A. Jane, "Systemic Misogyny Exposed: Translating Rapeglish from the Manosphere with a Random Rape Threat Generator," *International*

Journal of Cultural Studies 21, no. 6 (2018): 7, accessed January 27, 2020, https://doi.org/10.1177/1367877917734042; Michael A. Messner, "The Limits of 'The Male Sex Role': An Analysis of the Men's liberation and Men's Rights Movements' Discourse," *Gender and Society* 12, no. 3 (1998): 269; Shawn P. Van Valkenburgh, "Digesting the Red Pill: Masculinity and Neoliberalism in the Manosphere," *Men and Masculinities* (2018), accessed January 31, 2019, https://doi.org/10.1177/1097184X18816118.

39 Nancy Fraser and Linda Gordon. "A Genealogy of Dependency: Tracing a Keyword of the U.S. Welfare State." *Signs* 19, no. 2 (1994): 309–36, accessed December 9, 2020. http://www.jstor.org/stable/3174801.

40 Fraser and Gordon, "A Genealogy of Dependency," 320.

41 Ibid., 318.

42 Baker, "The Domestication of Politics."

43 Catherine Rymph, *Republican Women: Feminism and Conservatism from Suffrage through the Rise of the New Right* (Chapel Hill: University of North Carolina Press, 2006).

44 Catherine Gilbert Murdock, *Domesticating Drink: Women, Men, and Alcohol in America, 1870–1940* (Baltimore, MD: John Hopkins University Press, 1998).

45 Coverture refers to the legal doctrine where a woman's rights and obligations become subsumed by her husband once they are married. Under coverture, a woman's wages and most of her property legally belong to her husband.

46 Amy Dru Stanley, "Conjugal Bonds and Wage Labor," *The Journal of American History* 75, no. 2 (1988): 471-500.

47 Amy Dru Stanley, *From Bondage to Contract: Wage Labor, Marriage, and the Market in the Age of Slave Emancipation*, (Cambridge: Cambridge University Press, 1998), Ch. 5.

48 Anne L. Schneider and Helen M. Ingram, eds., *Deserving and Entitled: Social Constructions and Public Policy* (Ithaca: State University of New York Press, 2004), 221, accessed January 6, 2021. ProQuest Ebook Central.

49 Curran and Abrams, "Making Men into Dads," 664.

50 Ibid.

51 Ibid.

52 de Coning, field notes, August 2019.

53 Ibid.

54 Ibid.

8

MISOGYNIST INCELS AND MALE SUPREMACIST VIOLENCE

Megan Kelly, Alex DiBranco and Julia R. DeCook

This is an excerpt of the 2021 report, "Misogynist Incels and Male Supremacism: Overview and Recommendations for Addressing the Threat of Male Supremacist Violence," co-published by New America and the Institute for Research on Male Supremacism.[1]

Mass violence connected to incel ideology has increased public and academic scrutiny of incel communities online. We recommend the term misogynist incel (which can be understood linguistically as similar to the construction of the term racist skinhead) to distinguish the male supremacist ideology and movement from personal identification with the term incel. In this chapter, we trace the history of the misogynist incel movement and describe its ideology. Misogynist incel beliefs develop from a male supremacist culture that consistently fails to mitigate violence against women and girls, and teaches men that they are entitled to women for sexual and romantic fulfillment and that women are only valued for their instrumentality to these ends. Although misogynist incels use more extreme dehumanizing language and glorification of violence, their belief systems and ideologies are developed from and supported by the cultural and societal contexts in which they live.

In Santa Barbara in May 2014, a 22-year-old man perpetrated the first attack connected to the "incel" community, a group of people who identify as "involuntarily celibate" due to a claimed inability to find sexual and romantic partners. He set out to kill women at a sorority but was unable to gain entrance, attacking passersby instead. At the time, most coverage mistakenly identified the perpetrator as a "failed pickup artist," due to his activity in an online forum oriented toward men dissatisfied with the industry that promised to teach them how to seduce women. For years after the attack, there was no substantial media attention to the incel community. Yet over that same time period, the manifesto and

DOI: 10.4324/9781003164722-11

videos produced by the Santa Barbara attacker influenced the development of a movement of misogynist incel men, shaped around entitlement to sex and dehumanization of women.

In 2018, an attack in Toronto perpetrated by a self-identified incel man, running over and killing ten people with a van, drew widespread attention from North American media to the incel community for the first time. This attack was followed six months later by a misogynist attack on a yoga class in Tallahassee, Florida, by a man who had previously compared himself to the Santa Barbara perpetrator.

In the years since, incel communities have captured a piece of the public, academic, and the policy world's imagination. Numerous news pieces, journal articles, policy papers, and other coverage have appeared. However, this attention has carried significant and potentially harmful oversights and misconceptions, beginning with the way the term "incel" is used. The (heterosexual, cisgender) men-only misogynist movement whose growth is of concern now should be differentiated from the original use of the term, which dates to a 1990s gender-neutral community founded by a bisexual woman. The Institute for Research on Male Supremacism recommends the term **misogynist incel** (similar to the construction of the term "racist skinhead") to distinguish the male supremacist *ideology* and *movement* from personal identification with the term incel. This term will be used throughout the report.

In this policy brief, we explore the history of incel identity and the development of a new misogynist ideology, explaining core concepts related to dehumanization and entitlement, significant frameworks such as the "red pill" and "black pill," and violence as central to the movement ideology. In this brief format, we provide only a short overview of additional issues worthy of extensive analysis, such as race in incel communities. Our focus here is on conveying information most relevant to understanding and addressing potential violence by misogynist incel perpetrators.

History

As the women's rights movement undermined the patriarchal status quo in the 1970s, the seeds for new ideologies and movements aiming to reinstate men's dominance were planted in the United States and Canada. This included new secular misogynist ideologies, like the "men's rights movement," which denies the existence of patriarchy and presents men, not women, as the true victims of sexism and discrimination.[2] The so-called seduction industry developed, an enterprise to sell seminars and media promising to teach men how to seduce or "pick up" women, leading to these men being called "pickup artists (PUAs)."

Women face disproportionate gender-based violence, from domestic abuse to sexual violence to serial killings. Their movements for equality have also been met with violence. Men—including police officers—assaulted women suffragists protesting for their right to vote in the early 1900s, responding to the threat to men's dominance. As the feminist movement further transformed the system of men's control, in 1989, a Canadian man perpetrated the first solo act of mass violence documented as primarily motivated by misogynist ideology. He stated his motivation for an attack on women engineering students at Montreal's École Polytechnique, as "fighting feminism." (Until 2020, the 14 women killed marked Canada's most deadly act of mass violence.)[3]

The expansion of internet access and online discussion forums in the 1990s and 2000s enabled new online communities and wider spread of ideologies—including cross-pollination by users bringing ideas and beliefs across forums. The first PUA forum, alt.seduction.fast, founded in 1994, facilitated the industry's expansion to a community subculture.[4] Among the new forums emerging in the 1990s was Alana's Involuntary Celibacy Project, where the term "incel" was coined. Founded by a bisexual woman in Toronto, the forum aimed to support people who wanted but lacked romantic relationships.[5] While this forum was not designed from a misogynist worldview, the audiences for PUA and incel communities overlapped with respect to men dissatisfied with their sexual experience and shaped by the sexual entitlement and dehumanization toward women endemic in society. (The anonymous forum 4chan, founded in 2003, became another favored space for PUAs, incels, and varied misogynist and racist perspectives to interact.)[6]

PUA belief in a "sexual marketplace" influences the misogynist element of the incel community. According to this framework, every person has a "sexual market value" (SMV) informed by characteristics including, but not limited to, physical looks, fitness, age, wealth, and social class. PUA forums claim that feminism brought about and women control this system, seeking men with a higher SMV than their own (termed "female hypergamy"). This leads, they assert, to a distribution of women following the 80/20 rule: 80% of women pursue the top 20% of men, leaving the bottom 20% of women for the remaining 80% of men.[7] PUAs suggest men improve their SMV by learning "game" (techniques to seduce women), earning more money, and/or improving their physical appearance through working out. This presents women as shallow, manipulatable, and undeserving of respect or empathy, and men as victims of an unfair feminist system. These beliefs also feed Red Pill philosophy (discussed later), which "awakens" men to the supposed reality of feminist control.

In the mid-2000s, game strategies and PUA culture gained pop culture recognition through the best-selling 2005 book *The Game* by journalist Neil Strauss, who immersed himself in PUA culture, followed by a 2007 VH1 reality show *The Pick-Up Artist*.[8] PUA sexual entitlement, objectification of women, and dismissiveness toward consent encourage sexual harassment and assault and has been connected to mass violence. In August 2009, a 48-year-old white man and devoted follower of the seduction industry killed three women at an aerobics class in Collier Township, Pennsylvania. His blog recounts his justifications for the attack: lack of sexual and romantic relationships, anger at sexually active girls and women, and rejection by all "30 million" single women.[9] Following PUA industry advice, he emphasized working out and financial security, expecting this formula should deliver women. PUA forums, which advise men in coercion and force under euphemisms such as defeating "last-minute resistance" (LMR), are rife with personal accounts of actions that amount to committing sexual assault. In a rare occurrence in which the perpetrators faced criminal repercussions, two instructors with a PUA company and their student were convicted for the 2013 rape of a San Diego woman, committed as part of their "bootcamp" training. Faced with police investigatory negligence, the survivor herself investigated and discovered her assault detailed in the student's online "field report" on a PUA forum.[10]

PUAHate.com launched a couple months after the Collier Township attack as a forum for men angry at the PUA industry for failing to deliver the promised results (sex with women) but unsurprisingly became a space for hatred against women. The vitriol toward women attracted incel men who had unsuccessfully attempted PUA techniques and those who never tried "game." One such 22-year-old perpetrated the first attack connected to the incel community, killing six people in Santa Barbara in May 2014. He wrote that PUAHate "confirmed many of the theories [he] had about how wicked and degenerate women really are" and "how bleak and cruel the world is due to the evilness of women."[11] PUAHate shut down after the spotlight from the attack, relaunching as SlutHate. com, a name that reflected its focus on women, becoming a major forum for misogynist incel men.

The Santa Barbara attack marks a point at which a men's misogynist incel ideology begins to coalesce as a separate movement organized online, characterized by dehumanization of women, male sexual entitlement, and glorification of violence. (Though little demographic data is available, user surveys and qualitative reviews suggest that the community is comprised mostly of boys and men in their teens and 20s, a slight majority of whom are white.[12]) Misogynist incels laud the Santa Barbara perpetrator, who killed himself after the attack, as a patron saint and martyr. His autobiographical manifesto became a foundational movement document. While it does not use the term "incel," the perpetrator posted on PUAHate.com encouraging incel violence and implying his identification. "If we can't solve our problems, we must DESTROY our problems," he wrote. "One day incels will realize their true strength and numbers, and will overthrow this oppressive feminist system."[13]

In assessing this movement, it is vital to distinguish identification as an incel, in line with its original meaning, from the *misogynist incel* ideology that develops later. Men, like women and non-binary people, can identify as incels or involuntarily celibate, or struggle with finding sexual relationships, without following male supremacist ideology. For instance, the subreddit r/ForeverAlone, named after a 4chan meme depicting (a man's) loneliness, intentionally distanced itself from the misogynist iteration of incel beliefs.

The 2014 Santa Barbara attack was one manifestation of the growth of misogynist online mobilization, as male supremacist forums grew to the tens of

168 Megan Kelly et al.

thousands. The attack preceded, by a few months, the well-known #Gamergate incident, a harassment campaign that targeted women and feminist video game developers and reviewers under the guise of defending ethics in journalism.[14] It brought initial mainstream media attention to the growth of misogynist and racist mobilization online, which by 2016 would be widely known as the alt-right and part of the support for the election of U.S. President Donald Trump.[15] While #Gamergate turned mainstream media attention to this phenomenon, it was but a symptom of a mobilization already well underway.

The Foundational Manifesto

The manifesto and videos created by the Santa Barbara perpetrator present his lack of sexual access to women on demand as not just individual grievance but an injustice, a frame that is found in both leftist and rightist social movement-building.[16] Prior research on mass shooters finds that a "sense of entitlement" to take "revenge against those who have wronged you" transmutes grievances into violence. Perpetrators need to believe their actions are "justified" and "legitimate." They believe in their own superiority and feel "humiliated by their presumed inferiors," as when the Santa Barbara perpetrator complains he is treated like a "mouse" when he is a "god."[17] He claims to be the "true victim," that women and humanity "struck first" in "the war" by denying the pleasure to which he felt entitled. He frames not having sexual access to women as an "injustice," a "crime" perpetrated against him, emphasizing that his attack is "retribution." References to himself as a "magnificent gentleman" and "supreme gentleman" underscore his self-image as the hero of the story.

His decision to target a sorority as a symbol of the most sexually desirable and unattainable women (i.e., white, blonde, and attractive) particularly demonstrates the terroristic intent in the 2014 attack. The perpetrator researched which sorority had "the most beautiful girls," to represent "the kind of girls I've always desired but was never able to have because they all look down on me." The manifesto states the desire to inspire terror in women: "I cannot kill every single female on earth, but I can deliver a devastating blow that will shake all of them to the core of their wicked hearts." Unable to gain access to the selected target on the day of his attack, the perpetrator opened fire on nearby pedestrians.

Dehumanization of women, in multiple forms, is central to the misogynist incel community, and a pervasive aspect of the Santa Barbara manifesto. This should raise significant concern, as research by the Dangerous Speech Project finds that dehumanization is a hallmark of dangerous speech that paves the way for ideological extremist violence by stripping away inhibitions for carrying out violence and removing victims from moral consideration.[18]

Core to male sexual entitlement is a dehumanizing view of women as objects to serve men; this "instrumentality" has been identified as the "defining feature of objectification." Objectified people are reduced to "things," to possessions to be owned, to a "means to goals."[19] Sexual objectification, specifically, "reduces women to their appearance, body, or individual body parts. This leads to a perception of women as interchangeable with others possessing the same physical characteristics."[20] The Santa Barbara perpetrator refers repeatedly to "blondes," depicted as interchangeable and nonunique, as the focus of his desire (demonstrating an obsession with white women). At one point, he describes "giving the female gender one last chance to provide me with the pleasures I deserved from them."[21] The phrasing of expectation that "the female gender" should "provide" sexual pleasure evokes objectification and instrumentality. He views women as wronging him by not performing their function (sexual gratification).

The manifesto also approaches women with a mix of animalistic dehumanization and demonization, asserting, "Women are vicious, evil, barbaric animals, and they need to be treated as such." The manifesto states that women "think like beasts, and in truth, they are beasts. Women are incapable of having morals or thinking rationally."[22] Animalistic dehumanization stimulates feelings of "contempt and disgust" and is commonly deployed in support of genocide.[23] The Santa Barbara perpetrator imagines a "pure" world where women are put in concentration camps to be "deliberately starved to death," using those who survive for "breeding." (Obsession with purity is another hallmark of dangerous speech.) Demonization amps up dehumanization to the level of a crusade, for instance, calling on incels to "overthrow this oppressive feminist system." It "creates moral justification to act against a group perceived as inherently [and irredeemably] evil."[24] Violence against the target becomes not only justified but a "moral good," even an imperative.

Men the Santa Barbara perpetrator perceives as sexually successful appear as secondary targets in his rhetoric. The perpetrator dehumanizes "popular" men as pleasure-seeking "brutes" and refers to both men and women with statements like, "you are animals and I will slaughter you like animals." Despite being half-Asian himself, the perpetrator expresses heightened rage when he sees "inferior" Black, Latino, or "full-blooded" Asian men with white women, and claims, "I deserve it more" as a "descendant of British aristocracy."[25]

Increasing Rhetoric of Dehumanization

The themes found in the Santa Barbara manifesto have been picked up, elaborated on, and evolved in new directions in misogynist incel discourse. A Sluthate. com comment six months after the 2014 attack, on a thread about "incel shooting sprees," explicitly stated the instrumentality toward and commoditization of women's bodies, asserting that every person deserves to have basic needs met like food, shelter, and, "if you are a male, sexual access to attractive females as that is considered a basic need for men as well."[26]

New objectifying terms in the guise of memes developed, growing through the online forum 4chan. The "beautiful blondes" of the Santa Barbara manifesto are exemplified by the meme of "Stacys" (also "Stacies"), sexually desirable (high SMV) white women stereotyped as blonde and curvy. Meanwhile, "attractive, popular men who are sexually successful with women" are memed as "Chads."[27] The 2018 Toronto van attack perpetrator called for the overthrow of "Chads and Stacys."[28] Memes are often taken as not serious, ironic, or humorous, but they also can be assessed as forms of objectification: all sexually desirable women are so interchangeable they are given the same name, a term that reduces them to a set of sexualized physical characteristics. (Another, meme "Becky," refers to women viewed as less desirable—but more attainable—however, this term appears infrequently in misogynist incel forums.) Even "Chads" are interchangeable and defined by appearance, significant given that such men have been secondary targets for violence. Misogynist incels have racialized—and racist—terms for non-white "Chads"; the most-used such term, "Tyrone," refers to Black men, who are viewed as having a sexual advantage with women.

Two other disparaging terms popularized through 4chan are used frequently by misogynist incels as well as the alt-right: "normies" and "cucks." The word "cuck," shortened from cuckold (a man whose wife or partner is sexually unfaithful), disparages certain men as servile, submissive, and weak. *Cucks, Chads, Stacys*, and *Beckys* are all "normies," men and women viewed as conforming to society, i.e., "normal," non-incels. This categorization sets up an in-group/out-group dynamic also characteristic of dangerous speech. Misogynist incel men have voiced support for violence committed even by non-incels because the victims were "normies." For instance, r/Incels posters lauded the 2017 Las Vegas shooter, who killed 58 people attending a concert, for killing "normies," sympathizing and identifying with the perpetrator, even though he had a live-in girlfriend and was not an incel.[29]

While most studies and media on incels have focused on the terms "Chads" and "Stacys" as distinguishing the community, this does not accurately reflect the severity and popularity of dehumanization toward women in contemporary misogynist incel forums. Mechanistic dehumanization, not significant in the Santa Barbara manifesto, has become central to misogynist incel rhetoric, reducing women to machines with no capacity for emotion. This "sanitizes violence against the target" so that killing is reduced to "pulling the plug of an inanimate object. In fact, sometimes denying the other group the ability to feel any emotion may motivate excusing one's own collective abuses against them."[30] It is similar to objectification in perceiving its targets as interchangeable and instrumental. The terms "femoid" or "foid," abbreviations for "female humanoid" or "Female Humanoid Organism," have far outpaced the use of the term "Stacy." On incels. co, *foid* is used four times as often as *Stacy/Stacie*. Yet "Chad" remains the primary term for "sexually successful" men. While other men can be targets, women are the focus of misogynist incel dehumanization and violence.

Beyond the memes and ubiquitous mechanistic dehumanization, misogynist incel men have developed an array of other dehumanizing and derogatory terms for women. In particular, objectifying language refers to women by demeaning terms for their genitalia, most popularly "roasties" (a vulgar way of describing labia), or just reduces women to "holes." On incels.co, *roastie* appears almost as much as *Stacy/Stacie*. Terms for women considered undesirable for lacking ideal-ized physical features include animalistic epithets, for example, "landwhales," and racist epithets, such as "noodlewhores," a term for Asian women. To give a sense of how common basic dehumanization is when making reference to women, *femoid(s)/foid(s)* alone are used a third as frequently as the neutral terms *women/woman/girl(s)* on incels.co.

Promotion and Glorification of Violence

Following the 2014 attack, positive references to the Santa Barbara perpetra-tor, such as "Supreme Gentleman," which he called himself, as a saint became popular in misogynist incel spaces such as SlutHate.com, 4chan, and later incels. co.[31] Encouraging others to "go ER" (the initials of the Santa Barbara perpetra-tor), meaning to commit mass murder and then kill oneself, is one of many ways violence is promoted and glorified. Misogynist incels celebrate the anniversary of the attack, May 23, as the perpetrator's saint's day. Supporters have lamented that the perpetrator failed to gain access to the sorority and kill more women as planned and suggested other targets, for instance, a post advocating, "If incels go ER they should target feminists. Gender studies class would be a good location to go ER."[32] Mass fear and intimidation through violence are often promoted as the only means of achieving change for "inceldom" (see "The Black Pill" section for more on this.)

Glorification of men's violence, whether perpetrated by an incel or not, has become a distinguishing characteristic of the misogynist incel movement, as with the support for the 2017 Las Vegas shooting. Posts tagged as "lifefuel" often cel-ebrate interpersonal or mass violence against women or "normies." Such posts range from sharing news articles about cases of sexual violence or murder of women to the celebration of school shootings or mass killings of "normies." Moonshot CVE tracked three categories of interpersonal violence that appear on incel forums: "violent criminal behavior—including violence against women; actions to emotionally hurt or humiliate women; and actions to make women physically uncomfortable and fearful."[33] "Based," which they define as "not car-ing about being politically incorrect," though can also be understood as calling something awesome or righteous, is also used to approve of interpersonal vio-lence. Misogynist incels claim a number of men who committed attacks before widespread use of the term incel, such as the Oklahoma City bomber and the Virginia Tech shooter, as sharing their identity and as "saints" or "heroes" (or "hERos").[34] The shared features of most of the chosen "saints" are men who perpetuated mass violence, had demonstrated some form of violence or animosity toward women, and in some cases had a history of isolation or social exclusion.

Misogynist incel men have advocated for the legalization of violent actions to punish and control women, such as rape and beating. Posts have suggested legal-ized violence against women partners as a justified response to disobedience, not providing sex, or otherwise failing to "fulfill their feminine role."[35] This aligns

172 Megan Kelly et al.

them with elements of the PUA and Red Pill movements that defend and seek to legalize violence against women. Nostalgia for traditional gender norms, for a past in which women were coerced by societal structure into marriage as a means of support, pervades male supremacist ideologies. Jordan Peterson, a psychologist and professor at the University of Toronto and an ideologue popular with Red Pill adherents, advocated the concept of "enforced monogamy" as the "cure" for mass violence like the 2018 Toronto van attack driven by anger over women's rejection.[36] This appeals to misogynist incels as a means of overcoming the 80/20 rule and distributing women, one to each man.

Another disturbing development in the past few years has been rhetoric supporting pedophilia. Some misogynist incel men attempt to justify pedophilia by stating that underage girls (particularly pre-teen) are more likely to be "pure" by not yet having had sexual contact and are easier to influence and control. They claim that being with a "pure" girl is the only way to truly "ascend inceldom," as women who have had previous sexual relationships are tainted, and sex with them borders on being cuckolded. Nathan Larson—creator of misogynist sites including incelopocalypse and "raping girls is fun," and an active participant on other misogynist incel forums—is a major promoter of pedophilia and rape. (He also ran for Congress in Virginia in 2018 to promote this agenda.)[37] The acceptance of Larson in these spaces (which practice gatekeeping around incel identity), despite not being an incel, suggests that his misogynist content and agenda were valued. On incels.co, he regularly posted advocating the legalization of pedophilia, incest, and rape, until being banned for in-fighting.

Red Pill to Black Pill

The "Red Pill," a term that comes from the 1999 film *The Matrix*, has become a framework for individuals to describe their awakening to some previously hidden supposed reality. The major contemporary secular male supremacist movements—PUAs, men's rights activists, The Red Pill, and Men Going Their Own Way (MGTOW)—all use this terminology to describe their "realization" that men do not hold systemic power or privilege. Instead, they awaken to the "truth" that socially, economically, and sexually men are at the whims of women's (and feminists') power and desires. As in the film, to be bluepilled is to accept the mainstream narrative and choose to live in ignorance of the "truths" of the world. Red Pillers see themselves as intellectually superior to bluepilled "normies." The Red Pill terminology grew in male supremacist forums and was adopted more broadly by far-right and white supremacist groups to describe their own versions of awakenings, conspiracist worldviews that often overlap with male supremacist positions, such as antifeminism.[38]

Beginning around 2016, misogynist incel forums began to shift from a "Red Pill" to an increasing "Black Pill" mentality. This belief system accepts the Red Pill view of a society dominated by women but rejects individual-level attempts such as learning "game" to achieve a sexual relationship with women as

Misogynist Incels and Male Supremacist 173

misguided, asserting that only change at a societal level has the possibility to be effective. Black Pill adherents believe that looks are genetically determined and that women choose sexual partners based solely on physical features ("lookism"), so whether or not a person will be an incel is predetermined.[39] Misogynist incels attempt to prove the "truth" of the Black Pill through misreadings of scientific studies, online dating datasets, and their own "experiments" to prove that women only care about a man's physical looks. Although some incels still seek out plastic surgery, work out ("gym maxxing"), or try to otherwise improve their physical features, many believe such strategies are pointless, as "inceldom" is a problem with society, not the individual. Blackpilled incels are aware of appearance and sociability/game strategies and reject them as solutions.

The Black Pill philosophy typically offers only two options for what to do with their new accepted reality: accept their fate as an incel or try to change society to their benefit—usually advocated as potentially achievable by means of mass violence and terror, not politics or other methods of change. "Copes" are looked down on as methods of coping without changing the unjust system, including denying the reality of the Black Pill.

For those who choose to accept their blackpilled fate, suicide is often presented as the most inevitable solution; it is also encouraged in misogynist incel communities as a form of sacrificial violence and/or martyrdom. Incels talk about potential self-harm, giving up hope, or suicide by using phrases such as "rope" (committing suicide by hanging oneself), "LDAR" (lay down and rot), or "suifuel" (suicide fuel). "Suifuel," "it's over," "brutal," and "it never began" are popular responses to and tags for posts that members feel exemplify the truth of the Black Pill. Internal polls shared on incels.co have asked members when they think they will "rope." In some cases, users explicitly state, "I have to kill myself," or say that they will commit suicide by the time they are a certain age if they are still an incel.[40] While some fellow members respond to suicidal comments with sympathy, others urge posters on with harmful comments, asking those who have expressed suicidal ideation why they are still posting and have not yet attempted suicide. When active members stop posting for an extended period of time, this frequently leads to forum speculation that they have completed suicide; however, that absence could instead represent men withdrawing from the online community, and data is not currently available to ascertain what is occurring.

Regardless, there is a substantial difference between a community being vulnerable to self-harm and promoting and threatening violence against others. Members expressing suicidal ideation on misogynist incel forums are also encouraged to "go ER" or "be a hERo," meaning to commit mass murder before committing suicide. Many misogynist incels don't just advocate for suicide as a solution to inceldom but also to create structural change through first committing mass violence. As with the Santa Barbara perpetrator, martyrdom is revered; the Toronto van attacker told police he had hoped to commit "suicide by cop," a common plan for perpetrators of mass violence.[41] For Black Pill adherents seeking to change society rather than simply accept their fate, the use of mass violence to

174 Megan Kelly et al.

forcibly overthrow the system and force "normies" to take notice is positioned as a key pathway to structural change.

A November 2014 Sluthate.com thread on "incel shooting sprees" demonstrates the roots of this thinking, arguing that such mass bloodshed is "the only way that sluts and alphas will realize and accept that there are serious consequences for allowing so many males to live their lives in misery."[42] This use of mass violence to create social change in favor of incels' worldview has been referred to as the "Incel Rebellion" or "Beta Uprising." The 2018 Toronto van attack perpetrator stated that the "Incel Rebellion has already begun" in a Facebook post just prior to his attack and two days before he had posted on 4chan that "there would be another beta uprising." Misogynist incels that glorify violence posit that by eliminating women and "Chads," they are working to "purify" society and to frighten those who have not taken the Red Pill or the Black Pill.[43]

A Brief Overview of Intersections with Race and Class

Another component of the Black Pill is the claimed realities of racial hierarchy in the pursuit of sexual and romantic relationships. In misogynist incel communities, the acronym "JBW" (Just Be White) is a popular expression of white men's perceived sexual advantages. Data released by dating websites and applications that point to a preference for white men over other ethnicities are pointed to as evidence of all women's racism, another justification for dehumanizing women. A catch-all label, "ethniccels," refers to non-white incels, with posts that aim to scientifically prove the undesirability of non-white men in the West and beyond. The "Scientific Blackpill" draws on studies that have shown how Black and Latino men are hypersexualized and viewed as hypermasculine, while Asian men are desexualized and seen as feminine/weak in Western countries.[44] In incel communities, labels such as "rice-cel" (an East or Southeast Asian incel) or "currycel" (a South Asian incel) are used to refer to the struggles of these incels as unique, pointing out their physical undesirability and emasculation. The Santa Barbara perpetrator (who had a white father and Asian mother) is presented as evidence that Asian men are viewed as less attractive in Western countries and to claim that mixed-race people (particularly men) are more mentally unstable as a result of this. These beliefs are presented as justification for the violent acts he committed, faulting women and a "degenerate society" that allowed for emasculation of Asian men and "race-mixing." The perspectives on race both demonstrate the influence of white supremacist beliefs and are used as grounds to further justify violence by non-white men.

A 2020 member survey of a misogynist incel forum found that the majority of respondents were young men under 25, living with their parents while working or attending school. The class dimension of incel communities has been a subject of speculation, particularly the use of the term "NEET": "not in employment, education, or training."[45] However, evidence to demonstrate that economic strain motivates incel misogyny and violence is lacking. The term "NEET" does

Misogynist Incels and Male Supremacist 175

not necessarily relate at all to sexual activity; men who do not identify as incel call themselves "NEET" on online forums like 4chan, and the majority of incels do work or attend school. Anecdotes describing being "NEET" in misogynist incel forums indicate it can be in part a choice to opt-out from the economy as part of a Black Pill mentality, permitting young men with familial safety nets to choose not to pursue employment as irrelevant to their incel status. Similarly, the term "LDAR" can be less suggestive of suicidal ideation and more of refusing to take an active part in society in the face of perceived systemic injustice.

On the other hand, when considering the potential impact of economic status, *higher* class status may increase a sense of entitlement for those adhering to a "red pill" philosophy that views wealth as part of SMV. The Santa Barbara perpetrator described attending red carpet premieres thanks to his director father; his parents paid for his college tuition, rent, car, and a monthly allowance of 500 dollars, plus monetary gifts from grandparents, which he saved to buy the guns for his attack. (Given that he dropped out of school and did not work, he could be categorized as "NEET," but this would certainly not imply his class privilege accurately.)[46] He viewed women's inattention even with his expensive car and designer clothes as part of the injustice against him, suggesting that money increased his expectation and feeling of entitlement.

Mass Violence and Terrorism Since Santa Barbara

Since 2014, multiple acts of mass violence and attempted violence in the United States and Canada have referenced the Santa Barbara perpetrator or been connected to misogynist incel ideology. In the first couple of years following the attack, there was one serious thwarted threat of mass violence and one successful attack that referenced the 2014 attack: in 2015, the Santa Barbara perpetrator was praised in the manifesto of the Umpqua Community College shooter, who also wrote about his own lack of sexual relationships.[47] (In December 2017 and February 2018, two mass shootings occurred in which the perpetrators had mentioned the Santa Barbara perpetrator positively online, though without indication that misogynist incel ideology motivated them.)

The media awareness of incels changed with the April 2018 Toronto van attack by a perpetrator who explicitly wrote before killing ten people, "The Incel Rebellion has already begun! We will overthrow all the Chads and Stacys! All hail the Supreme Gentleman [Santa Barbara perpetrator]!"[48] While most of these perpetrators of mass violence killed themselves at the end of their attacks, the Toronto van perpetrator survived and went on to describe his knowledge of misogynist incel ideology in a police interview (he is now undergoing trial). This attack was followed six months later by a 40-year-old man, who had compared his younger self to the Santa Barbara perpetrator, who opened fire at a yoga class in Tallahassee, Florida, killing two women, cementing the new attention to the ideology.[49] Any time perpetrators choose spaces associated symbolically with young attractive women, such as a sorority or yoga class, that suggests a

176 Megan Kelly et al.

misogynist and potentially terrorist motivation, similar to the targeting of synagogues or mosques to represent anti-Semitic and anti-Muslim ideologies.

Military and law enforcement in the United States began to pay more attention to incels following the June 2019 shooting (no fatalities) at the Earle Cabell Federal Building in Dallas, Texas, by a perpetrator who had posted memes associated with incel communities.[50] In Canada, another attack in Toronto in February 2020, in which a man used a machete to kill one woman and injure another who worked at Crown Spa erotic massage, was charged for the first time as incel extremist terrorism.[51] In May 2020, at the Westgate shopping center in Arizona, a man shot three people while live-streaming video before being arrested. (None of the victims died.) He identified himself as an incel who had been rejected by women, seeking to target couples, to make them feel his pain.[52] In June 2020, a Virginia bomb-maker was arrested after injuring himself with his own explosives. Investigators found a letter imagining targeting "hot cheerleaders," with the statement, "I will not be afraid of the consequences no matter what I will be heroic I will make a statement like Elliott Rodgers did."[53]

While focused on North America, as thus far related mass violence has been geographically circumscribed, the online nature of this movement facilitates its influence across countries with English-speaking populations and should be approached as a transnational threat. In 2020, for instance, a bomb-maker connected to the misogynist incel movement was arrested in Britain.[54] And a recent report by the Swedish Defence Research Institute found that the United States and United Kingdom were the most common nationalities across incel forums but that Sweden had the most participants on a per capita ratio.[55]

The question of whether to label acts of misogynist incel violence as terrorism has been ongoing. Namely, the debate centers around both what movements and acts are included under the definition of terrorism, as well as the discussions over the pros and cons of labeling a group or an act "terrorist." Not all attacks perpetrated by misogynist incels should be categorized as terrorist acts; however, acts of mass violence with clear ideological motivations and goals, like the 2014 Santa Barbara attack and 2018 Toronto van attack, fit the category of terrorism. The Santa Barbara perpetrator makes clear that because he "cannot kill every single female on earth," he plans an attack to create fear and hopes to inspire others.[56]

Though misogynist incels are often perceived as a movement without political aims, violent perpetrators have the same type of far-reaching aims that white nationalists have: to completely change the culture and politics of society to favor their own group. Political ideas supported by misogynist incels range from concentration camps for women to mandating government-sponsored girlfriends and enforced monogamy to wiping out most of the existing "alpha" men and women. The Santa Barbara perpetrator had his own vision for an ideal society that his manifesto conveys. The specifics of a political agenda are not cohesively developed for the overall movement; however, they see themselves as an oppressed group that can only improve their situation through a total overthrow and restructuring of society.

Misogynist Incels and Male Supremacist **177**

While incels have taken up a prominent place in popular consciousness since 2018, approaches that remain aware of other forms of male supremacism will be more effective. Some mainstream journalists have erred in attempting to connect unrelated misogynist violence in Europe and North America to incels. In the case of the February 2020 attack in Hanau, Germany, by a far-right perpetrator, some outlets rushed to claim the attacker was an incel because of a passage in his manifesto stating that he had not been in a relationship with a woman for 18 years. The manifesto demonstrated misogynist beliefs, but not a connection to incel ideology. As scholars Greta Jasser, Megan Kelly, and Ann-Kathrin Rothermel have written, this focus only on incels obscures the extent to which male supremacism and misogyny animate beliefs and violence outside that specific movement.[57]

A note from the authors: Both the risks of work on male supremacism and the strain of the dehumanizing subject matter itself impact the ability of researchers to do this work. Many researchers, journalists, and activists lack access to mental health services to help them process the psychological impact of studying misogynist content and violence. Many therapists may not be well-equipped themselves to support clients doing this kind of work. An investment in designing and creating services to support researchers working on these topics, in addition to more funding and resources for conducting research projects, are much-needed components toward enabling this type of vital research to continue.

Notes

1 Available at https://www.newamerica.org/political-reform/reports/misogynist-incels-and-male supremacism/ and used under CC BY 4.0 license.
2 See, for instance, Warren Farrell, *The Myth of Male Power* (New York: Simon and Schuster, 1993); Christina Hoff Sommers, *Who Stole Feminism?: How Women Have Betrayed Women* (New York: Simon and Schuster, 1994); Alex DiBranco, "Mobilizing Misogyny," *The Public Eye* (Winter 2017): 11–16, https://www.politicalresearch. org/2017/03/08/mobilizing-misogyny.
3 Alex DiBranco, "The First Anti-feminist Massacre," *Political Research Associates*, December 6, 2019, https://www.politicalresearch.org/2019/12/06/first-anti-feminist-massacre.
4 Alice Marwick and Rebecca Lewis, *Media Manipulation and Disinformation Online* (Data & Society Research Institute, 2017), https://datasociety.net/wp-content/uploads/2017/05/DataAndSociety_MediaManipulationAndDisinformation Online-1.pdf.
5 Jim Taylor, "The Woman Who Founded the 'Incel' Movement," *BBC News*, August 29, 2018, https://www.bbc.com/news/world-us-canada-45284455.
6 Caitlin Dewey, "Absolutely Everything You Need to Know to Understand 4chan, The Internet's Own Bogeyman," *Washington Post*, September 25, 2014, https://www. washingtonpost.com/news/the-intersect/wp/2014/09/25/absolutely-everything-you-need-to-know-to-understand-4chan-the-internets-own-bogeyman/.
7 "Incels (Involuntary Celibates)," *ADL*, accessed December 14, 2020, https://www. adl.org/resources/backgrounders/incels-involuntary-celibates.
8 Alex Williams, "Would the Pickup Artist Stand a Chance in the #MeToo Era?," *New York Times*, July 13, 2018, https://www.nytimes.com/2018/07/13/style/the-game-pickup-artists-post-metoo.html.

9 ABC News, "George Sodini's Blog: Full Text by Alleged Gym Shooter," *ABC News*, August 5, 2009, https://abcnews.go.com/US/story?id=8258001&page=1.

10 Brandy Zadrozny, "The Pickup Artist Rape Ring," *Daily Beast*, September 21, 2016, https://www.thedailybeast.com/pickup-artists-preyed-on-drunk-women-brought-them-home-and-raped-them.

11 Elliot Rodger, "My Twisted World: The Story of Elliot Rodger," 2014, 118.

12 "Online Poll Results Provide New Insights into Incel Community," *ADL*, September 10, 2020, https://www.adl.org/blog/online-poll-results-provide-new-insights-into-incel-community.

13 Josh Glasstetter, "Shooting Suspect Elliot Rodger's Misogynistic Posts Point to Motive," Southern Poverty Law Center, 2014, https://www.splcenter.org/hatewatch/2014/05/23/shooting-suspect-elliot-rodgers-misogynistic-posts-point-motive.

14 Caitlin Dewey, "The Only Guide to Gamergate You Will Ever Need to Read," *Washington Post*, October 14, 2014, https://www.washingtonpost.com/news/the-intersect/wp/2014/10/14/the-only-guide-to-gamergate-you-will-ever-need-to-read/.

15 Matt Lees, "What Gamergate Should Have Taught Us about the 'Alt-Right'," *The Guardian*, December 1, 2016, https://www.theguardian.com/technology/2016/dec/01/gamergate-alt-right-hate-trump.

16 Karl-Dieter Opp, "Grievances and Participation in Social Movements," *American Sociological Review* 53 (December 1988): 853–64; Kristin Luker, *Abortion and the Politics of Motherhood* (Berkely: University of California Press, 1984).

17 Rachel Kalish and Michael Kimmel, "Suicide by Mass Murder: Masculinity, Aggrieved Entitlement, and Rampage School Shootings," *Health Sociology Review* 19, no. 4 (2010): 451–64, Rodger, "My Twisted World."

18 Susan Benesch et al., "Dangerous Speech: A Practical Guide," *Dangerous Speech Project*, December 31, 2018, https://dangerousspeech.org/guide/.

19 Edward Orehek and Casey G. Weaverling, "On the Nature of Objectification: Implications of Considering People as Means to Goals," *Perspectives on Psychological Science* 12 (August 2017): 720.

20 Ibid.

21 Rodger, "My Twisted World," 121.

22 Ibid., 136.

23 Roger Giner-Sorolla, Leidner Bernhard, and Emanuele Castano, "Dehumanization, Demonization, and Morality Shifting," in *Extremism and the Psychology of Uncertainty*, eds. Michael A. Hogg and Danielle L. Blaylock (Oxford: Blackwell Publishing Ltd, 2012), 169.

24 Giner-Sorolla et al., "Dehumanization, Demonization, and Morality Shifting," 169.

25 Rodger, "My Twisted World," 121, 84.

26 "Why Are So Many of You against Incel Shooting Sprees?" *Sluthate*, archived February 26, 2015, *Internet Archive*, https://web.archive.org/web/20150226223226, http://sluthate.com/viewtopic.php?f=2&t=41005.

27 "Incels (involuntary celibates)."

28 John Bacon, "Incel: What It Is and Why Alek Minassian Praised Elliot Rodger," *USA Today*, April 25, 2018, https://www.usatoday.com/story/news/nation/2018/04/25/incel-what-and-why-alek-minassian-praised-elliot-rodger/549577002/.

29 David Futrelle, "Reddit Incels Celebrate Deaths of 'Normies' in Las Vegas Mass Shooting," *We Hunted the Mammoth*, October 2, 2017, http://wehuntedthemammoth.

com/2017/10/02/reddit-incels-celebrate-deaths-of-normies-in-las-vegas-mass-shooting/.

30 Giner-Sorolla et al., "Dehumanization, Demonization, and Morality Shifting," 169.

31 Stassa Edwards, "Saint Elliot Rodger and the 'Incels' Who Canonize Him," *Jezebel*, April 27, 2018, https://jezebel.com/saint-elliot-rodger-and-the-incels-who-canonize-him-1825567815.

32 Robyn Pennacchia, "'Beta Males' Want to Kill Women Because They Can't Get Laid," *Bust Magazine*, February/March 2016, https://bust.com/feminism/15551-beta-males-want-to-kill-women-because-they-can-t-get-laid.html.

33 *Incels: A Guide to Symbols and Terminology* (Moonshot CVE, May 2020), http://moonshotcve.com/incels-symbols-and-terminology/.

34 "Happy Birthday, Theodore J. Kaczynski," *Incels.co*, May 22, 2020, https://incels.co/threads/happy-birthday-theodore-j-kaczynski.207162/.

35 "[Rant] Why Aren't Beatings against Women Legalized?" *Truecels*, archived November 24, 2018, PDF. Personal Dataset. Available Upon Request.

36 Tabatha Southey, "The Context of Jordan Peterson's Thoughts on 'Enforced Monogamy'," *Maclean's*, May 25, 2018, https://www.macleans.ca/opinion/the-context-of-jordan-petersons-thoughts-on-enforced-monogamy/.

37 Tim Squirrell, "Nathan Larson, The Self-Described Incel Paedophile, Is Running for Congress. This Is How He Groomed Vulnerable Young Men," *Independent*, June 5, 2018, https://www.independent.co.uk/voices/nathan-larson-incel-paedophile-dark-web-congress-virginia-a8384391.html.

38 *Incels.*

39 Ibid.

40 "I Have to Kill Myself," *Incels.co*, November 28, 2019, https://incels.co/threads/i-have-to-kill-myself.160889/.

41 Liam Casey, "Alek Minassian's Former Classmates Hope for Answers at Upcoming Toronto Van Attack Trial," *Canadian Broadcasting Corporation*, November 8, 2020, https://www.cbc.ca/news/canada/toronto/alek-minassian-toronto-van-attack-trial-1.5794539.

42 "Why Are So Many of You against Incel Shooting Sprees?"

43 Anders Wallace and Julia DeCook, "The Gods and Monsters of Incelistan," *The Good Men Project*, June 19, 2018, https://goodmenproject.com/featured-content/the-gods-and-monsters-of-incelistan-phtz/.

44 "Scientific Blackpill," *Incels Wiki*, accessed December 14, 2020, https://incels.wiki/w/Scientific_Blackpill.

45 "Online Poll Results Provide New Insights into Incel Community."

46 Rodger, "My Twisted World."

47 Rick Anderson, "'Here I Am, 26, with No Friends, No Job, No Girlfriend': Shooter's Manifesto Offers Clues to 2015 Oregon College Rampage," *Los Angeles Times*, September 23, 2017, https://www.latimes.com/nation/la-na-school-shootings-2017-story.html. The perpetrators of the December 2017 Aztec High School shooting and the February 2018 Parkland shooting had both mentioned the Santa Barbara perpetrator positively online, though their attacks did not appear to be directly motivated by misogynist incel ideology.

48 Bacon, "Incel."

49 Madeline Holcombe, Nicole Chavez, and Marlena Baldacci, "Florida Yoga Studio Shooter Planned Attack for Months and Had 'Lifetime of Misogynistic Attitudes,' Police Say," *CNN*, February 13, 2019, https://www.cnn.com/2019/02/13/us/tallahassee-yoga-studio-shooting/index.html.

50 Kelly Weill and Justin Glawe, "Dalla Federal Building Shooter Posted Far-Right Memes about Nazis and Confederacy," *Daily Beast*, June 17, 2019, https://www.thedailybeast.com/dallas-federal-building-shooter-posted-far-right-memes-about-nazis-and-confederacy.

51 Stewart Bell, Andrew Russel, and Catherine McDonald, "Deadly Attack at Toronto Erotic Spa Was Incel Terrorism, Police Allege," *Global News*, May 19, 2020, https://globalnews.ca/news/6910670/toronto-spa-terrorism-incel/.

52 Ray Stern, "The Westgate Shooter Was an Incel Who Wanted Couples to Feel 'Pain,'" *Phoenix New Times*, May 22, 2020, https://www.phoenixnewtimes.com/news/arizona-westgate-glendale-shooter-was-an-incel-who-targeted-couples-armando-hernandez-11471873.

53 "Incels (involuntary celibates)."

54 "Middlesbrough Fantasist Anwar Driouich Jailed for Explosive Substance," *BBC News*, March 27, 2020, https://www.bbc.com/news/uk-england-tees-52071379.

55 "Reader's Digest – 13 March 2020," *Tech Against Terrorism*, March 13, 2020, https://www.techagainstterrorism.org/2020/03/13/readers-digest-13-march-2020/.

56 Rodger, "My Twisted World."

57 Greta Jasser, Megan Kelly, and Ann-Kathrin Rothermel, "Male Supremacism and the Hanau Terrorist Attack: Between Online Misogyny and Far-Right Violence," International Centre for Counter-Terrorism – The Hague, 2020, https://icct.nl/publication/male-supremacism-and-the-hanau-terrorist-attack-between-online-misogyny-and-far-right-violence/.

PART IV
Intersections

9

FIGHT CLUB

Gavin McInnes, the Proud Boys, and Male Supremacism

Meadhbh Park

The new far right markets itself as an ideology to counteract multiculturalism, political correctness, and leftist social issues and portrays itself as an avenue to regain status and control. It also positions itself as an antidote to feminism, which is conveyed as an immediate threat to men, masculinity, and the continuation of Western civilization in general. At its core, the new far right perpetuates nostalgia for a past where white men dominated the powerful positions of society, both socially and politically. The motivations of individuals who join the new far right are varied, and the means of radicalization are multifaceted. This essay explores male supremacy as a leading motivator for men to join "alt-right" groups, by analyzing the rhetoric of Gavin McInnes, the founder of the Proud Boys. This essay situates the Proud Boys in the sphere of male supremacism and shows that the new far right is heavily influenced by male supremacist ideology and masculinity. This chapter hopes to demonstrate that we can better understand "alt-right" groups such as the Proud Boys through the lens of male supremacism and masculinity rather than solely through the lens of white supremacy.

> You're not a man unless you have beaten the shit out of someone, had the shit beaten out of you, had your heart broken and broken a heart—those are the four minimums.
>
> *Gavin McInnes*

The Proud Boys, a far-right group that only allows cisgender men to join, gained substantial public notoriety in 2020 when their name was tied with white supremacy during the first United States presidential debate between Donald Trump and Joe Biden. Once portrayed as an obscure "fraternity of 'western chauvinists'"[1] with a flair for street fighting and intimidation, they have grown and morphed since their founding during the 2016 U.S. election season. They have claimed

DOI: 10.4324/9781003164722-13

many forms, including "a men's club that meets about once a month to drink beer,"[2] an unofficial security force for far-right personalities, and a semi-para-military force. Their presence is consistently found at far-right rallies, including QAnon marches,[3] and they organize their own demonstrations and rallies. The Proud Boys have embedded themselves into the landscape of the contemporary far right in the United States and Canada, including the primarily online movement known as the "alt-right," and made a home for themselves among the conspiracy theorists, Islamophobes, neo-Nazis, white supremacists, and male supremacists.

Although the "alt-right" has most often been analyzed through the lens of white supremacist ideology (with the exception of works like those of Matthew N. Lyons, Chapter 3 of this volume), it is important to also assess the movement through the framework of male supremacist ideology and rigid views of masculinity. This chapter demonstrates how masculinity can supersede the racial aspects of the "alt-right" in multiracial groups like the Proud Boys and explores the possibility that cis men join these groups due to the appeal of performative masculinity and male supremacist ideology. Though termed alt-right, the Proud Boys' expanded offline activity argues for categorizing the group more generally as far right, an approach this chapter will largely take.

Masculinity and male supremacism have been frequently overlooked in analysis of the far right, even though these discourses dominate the rhetoric of far-right spaces, including 4Chan, the Daily Stormer, Parler, and 8Kun. In 2016 and 2017, some mainstream media outlets, such as the Associated Press, even created policies to replace the term "alt-right" with white nationalist or white supremacist, ignoring and erasing the role of misogyny as one of the significant pillars of the movement.[4] Casting the alt-right as solely a racially motivated movement has undergone criticism in recent years, as scholars and journalists have argued that a key motivating factor may be masculinity and a so-called crisis of masculinity— or as Chowdhury more accurately calls it, a "crisis of male supremacy." Or to use another term, a crisis in "hegemonic masculinity," the undermining of a system in which cisgender men are dominant.[567] This chapter argues for an intersectional approach that recognizes how appeals to whiteness and masculinity both function within the alt-right and broader far right.

This chapter offers an in-depth analysis of one far-right "thought leader," Proud Boys' founder Gavin McInnes. The aim is to provide an illustrative example of how future research might interrogate the default of focusing narrowly on white supremacist ideology. As a well-known far-right organization often called "white nationalist" rather than "male supremacist" despite its actual demographic makeup and ideology—a group exclusively for cis men that encourages men of color to join and frames itself as pro-Western—the Proud Boys provides an excellent descriptive case.

Crisis of Masculinity

Lamenting a supposed "crisis in masculinity" has become almost a battle cry for the far right. With it comes a sense of impending catastrophe and a call to action. Chowdhury describes this as masculinity's "crisis tendency," wherein masculinity is, at its core, fragile and insecure, requiring constant affirmation to mediate the perpetual crisis.[8] Roose notes shame, humiliation, perceived deep-seated social injury and wounded masculinity are significant factors when analyzing what pushes individuals to violent extremism.[9] Roose also notes that with the decline of the traditional working-class masculinity, and the increase of competition in the workplace from women and non-white men, there has been an increase of "hypermasculinity."[10] In hypermasculinity, "macho" traits and characteristics are performed "to the point of exaggeration."[11] It amplifies the reinforcement of gendered binaries and strict rejection of femininity,[12] glorifying the negative traits often associated with masculinity: violence,[13] hardened sexual attitudes, a view of women as mere conquests, a desire for action and danger, domination and control over all aspects of life, and displays of "virility and physicality."[14]

Raewyn Connell, whose work has been central to the study of masculinities, defines hegemonic masculinity as the "culturally idealized form"[15] of masculinity that encapsulates "the currently most honored way of being a man" and therefore "require[s] all other men to position themselves in relation to it."[16] It has ideologically legitimated the global subordination of women to men.[17] (Connell notes that hegemonic masculinity may not be the most common form of masculinity found in society, instead enacted by only a minority of men.) Beesley and McGuire identify the characteristics of hegemonic masculinity as "physical strength or power, aggressiveness, risk-taking, emotional control, and sexual potency."[18]

Femininity and women are denigrated and subjugated, and the only women considered deserving of respect are those who embody the roles of mother and housewife.[19] Traditional white masculinity casts itself in opposition to other masculinities deemed subordinate; a white man is not a Jewish man nor a black or Asian man. A man is also not homosexual or feminine.[20] Masculinity is set in the context of rigid binaries with no room for deviation or fluidity, such as transgender and non-binary identities.

The form of masculinity, or hypermasculinity, promoted by the Proud Boys deviates from traditional white masculinity in that it makes space for non-white men and homosexual men, while more strictly focusing on the exclusion of trans men and maintaining a somewhat complicated (by the occasional participation of mothers and sisters and "Proud Girls" in supporting the organization's activities) but largely hostile, exclusionary, and disrespectful position toward even white women (including a backlash against the Proud Girls, which was not recognized as an official part of the Proud Boys). A resource mobilization challenge for exclusionary social movements is that the exclusion of more groups of people limits the recruiting ground. White cisgender women have been an important resource in the past for white supremacist and far-right organizing, but the Proud Boys' strong antifeminist position, which on the far right today often encompasses Western white women broadly as all tainted, positions women as the "Other," the enemy. As cis men-only, far-right groups limit their recruiting ground by gender, they have simultaneously loosened the traditional exclusion of cis men of color and gay men, incorporating these men into a new construction of masculinity.

The Roots of the Proud Boys

Proud Boys' leader Gavin McInnes is known both inside the movement and in mainstream media, where he has been featured in hundreds of videos expressing his views. A Canadian born in Glasgow, McInnes was one of the founders of *Voice of Montreal* in 1994, which later turned into *Vice* magazine. He was bought out in 2008 due to his publicly emerging far-right beliefs,[21] after which he founded Rooster advertising agency in 2010. McInnes wrote a memoir, *The Death of Cool*, published in 2012, where he laid out some of his ethnonationalist and racist beliefs.[22] He hosted his own show on the Canadian conservative network Rebel Media and Compound Media, where he has produced many videos espousing his political and social views. His videos have garnered millions of views, and he has appeared on popular online mainstream channels such as the Joe Rogan Experience (JRE), gaining him a level of notoriety noteworthy in the alt-right. McInnes is a member of the *Order of the Knights of Columbus*, a Catholic fraternity with ties to fundamentalist right-wing think tanks,[23] though he typically does not talk about God or religion publicly.

McInnes disguises his beliefs through the use of crypto-fascism, which is the subtle admiration of fascistic ideology and policies concealed by wit, sarcasm, and, at times, outlandish humor.[24] He adamantly denies being alt-right, maintaining a shield of plausible deniability enabled by the mainstream tendency to only associate the alt-right with outright white nationalism. McInnes portrays himself as a political and social pundit and provocateur, using persuasion and charisma, humor and satire, to create accessible and entertaining videos for his audience. He is known to dress in costumes and to perform physical stunts, all of which are designed to push his far-right political agenda.

McInnes's most notable contribution to the alt-right movement was founding the now notorious Proud Boys in 2016, marketing the group as a "pro-West fraternal organization"[25] and "a men's club that meets about once a month to drink beer."[26] The group explicitly excludes women and trans men. It is fashioned after late 19th century U.S. men's clubs that had a "preoccupation with masculine ideals of physique and behaviour" and "manly virtues" such as "willpower, honour, courage, discipline, competitiveness, quiet strength, stoicism, sang-froid, persistence, adventurousness, independence, sexual virility tempered with restraint, and dignity." The core beliefs of the Proud Boys were listed on their website: "minimal government, maximum freedom, anti-political correctness, anti-drug war, anti-masturbation, closed borders, anti-racial guilt, anti-racism, pro-free speech, pro-gun rights, glorifying the entrepreneur, venerating the housewife, and reinstating a spirit of Western chauvinism."[27] It markets itself to men through heavy use of social media, meme sharing, and online platforms.[28]

The group has four degrees of membership with trials to pass through, from reciting the Proud Boys' creed, "I am a Western chauvinist who refuses to apologize for creating the modern world," to a series of violent actions.[29] Advancing to the second degree requires initiates to be punched in the stomach by other members until they can name five breakfast cereals and to give up masturbation.[30] (Despite the lack of explicit religious references, the emphasis on opposing masturbation and McInnes's involvement with a right-wing Catholic group suggests Christian Right influence on the ideology.) On successful completion of this second stage, the initiate becomes an official member. The third degree involves getting a Proud Boys tattoo, or branding, and the fourth involves carrying out violence, or "a major fight for the cause"[31] on behalf of the group. Perceived adversaries include members of Antifa and Black Lives Matter, Muslims, and other groups deemed enemies to the Western cause.[32] The Proud Boys have thus become notorious for their participation in and instigation of street brawls.

The organization is part of a trend in the far right over the past few years toward the exclusion of women and the admittance of men of other ethnicities and sexual orientations. The group demands that all members recognize that "(1) Whiteness is not the problem in modern society and (2) That Western civilization is superior to all others."[33] This allows non-white men to join so long as they believe systemic racism does not exist and that there should be no "racial guilt," as the Proud Boys put it. Their initiation, which requires men to say they "refuse to apologize for creating the modern world," can be inferred to mean that the history of the West is justified, including the confiscation of land from indigenous peoples and the trans-Atlantic slave trade among other atrocities which underlay the creation of modern Western civilization.

Multiracial and White Supremacist

The Proud Boys organization has attempted in some of its public rhetoric to distance itself from the alt-right. An article by McInnes on their website attempted to highlight the difference between the Proud Boys and the alt-right, noting, "[T]he two big differences we have with them is the 'JQ' and racial identity politics. They think the Jews are responsible for America's problems and they think 'Western' is inseparable from 'white.'"[34] ("JQ" is an abbreviation referring to the "Jewish Question," which alludes to anti-Semitic conspiracy theories that permeate the far right.) Yet McInnes himself appears in videos on YouTube defending far-right Holocaust denial, including the assertion that the Nazis did not use gas to murder Jewish people, and has previously tied white and Western culture together: "I love being white and I think it's something to be very proud of. I don't want our culture diluted. We need to close the borders now and let everyone assimilate to a Western, white, English-speaking way of life."[35] McInnes leaves ambiguity as to whether he is a white supremacist; he often flirts with this ideology in his videos, allowing room for interpretation while still aiming to appeal to non-white men.

Proud Boys—along with its sister organization, Fraternal Order of Alt-Knights or FOAK—is listed as a hate group by the Southern Poverty Law Center (SPLC). The SPLC describes the Proud Boys as "reject[ing] white nationalism and, in particular, the term 'alt-right' while espousing some of its central tenets" and notes that members of the group "have appeared alongside other hate groups at extremist gatherings like the 'Unite the Right' rally in Charlottesville."[36] A former Proud Boy, Jason Kessler, was one of the organizers of that event.[37] Their association with other groups in the alt-right movement, such as during Charlottesville Unite the Right Rally and the January 6 Capitol Attack, shows a common bond between this group and others in the alt-right movement, despite their protestations. In other words, though they hide behind plausible deniability and reject being defined as a white nationalist organization, the Proud Boys are not an outlier but a mostly representative group within the contemporary far-right, or alt-right, ecosystem.

The far right is not a monolith, and proponents of far-right ideology often differ on and debate issues such as race. Some far-right actors advocate an overt white supremacy where all non-Aryan races should be excluded from the nation, while others promote more of an "America-first" nationalism that is not explicitly racially discriminatory but still upholds far-right principles underlain with the white supremacy embedded in U.S. structure.[38] HoSang and Lowndes argue that the so-called alt lite, where McInnes places the Proud Boys, "is the liminal space in which white supremacy and multiculturalism interact."[39] By incorporating people of color, the far right and white supremacy become "a more durable force."[40] Masculinity "bridges racial difference," and the disavowal of white supremacy "allows the far right to draw in more recruits and allows participants a certain racial innocence—a plausible deniability of open racism."[41] HoSang and Lowndes point to the Proud Boys as a group that is simultaneously multicultural and racist that incorporates nationalism, racism, and patriarchy while symbolically distancing itself from the far right.[42] Cooper and Jenkins (2019) note on the subject of a "contemporary multiracial far-right,"

> With Patriot Prayer and Proud Boys combining support for restrictive gender roles with a fantasy of a new male supremacy and embrace of Western culture, they invoke a new version of the traditional Judeo-Christian values that defined the Christian Right over the past four decades.[43]

The role of masculinity and a return to patriarchy is especially salient in literature that attempts to explain the allure of the far right to men of color. The rejection of people of color into other far-right groups that take a different approach, or a stronger stance, in white supremacy does not negate the seriousness of the threat, or the level of extremism, of groups that are multiracial and far right. This chapter illustrates how masculinity and male supremacist ideology are key motivators for joining the Proud Boys and the "alt-right," contributing to our understanding of why men from various ethnicities are enticed to join a group whose rhetoric on "Western values" appear underlaid with supremacist beliefs.

Method

The purpose of this study is to examine if and how masculinity and male supremacy are motivating factors for joining the far right. Free and publicly accessible videos uploaded to YouTube between 2015 and 2018 that feature McInnes were selected for the dataset. This period coincides with the formation and early growth of the Proud Boys, when McInnes was most actively involved as leader of the group until he officially stepped down in 2018. Forty-three videos featuring Gavin McInnes on YouTube had one million views or more at the time of collection. Of those 43 videos, 26 focus specifically on women, gender, and feminism, while only three have a clear racially motivated agenda. (Some of the other videos centered around themes such as Obama, the baby boomer generation, fashion, and children, which may have had racial or gender undertones but did not speak primarily to these issues.) The videos used for this study included interviews with McInnes as well as the videos he produced and wrote himself. The most viewed videos featuring McInnes were two interviews on JRE.[44] After those two videos, his video entitled "10 Things Canadians Don't Know about Americans" was the most viewed, at 5.5 million views. From the full sample available of videos posted, 46 videos in total were analyzed for this research, including most of the videos that had one million views or more, as well as five videos that had under one million views, the least popular of which reached nearly 100,000 views. (All videos are listed in the Appendix Table.) Titles of some of videos include "Feminism Is a War on Masculinity" (215,000 views), "Feminist Gets Trolled by Gavin McInnes Until She's Shaking with Rage" (1.8 million views), "How to Rate Women from 1 to 10 the RIGHT Way" (1.5 million views), and "Single Moms: Stop Talking about How Brave and Cool You Are" (2.1 million views).

This study analyzes the videos through deductive thematic analysis, a qualitative method that allows the researcher to bring "a series of concepts, ideas, or topics that they use to code and interpret the data."[45] The frameworks of hypermasculinity and male supremacism were brought to the data, coding the videos as "acceptance of violence as a core part of manhood," "strict adherence to traditional gender roles," "villainization of feminism," "rejection of femininity in men," "way of life under attack," "male victimhood," and "male supremacism." The videos were viewed six times each and sentences relating to any of these codes were noted in a table. Three major themes[46] emerged from the interaction of these codes: "Violence and Manhood" (8 videos) "Frantic Call for Patriarchal Traditionalism" (a theme that includes the codes "male victimhood," "male supremacism," "rejection of femininity in men," and "strict adherence to traditional gender roles"; 33 videos), and "Perceived Enemies of Men" (constructed through merging the codes "villainization of feminism" and "way of life under attack"; 22 videos). Themes act as excellent devices by eliciting fear, rage, resentment, and a call to action through glorified violence. McInnes elicits these emotions while appearing to remain logical, reasonable, intelligent yet colloquial, which adds a candid element to his messages. He uses his age to his benefit; as a middle-aged man with a degree of fame, he fills younger men with the sense that he has wisdom to depart and the life experience and knowledge to comment on today's society and where society is failing. Racism, antisemitism, xenophobia,

190 Meadhbh Park

and Islamophobia were also present in the selected videos and future research could analyze the intersection of those themes with male supremacism.

Violence and Manhood

As expected, given how well-documented Proud Boys' glorification of and participation in violence is, McInnes often describes the relationship between masculinity and violence. Violence is a means to achieve status, defend oneself and one's masculinity, and an essential step in becoming a "real" man. McInnes's frequent mantra is, "You're not a man unless you have beaten the shit out of someone, had the shit beaten out of you, had your heart broken and broken a heart—those are the four minimums," a conflation of violence and emotion.[47] As combat has often been perceived as an arena where "boys become men," so too do McInnes and the Proud Boys view their street fights. Though he sometimes complains about the necessity for men to perform violence, overwhelmingly, violence in his view provides men with honor and glory, an inducement to potential recruits to the Proud Boys. His messaging makes use of cisgender men's sense of masculinity under assault and loss of their traditional power by offering violence as a means to reclaim status and power as a dominant, hypermasculine male.

McInnes conveys violence as an acceptable, honorable, and most of all inevitable part of manhood. In one Rebel News video mockingly directed toward "transman" (whose identity as men McInnes does not recognize), he states that being a man means "[y]ou have to fight" and "you're essentially in the National Reserves," ready to be drafted at any time to, for instance, protect a woman from harassment from another man or to defend your masculinity from a challenge by another man whose girlfriend falsely claims you sexually assaulted her. This echoes long-standing rhetoric deployed by men's rights activists such as Warren Farrell with respect to their gender role obligation to physically fight to defend women. Another Rebel News video, "Women in Combat? In Reality, Feminists Only Want Equality for the 'Fun' Stuff," evokes men's rights rhetoric about men as "disposable" and pushed into "death professions." McInnes tells women, "Come on into combat, come on into our world, we die at our jobs."[48] (McInnes holds a professional media job and has never served in the military.) He disdains women as physically inferior, even decrying the portrayal of women as heroes in action movies. ("By the way, women cannot beat up Russian agents, okay! Maybe Ronda Rousey [professional wrestler and retired mixed martial artist]. Maybe, and I doubt it."[49])

As violence is the sole domain of (cisgender) men, McInnes not only excludes women from the honor and prestige he associates with masculine violence but also from political power. In another video innocuously titled, "How to Replace a Transmission," McInnes ties violence, nationalism, and politics together under the umbrella of masculinity. "It's macho to be patriotic, it's macho to fight, it's macho to have to be tough and that's a politician's job,"[50] McInnes states. Women cannot enact the type of "macho" behavior necessary for politics, which justifies, for McInnes, opposing change to cis men's dominance in policies and government.

The far right's fear and frenzy over a perceived crisis in masculinity—an actual undermining of cis men's supremacy—inspired the movement to market hyper-masculine traits, such as a willingness to partake in violence. If leftist and liberal men are "soy boys" (a pejorative term meaning men who lack masculine traits used as an insult mainly on online forums), according to far-right leaders like McInnes, right-wing men are the exact opposite. They are warriors. They are the vanguard of conservative values and traditions, in a cultural and, sometimes, physical fight with liberal and leftist policies and people. In order to "defeat" their enemies, they must be prepared and eager to fight. This version of masculinity is alluring to men who feel powerless or denigrated by society, as it legitimizes vio-lence as an admirable means to achieve power, status, and manhood. As McInnes does not emphasize white masculinity, at least overtly, in his messaging around manhood and violence, he communicates a feeling of universality and inclusivity to cisgender white and non-white men who feel similar grievances and resonate with the desire for power, action, and warrior-type status. It is an opportunity to go from the mundanity or depressiveness of reality, where they may feel mean-ingless and emasculated, to an imagined version of an American warrior hero. Rallies, protests, and streets morph into actual warzones and battlefields where men can achieve power, respect, and glory through combat. The Proud Boys often call out for Antifa, their preferred enemy, during rallies and protests and actively search for resistance. They show an enthusiasm for real and bloody vio-lence or insurgency, which could be linked to the far right's appetite for an armed resistance, as detailed in the "Turner Diaries." The Capitol attack on January 6 was in part driven by the efforts of Proud Boys who helped to organize the demonstration and incited aggression and violence in the days leading up to the protest and on the day itself.[51]

Frantic Calls for Patriarchal Traditionalism

McInnes repeatedly promotes a return to patriarchal traditionalism and has bla-tantly stated that this is his ultimate desire for society, often shielding his far-right beliefs behind more mainstream conservatism. His beliefs around women in the workforce, relationship dynamics between men and women, and the growing trend of men taking on roles and responsibilities that would have once been deemed feminine align with patriarchal traditionalism. McInnes argues for men's superiority over women in almost all areas of life (except for parenting) but combines his claims with an anxiety related to fear of losing status and power to women in political, as well as social, spheres. This anxiety appears in his intense vitriol against feminism, with references to feminism in nearly all of the videos studied. He views feminism as a means for women to take on roles that should be held by men and claims that women are unable to adequately fulfill these roles, saying, "I'm not disparaging women here, natural women who create lives and shape lives, they all seem pretty reasonable, it's the ones that we forced into this male position that are a complete mess, I call them shitchests."[52] This anxiety around women infringing on men's spaces and threatening the historical status quo speaks to many men's feelings of frustration and loss of power as gender equality progresses in the workplace, dismantling their traditional privileged status. The message that a return to patriarchy could restore their dominance in society and lead to better and easier lives for men is extremely attractive and acts as an excellent recruitment tool. Despite that gender inequity and racial inequity have gone hand in hand, McInnes speaks to masculinity as encompassing all cisgender men, creating a space where men of color can blame women for competing in job opportunities and undermining their power, ignoring the centrality of white supremacy to the "traditional" system (as it is part of the Proud Boys' framework to require).

McInnes's frustration toward women encroaching in "male spaces" spans from women starring in action movies, to women in military combat positions, to women entering the workforce in general ("there are some of you who should be in the workforce, about 5%...the rest of you should be looking for a mate").[53] Echoing long-standing Christian Right frames, McInnes argues that women are better off as housewives, telling them, "You would be much happier at home with a husband and children!"[54] McInnes claims 95 percent of women inevitably become depressed in their careers and would be happier as stay-at-home mothers. His explanation for his fixation on women in the workforce oscillates from claiming that he is concerned about women's mental and physical well-being, stating explicitly, "the patriarchy is best for women," to his belief that women are simply incapable of working in most jobs.[55]

> They don't belong there, in the workforce, for the most part. Of course, there's exceptions, like Barbara Corcoran, Maggie Thatcher, there's tons of alpha females who fucking rock. Oprah, she's great. But my experience has been, when a woman contributes to the workforce, I want to say about 80% of the time it's just *makes exasperated gesture*.[56]

McInnes seeks to reclaim the traditional position of breadwinner and head of household held by men in patriarchy, with a strict division of gender roles, telling women, "[W]e would like you to let us provide for you."[57] Men who deviate from their appropriate role in the patriarchy also come under attack. "Being a stay-at-home dad is for losers, the acronym is accurate—SAD," McInnes mocks.[58] McInnes further denigrates stay-at-home fathers by questioning their masculinity using sexual disparagement, stating, "[S]tay-at-home dads do not receive fellatio ever," and "I read a study that said men who do chores at home get less sex."[59] His statements link gender, sex, relationships, and power by claiming if women become breadwinners and take on powerful positions in business, they would not do "anything remotely subservient in bed."[60]

McInnes's view that relationships are places where power is performed represents how he expects the dynamic between men and women, even in romantic relationships, to be one where men dominate and women are subservient. He does not view relationships as a place for equality between individuals but as a place where men should exert control and dominate, just as he desires men to do in broader society. In an interview with Joe Rogan on the topic of divorce, McInnes stresses that men who get divorced are failures, as they should have complete control over their wives; therefore, if their wives decide to leave, they are ultimately to blame. He tells Rogan, "That's what I'm saying, captain of the ship, *you* control their change if you're a real man, *you* control her and the kids!"[61] Undertones of domestic abuse come through in this assertion of control; other alt-right and male supremacist actors have explicitly promoted abuse as a form of controlling women.

McInnes attempts to personalize the alt-right agenda and create a sense that not only is public masculinity at stake but private masculinity as well, in terms of power in the home. Emasculation is portrayed as a direct effect of women taking on roles of responsibility outside the home, as well as of men opting to become stay-at-home fathers or expressing their own femininity. Men are encouraged not to be emotionally vulnerable with their partners; instead, McInnes romanticizes the stoicism of traditional masculinity, ranting in "10 Reasons Baby Boomers Are the Worst Generation":

> The Greatest Generation never talked about that. You'd say, "how are you doing?" to a man working the dock in the 1930s and he'd say, "what? I don't know". His whole existence was predicated on, is his wife happy, are his kids fed. [...] He didn't take Xanax to go to sleep at night, he didn't have a therapist![62]

McInnes denigrates women's ability to be in spaces traditionally deemed masculine—essentially anywhere outside the home and childrearing—as well as in their ability to think rationally or independently. This especially appears in his discussion of politics: "Women should have the right to vote, but should they vote?" he says. "It seems like every time I look at a political catastrophe, I see a bunch of ladies who were sort of torn out of the kitchen and forced into some position of power."[63] A master of creating plausible deniability, McInnes is careful to show that he does not believe *all* women are incapable of taking part in the public sphere:

> Ladies, you deserve all the same rights as we do. That doesn't mean you have to stand up when you pee. If you don't know about politics, please don't vote. And, if you're there just because you're a woman, please don't run.[64]

This statement insinuates that his frustrations are only directed toward women who "don't know about politics." This kind of smokescreen by male supremacists—that they are not talking about all women but only a certain kind of woman, often using "feminists" to mean all Western women—obscures or creates plausible deniability for their misogyny in the public eye.

194 Meadhbh Park

McInnes's disparagement toward women is coupled with the anxiety that women are increasingly entering the workforce and participating in politics, causing men to have to compete for roles traditionally reserved for (white) men. The changing of gender relations, both in the public and private sphere, clearly concerns McInnes, who sees any changes to the strict gender roles that would have been more prevalent in the 1950s as threatening to men. The sense of urgency and panic, especially around sexual relations and relationship dynamics, makes his message seem full of anxiety and as though a way of life is under immediate attack.

Perceived Enemies of Men

The last major gendered narrative that appears frequently in McInnes's public videos is the concept of a war on men or on masculinity. As white supremacist ideology creates narratives where white people are "under attack" from a foreign enemy that threatens their very existence and survival, male supremacists cling to narratives around male victimhood and view men and masculinity as under attack, most notably by feminists. The construction of an enemy that men can lay all of, or most of, the blame for their personal misfortunes, failings, or general feelings of victimhood and frustration provides a collective sense of injustice, core to any social movement recruitment. By providing a physical enemy, who is within reach, such as immigrants or feminists, McInnes and the far right can more easily mobilize men who are dissatisfied in their current situations. An invisible or more powerful enemy, such as capitalism, may not as easily motivate. Furthermore, with the exception of being anti-Muslim, McInnes does not bring racial, ethnic, or other religious tones into this message, allowing space for men of different ethnicities, sexualities, and religious backgrounds to join against feminism as the ultimate enemy to men's survival.

McInnes criticizes feminism from three angles. First, he claims that feminism allows women to fall for "myths," such as that they can take on traditionally masculine roles and live as freely in society as men, that ultimately harm women. For instance, in his video "Feminism Kills Women" he says to women, "[Y]ou're going to be safe at 4.20am? That's the myth of feminism, I blame feminism."[65] McInnes does not address the violence from men that threatens women's safety, instead blaming feminism for enabling women's independence. Second, McInnes views feminism as a direct threat to men and masculinity, in terms essentially identical to those used by men's rights activists: "[F]eminism isn't about equality anymore, it's about taking masculinity away from men."[66] Finally, he views feminism as a threat to the Western family and way of life, seeing them as enabling other threats to "Western" (a euphemism for white Christian) culture—for instance, his claims that feminists "keep pulling in these Islamic terrorists like Linda Sasour [Muslim American political activist]…that's really what feminism is, it's a giant suicide bomber that's meant to blow up tradition, and I'm telling

Fight Club **195**

you it only leads to death and suffering."[67] Note the escalation here of feminism, as an ideology, into being perceived as terrorism.

McInnes perpetuates a strong narrative that men are victimized by the forces of feminism and the Left. Continuing to use men's rights talking points, McInnes states in his video, "Feminism Is a War on Masculinity,"

> There's a brutal suicide rate going on with males, especially white males, and it's linked to opioids and cirrhosis of the liver, and I think it all comes from depression, and I think it all comes from a lifetime of being "you suck."[68]

He places men as both victims and victors in the perceived "war" on men. "Now, when you say there's a war on men, it's like when you say there's a war on Christmas and people go 'well, Christmas is still around.' Yeah, we're still winning. It doesn't mean you're not trying to shut us down," McInnes explains.[69] McInnes invokes warlike rhetoric and uses inclusive first-person plural pronouns, such as *we* and *our*, to suggest there is an in-group in which all men who adhere to his version of masculinity, traditional white masculinity, and hypermasculinity are inherently included. This both encompasses the narrative that a way of life is under attack and insinuates it can be reclaimed with a militaristic, or violent, approach.

Fighting against feminism is also a fight to secure potential future generations. It also fulfills a historically "chivalrous" act of protecting and saving women from something portrayed as endangering their lives and happiness, aligned with their self-presentation as "Western chauvinists." The "fight" against feminism clearly overlaps with the theme of "Violence and Manhood." While McInnes does not go so far as to explicitly suggest violence against women (though he has heavily implied this at times), McInnes views feminism as an evil force that needs to be stopped. The rage he attempts to elicit against feminist women mirrors the rage neo-Nazi groups have for Jewish people. Feminism is viewed as a shadowy, allusive yet powerful enemy that pulls the strings of the media, politics, and broader society in general. This kind of antifeminist conspiratorial thinking has grown in the past decade in misogynist groups such as the Red Pill, a forum started on Reddit. McInnes helps men to feel justified in their feelings of victimhood and fuels those feelings by disseminating biased studies, partial facts, and claims to back up his argument that men are being oppressed. For men who have had disappointing experiences with women in their lives, it is appealing to blame their negative experiences with women on feminism. Even more broadly, for men who are unhappy in their work lives and feel resentful toward women colleagues or superiors, feminism provides the perfect scapegoat.

McInnes understands the appeal of having a designated enemy to blame that also feels familiar, accessible, and potentially defeatable. Feminism, or feminist women, are accessible and can be attacked, whether it be online, at Women's Marches, pro-choice marches, universities, etc. McInnes's passionate beliefs in strict gender roles and gender binaries and his emphasis on their importance in order to uphold society coupled with his vehement disgust of feminism for daring to attempt to shift this status quo speaks to his inner far-right and male supremacist beliefs. McInnes offers men a dream, where they can be macho, powerful, and dominant; have a doting, submissive housewife; and be fully in charge of running society. And he offers them an enemy that is preventing that utopia: feminism. This is a very alluring narrative for many men seeking to view increasing gender equality and the loss of unjust privileges for cis men as disenfranchisment.

Conclusion

It is difficult to separate McInnes's political ideology and his views on masculinity, which implies a deep connection between the promoted ideal of manhood and the far right. Based on McInnes's rhetoric, men—without much understanding of far-right ideology and who may not consider themselves racist—may be drawn to the movement for its hypermasculine allure and male supremacist ideology. Men who want to find a group, or an outlet, where they can express themselves through physical violence or seek to restore a sense of status and superiority in an environment that encourages a deep sense of fraternity and male supremacism could be attracted by McInnes's rhetoric.

The male supremacism McInnes evokes may be perceived as an antidote by many men for their personal suffering in a world where they perceive themselves to be the main victims facing a downward economic trajectory. Feminism is most notably displayed as an enemy of men's survival and represents an adversary that subdues and feminizes men, casting them into the inferior position that hypermasculinity relegates women to. In order to subscribe to this ideology, members would most likely feel a sense of loss and entitlement. McInnes promotes a brand of masculinity that would be attractive to men who feel emasculated, either economically, politically, or socially and who may be looking for a means to feel a sense of power, status, and control in their lives. The enthusiasm to return to a past where men held dominant positions without competition from women is attractive to these men. The eagerness to create a world where men are legitimized in partaking in violence and where violence is acceptable and honorable is also attractive, as it lends an opportunity for men to achieve valor on a level that is most commonly associated with soldiers and warriors. This allows men to feel a further sense of importance and dominance in their lives.

These messages may appear to transcend racial lines, and for men of color who seek a space to vocally protest political correctness, feminism, and Communism, and protect "Western" values, the Proud Boys on the surface seems to be a group that does not discriminate based on race and is open to accepting these men. Occasionally, the Proud Boys will commandeer language and symbols of non-white cultures in order to bolster their image as a mainstream right-wing movement that advocates primarily for free speech. The level of racism in the Proud Boys may differ between groups—for example, the Wisconsin Proud Boys have been exposed as having especially extreme racist tendencies, but due to the relative secrecy of the groups, it is difficult to know if this level of extremism exists within all chapters. Proud Boys of color are not exempt from taking part in these discussions, and it was clear on the public Proud Boy Parler page that there was an expectation among members to accept and encourage posts that pushed the boundaries of mainstream right-wing talking points to include more overtly racist and misogynistic rhetoric. Often Proud Boys of color will make distinctions between themselves and the people of color the group mocks, insults, or attacks such as saying that they are "legal" immigrants, or descendants of "legal immigrants," or that they reject the idea of systematic racism and the harmful legacy of slavery.

This study of McInnes's rhetoric shows how focusing on the new far right solely through the lens of white supremacy is, in fact, a flaw of much of the literature and research, as the new far-right movement is equally drawn from ideas of masculinity and male supremacy. Analyzing McInnes's rhetoric through the lens of male supremacy and masculinity gives us a greater understanding of his views, therefore also a greater understanding of the views of the Proud Boys and the far right more generally. It is important to pay attention to the role of male supremacism as a key tenet in the far right and also as a link that ties different and often seemingly disparate groups in the far right together. McInnes's male supremacist ideology did not occur in a vacuum, and there are examples of male supremacism in various far-right forums, groups, and militias. Further research into the intersection between male supremacy and violent extremism deserves to be conducted, as well as the role of masculinity in the current far-right movement. To leave out, or ignore, male supremacist ideology and beliefs as a key motivating factor for men joining the far right would be detrimental to furthering our understanding of the rapidly evolving movement and of ever finding an effective means of prevention.

Appendix Table

Video	View Count
Career Women: Stop Throwing Away Your Ovaries	221k
"Cuck-mercials" Portray Men as Wimps; Lies about Race and Crime	923k
10 Reasons Baby Boomers Are the Worst Generation	1.5M
10 Reasons Obama Was the Worst President Ever	1.6M
10 Things Canadians Don't Know about Americans	5.5M
20 Ways to Ensure a Happy Life	
5 Ways to Know If You're a Sexist	999k
A Message to the Feminists Who Attacked Lauren Southern with Urine	1.3M
Amy Schumer: Joke Thief? Maybe—but She's Done Something WAY Worse	1.3M
BuzzFeed's 'Plus Size Fashion' Video Is Cruel and Stupid	1.5M
Cover Girl's New Model Is a Boy: Part of War on Men	774k
Debunking MTV's '2017' Resolutions for White Guys	1.7M
Defeating the Left's Strawman Arguments (I'm Looking at You, Bill Maher)	1.2M

198 Meadhbh Park

Video	View Count
Everything Wrong with HuffPo's "Why Feminism Is Good for Men"Video	886k
Feminism Is a War on Masculinity	215k
Feminism Kills Women	271k
Feminism Makes Women Ugly	375k
Feminist Gets Trolled by Gavin McInnes Until She's Shaking with Rage	1.8M
Feminists Are 7-Year-Old Boys	644k
FILFs: Feminists I'd Like to, Uh, Have Relations With	1.1M
Gavin McInnes: 10 Jobs That Are Bullsh*t	1.4M
Gavin McInnes: 10 Things Transmen Should Know about Men	918k
Gavin McInnes: 20 Reasons Why School Sucks	1.1M
Gavin McInnes: How *The Daily Show* tried (and failed) to Make Me Look Stupid	2.2M
Gavin McInnes: My 15 Most Controversial Moments	1.3M
Gavin McInnes: Some 'Myths' about Native Americans Are True	1.3M
Gavin McInnes: Stop Making Our Movies Politically Correct	1.6M
Gavin McInnes: Top 5 Things Men Need to Know	96k
Here's Why the New All-Female Ghostbusters Movie Will Bomb	904k
How to Dress Your Age, with Gavin McInnes	1.3M
How to Move to Canada (If Trump Becomes President)	2.5M
How to Rate Women from 1 to 10 the RIGHT Way	1.5M
How to Replace a Transmission	378k
I Predicted Ghostbusters Would Suck, and I Was Right	1M
Joe Rogan Experience #720	[a]
Millennials Aren't Interested in Having Sex. Here's Whose Fault That Is	1.3M
'Naked and Afraid' Offers Lessons in Gender and Feminism	2M
Single Moms: Stop Talking about How Brave and Cool You Are	2.1M
SNL's Trump Sketch Shows That America Finally Gets It	
Top 10 Things Wrong with Kids These Days	1.2M
We Need More Families	136k
What the Hell Happened to Athletic Shoes?	1.2M
Why Are Women so Fat?	1.1M
Woman's March: Idiots Duped by Muslim Con Artist	1.1M
Women in Combat? In Reality, Feminists Only Want Equality "for the Fun Stuff"	1.2M
You're Not "Plus Size"—You're Dying	1.2M

a Above five million views at the time of collection; the video has since been removed from YouTube.

Notes

1 Staff/gaby-del-valle, "Bathing in Pig's Blood: Inside the Alt-Right's Pro-Trump Art Show," *Gothamist*, October 10, 2016, https://gothamist.com/arts-entertainment/bathing-in-pigs-blood-inside-the-alt-rights-pro-trump-art-show.
2 Gavin McInnes, "WE ARE NOT ALT-RIGHT – Proud Boy Magazine," official-proudboys.com, n.d., accessed June 22, 2020, https://officialproudboys.com/proud-boys/we-are-not-alt-right/.

Fight Club **199**

3 Michael Futch and Rachael Riley, "The Latest: People Chanting 'Save the Kids' March through Downtown Fayetteville," *The Fayetteville Observer*, accessed July 2, 2021, https://eu.fayobserver.com/story/news/2020/08/29/fayetteville-downtown-businesses-advised-close-early-before-march/5668323002/.

4 John Daniszewski, "Writing about the 'Alt-Right'," *The Associated Press*, November 28, 2016, https://blog.ap.org/behind-the-news/writing-about-the-alt-right.

5 Alex DiBranco, "Mobilizing Misogyny," *Political Research Associates*, March 2017, https://www.politicalresearch.org/2017/03/08/mobilizing-misogyny.

6 Cas Mudde, "Why Is the Far Right Dominated by Men? | Cas Mudde," *The Guardian*, August 17, 2018, https://www.theguardian.com/commentisfree/2018/aug/17/why-is-the-far-right-dominated-by-men.

7 Elizabeth Ralph-Morrow, "The Right Men: How Masculinity Explains the Radical Right Gender Gap," *Political Studies* (July 22, 2020): 003232172093604, https://doi.org/10.1177/0032321720936049.

8 Romit Chowdhury, "Conditions of Emergence: The Formation of Men's Rights Groups in Contemporary India," *Indian Journal of Gender Studies* 21, no. 1 (February 2014): 27–53, https://doi.org/10.1177/0971521513511199.

9 Joshua M. Roose, *The New Demagogues: Religion, Masculinity and the Populist Epoch* (Abingdon and New York: Routledge, Taylor & Francis Group, 2021), 82–4.

10 Ibid., 84.

11 Erica Scharrer, "Virtual Violence: Gender and Aggression in Video Game Advertisements," *Mass Communication and Society* 7, no. 4 (September 2004): 393–412, https://doi.org/10.1207/s15327825mcs0704_2.

12 Bridget Blodgett and Anastasia Salter, "Ghostbusters Is for Boys: Understanding Geek Masculinity's Role in the Alt-Right," *Communication, Culture and Critique* 11, no. 1 (March 1, 2018): 133–46, https://doi.org/10.1093/ccc/tcx003.

13 Karen E. Dill-Shackleford and Kathryn P. Thill, "(PDF) Video Game Characters and the Socialization of Gender Roles: Young People's Perceptions Mirror Sexist Media Depictions," *Sex Roles* 57, no. 11 (December 2007): 852, https://www.researchgate.net/publication/225733100_Video_Game_Characters_and_the_Socialization_of_Gender_Roles_Young_People.

14 Erica Scharrer, "Virtual Violence: Gender and Aggression in Video Game Advertisements," *Mass Communication and Society* 7, no. 4 (September 2004): 397, https://doi.org/10.1207/s15327825mcs0704_2.

15 Rachel Jewkes et al., "Hegemonic Masculinity: Combining Theory and Practice in Gender Interventions," *Culture, Health & Sexuality* 17, no. 2 (October 16, 2015): 112–27, https://doi.org/10.1080/13691058.2015.1085094.

16 R. W. Connell and James W. Messerschmidt, "Hegemonic Masculinity: Rethinking the Concept," *Gender & Society* 19, no. 6 (December 2005): 829–59, https://doi.org/10.1177/0891243205278639.

17 Connell and Messerschmidt, "Hegemonic Masculinity," 832.

18 Francis Beesley and James McGuire, "Gender-Role Identity and Hypermasculinity in Violent Offending," *Psychology, Crime & Law* 15, no. 2–3 (February 2009): 251–68, https://doi.org/10.1080/10683160802190988.

19 Joane Nagel, "Masculinity and Nationalism: Gender and Sexuality in the Making of Nations," *Ethnic and Racial Studies* 21, no. 2 (January 1998): 246, https://doi.org/10.1080/014198798330007.

20 Ibid.

21 Kerry Flynn Business CNN, "Vice Distances Itself—Again—From Co-Founder Who Started Proud Boys," *CNN*, October 1, 2020, https://edition.cnn.com/2020/10/01/media/vice-gavin-mcinnes-proud-boys/index.html.

22 Samantha Kutner, "Swiping Right: The Allure of Hyper Masculinity and Cryptofascism for Men Who Join the Proud Boys," *ICCT*, 2020, https://doi.org/10.19165/2020.1.03.

23 Roose, *The New Demagogues*.

24 Julia Rose DeCook, "Trust Me, I'm Trolling: Irony and the Alt-Right's Political Aesthetic," *M/c Journal* 23, no. 3 (July 7, 2020), https://doi.org/10.5204/mcj.1655.

25 Julia R. DeCook, "Memes and Symbolic Violence: #Proudboys and the Use of Memes for Propaganda and the Construction of Collective Identity," *Learning, Media and Technology* 43, no. 4 (October 2, 2018): 485–504, https://doi.org/10.1080/17439884.2018.1544149.

26 McInnes, "WE ARE NOT ALT-RIGHT."

27 "Proud Boys," n.d. Proud Boys, https://proudboysusa.com/.

28 DeCook, "Memes and Symbolic Violence," 485–504.

29 "Proud Boys."

30 Lux Alptraum, "Why Are the Proud Boys So Obsessed with Masturbation?" *Medium*, October 19, 2018, https://gen.medium.com/why-are-the-proud-boys-so-obsessed-with-masturbation-c9932364ebe2.

31 Kimberly M. Aquilina, "Gavin McInnes Explains What a Proud Boy Is and Why Porn and Wanking Are Bad," *Metro US*, February 7, 2017, https://www.metro.us/gavin-mcinnes-explains-what-a-proud-boy-is-and-why-porn-and-wanking-are-bad/.

32 Kutner, "Swiping Right."

33 DeCook, "Memes and Symbolic Violence," 485–504.

34 McInnes, "WE ARE NOT ALT-RIGHT."

35 Vanessa Grigoriadis, "The Edge of Hip: Vice, the Brand (Published 2003)," *The New York Times*, September 28, 2003, sec. Style, https://www.nytimes.com/2003/09/28/style/the-edge-of-hip-vice-the-brand.html.

36 Southern Poverty Law Centre, "Proud Boys," Southern Poverty Law Center, 2016, https://www.splcenter.org/fighting-hate/extremist-files/group/proud-boys.

37 Jesse Ferraras, "The FBI Doesn't Consider the Far-Right Proud Boys an Extremist Group, and They Never Did: Reports," *Global News*, December 8, 2018, https://globalnews.ca/news/4742930/proud-boys-fbi-extremist-group/; Jason Wilson, "FBI Now Classifies Far-Right Proud Boys as 'Extremist Group', Documents Say," *The Guardian*, November 19, 2018, sec. World News, https://www.theguardian.com/world/2018/nov/19/proud-boys-fbi-classification-extremist-group-white-nationalism-report.

38 Cloee Cooper and Daryle Lamont Jenkins, "Culture and Belonging in the USA: Multiracial Organizing on the Contemporary Far Right," *Escholarship.org*, October 7, 2019, https://escholarship.org/uc/item/1q86f20p.

39 Daniel Hosang and Joseph E. Lowndes, *Producers, Parasites, Patriots: Race and the New Right-Wing Politics of Precarity* (Minneapolis: The University Of Minnesota Press, 2019), 125.

40 Ibid., 104.

41 Ibid.

42 Ibid., 122.

43 Cooper and Jenkins, "Culture and Belonging in the USA."

44 During the course of this research, both videos were removed before their view counts could be recorded. There was an attempt to contact the JRE for an official reason for this decision; however, there was no response.

Fight Club **201**

45 Victoria Clarke and Virginia Braun, "Thematic Analysis," *The Journal of Positive Psychology* 12, no. 3 (December 9, 2016): 58, https://doi.org/10.1080/17439760.2016.1262613.

46 Lorelli S. Nowell et al., "Thematic Analysis: Striving to Meet the Trustworthiness Criteria," *International Journal of Qualitative Methods* 16, no. 1 (October 2, 2017): 2, https://doi.org/10.1177/1609406917733847.

47 Rebel News, "Everything Wrong with HuffPo's 'Why Feminism Is Good for Men' Video," YouTube Video, *Rebel News*, June 10, 2016, https://www.youtube.com/watch?v=KhQ2EgS-Enw.

48 Rebel News, "Women in Combat? In Reality, Feminists Only Want Equality 'for the Fun Stuff,'" www.youtube.com, February 10, 2016, https://www.youtube.com/watch?v=q-J44jEaD30&t=29s.

49 Rebel News, "Gavin McInnes: Stop Making Our Movies Politically Correct," YouTube Video, *Rebel News*, July 25, 2017, https://www.youtube.com/watch?v=ca4lnPwnX3E.

50 Rebel News, "How to Replace a Transmission." YouTube Video, *Rebel News*, December 31, 2015, https://www.youtube.com/watch?v=qllv1kqAG5I.

51 Lois Beckett, "Enrique Tarrio, Leader of Rightwing Proud Boys, Arrested Ahead of Rallies," *The Guardian*, January 5, 2021, https://www.theguardian.com/world/2021/jan/04/enrique-tarrio-rightwing-proud-boys-arrested.

52 Rebel News, "Feminists Are 7-Year-Old Boys," YouTube Video, *Rebel News*, February 28, 2017, https://www.youtube.com/watch?v=JSfLAXLR2rI.

53 Rebel News, "20 Ways to Ensure a Happy Life," YouTube Video, *Rebel News*, October 17, 2016, https://www.youtube.com/watch?v=KLu_PogFGEw.

54 Rebel News, "Career Women: Stop Throwing Away Your Ovaries!," YouTube Video, *Rebel News*, May 19, 2015, https://www.youtube.com/watch?v=LMKvbU8cxHU.

55 Rebel News, "Cover Girl's New Model Is a Boy: Part of War on Men," YouTube Video, *Rebel News*, October 14, 2016, https://www.youtube.com/watch?v=2f7q9XxnmtM.

56 Joe Rogan Podcast, "Joe Rogan Experience #710 - Gavin McInnes," *JRE Podcast*, November 19, 2015, https://www.jrepodcast.com/episode/joe-rogan-experience-710-gavin-mcinnes/.

57 Rebel News, "Everything Wrong with HuffPo's 'Why Feminism Is Good for Men' Video."

58 Ibid.

59 Ibid.

60 Ibid.

61 Joe Rogan Podcast, "Joe Rogan Experience #710—Gavin McInnes."

62 Rebel News, "10 Reasons Baby Boomers Are the Worst Generation," www.youtube.com, January 15, 2016, https://www.youtube.com/watch?v=V9bVnQPaj48.

63 Rebel News, "How to Replace a Transmission."

64 Ibid.

65 Rebel Edge, "Gavin McInnes: Feminism Kills Women," YouTube Video, *Rebel Edge*, May 8, 2017, https://www.youtube.com/watch?v=ducNreliCS4.

66 Rebel News, "Gavin McInnes: Feminism Is a War on Masculinity," YouTube Video, *Rebel News*, April 24, 2017, https://www.youtube.com/watch?v=vaVs4Ey5x8E.

67 Ibid.

68 Ibid.

69 Rebel News, "Cover Girl's New Model Is a Boy: Part of War on Men."

10

WATCHING AWAKENING

Violent White Masculinity in *Cuck*

Meredith L. Pruden

> So, are you ready to take the red pill, or are you just another cuck?
>
> *Chance Dalmain,* Cuck

Cuck is a (2019) fictional film chronicling the life of discontented loner Ronnie Palicki as he is red-pilled[1] and radicalized in online spaces, such as message boards and video sharing platforms, before ultimately murdering a number of people. The term "cuck" was popularized as a genre of pornography and is short for cuckold.[2] Since then, the word has become a popular slur among white supremacists, violent misogynists, and the far right characterizing "weak, effeminate, unmanly or inadequate men" who let their women partners dominate them.[3] According to an interview with writer-director Rob Lambert, he intended the film to be a "gritty character study" exploring "lone wolf shooters" besieged by the "economic stress caused by outside groups … taking away the American dream," as well as an exploration of the themes of "sexual frustration, political recruitment, and online shaming" and obsession with U.S. patriotism and the country's military apparatus.[4] Lambert conceptualized Ronnie as a portmanteau of infamous lone shootings, including the white supremacist Emanuel African Methodist Episcopal Church shooting in Charleston in 2015 and the violent misogynist mass murders near the University of California Santa Barbara in 2014.[5] The film culminates in Ronnie's rampage killing, during which he murders his mother and the couple who "cuck" him, nearly kills his former employer (an Iranian American immigrant) and his son, and randomly shoots at a group of people standing on the street before committing "suicide by cop."[6]

Following its premiere at the Cleveland International Film Festival (CIFF), *Cuck* launched nationwide with a limited theatrical release before becoming available on streaming services. It isn't clear for what audience Lambert intended the film. Early online reception from far-right circles labeled it "leftist propaganda,"[7]

DOI: 10.4324/9781003164722-14

while left-leaning media called it "bigoted" and "pornography."[8] Box office numbers and other financials have not been made publicly available, but the film received mixed reviews from audiences and critics, with comments on review sites polarized along ideological lines.[9] There is, however, evidence some viewers sympathized with Ronnie. Actor Zachary Ray Sherman (Ronnie) said his goal was to portray a "whole" character and "full portrait of a person" that provided a "different experience than what's in the news" [about lone shooters].[10] He went on to say he has heard from "a lot" of fans who empathized with Ronnie. The film has also received accolades. It was nominated for Best American Independent Feature Film at CIFF, and Sherman was the Seymour Cassel Award winner for Outstanding Performance for his portrayal at the 2019 Oldenburg Film Festival. The film was also nominated for the German Independence Award (Audience Award) at Oldenburg the same year.

Regardless of the mixed reception *Cuck* received, art is a window into the cultural imagination. Film is capable of recording "ordinary life" and presenting it "for thoughtful reflection."[11] This is possible because films are "structured to appeal to audience emotions" and create specific moods.[12] Moreover, images in film are not strictly representative; they can also discursively constitute identities through affective excesses and material embodiment.[13] In this way, films not only "reflect social norms and play a key role in circulating and perpetuating values about identities, communities, and cultures" but also bring the same into being.[14]

Unpacking and critiquing the fictional world of *Cuck* provides a window into common social narratives about right-wing whiteness and male supremacism and helps to show how these movements draw from and deploy digital and visual culture to recruit and mobilize their base. This chapter asks four related questions. First, what does *Cuck* say about the interrelatedness of right-wing whiteness and male supremacy? Second, how does the film position the audience with regard to the same? Third, what gets lost when we use the lone wolf metaphor to describe single-shooter white nationalists and violent misogynists? Finally, what does the film tell us about the ways in which these movements use and are influenced by visual and digital culture?

In asking these questions about *Cuck*, this chapter argues the film illuminates some of the ways right-wing whiteness and violent misogyny are deeply entangled and begins to tease out these connections. Second, it suggests the film reinforces white men's sense of victimhood and encourages a sympathetic identification with the white male anti-hero in the same ways as mainstream media coverage. This, in turn, helps to uncover and illustrate the institutional structures and motivations for the widespread portrayal of single-actor shooters as young, white "lone wolf" losers, as well as the possible repercussions of this representation. Finally, this chapter explores Ronnie's use of images within his environment, as well as his prolific use of online chat rooms/discussion forums, a YouTube-like digital streaming video channel, dating, and pornography sites to demonstrate how the far right and violent misogynists are influenced by visual culture even as they deploy the same for recruitment and mobilization.

204 Meredith L. Pruden

Setting the Stage

> If a man makes himself a worm he must not complain when he is trodden on.
> *Immanuel Kant, quoted in Cuck's opening "over black"*

Cuck opens on an all-black screen with three lines of stark white lettering in all uppercase type. It is a quote by Enlightenment-era philosopher Immanuel Kant that foretells Ronnie's "awakening" or red-pilling to the supposed truth of the world. Ominous bass tones play from the ether and set the somber mood. The abyss of the deep black screen fades into an aerial view of an entangled mass of highways bifurcating a desolate industrial landscape. The scene is colored in melancholic sepia tones. Cars whiz across the screen in some lanes while others crawl slowly forward, snarled in traffic. The scene is a visual metaphor for Ronnie's life—dismal, fragmented, and stuck in place as the world carries on around him.

As the aerial view continues, a low rumbling static comes into focus as the tuning of a car radio. A cacophonous rush of changing channels plays frenetically, jumping from an advertisement for a local credit union to a Spanish language station and foreshadowing the film's focus on the failed promise of the American dream. While blame for this failure is largely placed on immigrants, it is also chalked up to organized efforts by the "deep state" to keep white people down financially and demographically.[15] The frenzied pace also matches Ronnie's disjointed affective state. The camera begins to jump to progressively tighter frames of what we now know is the Los Angeles, California, suburb of Van Nuys. The changing stations continue, taking us through advertisements for the U.S. Army and L.A. real estate, Spanish music, a brief period of unintelligible noise, and a variety of conservative and religious talk radio programs discussing prayer, top-down politics, diversity, and "the male gaze." It is a 30-second auditory snapshot of the hot button issues Ronnie perceives as plaguing America.

Passing over busy intersections, faded whitewashed office buildings, train yards, and flat suburban landscapes, the drone footage hovers above one muted gray house in a debris-filled brown yard in a working-class neighborhood. The single-shot drone footage of the opening scene conveys a sense of disembodied surveillance reminiscent of white supremacist conspiracy theories about government overreach. It also serves as a commentary on the systems of capitalist surveillance inherent to online environments and social media.[16] Finally, the camera alights on the roof. Smack in the center sits an old school, Yagi-style television broadcast antenna with wires snaking across the shingles and dropping into microscopic holes. Shadows of small birds dance across the roof.

The birds, in their easy freedom, are the antithesis of Ronnie, who sits below in his dimly lit and dirty bedroom—surrounded by soft-core photographs of nearly naked women, U.S. Army paraphernalia, and a large American flag—polishing a pair of military-issue boots and listening to alt-right VlogTubes celebrity Chance Dalmain.[17] The fictional Dalmain bears a striking resemblance to a young Richard Spencer (the real-life neo-Nazi, white nationalist, and misogynist alt-right leader at the helm of the National Policy Institute and AltRight.com) right down to his suited and booted apparel, high and tight combover, and rhetorical speaking style. We see Dalmain has 1.6 million VlogTube subscribers, and the video currently playing has been viewed more than 337,000 times. It is here we recognize the opening sequence soundtrack has changed from rotating stations on the radio dial to Dalmain's soliloquy against progressive media and academic narratives of the white male as villain. As Ronnie finishes polishing his boots and stands to face a sliding closet door mirror, we note he is wearing ill-fitting U.S. Army fatigues, which we later learn belonged to his dead father.

This opening sequence, while perhaps a little too "on the nose," positions its protagonist as the stereotypical lone shooter—a young, white, cis heterosexual man living with his mother who spends too much time online. He is, to use Kant's terms featured in the opening "over black," "making himself a worm." Throughout the film, Ronnie becomes increasingly radicalized through online videos and discussion forums (which, as we will see, belies the lone wolf metaphor) and, ultimately, becomes an online alt-right sensation before experiencing a fall from grace through online shaming as a cuck in the world of webcams and sex for sale.[18]

Right-Wing Identity and Ideology: Whiteness and Male Supremacy

> You can't be proud to be white and male anymore. It's not politically correct.
> *Ronnie,* Cuck

Ronnie is constructed as a fictional embodiment of the quintessential victim swept up in the so-called crisis of white men's identity. The military rejected him, and he's unable to find employment. He's awkward, unsuccessful with women, and frequently abused and emasculated by his mother. To Ronnie, his inability to be a "real man," like his father, is not, and never could be, his fault. Rather than acknowledging he was rejected by the military for possessing a criminal history and negative psychological evaluation, Ronnie believes the military accepts too many "queers."[19] Rather than attributing an inability to get a better job to his lack of education, Ronnie blames immigrants for "running the show and looking down on him."[20] Rather than admitting his aggressive and socially awkward behavior and misogynistic language offend the women with whom he's trying to connect, Ronnie puts the fault on higher education as a "breeding ground for liberal communism ... and turning women into feminazis."[21] In this way, the *Cuck* story arc plods along, failing to problematize these narratives and placing the blame on society—in particular, feminists, social justice warriors, progressives, and all those Ronnie sees as enforcing unfair standards around so-called political correctness.

The anonymous power of hegemonic whiteness is universal, invisible, and naturalized, synonymous with rationality and European ancestry.[22] Traditionally, whiteness has been understood as seeable only in its relationality to other identity categories while nevertheless managing to, paradoxically, reproduce itself.[23] This phenomenon is a public pedagogy that continues white dominance at the structural level.[24] This does not mean individual white folks always enjoy the "good life"; however, it does indicate society is systematically structured to afford white people a leg up. Maintaining the indeterminant visibility of whiteness becomes increasingly complex in the context of white nationalism since adherents do not seek to be unmarked. Instead, the white right has constructed an insular in-group around the notion of an ethno-European identity (e.g., "pure" whiteness).

Contrary to historical notions of the invisible power of whiteness, these groups seek to make their whiteness visible. And yet, even as white supremacists explicitly stake a claim to their ethno-European identity, they simultaneously profess they are unfairly disadvantaged by nefarious outside actors who take the form of everything from a transnational deep-state cabal to immigrant families illegally crossing the southern border. In the last several decades, fear of these out-group actors has coalesced into theories about white genocide (i.e., the belief there's a global plot to exterminate the white race through immigration, miscegenation, and falling white birth rates). These "myths of victimhood" and white imperilment frame problems and propose solutions that may not always look like explicit calls to violence but which nevertheless provide justification for it.[25] Bharath Ganesh (2020) suggests this may work as the far right weaponizes affect as a sort of white thymos wherein pride, rage, and indignation converge.[26] It is this logic of victimhood that provides the easy slippage between and among white and male supremacist ideologies.

Hegemonic whiteness is often intertwined with hegemonic masculinity in much the same way, as are the associated ideologies of male and white supremacism. Mitch Berbrier suggests a white supremacist strategy has been to play on the backlash politics of angry white men to invoke a "broader sentiment of the victimized white male," which they use to recruit and mobilize to their cause.[27] A victim "is a type of person whose basic characteristic is the experience of harm" but is also blameless for the harm enacted upon them and, thus, a sympathetic character.[28] This plays out across five themes, including white people as (1) "oppressed victims of discrimination," (2) the denial of white rights to heritage and culture, and (3) a double standard in which pride is "expected of nonwhites" but "unacceptable for whites" that contributes to (4) "deflated self-esteem" and, ultimately "threatened survival."[29] These strategies coalesce into a logic of white male victimhood that is societally pervasive and present in media artifacts.

Both white and male supremacist worldviews adhere to a strict, naturalized two-sex system in which men are in charge in the public and private spheres, and women are reduced to their reproductive or sexual functions. Transgender folks have no place in this schema because they do not fit within its biologically deterministic framework. To perpetrators of ideological killings, only a violent hero's quest can restore the good and just balance in their favor. Each of these attitudes is marked by oppositional, or backlash, politics that reflect feelings of superiority toward racialized, gendered, and sexualized Others that become further entrenched because they are bounded by impermeable in- (e.g., ethno-European whites) and out-groups (e.g., socialists, immigrants, Jews, LGBTQ folks, and people of color).

When films build their narratives around social interactions between binary racial categories, as in the case of *Cuck*, Thomas K. Nakayama and Judith N. Martin argue these films "encourage a spectatorial position that understands events in the film as they relate to the white characters" and, thus, marginalize the Other.[30] In other words, these filmic narratives are filtered "through the lens of whiteness."[31] The same could be said of "maleness"—these films encourage a spectatorial position that understands events in the film as they relate to *male* characters through the lens of a biologically essentialized *maleness*. These types of media texts not only center whiteness but also foreground wounded white masculinity, which functions as a genre convention connected to neoliberalism through its emphasis on professional success.[32] In *Cuck*, as in life, white (cis) men's success is measured in terms of upwardly mobile professional achievement and sexual conquest. Marginalized men are barriers to Ronnie's success in both areas, while white women are simply objects to be won. When Ronnie fails to attain professional and sexual success, he feels victimized.

Victimhood and the White Male Anti-hero

> I'm frustrated. No one listens to me. I feel like shit. I can't be anything I need to be in this fucking country.
>
> *Ronnie,* Cuck

In *Cuck*, Ronnie is constructed as frustrated by his perpetual victimization at the hands of those around him, including his family, extended circle, and even strangers. He is portrayed as suffering from mental illness, as evidenced by his early web search for "probation + psych eval + ARMY" and several scenes in which he physically shakes from anger. The filmmakers, apparently, called this the "silent scream" and intended it to signify trauma-induced rage.[33] Yet Ronnie's actual trauma (his father's suicide and mother's abuse) is hidden, in the first case, or downplayed in the latter throughout the film, leaving the viewer to imagine this trauma arises from his professional and sexual failures at the hands of racialized Others and women, which leaves him feeling "like shit" and professionally stunted. Because of this narrative choice, the silent scream comes across not as a trauma response but rather as the physical manifestation of an emotionally stunted man who never learned to appropriately express his feelings.

At home, Ronnie's deeply religious mother, whom he ultimately strangles to death, is the quintessential "mommy dearest."[34] Each time she appears, she

208 Meredith L. Pruden

berates and belittles Ronnie, leaving him little room for a response. In one particularly disturbing bathtub scene, she forces Ronnie to wash her naked body as she caresses his hand, moving it to her breast and coyly smiling through pursed lips. This incident elicits a rage-fueled inner monologue that segues into a VlogTubes confessional video, wherein Ronnie bemoans "sluts" who "get more comfortable than they deserve" and the need to be an alpha male.[35] The structure of this scene exemplifies the ways in which the material world becomes folded into the digital one, and vice versa, both in the fictional world of *Cuck* and in everyday life.

While the scenes with Ronnie's mother clearly point to emotional and sexual abuse, the mother character also reflects the deep internalized misogyny of the filmmakers. To fail as a mother is not an individual flaw but a failure due to aberrant femininity.[36] Depicted in this film, particularly when read against the few other women characters (who also are portrayed as failing to perform "appropriate" femininity), these failures become representative of all women and reinforce problematic tropes rooted in misogyny.

Ronnie's mother is not the only woman with whom he has problems. Out in the world, he follows VlogTuber Dalmain's advice[37] and attempts to channel a Chad—a professionally and sexually successful alpha male—to make conversation with a woman at the bus stop. When she rebuffs him with a curt "fuck off," Ronnie appears dejected and begins to slink away. Then, visibly frustrated, he returns to tell the woman she "doesn't have to be a bitch."[38] The woman begins as a feminine object of Ronnie's sexual desire but is effectively stripped of her feminine status through her obscenity-laced rejection. Although Ronnie interrupts the woman, who is listening to her headphones, with his uninvited advances, the filmmakers lean hard into the affect around the embarrassment of rejection. They portray Ronnie as initially nervous and unassuming, while the woman is painted as unnecessarily hostile. In so doing, the viewer is encouraged to relate to Ronnie's suffering at her hand, rather than recognize the dangers women face from pervasive sexual/street harassment and violence. This scene also conjures real life. The violent misogynist who committed mass murder near the University of California Santa Barbara in 2014, on which the film is partially based, wrote that he once threw coffee on two "hot blonde girls" at a bus stop.[39] In both cases, the message is that the women "deserved" it.

Following the bus stop encounter, Ronnie is emboldened and asks a woman out through an online dating platform. The woman attempts to end the date when conversation sours in response to Ronnie's derogatory use of the word "pussies" to describe the state of men and masculinity, but Ronnie grabs her and tells her she can't leave because he bought her a coffee. This scene illustrates a transactional view of dating in which men believe they are entitled to some next step, often sex, when they buy dinner, drinks (or, in this case, coffee) for women. It is an example of what Emma Beckett has termed "gendered capital," reflecting a phenomenon in which patriarchy and capitalism are "perfectly intertwined."[40] Bystanders intervene and throw Ronnie out of the shop but not before he tells her she's "being a fucking bitch."[41] Ronnie sees the other patrons as white knighting[42] cucks and the woman as a gold-digging vulture indoctrinated into feminazi culture during her college experience, which we learn through Ronnie's increasingly popular VlogTube channel where he posts responses to life events.

It's not just women who are framed as mistreating Ronnie. An Asian-American ride share service representative declines to give Ronnie a job because he fails to produce a driver's license, a phone that can run the necessary app, or a clean and functional car. A nonwhite pawnshop owner condescends to Ronnie, telling him guns aren't toys. Two military veterans (one Black and one white) in the shooting range interrogate and mock Ronnie for wearing a first Gulf War uniform that's obviously not his own. Finally, in a scene that culminates in Ronnie's termination from his job at a local market owned by an Iranian American family, Ronnie is beaten by three young Black men. Although Ronnie instigates the violence by spraying water on the trio's BMW sports car, the movie situates the men as ganging up on Ronnie. They're shown as escalating a petty altercation into physical violence by calling Ronnie "Forest Gump" and "Opie."[43] This scene illustrates the belief that white people are the oppressed party, and there is a double standard elevating the Other while victimizing white men. In every case, Ronnie should be construed as *at least* partially at fault, but the film never fails to diminish his culpability to heighten the perception of him as a victim.

The constant barrage of people who are unkind to Ronnie, whether deserved or otherwise, positions him as an oppressed victim of discrimination and functions to draw clear attention to the few who show him any goodwill. The first is a middle-aged white man, a U.S. veteran and NRA supporter, who is featured sporadically throughout the film speaking with Ronnie about the disappearing American dream (at the hands of immigrants), dating (e.g., women don't like weakness), and being a man (e.g., get knocked down, get up and keep swinging). The second person who *initially* shows Ronnie kindness is webcam model Candy who, with the help of her white supremacist husband Bill, lures Ronnie into her world of sex for sale. As an embodied visual indicator of character ideology, Bill wears several common white supremacist tattoos, including a Norse valknut or "knot of the slain," an Aryan Brotherhood "AB" insignia, and the number 88, which stands for Heil Hitler. He also has the clean shaved head and horseshoe mustache common in some biker gangs, specifically the Nazi Low Riders. Ironically, Bill and Candy never discuss white supremacist ideology with Ronnie and, in fact, cast Ronnie in the role of the cuck husband for Candy's webcam videos. In these videos, which Bill films, Ronnie watches and often masturbates as Candy has sex with Black and Hispanic men—one of whom Candy instructs to ejaculate in Ronnie's face. Despite the white supremacist tattoos and Ronnie's casting as a cuck, one could argue it's Bill who is the cuck since he runs the camera as his wife has sex with nonwhite men (whom his tattoos indicate he would not normally welcome into his home).

When we consider who, exactly, is the cuck in the Candy–Bill–Ronnie triad, contradictions and tensions arise. As Candy's husband, camera operator and, ostensibly, her pimp, Bill seems to be the cuck. However, Bill performs white masculinity (i.e., tall, strong, in control as the king of his castle) according to social norms and, thus, is not equated with cuckoldry in the film. This is cemented when he threatens Ronnie for having sex with Candy without paying. Bill cannot allow Candy to "give it away" because it would undermine his masculine performance. Bill sees Candy having sex with other men as a transaction for which she must be paid. In most cases, Candy's webcam viewers pay to watch her have sex online. Ronnie, however, got it for free. This threatens Bill's masculinity. To rectify this situation and restore Bill's fragile masculinity, Ronnie must be made to pay post facto. This transactional view of sex further distances Bill from being labeled a cuck. Alternatively, Ronnie is paid to perform as a cuck because he fails to appropriately perform white masculinity. In this way, Ronnie is doubly cucked. He is paid to play the role of a cuck for Candy and remains weak and inadequate even when the cameras aren't rolling.

Over the course of the film, Ronnie becomes further enmeshed in the demeaning cuck role of Candy's webcam world, falling in love with her even as he is visibly disgusted by her sexual contact with nonwhite men. At the same time, he also gains increasing notoriety as a far-right white supremacist vlogger. This activity draws the attention of Dalmain, who initially becomes the third person to show interest in Ronnie, recruiting him to the white nationalist cause over dinner following a Trump rally.[44] However, when the videos of Ronnie playing Candy's cuck husband surface online, Dalmain uses his VlogTube channel to publicly "cancel" Ronnie, and Ronnie's imagined romantic relationship with her quickly deteriorates.[45] Ultimately, the deterioration of their relationship leads to Ronnie murdering Candy and Bill.

By visually positioning Ronnie as a loser with low self-esteem through his surroundings and physical appearance, the viewer is guided to see Ronnie's circumstances as largely beyond his control. *Cuck* becomes a story not about the people Ronnie ultimately murders—because, according to the implicit narrative of the film, they deserved it—but about a sympathetic representation of Ronnie as a person in need of redemption because he has been mistreated and handed an unfair lot in life. In this way, the film reproduces the right-wing fetishization of killers and disregard for victims and functions as a form of apologia for white male racism and misogyny. As Sherman's earlier statements suggest, at least some fans identified with the sympathetic portrayal of Ronnie as a white male antihero, which raises concerns about the level of identification individuals may have with real-life lone wolf killers when framed by the mainstream news media as sympathetic and, therefore, somehow justified. In short, the film asks us to empathize with Ronnie as an individual due to circumstances beyond his control, and in the process legitimates his actions, without any serious consideration of how those same circumstances impact many people—most of whom do not commit mass violence—across racial and gender lines every day.

The Not-So-Cunning, Not-So-Lone Wolf

Mr. Dalmain called on us, so we've come.

Ronnie, Cuck

Lone wolves are not quite so lone as the name conveys. Ronnie's involvement with online communities, as well as his material involvement with other people, reflects the falsity of the lone wolf metaphor. As Bart Schuurman et al. (2019) have found, so-called lone wolves are not particularly cunning, as the wolf metaphor implies, but do tend to have ties to larger networks that provide justification and encouragement.[46] This research suggests true lone actors are outliers who often try to recruit others to their cause but fail due to a lack of social skills. Nevertheless, they do typically maintain weak ties to networks while being able to plan effectively and "maintain operational security."[47] Additionally, in their meta-analysis of 119 lone actor terrorists, Paul Gill, John Horgan, and Paige Deckert found evidence of some telling markers that speak to the not-so-loneness of the so-called lone wolf.[48]

First, many of these men had recent exposure to new extremist movements (including related media and propaganda) and links to networks, including efforts to seek legitimization from movement leaders. Many of the most high-profile recent mass shooters have had prolific online footprints and sought connections with like-minded others—the Christchurch shooter, for example, wrote the names of other infamous mass killers on his weapons and livestreamed the event. Similarly, in *Cuck,* Ronnie spends a lot of time online viewing increasingly extreme videos spiraling out from porn and guns and ultimately connecting him with Dalmain from whom he seeks legitimization. Second, many of these men have recently joined politically contentious groups and interacted in the material world with other activists. White supremacists gathered in 2017 at the Unite the Right rally and, more recently, a who's who of far-right extremists intermingled during the January 6 Capitol coup. Likewise, in *Cuck,* Ronnie attends a rally because "Mr. Dalmain called on us."[49] Third, many of these men have friends or family involved in political violence. In *Cuck,* Ronnie's veteran friend leans far right, and Ronnie's proximity to Nazi Bill is illustrative even if the two don't directly talk politics. Finally, to a lesser degree, some of these men have links to a "wider command and control" network that was "specifically associated with the violent event that was planned or carried out."[50] Unsurprisingly, this element is not portrayed in *Cuck,* as to do so would belie the victimized white male anti-hero narrative.

Cuck writer-director Lambert seems to see so-called lone wolf shooters as sympathetic anti-heroes, viewing them as angry, lonely, "confused," and "easily manipulated" "lost boys."[51] Ronnie fits the stereotype in the popular imagination and, unsurprisingly, conforms to Lambert's understanding of lone wolves. It also situates Ronnie as being enmeshed in an online world that reinforces far-right views. This is the baseline for Ronnie's online interactions, which escalate across

212 Meredith L. Pruden

the story arc, as he becomes further entrenched in the digital world of far-right content and the rabbit hole of recommendations and click-throughs. Ronnie's VlogTubes recommendations are a hodgepodge of extremist content that leads him to a real-world rally in support of President Donald Trump. Meanwhile, the America First subREADIT[52] offers ripped-from-the-headlines titles including:

> Parkland crisis actors to receive $100,000 in Federal funds
> False Pizzagate location intentionally leaked
> Patriots Flood Florida in support of Stand Your Ground
> Transgender activist outed as child molester
> Illegals Tried to Rape Me, Texas Mom says
> Black Lives looters set to burn Ferguson again[53]

As Paul Gill, John Horgan, and Paige Deckert (2014) demonstrated, these fictional events provide evidence of Ronnie's links to larger networks. Like so many of the lone wolf shooters on whom the character is purportedly based, Ronnie carries out the final act of violence alone but was radicalized as part of an extremist movement.

Yet, Lambert is quick to point out the film is not intended to be political.[54] Of course, there's absolutely nothing apolitical about gendered mass violence and lone wolf shooters. Wrapping these phenomena in the cloak of a feature film doesn't miraculously strip the politics out of it. There isn't enough movie magic in the world for that. Lambert can pretend *Cuck* is nonpolitical because of the hegemony of white and male supremacism. These ideologies are so systemic, so structural, so pervasive, so taken for granted, they can be framed as apolitical. They seem natural, and what is natural is, by default, outside of human-orchestrated politics. The expectation of militancy in patriotic masculinity is, similarly, naturalized. In Ronnie, we see how this well-established display of real manhood is also highly performative and always politically charged.

Visual and Digital Culture of the Far Right

> Us real patriots, we gotta have each other's backs.
>
> *Ronnie*, Cuck

In early scenes, the film uses stickers on cars and other objects to foreshadow Ronnie's trajectory into the misogynist white right, and the ideas they symbolize are reflected in the digital spaces he traverses. Indeed, they call visual attention to the white man's "victim ideology."[55] The entanglement of material stickers into symbolic digital representation and back into the "real" world again provides evidence of the blurred boundaries between spheres that often—but certainly not always—remain distinct in scholarship. Visual representations of the "crisis" of white male identity and white supremacism aren't confined to one's immediate physical surroundings but also circulate cognitively and affectively in online spaces, where they provide one way for "real patriots" to find one another and "have each other's backs."[56] This is particularly true of social media, where the dominant and naturalized power of whiteness connects otherwise diverse audiences via nostalgic gender conservatism and global antifeminism in a new sort of culture war.[57] For example, Julia DeCook (2018) found the far-right Proud Boys use fascist aesthetics to disseminate the movement's political ideology and propaganda, as well as affirm and visualize their membership in the violent, militaristic, and universally male group.[58]

Similarly, Lisa Nakamura (2007) suggests the computer is a cinematic space where "screen culture is ... the hegemonic cultural interface" for identity work through visual culture.[59] When these far-right messages and fascist aesthetics, engorged with white and male supremacist symbolism, circulate via social media, the result is often increased engagement for the posters and increased political anxieties and extremist attitudes for their followers.[60] This is, in part, because extremist content proliferates in social digital spaces characterized by interactivity and perceived anonymity that drive a propensity for vilification and the "performance of outrage" in identity construction.[61] For the far right and other extremist identities, this can coalesce and emerge as what Kevin Michael DeLuca and Jennifer Peeples (2010) have called "the productive role of violence in social protest on the public screen."[62]

The *Cuck* team is clearly aware of this phenomenon to some degree, and the skillful way in which they fold these representations in on themselves is one of the few elements of the film that can't be faulted. Peppered throughout Ronnie's environment, these visual artifacts symbolize his ideology and are widely circulated within the digital ecosystem of which he is a part, both by Ronnie and others. Images that symbolize patriotism feature prominently in *Cuck*. From military fatigues and other regalia, to the U.S. flag—which emerges as room decor, animated online video background, draped across shoulders in a stock image for a protest flyer, and even as a folding chair—these symbols of U.S. nationalism stand in for Ronnie's military rejection but also become markers of his gradual awakening to the red pill, white nationalism, and, ultimately, fascistic authoritarian thinking. This becomes most clear when Ronnie attends the rally and encounters counterprotesters wielding hand-scrawled signs reading "Dump Trump" and a giant papier-mâché Trump doppelgänger complete with Ku Klux Klan hood in hand. Ronnie appears confused by the disrespect shown to a sitting U.S. president but records the scene for posterity and his VlogTubes channel, where he calls the protesters, among other things, anti-American "lib-cucks."

The far-right movement tends to elevate so-called lone wolves to the level of warrior-saint-martyr as a form of motivation for others to emulate the act of mass violence, and one of the ways by which they do this is reframing images as propaganda.[63] This is effective for recruitment and mobilization because, according to W.J.T. Mitchell, pictures have a sort of "visual reciprocity" by which they are "not merely a by-product of social reality but actively constitutive of it."[64]

The role of visual reciprocity in the radicalization of far-right actors is made clear in the fictional world of *Cuck*, with visual markers of far-right male whiteness prevalent throughout the film. Ronnie materially surrounds himself with nationalistic and military iconography, as well as soft-core pornography, from the film's outset and becomes increasingly enmeshed in the far-right digital world throughout the course of the film. Across the process of Ronnie's "awakening," it becomes progressively more difficult to tell if the images reflect his reality or are radicalizing him into a new one.

Conclusion

In *Cuck*, the depiction of Ronnie's imperiled white masculinity, which is attached to his inability to achieve professional and sexual success, conforms to the common belief that male supremacy is a gateway to the white right. Ronnie has been unable to achieve an idealized masculinity and so descends into extremism where he finds validation as his online channel gains followers and keyboard warriors egg him on. The film narrativizes the gateway metaphor to situate its protagonist as a sympathetic victim triggered by circumstances beyond his control and, in this way, reinforces the myth of white male victimhood. By the time the film climaxes with Ronnie's violent rampage—during which he strangles his mother, shoots Candy and Bill in their home, and nearly kills the shop owner and his son—he has been positioned as justified in this act of retributive mass violence.

It is only after this final violent act that we finally learn Ronnie's father killed himself with baby Ronnie in his arms, reinforcing the perception that Ronnie has been a victim effectively from birth. Since that time, his life has been a series of letdowns, rejections, and an endless assault on his white masculinity. When he finally thinks he has it all together, with a job, love, and a place of respect in the white nationalist community, everyone turns on him again—only now the ridicule is quickly circulated online. In the face of this new emasculation, the film frames Ronnie as having no other recourse than to don his father's U.S. Army uniform one last time and wage war against those who wronged him before committing suicide by cop. This is an anti-hero's death. As he lies in a pool of his own blood, war paint streaked across his face, his open yet lifeless eyes staring up at the night sky, the film cuts to a clip Ronnie filmed on his trip to the rally that's been posthumously posted to VlogTubes as *Van Nuys Shooter—Lost Tape*:

> I had the opportunity to meet one of my … heroes… I feel like someone's … listening to me. … All you patriots who keep subscribing … that means the world to me. … I feel like … we are gonna change the world. This year has been the best. … Stay strong patriots.

In the clip, the sun is shining and reflects Ronnie's unusually chipper mood. He feels seen and productive for the first time and is certain things are changing for the better. Leaving the viewer with this image confirms our understanding of Ronnie as a sympathetic anti-hero thwarted by external forces and triggered to commit violence by circumstances beyond his control. It also reminds us, no matter what Lambert says, that this film is equivocally not apolitical, and Ronnie is not a "lone wolf."

Continuing to frame white male mass killers as lone wolves individualizes and pathologizes their violence as the act of one deranged or triggered man while failing to recognize any contributing structural components—namely, white and male supremacism. For example, many lone wolf killers have a documented history of violence against women that, because it is generally interpersonal in nature and takes place in the private sphere, is not considered "real" violence and remains disconnected from conversations about lone wolf terrorism as a global security threat.[65] This "oversight" allows aggrieved white men, and apparently filmmakers, to discursively construct themselves as occupying an oppressed position from which they can deploy strategies of hegemonic whiteness while at the same time appropriate the tactics of subaltern counterpublics. When these narratives are perpetuated by the media, they end up reinforcing whiteness as unmarked, invisible, and rational power as individual white men become visible only when they make explicit claims to their ethno-European identity because they have been "victimized" by cultural Marxism and are triggered to commit retributive violence. In other words, centering wounded white masculinity winds up sanctioning white male violence.

Notes

1 Red pill theory originated in far-right message boards and is a nod to the *Matrix* franchise. In the film, the protagonist chooses whether he'll take the red pill and see the world for what it is or take the blue pill and go back to his former state of blissful ignorance. While there are gradations of red pill theory, most are rooted in the belief that feminism has ruined society and left women unfairly in charge (thereby oppressing men).

2 Cuckold is an Old English word describing the husband of an unfaithful wife. In contemporary usage, it often has a racialized meaning, signifying a white man whose white wife has sex with a Black man. The term has evolved to become a popular insult among the far-right—and more recently conservatives at large—meant to describe weak men. This could be liberals or conservatives, aka "cuckservatives," deemed complicit in liberal politics.

3 Dictionary.com, s.v. "Cuck," accessed September 2, 2020, https://www.dictionary.com/e/slang/cuck/.

4 R.J. Frometa, "What the Cuck? An Exclusive Interview with Director Rob Lambert," *VENTS Magazine*, May 17, 2018, https://ventsmagazine.com/2018/05/17/what-the-cuck-an-exclusive-interview-with-director-rob-lambert/.

5 Frometa, "What the Cuck?" It should be noted, despite the film's emphasis on whiteness, the Santa Barbara killer was half-Asian.

6 See, for example, Mark Lindsay and David Lester, "Suicide-by-Cop: Committing Suicide by Provoking Police to Shoot You (1st ed.)" (Amityville, NY: Baywood Publishing Company, 2004).

216 Meredith L. Pruden

7 Aaron Berry, "Cuck: A Cautionary Tale for No One," *Film Inquiry*, October 3, 2019, https://www.filminquiry.com/cuck-2019-review/.

8 Glenn Kenny, "'Cuck Review: When Bigotry Meets Pornography. Yes, It's That Bad," *New York Times*, October 3, 2019, https://www.nytimes.com/2019/10/03/movies/cuck-review.html.

9 4.1/10 on IMDB; 44/100% "Tomatometer" score and 64% audience score on Rotten Tomatoes; 40/100 metascore and 4.4/10 user score on Metacritic; 3.5/5 on Amazon Prime Video.

10 Chance Solem-Pfeifer, "An Oregon-Bred Actor Takes on One of the Most Challenging Roles of His Career," *Willamette Week*, October 15, 2019, https://www.wweek.com/arts/2019/10/15/an-oregon-bred-actor-takes-on-one-of-the-most-challenging-roles-of-his-career/.

11 Robert Hariman and John Louis Lucaites, *The Public Image: Photography and Civic Spectatorship* (Chicago, IL: University of Chicago Press, 2016), 14.

12 Greg M. Smith, *Film Structure and the Emotion System* (Cambridge: Cambridge University Press, 2003), 41.

13 Derek P. McCormack, "Moving Images for Moving Bodies," in *Refrains for Moving Bodies: Experience and Experiment in Affective Spaces* (Durham: Duke University Press, 2014), 141–64.

14 Alison Harvey, *Feminist Media Studies* (Cambridge: Polity Press, 2020), 59.

15 Many far-right and white nationalist actors believe in a Jewish-led transnational cabal (the Zionist Occupied Government or ZOG) that controls world banking institutions, media outlets, and federal governments and which actively seeks to demographically reduce and financially harm white populations.

16 Surveillance capitalism is a powerful "invisible hand ... used to deprive populations of choice in the matter of what about their lives remains secret" online and redistributes rights into the hands of the "Big Other" (i.e., tech firms like Google, Facebook, etc.) through a "logic of accumulation" for profit. Shoshana Zuboff, "Big Other: Surveillance Capitalism and the Prospects of an Information Civilization," *Journal of Information Technology* 30 (2015): 75–89. Importantly, much of this is premised on an improved online experience for consumers, who opt-in to being surveilled.

17 VlogTubes is a riff on the online video-sharing platform YouTube.

18 I have used the term "lone wolf" in places throughout this chapter because the film's director uses it to describe Ronnie, but I don't agree with this stereotype of violent misogynists and white supremacists. For an overview and/or critique of this concept, see John G. Horgan, Paul Gill, Noemie Bouhana, James Silver, and Emily Corner, "Across the Universe? A Comparative Analysis of Violent Behavior and Radicalization across Three Offender Types with Implications for Criminal Justice Training and Education" (U.S. Department of Justice, Washington D.C., 2016); Bart Schuurman, Masse Lindekilde, Stefan Malthaner, Francis O'Connor, Paul Gill, and Noémie Bouhana, "End of the Lone Wolf: The Typology That Should Not Have Been," *Studies in Conflict & Terrorism* 42, no. 8 (2019):771–78; Jude McCulloch, Sandra Walklate, JaneMaree Maher, Kate Fitz-Gibbon, and Jasmine McGowan, "Lone Wolf Terrorism through a Gendered Lens: Men Turning Violent or Violent Men Behaving Violently?" *Critical Criminology* 27 (2019): 437–50.

19 This exchange happens while Ronnie is talking with a friend. The friend initiates the hate speech, and Ronnie agrees with and expands upon it.

20 *Cuck*, directed by Rob Lambert (2019; Los Angeles, CA: Rimrock Pictures), Amazon, 2019.

21 *Cuck*, 2019.
22 Thomas K. Nakayama and Judith N. Martin, *Whiteness: The Communication of Social Identity* (Thousand Oaks, CA: Sage, 1999).
23 Ibid.
24 Rachel Alicia Griffin, "Problematic Representations of Strategic Whiteness and 'Post-racial' Pedagogy: A Critical Intercultural Reading of The Help," *Journal of International and Intercultural Communication* 8, no. 2 (2015): 147–66.
25 Holger Marcks and Janina Pawelz, "From Myths of Victimhood to Fantasies of Violence: How Far-Right Narratives of Imperilment Work," *Terrorism and Political Violence* (2020): 1–18, https://doi.org/10.1080/09546553.2020.1788544.
26 Bharath Ganesh, "Weaponizing White Thymos: Flows of Rage in the Online Audiences of the Alt-Right," *Cultural Studies* (2020): 1–33, https://doi.org/10.1080/09502386.2020.1714687. Ganesh uses thymos to describe "the part of our souls that desires recognition of injustices done to us," 2.
27 Mitch Berbrier, "The Victim Ideology of White Supremacists and White Separatists in the United States," *Sociological Focus* 33, no. 2 (2000): 175–91, 187.
28 Ibid., 187.
29 Ibid., 179–84.
30 Nakayama and Martin, *Whiteness*.
31 Brian L. Ott and Greg Dickinson, "Visual Rhetoric and/as Critical Pedagogy," in *The SAGE Handbook of Rhetorical Studies*, eds. Andrea A. Lunsford, Kirt H. Wilson, and Rosa A. Eberly (Thousand Oaks, CA: Sage, 2008), 325.
32 Paul Elliot Johnson, "Walter White(ness) Lashes Out: Breaking Bad and Male Victimage," *Critical Studies in Media Communication*, vol. 34, no. 1 (2017): 14–28.
33 Solem-Pfeifer, "An Oregon-Bred Actor."
34 *Mommy Dearest* was a 1978 memoir written by actress Joan Crawford's adopted daughter detailing her upbringing. In 1981, the book was adapted to a film starring Faye Dunaway as an alcoholic mother (Crawford) who manipulated and abused her adopted children.
35 According to manosphere and far-right terminology, alpha males are at the top of the social hierarchy. They're the most attractive, sexually desirable, and financially successful men. From a gender studies perspective, they're the heteronormative men who best conform to a normalized male-identified gender performance according to ideal societal standards.
36 Laura Sjoberg and Caron E. Gentry, *Mother's, Monsters, Whores: Women's Violence in Global Politics* (London: Zed Books, 2007), 12.
37 Ronnie has just finished watching an online video explaining the 80/20 rule, "It's just math. Eighty percent of women are seeking that top 20 percent of men. And, if you wanna compete with the Chads, that's who you gotta be."
38 *Cuck*, 2019.
39 Elliot Rodger, "My Twisted World: The Story of Elliot Rodger," [manifesto], 2014.
40 Sophie Gallagher, "I Bought Your Drinks, So You Owe Me Sex – Why Do Some Men Believe Dating Is a Transaction," *HuffPost*, June 18, 2019, https://www.huffingtonpost.co.uk/entry/i-bought-your-drinks-so-you-owe-me-sex-why-do-some-men-believe-dating-is-a-transaction_uk_5cf6a9cce4b0a1997b724e30.
41 *Cuck*, 2019.
42 White knighting is a derogatory term commonly used by the far-right and male supremacists describing when men come to the aid of women who are being harassed and abused.

43 These names are used in a pejorative and anti-disability manner, reflecting an ableist viewpoint. *Cuck*, 2019.
44 The rally depicted in *Cuck* is a real-life rally that took place in Beverly Hills, California. Sherman has said it was the hardest part of the movie to shoot because he's personally left-leaning. Solem-Pfeifer, "An Oregon-Bred Actor."
45 In the montage released online, Candy has sex with a string of men as Ronnie watches. Throughout the scene, she verbally berates and belittles Ronnie as he masturbates. In one particularly graphic scene, which we see earlier in the film as well, Candy instructs her partner to ejaculate on Ronnie's face.
46 Shuurman et al., "End of the Lone Wolf," 771–78.
47 Ibid., 774.
48 Paul Gill, John Horgan, and Paige Deckert, "Bombing Alone: Tracing the Motivations and Antecedent Behaviors of Lone-Actor Terrorists," *Journal of Forensic Sciences* (2013): https://doi.org/10.1111/1556-4029.12312.
49 *Cuck*, 2019.
50 Gill, Horgan, and Deckert, "Bombing Alone," 430.
51 Frometa, "What the Cuck."
52 The America First subREADIT is a spinoff of earlier far-right message boards on Reddit.
53 *Cuck*, 2019.
54 Frometa, "What the Cuck."
55 Berbrier, "The Victim Ideology."
56 *Cuck*, 2019.
57 Agneiszka Graff, Ratna Kapur, and Suzanna Danuta Walters, "Introduction: Gender and the Rise of the Global Right," *Signs: Journal of Women in Culture and Society* 44, no. 3 (2019): 541–60; Johnson, "Walter White(ness) Lashes Out."
58 Julia R. DeCook, "Memes and Symbolic Violence: #Proudboys and the Use of Memes for Propaganda and the Construction of Collective Identity," *Learning, Media and Technology* 34, no. 4 (2018): 485–504.
59 Nakamura, Digitizing Race: Visual Cultures of the Internet, (Minneapolis: University of Minnesota Press, 2008).
60 Raffael Heiss and Jörg Matthes, "Stuck in a Nativist Spiral: Content, Selection, and Effects of Right-Wing Populists' Communication on Facebook," *Political Communication* 37, no. 3 (2020): 303–28.
61 Thomas K. Nakayama, "What's Next for Whiteness and the Internet," *Critical Studies in Media Communication* 34 (2017): 68–72, 70.
62 Kevin Michael DeLuca and Jennifer Peeples, "From Public Sphere to Public Screen: Democracy, Activism, and the 'Violence' of Seattle," *Critical Studies in Media Communication* 19, no. 2 (2002): 125–51. These authors examine World Trade Organization protests and are not focused on the far right; however, their assertion—that images of violence in the service of a cause shared online have power—is relevant here.
63 Ari Ben Am and Gabriel Weimann, "Fabricated Martyrs: The Warrior-Saint Icons of Far-Right Terrorism," *Perspectives on Terrorism* 14, no. 5 (2020): 219–35.
64 W.J.T. Mitchell, *What Do Pictures Want?* (Chicago, IL: University Of Chicago Press, 2004), 47.
65 McCulloch et al., "Lone Wolf Terrorism."

11

TRANS WOMEN AND THE INVISIBLE SISTERHOOD

Katherine Cross

> This is a lightly edited reprint of a speech delivered at the opening plenary of the 2013 State University of New York—New Paltz Women's Studies Conference.

Patriarchy does not begin in our bodies.

Contrary to those theories, feminist and otherwise, that seek an "origin myth" for patriarchy somewhere in the uterus, patriarchy has no starting point in reproductive organs of any kind—there is nothing in our marrow as women that sets us up as ontological victims of men whose bodies, whose bits, predispose them to oppression.

In the words of legal scholar Catharine MacKinnon:

> It is one thing to identify woman's biology as part of the terrain on which a struggle for dominance is acted out; it is another to identify woman's biology as the source of that subordination. The first approach certainly identifies an intimate alienation; the second predicates woman's status on the facticity of her biology.[1]

While there's much to dispute in her whorephobic oeuvre, she was certainly right about *this*.

Put bluntly, there is no truly feminist or social-scientific way to reason that patriarchy begins in a womb, an ovary, or a vagina. Rather, it is the *meaning* society gives our bodies that oppresses us—and also what binds us together, however unwillingly. I begin here because if I am to speak about trans women's experience of reproductive injustice, I cannot indulge the false premise that women are born to be oppressed—a very different proposition from saying we are born

DOI: 10.4324/9781003164722-15

into a world that oppresses us. After all, much searing truth remains in Simone de Beauvoir's timeless assertion, "One is not born, but rather becomes, woman."[2]

The oppression of other genders by cisgender men does not begin in any of our bodies, but it is often very intimately concerned with them. Patriarchy powerfully regulates and controls women's bodies, for instance—not because a sizeable percentage of women have ovaries (not all of us do), nor because many women menstruate (not all of us do), nor because every woman can get pregnant (many of us can't)—but because there is a powerful, controlling ideology about what bodies are *for* that transcends the particulars of any one woman's embodiment.

Feminism has often been accused—sometimes wrongly, sometimes rightly—of essentialising and universalising "woman." Yet more often than not it is feminism that has been the necessary antidote to the patriarchal myth that all women are the same bundle of incapabilities imbuing an alabaster, pedestalised angel who exists only for man's pleasure. Every woman who does not fit is cast into the fires of violent oppression at its most naked; women of colour, transgender women, poor women, women with disabilities, loud and outspoken women, sex working women, any woman regardless of race and class who refuses the objectification of that invisible cage. As we are tortured in the shadows, the myth of patriarchal essentialism—centred on a mythic, silent, and obedient white cis virgin upon her pedestal—beats on. This, too, impacts how patriarchy treats nonbinary people as well, brutalised for their perceived failure to *be* either men or women as assigned at birth.

Male dominance gives our bodies a very particular meaning, one that purportedly unites us and submerges all particularity, all individuality, beneath its event horizon. Our bodies are meant for one thing, and one thing alone. Ours is to reproduce; if we cannot, we are condemned—we join those considered unable to fulfil their supposedly naturally ordained functions. And yet, we know patriarchy does not apply this meaning equally; for all its mythologising about the eternal feminine and the ultimate indistinguishable unity of women, it is cognisant of our differences. This gendered oppression is not just patriarchal but also homo/transphobic, white supremacist in many places, and classist. As a system, it has striven to prevent some women from reproducing—killed or sterilised by the hundreds of thousands, targeted daily by microaggressions writ painfully small and propaganda writ blazingly large.

Yet even in this case, we see where patriarchy begins and ends: its alpha and omega is the *meaning* forced on people's bodies, and so much hinges on how suited we are judged to be for reproductive purposes. So much hatred is directed at us around the issue of reproduction—whether it is forcing white women to have children or forcing Black women, Native women, and Latinas not to. Patriarchy really cares about what we're doing with our bodies.

Consider, no less, how the interventions of women of colour have broadened feminist understandings of reproductive justice: reminding us that reproductive injustice happens when we are forced not to bear children or adopt, as when we are forced to do so. In every case, what links them is both a denial of women's agency—our right to choose—and a meaning imposed on our bodies by a sexist society that seeks to stifle and suffocate our humanity beneath that overriding myth of idealised motherhood. Motherhood on the terms of cisgender men, particularly white men: composed of the right kind of mothers, doing the right and proper things—mostly involving keeping our mouths shut and bearing our pain with silence and obedience.

Where does one suppose trans women fit into this?

Feminist activist and former city councillor Sarah Brown once posted a conversation between herself and a cisgender man who was sexually harassing her, fetishising her for being a trans woman. He cack-handedly asked her whether she was trans or cis by saying, "so r u a natural woman?"

Her reply: "What, like the song? Or do you mean, do I occur in the universe? Because, I like to think so."

That natural occurrence is, perhaps, one of the more troubling aspects of our existence, so far as patriarchy is concerned. For a society that believes so very passionately that women are made to reproduce—and to do so in a certain way—the fact that we keep damnably and insistently popping up is a source of unending consternation to those most invested in biologist myths. Put plainly, I am not supposed to exist. I shouldn't be here, and my occurrence in the universe not only disrupts what is meant by "natural" but also what is meant by "woman." I share that quality, as I alluded to earlier, with many women whose bodies are not capable of reproducing in the way women are presumed to be universally able to.

You may wonder why I spent the last couple of minutes on so much foreground, by the way, barely mentioning transgender people at first. The reason for this, for summoning up theoretical arguments against essentialism that underlay the best of the feminist tradition, is explained by the following comment from a cisgender woman replying to an article I wrote on Feministing about why "trans rights are reproductive rights":

> Reproductive rights are at their core the right not to die or be crippled or to be left destitute or be trapped in a violent relationship by an unwanted/ unplanned … pregnancy. / Trans women cannot get pregnant, this is not about trans women.[3]

One supposes that this isn't about all the *cisgender* women out there who can't get pregnant either.

Statements like this, which appear well-meaning, mistake the terrain of reproductive injustice for its fundamental cause. There is no doubt that women who get pregnant are ruthlessly targeted by our society for dehumanisation and shackled by a regime of bodily control, one way or the other. But for those of us who cannot, we are in many cases ruthlessly attacked in part because we are unable or unwilling to fulfil the patriarchal mandate that says women must bear children in order for them to be both legitimate and successful women. We all feel that pressure, whatever our bodily configurations may be. That's because it doesn't arise from our bodies or begin in the shape of our genitalia but instead is projected onto us by the society in which we live.

When I came out, one of the first things my father lamented was the loss of his grandchildren, the loss of progeny who would—by blood—carry his name and his "legacy." Then came the recriminations about what my body was "for" and what "God put us on this earth to do." I was no good to my family as a woman if I could not bear children. Interwoven in all of this is that very ideology about what bodies are for. It is precisely the same ideology that has seen women coerced into having children, that has seen people of colour brutalised under eugenics programmes that sterilised them, and that has created a byzantine web of regulations regarding what trans people can and cannot do with their bodies.

It is the ideology behind laws in many countries that require trans people to be sterilised before our gender markers can be changed on various IDs and the ideology that still sees too many psychiatrists enforcing gender norms on their trans patients as a pre-requisite of trans healthcare. We all have different medical needs as trans people, but for those of us who require hormones and surgery, we are often spiritually blackmailed for them ("wear this skirt and makeup, or I won't see you as a serious woman"). We may be charged dearly for the pleasure and then laughed at if we suggest such things should be covered by either public or private insurance. We may also be denied transition altogether.

All in the name of what some people—particularly men—think our bodies are for. What they think a woman's body should be.

One of the central reasons that what we do is considered "self-mutilation" is that we are seen to be destroying our purportedly natural reproductive capacity. We are seen to be revolting against a genetic inheritance that should obviate the very existence of transgender people; sinful enough. Yet, far worse in the eyes of many petty patriarchs is when trans people express their biological reproductive capacity. All the consternation over Thomas Beatie, a trans man who made headlines with his pregnancies, makes this plain. Until recently, laws in Australia, in the United Kingdom, and in several American states prohibited trans people from changing the gender markers on identity documents until we could prove we've surgically altered our genitals.[4]

Our limited access to reproductive care facilities illustrates our ongoing illegibility in this area. All such facilities expect an unproblematically cisgender man or woman. So when a Planned Parenthood clinic is confronted with a transgender man who needs a gynaecologist, or when a sperm bank is confronted with a trans woman who wants to have children of her own someday, or when a nonbinary person merely asks for recognition of their true selves, it occasions the medical equivalent of a constitutional crisis that sees these trans people shown the door more often than not, left to fend for ourselves.

When trying to bank her sperm, one trans woman I know was asked by the attendant on the phone why she was doing this. When my friend explained, the staffer abruptly said, "That's not real" and hung up on her. Meanwhile, a close

Trans Women and the Invisible Sisterhood **223**

friend simply got the "don't call us, we'll call you" treatment when she revealed she was trans.

We are damned because through transition, we may sterilise ourselves, but we are equally damned if we try to preserve and express biologic reproductive capacity. We transition; therefore, we upend naturalist myths—which is bad enough—but to make sure we don't pass on our cooties and do even more violence to that patriarchal mythology, the state demands that we become sterile anyway if it is to suffer our insistent existence.

Little medical research is done on trans people and reproduction—whether to simply collect data or to create organs that might allow me to bear the child I should love to have someday—we are not supposed to exist, after all.

Yet that existence threatens patriarchy on a more existential level. We as trans people—whether we are trans women, trans men, or genderqueer—expose the fatal flaw of naturalism, just as many before us have in ways great and small. But in our way, we put the lie to the idea that to be a woman, or a man, means fulfilling some evolutionary imperative or to silently obey the edicts of our selfish genes while using the bits we were born with.

We upend the idea that one is born anything and tacitly remind all that we "become" something.

When I go out into the world and have a gender ascribed to me—one that is almost always some kind of woman—the people who gender me are not thinking about my genitals, or my chromosomes, or what is on my birth certificate. I present as a woman, according to the various cues that our society assigns to the gender of "woman"; therefore, I am one so far as they are concerned. Therefore I am treated as one.

I run the same risk as cis women do of going into a job interview and being silently judged because I'm a young woman who "might get pregnant and leave"—I might get mommy-tracked if I'm hired, and if I come out, I run the risk of being fired because I'm trans. No uterus required, just patriarchy.

In the street, I face men who sexually harass me because they see me as a woman, and therefore they feel entitled to my body, whatever its configuration. No uterus required, just patriarchy.

I find myself condescended to and mansplained to; I've been the target of rape threats; I have been stalked and harassed online; I've been called every sexist and transmisogynist slur in the book—including ones I hadn't heard of. I was told that I was a "feminazi whore with too much sand in her fake vagina." I'd never spoken to this man about my body—and but for the word "fake" he merely said what he might've said to any cis woman. No uterus required, just patriarchy.

Until very recently, it was legal for police to raid the handbags of trans women of colour in New York City and then arrest them on prostitution charges if they're found to be carrying condoms. Police abuse continues in other ways. Where are their reproductive rights, one wonders? No uterus required, just patriarchy.

Women are not wombs; that is one of the most powerful lessons that feminism has tried to teach a stricken world.

Women are not oppressed because we have wombs; wombs are attacked because *they are perceived to belong to women*. For those of us without wombs, because we are still seen as women, our bodies are disciplined and controlled in other ways. For trans men, genderqueer, and nonbinary people with wombs, who all refuse a womanhood patriarchy relentlessly tries to foist upon them, they too find themselves viciously attacked in part because they refuse to adhere to naturalism—they may dare to show that pregnancy does not *only* define the condition of woman. It is just another way of being a *person*. That sort of universal humanity dissolves the fibrous logics of oppression.

We as trans women are not an entryist plot trying to distract from "the real issues," we are women who are simply trying to get by, trying to move around, trying to live, and to claim the humanity that is our common birthright. We bring not dissension and dissolution, but the same truths that women down the centuries from Sojourner Truth to the "Lavender Menace" have brought. The truth of feminism's promise: that none of us will win unless all of us do and that we are all ultimately united in struggle.

We as trans women have always been here—for while theoretical debates about our womanhood prevail, the fact of our womanhood prevails in the world out there. Patriarchy makes no mistakes about us; we are targeted because we are women, uniting us in a great, if at times unwilling, sisterhood invisible.

That notion of sisterhood, battered over the years by so much needful criticism, still thrums through so many trans women who find comfort and refuge among other women like them—and sometimes, as has been blessedly true with me, cisgender women who see in me their lives and struggles recited back to them in a different voice that resonates with theirs.

What links us is not our scars or the ways we have been hurt but our aspirations to rise above oppression's fetters and claim our bodies for ourselves. We share something far more essential than a body: we share the fact that we are survivors. We share the fact that patriarchy imposes a meaning on our bodies that demands something soul-wrenching from us. And yet that "we" remains riven by the illimitable strikes of white supremacy; as a Latina, I often feel furthest away from other women not because of transphobia but because of white supremacy. Universalist identity has taken a beating for good reason. What is "woman" if not just another white supremacist construct that privileges white women over everyone else? What is "woman" to nonbinary people who find the very notion a straitjacket?

Instead of seeing "woman" as one pole at the end of an iron dyad, it should be viewed as one voice in a chorus. A shared identity that has profound social meaning and a standpoint from which we can share in the fight against oppression and marginalisation. But we should resist the urge—as I have had to here, in both writing and editing this piece—to lionise womanhood in such a way that it recreates patriarchal mythology in feminist colours. What remains true is that cisgender and transgender women are oppressed by very similar forces. I am not "just like you" any more than you are just like me, but our political situations are inextricably bound together. Patriarchal bathroom policing of trans people inevitably comes around to gender non-normative cis women; the same laws, norms, and rules that police how I can alter my body also stem from the logics inhibiting cis women's reproductive freedom; the laws governing who I can and cannot love, and how, affect you too. This is not a paean to selfishness, to claim that we should only stand together because of this shared interest. It is simply a fact.

And in that very specific way, I am you and you are me. To view trans women as sisters is simply another step towards survival.

Notes

1 Catharine MacKinnon, *Toward a Feminist Theory of the State* (Cambridge: Harvard University Press, 1989), 54.
2 Simone de Beauvoir, *The Second Sex*, trans. Constance Borde and Sheila Malovany-Chevallier (New York: Vintage Books, 2011), 283.
3 Phorest Phire, April 21, 2012 6:26pm, "comment on," Katherine Cross, "Trans Rights Are Reproductive Rights," *Feministing* (blog), April 10, 2012, https://web.archive.org/web/20140724123343/http:/feministing.com/2012/04/10/trans-rights-are-reproductive-rights/.
4 As I updated this article, nonbinary and intersex people were finally offered access to a gender marker of X on U.S. passports in mid-2021, at last severing the link between perceived reproductive status and identity in government documentation. But much work remains to be done in a time when attacks on transgender people are renewed in their vigour and anti-trans "feminism" allies itself with the far right.

BIBLIOGRAPHY

"A New Paradigm for Welfare Policy: Recommendations to Congress on the Reauthorization of PRWORA." Staff Draft, United States Commission on Civil Rights, July 2002. Accessed January 4, 2020. https://www.usccr.gov/pubs/prwora/old.htm

"False Reporting." National Sexual Violence Resource Center, 2012. https://www.nsvrc.org/sites/default/files/Publications_NSVRC_Overview_False-Reporting.pdf

"Pro-life Activists Confronted, Attacked on Camera." *Fox News 11*, July 2014. https://video.foxnews.com/v/3669804665001#sp=show-clips

"Table A-1. Employment Status of the Civilian Population by Sex and Age." *Bureau of Labor Statistics*, January 6, 2017. https://www.bls.gov/news.release/empsit.t01.htm

"The American National Election Studies, 2016 Time Series Study." *Stanford University and the University of Michigan*, December 2017. http://www.electionstudies.org/studypages/anes_timeseries_2016/anes_timeseries_2016.htm

"'Welfare Queen' Becomes Issue in Reagan's Campaign." *The New York Times*, February 15, 1976. Accessed https://www.nytimes.com/1976/02/15/archives/welfare-queen-becomes-issue-in-reagan-campaign-hitting-a-nerve-now.html

Agrikoliansky, Eric, and Annie Collovald. "Mobilisations Conservatrices: Comment les Dominants Contestent?" *Politix* 106, no. 2 (2014): 7–29.

Allen, Silas. "Anti-abortion Group Sues Oklahoma State University." *The Oklahoman*, January 29, 2013. https://oklahoman.com/article/3749938/anti-abortion-group-sues-oklahoma-state-university?page=1

Almog, Ran, and Danny Kaplan. "The Nerd and His Discontent." *Men and Masculinities* 20, no. 1 (2017): 27–48. https://doi.org/10.1177/1097184X15613831

American Bible Society. *Stand in the Gap: A Sacred Assembly of Men. Commemorative Edition New Testament. Contemporary English Version.* Nashville, TN: Thomas Nelson Publishers, 1997.

American College of Obstetricians and Gynecologists. "Increasing Access to Abortion." https://www.acog.org/clinical/clinical-guidance/committee-opinion/articles/2020/12/increasing-access-to-abortion

Bibliography   **227**

Anderson, Dianna. "MRAs for Jesus: A Look Inside the Christian 'Manosphere'." *Rewire*, September 30, 2014. https://rewire.news/article/2014/09/30/mras-jesus-look-inside-christian-manosphere/

Anderson, Kristin J. *Modern Misogyny: Anti-feminism in a Post-Feminist Era*. New York: Oxford University Press, 2015.

Aosved, Allison C., and Patricia J. Long. "Co-Occurrence of Rape Myth Acceptance, Sexism, Racism, Homophobia, Ageism, Classism, and Religious Intolerance." *Sex Roles* 55, no. 7–8 (2006): 481–92.

Bacarisse, Bonnie. "The Republican Lawmaker Who Secretly Created Reddit's Women-Hating 'Red Pill'." Accessed February 11, 2021. https://www.thedailybeast.com/the-republican-lawmaker-who-secretly-created-reddits-women-hating-red-pill

Baele, Stephane J., Lewys Brace, and Travis G. Coan. "From "Incel" to "Saint": Analyzing the Violent Worldview Behind the 2018 Toronto Attack." *Terrorism and Political Violence* (2019): 1–25. https://doi.org/10.1080/09546553.2019.1638256

Baird-Windle, Patricia, and Eleanor J. Bader. *Targets of Hatred: Anti-Abortion Terrorism*. New York: Palgrave, 2001.

Baker Beck, Debra. "The 'F' Word: How the Media Frame Feminism." *NWSA Journal* 10, no. 1 (Spring 1998): 139–53.

Baker, Paula. "The Domestication of Politics: Women and American Political Society, 1780–1920." *The American Historical Review* 89, no. 3 (1984): 620–47. Accessed December 9, 2020. https://doi.org/10.2307/1856119

Balmer, Randall. *Thy Kingdom Come*. New York: Basic Books, 2006.

Bard, Christine, ed. *Un Siècle d'Antiféminisme*. Paris: Fayard, 1999.

Barreto, Manuela, and Naomi Ellemers. "The Perils of Political Correctness: Men's and Women's Responses to Old-Fashioned and Modern Sexist Views." *Social Psychology Quarterly* 68, no. 1 (2005): 75–88.

Barthélemy, Hélène. "How Men's Rights Groups Helped Rewrite Regulations on Campus Rape." *The Nation*, August 14, 2020. https://www.thenation.com/article/politics/betsy-devos-title-ix-mens-rights/

Basu, Srimati. "Looking through Misogyny: Indian Men's Rights Activists, Law, and Challenges for Feminism." *Canadian Journal of Women and the Law* 28, no. 1 (2016): 45–68. https://doi.org/10.3138/cjwl.28.1.45

Beauchamp, Zack. "Incel, the Misogynist Ideology That Inspired the Deadly Toronto Attack, Explained." Accessed February 10, 2021. https://www.vox.com/world/2018/4/25/17277496/incel-toronto-attack-alek-minassian

Beinart, Peter. "Fear of a Female President." *The Atlantic*, September 8, 2016. http://www.theatlantic.com/magazine/archive/2016/10/fear-of-a-female-president/497564/

Belonsky, Andrew. "Michelle Bernard: 'The Republican Party Needs to Find Its Soul'." *Independent Women's Forum*, April 9, 2009. http://www.iwf.org/news/2435006/Michelle-Bernard:-'The-Republican-Party-Needs-to-Find-Its-Soul'

Ben Am, Ari, and Gabriel Weimann. "Fabricated Martyrs: The Warrior-Saint Icons of Far-Right Terrorism." *Perspectives on Terrorism* 14, no. 5 (2020): 219–35.

Benford Robert, D., and David A. Snow. "Framing Processes and Social Movements: An Overview and Assessment." *Annual Review of Sociology* 26, no. 1 (August 2000): 611–39.

Berbrier, Mitch. "The Victim Ideology of White Supremacists and White Separatists in the United States." *Sociological Focus* 33, no. 2 (2000): 175–91.

Berkowitz, Bill. "'Cultural Marxism' Catching On." Southern Poverty Law Center, August 15, 2003. https://www.splcenter.org/fighting-hate/intelligence-report/2003/cultural-marxism-catching

228 Bibliography

Berman, Mark. "Prosecutors Say Dylann Roof 'Self-Radicalized' Online, Wrote Another Manifesto in Jail." *The Washington Post*, August 22, 2016. https://www.washingtonpost.com/news/post-nation/wp/2016/08/22/prosecutors-say-accused-charleston-church-gunman-self-radicalized-online/?utm_term=.0afcab8108f7

Bertois, Carl, and Janice Drakich. "The Fathers' Rights Movement." *Journal of Family Issues* 14, no. 4 (1993): 592–615. https://doi.org/10.1177/019251393014004007

Bishop, George F. "Experiments with the Middle Response Alternative in Survey Questions." *Public Opinion Quarterly* 51, no. 2 (1987): 220–32.

Blake, Mariah. "Mad Men: Inside the Men's Rights Movement—And the Army of Misogynists and Trolls It Spawned." *Mother Jones*, January/February 2015. http://www.motherjones.com/politics/2015/01/warren-farrell-mens-rights-movement-feminism-misogyny-trolls

Blee, Kathleen M. "Women in the 1920s' Ku Klux Klan Movement." *Feminist Studies* 17, no. 1 (1991): 57–77.

Blee, Kathleen M., and Kimberly A. Creasap. "Conservative and Right-Wing Movements." *Annual Review of Sociology* 36, no. 1 (2010): 269–86.

Bloch, Ruth H. "American Feminine Ideals in Transition: The Rise of the Moral Mother, 1785-1815." *Feminist Studies* 4, no. 2 (June 1978): 100–26.

Blommaert, Jan. "Online-Offline Modes of Identity and Community: Elliot Rodger's Twisted World of Masculine Victimhood." *Tilburg Papers in Culture Studies*, no. 200 (2017).

Bourdieu, Pierre. *La Domination Masculine*. Paris: Éditions du Seuil, 1998.

Bourne, Lisa. "Ohio Woman Must Pay." *LifeSite News*, August 26, 2014. https://www.lifesitenews.com/news/ohio-woman-must-pay-80-after-attack-on-pro-lifers-assault-charge-dropped

Bowles, Nellie. "Push for Gender Equality in Tech? Some Men Say It's Gone Too Far." *The New York Times*, September 23, 2017. https://www.nytimes.com/2017/09/23/technology/silicon-valley-men-backlash-gender-scandals.html

Boyd, Susan B. "Backlash against Feminism: Canadian Custody and Access Reform Debates of the Late Twentieth Century." *Canadian Journal of Woman and the Law* 16 (2004): 255–90.

Braine, Naomi. "Terror Network or Lone Wolf? Disparate Legal Treatment of Muslims and the Radical Right." *Political Research Associates*, June 19, 2015. https://www.politicalresearch.org/2015/06/19/terror-network-or-lone-wolf/

Brandon, Alex. "Trump Says His Supreme Court Nominees Will Be Ready to Take on Abortion Ruling." *The Columbus Dispatch*, November 27, 2016. http://www.dispatch.com/content/stories/insight/2016/11/27/1-trump-says

Bratich, Jack, and Sarah Banet-Weiser. "From Pick-up Artists to Incels: Con(Fidence) Games, Networked Misogyny, and the Failure of Neoliberalism." *International Journal of Communication* 13 (2019): 5003–27.

Bray, Michael. *A Time to Kill*. Portland, OR: Advocates for Life, 1994.

Bridges, Tristan, and C. J. Pascoe. "Hybrid Masculinities: New Directions in the Sociology of Men and Masculinities." *Sociology Compass* 8, no. 3 (2014): 246–58. https://doi.org/10.1111/soc4.12134

Bromley, David G., and Anson Shupe, eds. *New Christian Politics*. Macon, GA: Mercer, 1984.

Buechler, Steven. *Women's Movement in the United States*. New Brunswick, NJ: Rutgers University Press, 1990.

Bibliography   **229**

Burnham, Linda. "The Absence of a Gender Justice Framework in Social Justice Organizing." Center for the Education of Women: University of Michigan, July 2008. http://www.cew.umich.edu/sites/default/files/BurnhamFinalProject.pdf

Byers, Dylan. "Conservative Female Pundits Want Donald Trump to Fire His Campaign Manager." *CNN Money*, March 30, 2016. http://money.cnn.com/2016/03/30/media/female-conservatives-fire-corey-lewandowski/

Campbell, Bernadette, E. Glenn Schellenberg, and Charlene Y. Senn. "Evaluating Measures of Contemporary Sexism." *Psychology of Women Quarterly* 21, no. 1 (1997): 89–102.

Carian, Emily K., Alex DiBranco, Pierce Dignam, and Megan Kelly. "The Origins of Contemporary Male Supremacism." Unpublished Manuscript, n.d.

Carian, Emily K., and Amy L. Johnson. "The Agency Myth: Persistence in Individual Explanations for Gender Inequality." *Social Problems* (2020). https://doi.org/10.1093/socpro/spaa072

Carian, Emily K. "'We're All in This Together': Leveraging a Personal Action Frame in Two Men's Rights Forums," Mobilization, forthcoming.

Carrigan, Tim, Bob Connell, and John Lee. "Toward a New Sociology of Masculinity." *Theory and Society* 14, no. 5 (1985): 551–604. http://www.jstor.org/stable/657315

Central Intelligence Agency. "The World Factbook: North America: United States," 2017. https://www.cia.gov/library/publications/resources/the-world-factbook/geos/us.html

Cernovich, Mike. "16 Feminists Who Have Taken over 'Conservative' Media." *Danger & Play*, March 30, 2016. https://www.dangerandplay.com/2016/03/30/16-feminists-who-have-taken-over-conservative-media/

Chamberlain, Pam, and Jean Hardisty. "Reproducing Patriarchy: Reproductive Rights under Siege." *Political Research Associates*, April 1, 2000. https://www.politicalresearch.org/2000/04/01/reproductive-patriarchy-reproductive-rights-under-siege

Charmaz, Kathy. "Constructionism and the Grounded Theory Method." In *Handbook of Constructionist Research*, edited by J. A. Holstein, and J. F. Gubrium, 397–412. New York: The Guilford Press, 2008.

Chuang, Angie, and Robin Chin Roemer. "Shifting Signifiers of Otherness: The 2002 'DC Snipers' in the U.S. Press." *Communication, Culture & Critique* 7 (2014): 541–58.

Chung, Grace S., Ryan E. Lawrence, Kenneth A. Rasinski, et al. "Obstetrician-Gynecologists' Beliefs about When Pregnancy Begins." *American Journal of Obstetrics and Gynecology* 206, no. 2 (2012): 132.e1–7. https://www.ajog.org/article/S0002-9378(11)02223-X/fulltext

Cirilli, Kevin. "Trump Reverses on Abortion Ban, Saying Doctors, Not Women, Would Be Punished." *Bloomberg Politics*, March 30, 2016. http://www.bloomberg.com/politics/articles/2016-03-30/trump-says-abortion-ban-should-carry-punishment-for-women

Clark-Flory, Tracy, and Leigh Cuen. "Donald Trump Has the Pickup Artist Vote in the Bag." *Vocativ*, August 24, 2015. http://www.vocativ.com/224810/donald-trump-anti-feminist-pickup-artists/

Cohen, David S. "Trump's Assassination Dog Whistle Was Even Scarier Than You Think." *Rolling Stone*, August 9, 2016. http://www.rollingstone.com/politics/features/trumps-assassination-dog-whistle-was-scarier-than-you-think-w433615

Cohen, Lizabeth. *A Consumers' Republic: The Politics of Mass Consumption in Postwar America*. New York: Vintage Books, 2004.

230 Bibliography

Comment on TheRedPill, an "official subreddit of TRP.RED." *Reddit* (blog). https://www.reddit.com/r/TheRedPill/comments/12v1hf/almost_a_hundred_subscribers_welcome_newcomers/

Condit, Celeste. *Decoding Abortion Rhetoric.* Urbana and Chicago: University of Illinois Press, 1994.

Congress.gov. "Text—H.R.3734—104th Congress (1995–1996): Personal Responsibility and Work Opportunity Reconciliation Act of 1996." August 22, 1996. https://www.congress.gov/bill/104th-congress/house-bill/3734/text

Connell, R. W., and James W. Messerschmidt. "Hegemonic Masculinity." *Gender & Society* 19, no. 6 (2005): 829–59. https://doi.org/10.1177/0891243205278639

Corredor, Elizabeth S. "Unpacking "Gender Ideology" and the Global Right's Antigender Countermovement." *Signs: Journal of Women in Culture and Society* 44, no. 3 (2019): 613–38. https://doi.org/10.1086/701171

Coston, Bethany M., and Kimmel, Michael. "White Men as the New Victims: Reverse Discrimination Cases and the Men's Rights Movement." *Nevada Law Journal* 13, no. 2 (2013): 5.

Cott, Nancy, ed. *No Small Courage: A History of Women in the United States.* Oxford: Oxford University Press, 2000a.

Cott, Nancy. *Public Vows: A History of Marriage and the Nation.* Cambridge MA and London: Harvard University Press, 2000b.

Created Equal. *Abortion: Doctrine of Demons.* January 7, 2020. https://www.createdequal.org/doctrine-of-demons/, https://www.youtube.com/watch?v=KI-BfncsYSw

Created Equal. "One Question Stumps College Student." https://www.createdequal.org/outreach/

CreatedEqualFilms. *Jumbotron College Campus Debut.* YouTube. Video. https://www.youtube.com/watch?v=7Nbp6ewiLPU&feature=emb_logo

Crenshaw, Kimberlé. "Mapping the Margins: Intersectionality, Identity Politics, and Violence against Women of Color." *Stanford Law Review* 43, no. 6 (1991): 1241–99.

Crenshaw, Kimberlé. "Race, Reform, and Retrenchment: Transformation and Legitimation in Antidiscrimination Law." *German Law Journal* 12, no. 1 (2011): 247–84.

Critchlow, Donald. *Phyllis Schlafly and Grassroots Conservatism: A Woman's Crusade.* Princeton, NJ and Oxford: Princeton University Press, 2005.

Critchlow, Donald, and Nancy MacLean. *Debating the American Conservative Movement: 1945 to the Present.* Lanham, MD: Rowman & Littlefield Publishers, 2009.

Crockett, Emily. "Did Roosh V Really Organize "Pro-rape Rallies"? No, but Here's Why People Are Protesting Him." Accessed February 11, 2021. https://www.vox.com/2016/2/6/10926872/roosh-pro-rape-rallies

Cross, Katherine. "What 'GamerGate' Reveals about the Silencing of Women." *Rewire,* September 9, 2014. https://rewire.news/article/2014/09/09/gamergate-reveals-silencing-women/

Cunningham, David. *Klansville USA: The Rise and Fall of the Civil Rights-Era Ku Klux Klan.* New York: Oxford University Press, 2012.

Curran, Laura and Laura S. Abrams. "Making Men into Dads: Fatherhood, the State, and Welfare Reform." *Gender and Society* 14, no. 5 (October 2000): 662–78.

Curry, Shirley. "Shirley Curry." Project Voices of Truth, 2016. http://eagleforumtruth.com/voices-of-truth/

Dame-Griff, Avery. "Herding the 'Performing Elephants': Using Computational Methods to Study Usenet." *Internet Histories* 3, no. 3–4 (2019): 223–44.

Bibliography **231**

Daniszewski, John. "Writing about the 'Alt-Right'." *Associated Press*, November 18, 2016. https://blog.ap.org/behind-the-news/writing-about-the-alt-right

Davis, Angela Y. *Women, Race and Class*. New York: Random House, 1983.

de Coning, Alexis. "Men's Rights Movement/Activism." In *The International Encyclopedia of Gender, Media, and Communication*, edited by Karen Ross, Ingrid Bachmann, Valentina Cardo, Sujata Moorti, and Marco Scarcelli, 1–9. Hoboken, NJ: John Wiley & Sons, Inc, 2020. https://doi.org/10.1002/9781119429128

DeCook, Julia R. "Memes and Symbolic Violence: #Proudboys and the Use of Memes for Propaganda and the Construction of Collective Identity." *Learning, Media and Technology* 34, no. 4 (2018): 485–504.

DeFoster, Ruth, and Natashia Swalve. "Guns, Culture or Mental Health? Framing Mass Shootings as a Public Health Crisis." *Health Communication* 33, no. 10 (2018):1211–22.

DeLuca, Kevin Michael, and Jennifer Peeples. "From Public Sphere to Public Screen: Democracy, Activism, and the 'Violence' of Seattle." *Critical Studies in Media Communication* 19, no. 2 (2002): 125–51.

Delwiche, Aaron. "Early Social Computing: The Rise and Fall of the BBS scene (1977–1995)." In *The SAGE Handbook of Social Media*, 35–52. London: SAGE Publications Ltd, 2018.

Demetriou, Demetrakis Z. "Connell's Concept of Hegemonic Masculinity: A Critique." *Theory and Society* 30, no. 3 (2001): 337–61. http://www.jstor.org/stable/657965

Department of Defense. "DoD Instruction 6130.03: Medical Standards for Military Service: Appointment, Enlistment, or Induction." May 6, 2018. https://www.esd.whs.mil/Portals/54/Documents/DD/issuances/dodi/613003v1p.PDF?ver=7cPFjXiGqfqNSF2HHw-X6w%3D%3D

DePue, Mark. Interview with Phyllis Schlafly. Abraham Lincoln Presidential Library, Oral History Program, "ERA fight in Illinois" Series, Clayton, Missouri, January 5–6, January 15, February 21–22, March 29–30, 2011.

Deutsch, James, and Levi Bochantin. "The Folkloric Roots of the QAnon Conspiracy." December 7, 2020. https://folklife.si.edu/magazine/folkloric-roots-of-qanon-conspiracy

Dewey, Caitlin. "The Only Guide to Gamergate You Will Ever Need to Read." *The Washington Post*, October 14, 2014. https://www.washingtonpost.com/news/the-intersect/wp/2014/10/14/the-only-guide-to-gamergate-you-will-ever-need-to-read/?utm_term=.d3cb125407d0

Diamond, Sara. *Not by Politics Alone: The Enduring Influence of the Christian Right*. New York: The Guilford Press, 1998.

Diamond, Sara. *Spiritual Warfare: The Politics of the Christian Right*. Boston, MA: South End Press, 1989.

DiBranco, Alex. "Men's Rights Conference Host Says Women Who Drink & Dance Are 'Begging' for Rape." *Political Research Associates*, July 2, 2014a. https://www.politicalresearch.org/2014/07/02/mens-rights-conference-host-says-women-who-drink-dance-are-begging-for-rape

DiBranco, Alex. "Profiles On The Right: Americans United For Life." *Political Research Associates*, April 7, 2014b. https://www.politicalresearch.org/2014/04/07/profiles-on-the-right-americans-united-for-life/#sthash.Zz04Fcm6.epvFr2db.dpbs

DiBranco, Alex. "Who Speaks for Conservative Women?." *Political Research Associates*, June 9, 2015. https://www.politicalresearch.org/2015/06/09/who-speaks-for-conservative-women/

232 Bibliography

DiBranco, Alex. "Mobilizing Misogyny." *The Public Eye*, Winter 2017. https://www.politicalresearch.org/2017/03/08/mobilizing-misogyny

DiBranco, Alex. ""The Incel Rebellion": Movement Misogyny Delivers Another Massacre." Accessed December 31, 2019. https://www.malesupremacism.org/publications/the-incel-rebellion-movement-misogyny-delivers-another-massacre/

DiBranco, Alex. "Male Supremacist Terrorism as a Rising Threat." Updated February 10, 2020a. Accessed June 21, 2021. https://icct.nl/publication/male-supremacist-terrorism-as-a-rising-threat/

DiBranco, Alex. "The Long History of the Anti-Abortion Movement's Links to White Supremacy." *The Nation*. February 3, 2020b. https://www.thenation.com/article/politics/anti-abortion-white-supremacy/

DiBranco, Alex. "Shooting in Tallahassee Illustrates Increasing Misogynist Violence." Accessed February 11, 2021. https://www.politicalresearch.org/2018/11/08/shooting-in-tallahassee-illustrates-increasing-misogynist-violence

DiBranco, Alex, and Chip Berlet. "The Ideological Roots of the Republican Party and Its Shift to the Right in the 2016 Election." Working draft. n.d. http://www.progressivemovements.us/now/site-guide/research-resources/#ideological

dictionary.com, s.v. "Cuck." Accessed September 2, 2020. https://www.dictionary.com/e/slang/cuck/

Dignam, Pierce Alexander, and Deana A. Rohlinger. "Misogynistic Men Online: How the Red Pill Helped Elect Trump." *Signs: Journal of Women in Culture and Society* 44, no. 3 (2019): 589–612. https://doi.org/10.1086/701155

Dobbins-Harris, Shyrissa. "The Myth of Abortion as Black Genocide: Reclaiming our Reproductive Cycle." *National Black Law Journal* 26, no. 1 (2017): 86–127.

Dooley, Erin, Janet Weinstein, and Meridith McGraw. "DeVos' Meetings with 'Men's Rights' Groups over Campus Sex Assault Spark Controversy." *ABC News*, July 14, 2017. http://abcnews.go.com/Politics/betsy-devos-meetings-mens-rights-groups-sex-assault/story?id=48611688

Doyle, Richard. Letter to Phyllis Schlafly. May 8, 1981 (Eagle Forum Archives, Collection Phyllis Schlafly, Series ERA, Subjects, Box 4, File 7).

Dragiewicz, Molly. "Patriarchy Reasserted." *Feminist Criminology* 3, no. 2 (2008): 121–44. https://doi.org/10.1177/1557085108316731

Dupuis-Deri, Francis. "Le Discours de la 'Crise de la Masculinité' comme Refus de l'Égalité Entre les Sexes: Histoire d'une Rhétorique Antiféministe." *Cahiers du Genre* 52, no. 1 (2012): 119–43.

Duxbury, Scott W., Laura C. Frizzell, and Sadé L. Lindsay. "Mental Illness, the Media, and the Moral Politics of Mass Violence: The Role of Race in Mass Shootings Coverage." *Journal of Research in Crime and Delinquency* 55, no. 6 (2018): 766–97.

DVD 261. "Phyllis and Fred on Good Morning America," January 1, 1978 (Eagle Forum Archives, Collection DVD).

DVD 291. "PS Speech for Families in Crisis Seminar: Homemakers as Policy Makers." May 8, 1981 (Eagle Forum Archives, Collection DVD).

DVD 1129. "How to Communicate Eagle Forum's Message: Appearance, Makeup and Dress." September 8, 2000 (Eagle Forum Archives, Collection DVD).

Dworkin, Andrea. *Right-Wing Women: The Politics of Domesticated Females*. London: The Women's Press, 1983.

Eagle Forum. "State Chapters President Applications." n.d.. (Eagle Forum Archives, Collection Eagle Forum, Series Organization, Box 11, File 4, 5, 6, 7, 8; Box 12, File 1, 2).

Editorial Staff. "ThinkProgress Will No Longer Describe Racists as 'Alt-Right'." *Think Progress*, November 22, 2016. https://thinkprogress.org/thinkprogress-alt-right-policy-b04fd141d8d4#.av5b2ftsm

England, Paula. "The Gender Revolution: Uneven and Stalled." *Gender & Society* 24, no. 2 (April 1, 2010): 149–66.

Epstein, Reid J. "Trump Refuses to Denounce White Supremacy in Chaotic Debate." *The New York Times*, September 29, 2020. https://www.nytimes.com/live/2020/09/29/us/presidential-debate-trump-biden

Exposed By CMD Editors. "'Independent' Women's Group Backing Trump Skirts Law to Influence Election." *Center For Media and Democracy*, November 1, 2016. http://www.exposedbycmd.org/2016/10/25/independent-womens-group-backing-trump-skirts-law-influence-elections/

Faludi, Susan. "How Hillary Clinton Met Satan." *The New York Times*, October 29, 2016. http://www.nytimes.com/2016/10/30/opinion/sunday/how-hillary-clinton-met-satan.html

Faludi, Susan. *The Undeclared War against American Women*. New York: Crown Publishing, 1991.

Faucet, Richard, and Allan Feuer. "Far Right Groups Surge into National View in Charlottesville." *New York Times*, August 13, 2017. https://www.nytimes.com/2017/08/13/us/far-right-groups-blaze-into-national-view-in-charlottesville.html

Feldberg, Roslyn L. "Comparable Worth: Toward Theory and Practice in the United States." *Signs* 10, no. 2 (Winter 1984): 311–28.

Felsenthal, Carol. *The Sweetheart of the Silent Majority: The Biography of Phyllis Schlafly*. New York: Doubleday, 1981.

Ferber, Abby L. "Racial Warriors and Weekend Warriors: The Construction of Masculinity in Mythopoetic and White Supremacist Discourse." *Men and Masculinities* 3, no. 1 (July 2000): 30–56.

Field Observation Notes, Eagle Council, Washington, DC, September 14–17, 2017.

Forney, Matt. "Who Cares What Women Think." *Alternative Right* (blog), January 29, 2015. http://alternative-right.blogspot.com/2015/01/who-cares-what-women-think.html

Forney, Matt. "Why Feminists Want Men to Rape Them." *Matt Forney.com*, February 26, 2016a. http://mattforney.com/feminists-want-men-rape/

Forney, Matt. "Why You Should Shun Girls Who Support Abortion." *Return of Kings*, August 18, 2016b. http://archive.is/zQwx4#selection-769.269-769.363

Fraser, Nancy, and Linda Gordon. "A Genealogy of Dependency: Tracing a Keyword of the U.S. Welfare State." *Signs* 19, no. 2 (1994): 309–36.

Friedan, Betty. *The Feminine Mystique*. New York and London: Norton & Company, 1997 [1963].

Friedman, Jaclyn. "A Look Inside the 'Men's Rights' Movement That Helped Fuel California Alleged Killer Elliot Rodger." *The American Prospect*, October 24, 2013. http://prospect.org/article/look-inside-mens-rights-movement-helped-fuel-california-alleged-killer-elliot-rodger

Frometa, R. J.. "What the Cuck? An Exclusive Interview with Director Rob Lambert." *VENTS Magazine*, May 17, 2018. https://ventsmagazine.com/2018/05/17/what-the-cuck-an-exclusive-interview-with-director-rob-lambert/

Gallagher, Sophie. "I Bought Your Drinks, So You Owe Me Sex — Why Do Some Men Believe Dating Is a Transaction." *HuffPost*, June 18, 2019. https://www.huffington-post.co.uk/entry/i-bought-your-drinks-so-you-owe-me-sex-why-do-some-men-believe-dating-is-a-transaction_uk_5cf6a9cce4b0a1997b724e30

234 Bibliography

Gambill, Edward. *Uneasy Males: The American Men's Movement 1970 – 2000.* New York: iUniverse, 2005.

Ganesh, Bharath. "The Ungovernability of Digital Hate Culture." *Journal of International Affairs* 71/2 (2018): 30–49. https://jia.sipa.columbia.edu/ungovernability-digital-hate-culture

Ganesh, Bharath. "Weaponizing White Thymos: Flows of Rage in the Online Audiences of the Alt-Right." *Cultural Studies* (2020): 1–33. https://doi.org/10.1080/09502386.2020.1714687

Geary, Daniel. *Beyond Civil Rights: The Moynihan Report and Its Legacy.* Philadelphia: University of Pennsylvania Press, 2015.

Gentry, Carol E and Sjoberg, Laura. *Mother's, Monsters, Whores: Women's Violence in Global Politics.* London: Zed Books, 2007, 12.

Gilbert, Sophie. "The Movement of #MeToo." *The Atlantic,* October 16, 2017. https://www.theatlantic.com/entertainment/archive/2017/10/the-movement-of-metoo/542979/

Gilgoff, Dan. *The Jesus Machine.* New York: St. Martin's Griffin, 2007.

Gill, Paul, John Horgan, and Paige Deckert. "Bombing Alone: Tracing the Motivations and Antecedent Behaviors of Lone-Actor Terrorists." *Journal of Forensic Sciences* (2013). https://doi.org/10.1111/1556-4029.12312

Ging, Debbie. "Alphas, Betas, and Incels." *Men and Masculinities* 19 (2017): 1097184X1770640. https://doi.org/10.1177/1097184X17706401

Glick, Peter, and Susan T. Fiske. "The Ambivalent Sexism Inventory: Differentiating Hostile and Benevolent Sexism." *Journal of Personality and Social Psychology* 70, no. 3 (1996): 491–512.

Glick, Peter, and Susan T. Fiske. "An Ambivalent Alliance. Hostile and Benevolent Sexism as Complementary Justifications for Gender Inequality." *The American Psychologist* 56, no. 2 (February 2001): 109–18.

Glover, Scott. "Colleague, Transcripts Offer Closer Look at Old Allegations of Racism against Sen. Jeff Sessions." *CNN,* January 10, 2017. http://www.cnn.com/2016/11/18/politics/jeff-sessions-racism-allegations/

Godin, Mélissa. "Canadian Teen Charged with Terrorism over Attack Allegedly Motivated by 'Incel Movement'." Accessed February 10, 2021. https://time.com/5839395/canada-teen-terrorism-incel-attack/

Goldberg, Michelle. "Obama Billboard Shows Anti-abortion Focus on African-Americans." *Daily Beast.* March 30, 2011. https://www.thedailybeast.com/obama-billboard-shows-anti-abortion-focus-on-african-americans

Goldwag, Arthur. "Leader's Suicide Brings Attention to the Men's Rights Movement." *Southern Poverty Law Center Intelligence Report,* March 1, 2012. https://www.splcenter.org/fighting-hate/intelligence-report/2012/leader%E2%80%99s-suicide-brings-attention-men%E2%80%99s-rights-movement

Goldwater, Barry. *Conscience of a Conservative.* Shepherdsville: Victor Publishing, 1960.

Gordon, Linda. *The Second Coming of the KKK: The Ku Klux Klan of the 1920s and the American Political Tradition.* New York: Liveright, 2017.

Gotell, Lise, and Emily Dutton. "Sexual Violence in the 'Manosphere': Antifeminist Men's Rights Discourses on Rape." *International Journal for Crime, Justice and Social Democracy* 5, no. 2 (2016): 65–80. https://doi.org/10.5204/ijcjsd.v5i2.310

Graff, Agnieszka, Ratna Kapur, and Suzanna Danuta Walters. "Introduction: Gender and the Rise of the Global Right." *Signs: Journal of Women in Culture and Society* 44, no. 3 (2019): 541–60.

Graves, Lisa. "Confirmation: the Not-So Independent Women's Forum Was Born in Defense of Clarence Thomas and the Far Right." *Center for Media and Democracy*, April 21, 2016. http://www.prwatch.org/news/2016/04/13091/confirmation-how-not-so-independent-womens-forum-was-launched-aid-clarence

Grether, Nicole. "Men's Right Activist: Feminists Have Used Rape 'as a Scam'." *Aljazeera America*, June 6, 2014. http://america.aljazeera.com/watch/shows/america-tonight/articles/2014/6/6/mena-s-rights-activistfeministshaveusedrapeaasascama.html

Griffin, Rachel Alicia. "Problematic Representations of Strategic Whiteness and 'Post-racial' Pedagogy: A Critical Intercultural Reading of the Help." *Journal of International and Intercultural Communication* 8, no. 2 (2015): 147–66.

Griffin, Roger. "From Slime Mold to Rhizome: An Introduction to the Groupuscular Right." *Patterns of Prejudice* 37, no. 1 (2003): 27–50. https://doi.org/10.1080/0031322022000054321

Haberman, Maggie, Alexander Burns, and Ashley Parker. "Donald Trump Fires Corey Lewandowski, His Campaign Manager." *The New York Times*, June 20, 2016. http://www.nytimes.com/2016/06/21/us/politics/corey-lewandowski-donald-trump.html

Hahn, Harley. "Newsgroups and Hierarchies." Harley Hahn's Usenet Center (2020). Retrieved from http://www.harley.com/usenet/usenet-tutorial/newsgroups-and-hierarchies.html

Hains, Tim. "Trump: Men Today 'Are Petrified to Speak to Women Anymore' 'Women Get It Better Than We Do, Folks'." *Real Clear Politics*, May 8, 2016. http://www.realclearpolitics.com/video/2016/05/08/trump_remember_this_when_you_see_hillarys_phony_paid-for-by-wall_street_ads.html

Hampson, Rich. "Exclusive: Fox anchor Megyn Kelly describes scary, bullying 'Year of Trump'." *USA Today*, November 15, 2016. http://www.usatoday.com/story/news/politics/elections/2016/11/15/megyn-kelly-memoir-donald-trump-roger-ailes-president-fox-news/93813154/

Hariman, Robert, and John Louis Lucaites. *The Public Image: Photography and Civic Spectatorship*. Chicago, IL: University of Chicago Press, 2016, 14.

Harkinson, Josh. "We Talked to Experts about What Terms to Use for Which Group of Racists." *Mother Jones*, December 8, 2016. http://www.motherjones.com/politics/2016/12/definition-alt-right-white-supremacist-white-nationalist

Harrington, Mark. "Social Justice Critical Theory and Christianity." *Radio Activist: The Mark Harrington Show*, December 31, 2020a. https://createdequal.podbean.com/e/social-justice-critical-theory-and-christianity-are-they-compatible-the-mark-harrington-show-12-31-2020/

Harrington, Mark. "Top Ten Reasons to Not Support the #BlackLivesMatter Movement." *Radio Activist: The Mark Harrington Show*, November 5, 2020b. https://markharrington.org/live/top-ten-reasons-to-not-support-the-blacklivesmatter-movement-the-mark-harrington-show-11-05-2020/

Harvey, Alison. *Feminist Media Studies*. Cambridge: Polity Press, 2020, 59.

Hatewatch Staff. "Update: 1,094 Bias-Related Incidents in the Month Following the Election." *Southern Poverty Law Center Hatewatch*, December 16, 2016. https://www.splcenter.org/hatewatch/2016/12/16/update-1094-bias-related-incidents-month-following-election

Havard, Sarah. "8 Worst Things Phyllis Schlafly Ever Said about Women's Rights." *Identities.Mic*, September 6, 2016. https://mic.com/articles/153506/8-worst-things-phyllis-schlafly-ever-said-about-women-s-rights#.4Wxyh3b3x

Bibliography

Hays, Charlotte. "Portrait of a Modern Feminist: Helen Smith." *Independent Women's Forum*, September 19, 2012. http://iwf.org/modern-feminist/2789205/Portrait-of-a-Modern-Feminist:-Helen-Smith

Hays, Charlotte. "'Toxic Feminism:' Cathy Young Dissects the Bizarre Response to a Mass Murder." *Independent Women's Forum*, May 30, 2014. http://www.iwf.org/blog/2794091/%22Toxic-Feminism:%22-Cathy-Young-Dissects-the-Bizarre-Response-to-a-Mass-Murder

Hays, Charlotte. "Donald Trump Breathes New Life into Left's War on Women." *Independent Women's Forum*, March 18, 2016. http://www.iwf.org/news/2799633/Donald-Trump-Breathes-New-Life-into-Left%E2%80%99s-War-on-Women

Heiss, Raffael, and Jörg Matthes. "Stuck in a Nativist Spiral: Content, Selection, and Effects of Right-Wing Populists' Communication on Facebook." *Political Communication* 37, no. 3 (2020): 303–28.

Hemmer, Nicole. "The Pre-Emptive #MeToo Backlash," January 16, 2018. https://www.usnews.com/opinion/thomas-jefferson-street/articles/2018-01-16/aziz-ansari-and-the-pre-emptive-metoo-backlash

Henderson, Nia-Malika. "Donald Trump's Nonexistent Problem with GOP Women." *CNN*, September 11, 2015. http://www.cnn.com/2015/09/10/politics/donald-trump-women/

Hersher, Rebecca. "Jury Finds Dylann Roof Guilty In S.C. Church Shooting." *NPR*, December 15, 2016. http://www.npr.org/sections/thetwo-way/2016/12/15/505723552/jury-finds-dylann-roof-guilty-in-s-c-church-shooting

Hess, Amanda. "Why Women Aren't Welcome on the Internet." *Pacific Standard Magazine*, January 6, 2014. https://psmag.com/why-women-aren-t-welcome-on-the-internet-aa21fdbc8d6#.mdzlvrvd4

Hill, Chelsea. "Data Point: 2018, A Year of the Woman Like 1992?" Center for American Women and Politics, Rutgers University, January 23, 2018. http://www.cawp.rutgers.edu/sites/default/files/resources/data-point-compare-1992-2018.pdf

Hoffman, Bruce, Jacob Ware, and Ezra Shapiro. "Assessing the Threat of Incel Violence." *Studies in Conflict & Terrorism* 43, no. 7 (2020): 565–87. https://doi.org/10.1080/1057610X.2020.1751459

Holland, Jennifer. *Tiny You*. Berkeley: University of California Press, 2020.

Holt, Earl III. "Media Interviews with the CofCC," June 21, 2015. https://web.archive.org/web/20150622033926/http://conservative-headlines.com/2015/06/media-interviews-with-the-cofcc/

Hong, Nicole, Mihir Zaveri, and William K. Rashbaum. "Inside the Violent and Misogynistic World of Roy Den Hollander." *The New York Times*, July 26, 2020. https://www.nytimes.com/2020/07/26/nyregion/roy-den-hollander-judge.html

Horgan, John G., Paul Gill, Noemie Bouhana, James Silver, and Emily Corner. "Across the Universe? A Comparative Analysis of Violent Behavior and Radicalization across Three Offender Types with Implications for Criminal Justice Training and Education." U.S. Department of Justice, Washington DC, 2016.

Hosang, Daniel Martinez, and Joseph E. Lowndes. *Producers, Parasites, Patriots: Race and the New Right-wing Politics of Precarity*. Minneapolis: University of Minnesota Press, 2019.

Israel, Josh. "Women From Koch-Funded Conservative Groups Lambaste Equal Pay Measure." *Think Progress*, April 9, 2014. https://thinkprogress.org/women-from-koch-funded-conservative-groups-lambaste-equal-pay-measure-d8eb0ea3edb7#.lj3d1onh2

Jabali, Malaika. "White People Are Killed by Cops Too. But That Doesn't Undermine Black Lives Matter. *The Guardian*, July 16, 2020. https://www.theguardian.com/commentisfree/2020/jul/16/trump-police-abolition-black-americans

Bibliography 237

Jaki, Sylvia, Tom de Smedt, Maja Gwóźdź, Rudresh Panchal, Alexander Rossa, and Guy de Pauw. "Online Hatred of Women in the Incels.Me Forum." *Journal of Language Aggression and Conflict* 7, no. 2 (2019): 240–68. https://doi.org/10.1075/jlac.00026.jak

Jane, Emma A. "Your a Ugly, Whorish, Slut." *Feminist Media Studies* 14, no. 4 (2014): 531–46. https://doi.org/10.1080/14680777.2012.741073

Jane, Emma A. "Systemic Misogyny Exposed: Translating Rapeglish from the Manosphere with a Random Rape Threat Generator." *International Journal of Cultural Studies* 21, no. 6 (2018): 661–80. https://doi.org/10.1177/1367877917734042

Jasper, James. "Emotions and Social Movements: Twenty Years of Theory and Research." *Annual Review of Sociology* 37 (2011): 285–303.

Jasser, Greta, Megan Kelly, and Ann-Kathrin Rothermel. "Male Supremacism and the Hanau Terrorist Attack: Between Online Misogyny and Far-Right Violence." *ICCT*. Accessed December 10, 2020. https://icct.nl/publication/male-supremacism-and-the-hanau-terrorist-attack-between-online-misogyny-and-far-right-violence/

Jeansonne, Glen. *Women of the Far Right: The Mothers' Movement and World War II*. Chicago, IL: University of Chicago Press, 1996.

Jefferis, Jennifer. *Armed for Life: The Army of God and Anti-Abortion Terror in the United States*. Santa Barbara, CA: Praeger, 2011.

Jeltsen, Melissa. "Trump's Election Raises Fears Of Increased Violence against Women." *The Huffington Post*, November 15, 2016. http://www.huffingtonpost.com/entry/trump-women-rights-violence-fears_us_582a0f63e4b02d21bbc9f186

Jesudason, Sujatha. "The Latest Case of Reproductive Carrots and Sticks: Race, Abortion and Sex Selection." *The Scholar and Feminist Online* 9.1–9.2 (Fall 2010/Spring 2011).

Joffe, Carole. "Working with Dr. Tiller: Staff Recollections of Women's Health Care Services of Wichita." *Perspectives on Sexual and Reproductive Health* 43, no. 3 (August 9, 2011): 199–204.

Johnson, Paul Elliott. "Walter White(ness) Lashes Out: Breaking Bad and Male Victimage." *Critical Studies in Media Communication* 34, no. 1 (2017): 14–28.

Johnston, Hank, ed. *Culture, Social Movements and Protest*. Farnham and Burlington, VT: Ashgate, 2009.

Jones, Callum, Verity Trott, and Scott Wright. "Sluts and Soyboys: MGTOW and the Production of Misogynistic Online Harassment." *New Media & Society* 200, no. 2 (2019): 1–19. https://doi.org/10.1177/1461444819887141

Jost, John T., Mahzarin R. Banaji, and Brian A. Nosek. "A Decade of System Justification Theory: Accumulated Evidence of Conscious and Unconscious Bolstering of the Status Quo." *Political Psychology* 25, no. 6 (2004): 881–919.

Joyce, Kathryn. "Abortion as Black Genocide." *Public Eye*, April 29, 2010. https://www.politicalresearch.org/2010/04/29/abortion-as-black-genocide-an-old-scare-tactic-re-emerges

Kalish, Rachel, and Michael Kimmel. "Suicide by Mass Murder: Masculinity, Aggrieved Entitlement, and Rampage School Shootings." *Health Sociology Review* 19, no. 4 (2010): 451–64. https://doi.org/10.5172/hesr.2010.19.4.451

Kandiyoti, Deniz. "Bargaining with Patriarchy." *Gender and Society* 2, no. 3 (September 1988): 274–90.

Kaplan, Esther. *With God on Their Side*. New York: The New Press, 2004.

Karet, Brendan. "Right-Wing Civil War: Megyn Kelly Trades Barbs With Breitbart Editor-at-Large over Dangers of Empowering 'Alt-Right'." *Media Matters for America*, December 7, 2016. https://mediamatters.org/blog/2016/12/07/right-wing-civil-war-megyn-kelly-trades-barbs-breitbart-editor-chief-over-dangers-empowering-alt/214754

238 Bibliography

Kassel, Hesse. "5 Lines That Potential Wives Cannot Cross." *Return of Kings*, November 11, 2014. http://www.returnofkings.com/47540/5-lines-that-potential-wives-cannot-cross

Katznelson, Ira. *When Affirmative Action Was White*. New York: W.W. Norton and Co., 2006.

Kearl, Michelle Kelsey. "WWMLKD?: Coopting the Rhetorical Legacy of Martin Luther King, Jr. and the Civil Rights Movement." *Journal of Contemporary Rhetoric* 8, no. 3 (2018): 184–99.

Kelly, Amita. "Hillary Clinton Becomes First Woman to Top Major-Party Ticket." *NPR*, June 6, 2016. https://www.npr.org/2016/04/27/475765145/clintons-road-to-the-nomination-was-paved-by-other-women-who-ran

Kelly, Megan, Alex Di Branco, and Julia R. DeCook. "Misogynist Incels and Male Supremacism." *New America*, February 18, 2021. Accessed July 5, 2021. https://www.newamerica.org/political-reform/reports/misogynist-incels-and-male-supremacism/

Kentucky Kernal. "Anti Abortion Protest on UK Campus," October 9, 2017. http://www.kykernel.com/opinion/editorial-no-matter-what-you-say-free-speech-belongs-to-everyone/article_28c7b132-b51a-11e7-a54a-df29910c49f6.html

Kerber, Linda. "The Republican Mother: Women and the Enlightenment-An American Perspective." *American Quarterly* 28, no. 2 (Summer 1976): 187–205.

Kerber, Linda. "Separate Spheres, Female Worlds, Woman's Place: The Rhetoric of Women's History." *The Journal of American History* 75, no. 9 (June 1988): 9–39.

Knoll, James L., and Ronald W. Pies. "Mounties, Cowboys, Avengers—and the Cultural Script of Gun Violence." *The Psychiatric Times* 33, no. 1 (2016): 9.

Kochavi, Adi. "The Sad Heroification of Elliot Rodger." *Vocativ*, May 25, 2014. http://www.vocativ.com/underworld/crime/sad-heroification-elliot-rodger/

Kollock, Peter and Marc A. Smith. "Communities in Cyberspace." In *Communities in Cyberspace*, edited by Marc A. Smith, and Peter Kollock. New York: Routledge, 1999/2005: 3–25.

Koster, Willem de, and Dick Houtman. "'Stormfront Is Like a Second Home for Me': On Virtual Community Formation by Right-Wing Extremists." *Information, Communication & Society* 11, no. 8 (2008): 1155–76. https://doi.org/10.1080/13691180802266665

Kraus, Michael W., E. J. Horberg, Jennifer L. Goetz, and Dacher Keltner. "Social Class Rank, Threat Vigilance, and Hostile Reactivity." *Personality & Social Psychology Bulletin* 37, no. 10 (October 2011): 1376–88.

Krzych, Scott. "The Price of Knowledge: Hysterical Discourse in Anti-Michael Moore Documentaries." *The Comparatist* 39 (2015): 80–100.

Kurtzleben, Danielle. "In Wage Gap Debate, a Fight over 77 Cents." *US News & World Report*, June 10, 2013. http://www.usnews.com/news/articles/2013/06/10/in-wage-gap-debate-a-fight-over-77-cents

Lambert, Rob, dir. *Cuck*. Los Angeles, CA: Rimrock Pictures, 2019. Amazon.

Landler, Mark. "Transition Team's Request on Gender Equality Rattles State Dept." *The New York Times*, December 22, 2016. https://www.nytimes.com/2016/12/22/us/politics/state-department-gender-equality-trump-transition.html

Langman, Lauren. "Cycles of Contention: The Rise and Fall of the Tea Party." *Critical Sociology* 38, no. 4 (July 2012): 469–94.

Legler, Paul K. "The Coming Revolution in Child Support Policy: Implications of the 1996 Welfare Act." *Family Law Quarterly* 30, no. 3 (1996): 519–63. http://www.jstor.org/stable/25740093

Lenz, Ryan. "The Battle for Berkeley," May 1, 2017. https://www.splcenter.org/hate-watch/2017/05/01/battle-berkeley-name-freedom-speech-radical-right-circling-ivory-tower-ensure-voice-alt

Lerer, Lisa, and Sydney Ember. "Kamala Harris Makes History as First Woman and Woman of Color as Vice President." *The New York Times*, November 7, 2020. https://www.nytimes.com/2020/11/07/us/politics/kamala-harris.html

Lerner, Gerda. *The Creation of Patriarchy*. New York and Oxford: Oxford University Press, 1986.

Lewis, Helen. "To Learn About the Far Right, Start with the 'Manosphere'." *The Atlantic*, August 7, 2019. https://www.theatlantic.com/international/archive/2019/08/anti-feminism-gateway-far-right/595642/

Lewis, Loree. "Court Rules on Miller-Young Case." *Daily Nexus*, August 27, 2014. https://dailynexus.com/2014-08-27/court-rules-on-miller-young-case/

Lewis, Rebecca, and Alice E. Marwick. "Media Manipulation and Disinformation Online." Data & Society Research Institute, n.d. https://datasociety.net/pubs/oh/DataAndSociety_MediaManipulationAndDisinformationOnline.pdf

Liebman, Robert C., and Robert Wuthnow, eds. *The New Christian Right*. New York: Aldine Publishing Company, 1983.

Lilly, Mary. "'The World Is Not a Safe Place for Men': The Representational Politics of the Manosphere." Université D'Ottawa / University Of Ottawa, 2016.

Lin, Jie Liang. "Antifeminism Online: MGTOW (Men Going Their Own Way): Ethnographic Perspectives across Global Online and Offline Spaces." In *Digital Environments: Ethnographic Perspectives across Global Online and Offline Spaces*, edited by Urte U. Frömming, Steffen Köhn, Samantha Fox, and Mike Terry, 77–96. Media studies 34. Bielefeld: transcript, 2017.

Lindsay, Mark, and David Lester. *Suicide-by-Cop: Committing Suicide by Provoking Police to Shoot You* (1st ed.). Amityville, NY: Baywood Publishing Company, 2004.

Lucas, Carrie L. "One in Four? Rape Myths Do Injustice, Too." *Independent Women's Forum*, April 27, 2006. http://www.iwf.org/news/2432517/One-in-Four-Rape-myths-do-injustice-too#sthash.EOyWF55L.dpuf

Lucas, Ryan. "4 Proud Boys Charged with Conspiracy over Jan. 6 Capitol Riot." *NPR*, March 19, 2021. https://www.npr.org/2021/03/19/979304432/4-proud-boys-charged-with-conspiracy-over-jan-6-capitol-riot

Luker, Kristin. *Abortion and the Politics of Motherhood*. University of California Press, 1984. http://www.jstor.org/stable/10.1525/j.ctt1ppck8

Luna, Zakiya. "'Black Children Are an Endangered Species': Examining Racial Framing in Social Movements." *Sociological Focus* 51 no. 3 (2018): 238–51.

Lyons, Matthew N. "Notes on Women and Right-Wing Movements – Part Two." *ThreeWayFight* (blog), October 1, 2005. http://threewayfight.blogspot.com/2005/10/notes-on-women-and-right-wing.html

Lyons, Matthew N. "Jack Donovan on Men: A Masculine Tribalism for the Far Right." *Three Way Fight*, November 23, 2015. http://threewayfight.blogspot.com/2015/11/jack-donovan-on-men-masculine-tribalism.html

Lyons, Matthew N. "Alt-Right: More Misogynistic Than Many Neonazis." *ThreeWayFight*, December 3, 2016. http://threewayfight.blogspot.com/2016/12/alt-right-more-misogynistic-than-many.html

Lyons, Matthew N. "Ctrl-Alt-Delete: The Origins and Ideology of the Alternative Right." *Political Research Associates*, January 20, 2017. https://www.politicalresearch.org/2017/01/20/ctrl-alt-delete-report-on-the-alternative-right/

Majeed, Muhammad Hassan, Donna M. Sudak, and Eugene Beresin. "Mass Shootings and the News Media: What Can Psychiatrists Do?." *Academic Psychiatry* 43 (2019): 442–47.

240 Bibliography

Malmsheimer, Taylor. "Conservatives Are Obsessed with Debunking the 1-in-5 Rape Statistic. They're Wrong, Too." *New Republic*, June 27, 2014. https://newrepublic.com/article/118430/independent-womens-forum-challenges-one-five-statistic

Manne, Kate. *Down Girl: The Logics of Misogyny*. New York: Oxford University Press, 2018.

Mantilla, Karla. "Gendertrolling: Misogyny Adapts to New Media." *Feminist Studies* 39, no. 2 (2013): 563–70. http://www.jstor.org/stable/23719068

Marantz, Andrew Marantz. "Trolls for Trump." *The New Yorker Magazine*, October 31, 2016. http://www.newyorker.com/magazine/2016/10/31/trolls-for-trump

Marcks, Holger, and Janina Pawelz. "From Myths of Victimhood to Fantasies of Violence: How Far-Right Narratives of Imperilment Work." *Terrorism and Political Violence* (2020): 1–18. https://doi.org/10.1080/09546553.2020.1788544

Marcotte, Amanda. "Missouri Lawmaker Uses 'Men's Rights' Talking Points to Justify Abortion Restriction." *Raw Story*, December 17, 2014. http://www.rawstory.com/2014/12/missouri-lawmaker-uses-mens-rights-talking-points-to-justify-abortion-restriction/

Marshall, Susan. *Splintered Sisterhood: Gender and Class in the Campaign against Women Suffrage*. Madison: University of Wisconsin Press, 1997.

Marwick, Alice E., and Robyn Caplan. "Drinking Male Tears: Language, the Manosphere, and Networked Harassment." *Feminist Media Studies* 18, no. 4 (2018): 543–59. https://doi.org/10.1080/14680777.2018.1450568

Mason, Carol. "Minority Unborn." In *Fetal Subjects, Feminist Positions*, edited by Lynn M. Morgan, and Meredith Wilson Michaels, 159–74. Philadelphia: University of Pennsylvania Press, 1999.

Mason, Carol. *Killing for Life: The Apocalyptic Narrative of Pro-Life Politics*. Ithaca, NY: Cornell University Press, 2002.

Mason, Carol. "Opposing Abortion to Protect Women: Transnational Strategy since the 1990s." *Signs: Journal of Women in Culture and Society* 44, no. 3 (2019): 665–692.

Massanari, Adrienne. "#Gamergate and the Fappening: How Reddit's Algorithm, Governance, and Culture Support Toxic Technocultures." *New Media & Society* 19, no. 3 (2017): 329–46. https://doi.org/10.1177/1461444815608807

Mathis-Lilley, Ben. "Trump Was Recorded in 2005 Bragging about Grabbing Women 'by the Pussy'." *Slate*, October 7, 2016. http://www.slate.com/blogs/the_slatest/2016/10/07/donald_trump_2005_tape_i_grab_women_by_the_pussy.html

Mattheis, Ashley. "Understanding Digital Hate Culture." Accessed September 17, 2019. https://www.radicalrightanalysis.com/2019/08/19/understanding-digital-hate-culture/

McCormack, Derek P.. *Refrains for Moving Bodies: Experience and Experiment in Affective Spaces*. Durham: Duke University Press, 2014, 141–64.

McCulloch, Jude, Sandra Walklate, JaneMaree Maher, Kate Fitz-Gibbon, and Jasmine McGowan. "Lone Wolf Terrorism through a Gendered Lens: Men Turning Violent or Violent Men Behaving Violently?" *Critical Criminology* 27 (2019): 437–50.

McGinty, Emma E., Daniel W. Webster, and Colleen L. Barry. "Effects of News Media Messages About Mass Shootings on Attitudes toward Persons with Serious Mental Illness and Public Support for Gun Control Policies." *The American Journal of Psychiatry* 170, no. 5 (2013): 494–501.

McKay, Tom. "College President's Horrifying Rape Comments Are Basically Conservative Dogma." *The Daily Banter*, November 12, 2014. http://thedailybanter.com/2014/11/college-presidents-horrible-remarks-campus-rape-basically-conservative-dogma/

Bibliography   **241**

McVeigh, Rory. *The Rise of the Ku Klux Klan*. Minneapolis: University of Minnesota Press, 2009.

Messerschmidt, James W. *Hegemonic Masculinities and Camouflaged Politics: Unmasking the Bush Dynasty and Its War against Iraq*. Florence: Taylor and Francis, 2010.

Messner, Michael A. *Politics of Masculinities: Men in Movements*. Lanham, MD: AltaMira Press, 1997.

Messner, Michael A. "The Limits of 'The Male Sex Role': An Analysis of the Men's Liberation and Men's Rights Movements' Discourse." *Gender & Society* 12, no. 3 (June 1998): 255–76.

Messner, Michael A. "Equality with a Vengeance: Men's Rights Groups, Battered Women, and Antifeminist Backlash." *Contemporary Sociology: A Journal of Reviews* 42, no. 3 (2013): 384–85. https://doi.org/10.1177/0094306113484702d

Messner, Michael A. "Forks in the Road of Men's Gender Politics: Men's Rights vs Feminist Allies." *International Journal for Crime, Justice and Social Democracy* 5, no. 2 (2016): 6–20.

Meyer, David S. Meyer, and Suzanne Staggenborg. "Movements, Countermovements, and the Structure of Political Opportunity." *American Journal of Sociology* 101, no. 6 (May 1996): 1628–60.

Meyers, Marian. *News Coverage of Violence against Women: Engendering Blame*. Thousand Oaks, CA: Sage, 1997.

Milkis, Sydney, and Marc Landy. "The Presidency in History: Leading from the Eye of the Storm." In *The Presidency and the Political System* (11th ed.), edited by Michael Nelson. Thousand Oaks, CA: Sage/CQ Press, 2018: 93–130.

Miller, Cassie, and Alexandra Werner-Winslow. "Ten Days after: Harassment and Intimidation in the Aftermath of the Election." *Southern Poverty Law Center*, November 29, 2016. https://www.splcenter.org/20161129/ten-days-after-harassment-and-intimidation-aftermath-election

Mitchell, W. J. T. *What Do Pictures Want?*. Chicago: University of Chicago Press, 2004, 47.

Morin, Aysel. "Framing Terror: The Strategies Newspapers Use to Frame an Act as Terror or Crime." *Journalism & Mass Communication Quarterly* 93, no. 4 (2016): 986–1005.

Mottl, Tahi L. "The Analysis of Countermovements." *Social Problems* 27, no. 5 (June 1980): 620–35.

Mulvey, Laura. "Visual Pleasure and Narrative Cinema." *Screen* 16, no. 3 (1975): 6–18.

Munson, Ziad W. *The Making of Pro-life Activists: How Social Movement Mobilization Works*. Chicago, IL: University of Chicago Press, 2009.

Murdock, Catherine Gilbert. *Domesticating Drink: Women, Men, and Alcohol in America, 1870-1940*. Baltimore, MD: John Hopkins University Press, 1998.

Murphy, Kate. "Students Sue Miami University." *Cincinnati Inquirer*, December 1, 2017. https://www.cincinnati.com/story/news/2017/11/30/students-sue-miami-university-over-anti-abortion-protest/908549001/

Nadasen, Premilla. "From Widow to "Welfare Queen": Welfare and the Politics of Race." *Black Women, Gender Families* 1, no. 2 (2007): 52–77. https://www.jstor.org/stable/10.5406/blacwomegendfami.1.2.0052

Nadasen, Premilla. *Rethinking the Welfare Rights Movement*. New York: Routledge, 2012.

Nagle, Angela. *Kill All Normies: The Online Culture Wars from Tumblr and 4chan to the Alt-Right and Trump*. Winchester and Washington: Zero Books, 2017.

Nakamura, Lisa. *Digitizing Race: Visual Cultures of the Internet*. Minneapolis: University of Minnesota Press, 2008.

Nakayama, Thomas K., and Robert L. Krizek. "Whiteness: A Strategic Rhetoric." *Quarterly Journal of Speech* 81, no. 3 (1995): 291–309.

242 Bibliography

Nakayama, Thomas K., and Judith N. Martin. *Whiteness: The Communication of Social Identity*. Thousand Oaks, CA: Sage, 1999.

Nakayama, Thomas K.. "What's Next for Whiteness and the Internet." *Critical Studies in Media Communication* 34 (2017): 68–72, 70.

Nash, Elizabeth, and Lauren Cross. "2021 Is on Track to Become the Most Devastating Antiabortion State Legislative Session in Decades," April 29, 2021. https://www.guttmacher.org/article/2021/04/2021-track-become-most-devastating-anti-abortion-state-legislative-session-decades

Nash, George H. *The Conservative Intellectual Movement in America since 1945*. Wilmington, DE: ISI Books, 2006 [1976].

National Coalition for Men. "Richard F. Doyle, MRA." https://ncfm.org/advisor-board/richard-f-doyle/

National Commission on the Observance of International Women's Year. "Legal Status of Homemakers: A Workshop Guide," March 1977 (Eagle Forum Archives, Collection Phyllis Schlafly, Series ERA, Series IWY, Box 1, File 6).

Neubeck, Kenneth J., and Noel A. Cazenave. *Welfare Racism: Playing the Race Card against America's Poor*. New York: Routledge, 2001.

New York Radical Women. "No More Miss America!," 1968. https://www.redstockings.org/index.php/no-more-miss-america

New, Jake. "More Students Punished over Sexual Assault Are Winning Lawsuits against Colleges." *Inside Higher Ed*, November 5, 2015. https://www.insidehighered.com/news/2015/11/05/more-students-punished-over-sexual-assault-are-winning-lawsuits-against-colleges

Newman, Karen. *Fetal Positions: Individualism, Science, Visuality*. Stanford, CA: Stanford University Press, 1996.

Newman, Louise M. *White Women's Rights: The Racial Origins of Feminism in the United States*. New York: Oxford University Press, 1999.

Newton, Judith. *From Panthers to Promise Keepers: Rethinking the Men's Movement*. Lanham, MD: Rowman & Littlefield, 2004.

Nickerson, Michelle M. *Mothers of Conservatism: Women and the Postwar Right*. Princeton, NJ: Princeton University Press, 2012.

O'Neill, Rachel. *Seduction: Men, Masculinity and Mediated Intimacy*. Cambridge, MA and Medford, OR: Polity, 2018.

Ohlheiser, Abby. "Just How Offensive Did Milo Yiannopoulos Have to Be to Get Banned from Twitter?." *The Washington Post*, July 21, 2016. https://www.washingtonpost.com/news/the-intersect/wp/2016/07/21/what-it-takes-to-get-banned-from-twitter/?utm_term=.69e3e83044cc

Oliver, Pamela E., and Hank Johnston. "What a Good Idea! Ideologies and Frames in Social Movement Research." *Mobilization: An International Quarterly* 4, no. 1 (2000): 37–54.

Ott, Brian L., and Greg Dickinson. "Visual Rhetoric and/as Critical Pedagogy." In *The SAGE Handbook of Rhetorical Studies*, edited by Andrea A. Lunsford, Kirt H. Wilson, and Rosa A. Eberly, 325. Thousand Oaks, CA: Sage, 2008.

Paquette, Danielle. "The Alt-Right Isn't Only about White Supremacy. It's about White Male Supremacy." *The Washington Post*, November 25, 2016. https://www.washingtonpost.com/news/wonk/wp/2016/11/25/the-alt-right-isnt-just-about-white-supremacy-its-about-white-male-supremacy/?utm_term=.25af1245eb6b

Payne, Diana L., Kimberly A. Lonsway, and Louise F. Fitzgerald. "Rape Myth Acceptance: Exploration of Its Structure and Its Measurement Using the Illinois Rape Myth Acceptance Scale." *Journal of Research in Personality* 33 (1999): 27–68.

Pepin, Joanna Rae. "Nobody's Business? White Male Privilege in Media Coverage of Intimate Partner Violence." *Sociological Spectrum* 36, no. 3 (2016): 123–41, for sanctioning male violence.

Petchesky, Rosalind. *Abortion and Woman's Choice*. Boston, MA: Northeastern University Press, 1984.

Petras, James, and Steve Vieux. "From Little Rock to Wall Street: Clinton's Journey beyond Reaganism." *Economic and Political Weekly* 30, no. 5 (1995): 251–53. Accessed December 10, 2020. http://www.jstor.org/stable/4402347

Phyllis Schlafly Eagles. "The Life and Legacy of Phyllis Schlafly." https://www.phyllis-chlafly.com/phyllis/

Podsakoff, Philip M., Scott B. MacKenzie, Jeong-Yeon Lee, and Nathan P. Podsakoff. "Common Method Biases in Behavioral Research: A Critical Review of the Literature and Recommended Remedies." *The Journal of Applied Psychology* 88, no. 5 (2003): 879–903.

Poland, Bailey. *Haters: Harassment, Abuse, and Violence Online*. Lincoln: Potomac Books an imprint of the University of Nebraska Press, 2016. http://search.ebscohost.com/login. aspx?direct=true&scope=site&db=nlebk&AN=1354282

Political Research Associates. *Defending Reproductive Justice: An Activist Resource Kit*. Somerville: Political Research Associates, 2013. https://www.politicalresearch.org/ sites/default/files/2018-10/Defending-Reproductive-Justice-ARK-Final.pdf

Polletta, Francesca. "'It Was like a Fever…:' Narrative and Identity in Social Protest." *Social Protest* 45, no. 2 (May 1998): 137–59.

Posner, Sarah. "How Stephen Bannon Created an Online Haven for White Nationalists." *Mother Jones*, August 2, 2016a. http://www.theinvestigativefund.org/ investigations/politicsandgovernment/2265/how_stephen_bannon_created_an_ online_haven_for_white_nationalists/

Posner, Sarah. "Meet the Alt-Right 'Spokesman' Who's Thrilled with Trump's Rise." *Rolling Stone Magazine*, October 18, 2016b. http://www.rollingstone.com/politics/ features/meet-the-alt-right-spokesman-thrilled-by-trumps-rise-w443902

Potok, Mark. "War on Women." *Southern Poverty Law Center Intelligence Report*, August 20, 2014. https://www.splcenter.org/fighting-hate/intelligence-report/2014/ war-women

Price, Greg. "Women in #MeToo Can 'Ruin a Man's Career' without Due Process, Morning Joe's Mika Brzezinski Says." *Newsweek*, December 19, 2017. https://www. newsweek.com/women-ruin-men-career-metoo-morning-joe-752386

Pruden, Meredith L., Ayse Lokmanoglu, Anne Peterscheck, and Yannick Veilleux Lepage. "Birds of a Feather: A Comparative Analysis of White Supremacist and Violent Male Supremacist Discourses." In *Far-Right Extremism in North America*, edited by Barbara Perry, Johannes Gruenwald, and Ryan Scrivens. Cham: Palgrave, forthcoming 2022.

Quadagno, Jill S. *The Color of Welfare*. Oxford and New York: Oxford University Press, 1994.

Rabin, Roni Caryn. "Nearly 1 in 5 Women in U.S. Survey Say They Have Been Sexually Assaulted." *The New York Times*, December 14, 2011. http://www.nytimes. com/2011/12/15/health/nearly-1-in-5-women-in-us-survey-report-sexual-assault. html?_r=0

Reagan, Ronald. "Inaugural Address." January 20, 1981a. Accessed at: https://www. reaganfoundation.org/media/128614/inaguration.pdf

Reagan, Ronald. "Address Before a Joint Session of Congress on the Program for Economic Recovery," February 18, 1981b. Accessed at: https://www.reaganlibrary.gov/archives/ speech/address-joint-session-congress-program-economic-recovery-february-1981

244 Bibliography

Reilly, Ryan J. "Jeff Sessions Now Admits Grabbing a Woman by the Genitals is Sexual Assault." *The Huffington Post*, January 10, 2017. http://www.huffingtonpost.com/entry/jeff-sessions-trump-sexual-assault_us_58753f08e4b043ad97e64369

Rhode, Deborah L. *Speaking of Sex: The Denial of Gender Inequality.* Cambridge: Harvard University Press, 1997.

Ribieras, Amélie. "The Sociocultural Discourse and the Social Movement Practices of Conservative Women in the United States. The Example of Phyllis Schlafly and Eagle Forum." PhD dissertation defended at La Sorbonne Nouvelle, France on November 29th, 2019 and supervised by Hélène Le Dantec-Lowry, 2019.

Ribieras, Amélie. "'Stop Taking Our Privileges:' Phyllis Schlafly's Traditional Womanhood and the Fight for Sociocultural Hegemony in the 1970–1980s." *USAbroad-Journal of American History and Politics* 4, March 2021. https://usabroad.unibo.it/article/view/11614/12363

Ribeiro, Manoel Horta, Raphael Ottoni, Robert West, Virgílio A. F. Almeida, and Wagner Meira. "Auditing Radicalization Pathways on YouTube." *FAT★ '20: Proceedings of the 2020 Conference on Fairness, Accountability, and Transparency* (2020b): 131–41.

Ribeiro, Filipe N., Jeremy Blackburn, Barry Bradlyn, Emiliano de Cristofaro, Gianluca Stringhini, Summer Long, Stephanie Greenberg, and Savvas Zannettou. "The Evolution of the Manosphere across the Web," 2020a. Accessed August 25, 2020. https://arxiv.org/abs/2001.07600

Riccardi, Nicholas. "Suspect in George Tiller's Slaying Reportedly Belonged to Anti-government Militia. *Los Angeles Times*, June 2, 2009. https://www.latimes.com/archives/la-xpm-2009-jun-02-na-tiller-suspect2-story.html

Rich, Spencer. "Schlafly: Sex Harassment on Job No Problem for Virtuous Women." *The Washington Post*, April 22, 1981.

Rivers, Caryl, and Rosalind C. Barnett. *The New Soft War on Women: How the Myth of Female Ascendance Is Hurting Women, Men—and Our Economy.* New York: Tarcher/Penguin, 2013.

Roberts, Bill. "BSU, Anti-abortion Group Settle Free Speech Lawsuit." *Idaho Statesman*, June 3, 2015. https://www.idahostatesman.com/news/local/education/boise-state-university/article40861854.html

Roberts, Dorothy. *Killing the Black Body: Race, Reproduction and the Meaning of Liberty.* New York: Vintage Books, 1998.

Roberts, Dorothy E. "Welfare Reform and Economic Freedom: Low-Income Mothers' Decisions about Work at Home and in the Market." *Faculty Scholarship at Penn Law* 584 (2004): 1029–63.

Romano, Aja. "How the Alt-Right's Sexism Lures Men into White Supremacy." *Vox*, April 26, 2018. https://www.vox.com/culture/2016/12/14/13576192/alt-right-sexism-recruitment

Ronan, Wyatt. "2021 Becomes Record Year For Anti-Transgender Legislation." *Human Rights Campaign*, March 13, 2021. https://www.hrc.org/press-releases/breaking-2021-becomes-record-year-for-anti-transgender-legislation

Rone, Julia. "Far Right Alternative News Media as 'Indignation Mobilization Mechanisms': How the Far Right Opposed the Global Compact for Migration." *Information, Communication & Society* (2021): 1–18. https://doi.org/10.1080/1369118X.2020.1864001

Rosenfeld, Megan. "Feminist Fatales." *The Washington Post*, November 30, 1995. https://www.washingtonpost.com/archive/lifestyle/1995/11/30/feminist-fatales/cfd56f87-296b-4580-9d76-fcfba15c6296/?utm_term=.93e2dd0b66d0

Bibliography **245**

Rosenthal, Lawrence, *Empire of Resentment: Populism's Toxic Embrace of Nationalism*. New York: The New Press, 2020.

Ross, Loretta. "White Supremacy in the 1990s." In *Eyes Right! Challenging the Right-Wing Backlash*, edited by Chip Berlet, 166–81. Boston, MA: South End Press, 1995.

Ross, Loretta. "Women's Rights Are Human Rights and the Women's March on Washington." *Rewire*, January 19, 2017. https://rewire.news/article/2017/01/19/womens-rights-human-rights-womens-march-washington/

Ross, Loretta J., and Rickie Solinger. *Reproductive Justice: An Introduction*. Berkeley: University of California Press, 2017.

Rothermel, Ann-Kathrin. "Die Manosphere. Die Rolle Von Digitalen Gemeinschaften Und Regressiven Bewegungsdynamiken Für on- Und Offline Antifeminismus." *Forschungsjournal Soziale Bewegungen* 33, no. 2 (2020a): 491–505. https://doi.org/10.1515/fjsb-2020-0041. https://www.degruyter.com/document/doi/10.1515/fjsb-2020-0041/html

Rothermel, Ann-Kathrin. "'The Other Side': Assessing the Polarization of Gender Knowledge through a Feminist Analysis of the Affective-Discursive in Anti-Feminist Online Communities." *Social Politics: International Studies in Gender, State & Society* (2020b). https://doi.org/10.1093/sp/jxaa024

Rudman, Laurie A., Corinne A. Moss-Racusin, Julie E. Phelan, and Sanne Nauts. "Status Incongruity and Backlash Effects: Defending the Gender Hierarchy Motivates Prejudice against Female Leaders." *Journal of Experimental Social Psychology* 48, no. 1 (2012): 165–79.

Ruthig, Joelle C., Andre Kehn, Bradlee W. Gamblin, Karen Vanderzanden, and Kelly Jones. "When Women's Gains Equal Men's Losses: Predicting a Zero-Sum Perspective of Gender Status." *Sex Roles* 76, no. 1–2 (2017): 17–26.

Ryan, Camille L., and Julie Siebens. "Educational Attainment in the United States: 2009." Vol. February. US Census Bureau, 2012.

Rymph, Catherine E. *Republican Women: Feminism and Conservatism from Suffrage through the Rise of the New Right*. Chapel Hill: The University of North Carolina Press, 2006.

Salter, Michael. "From Geek Masculinity to Gamergate: The Technological Rationality of Online Abuse." *Crime, Media, Culture: An International Journal* 14, no. 2 (2018): 247–64. https://doi.org/10.1177/1741659017690893

Santoro, Nadine. "USU Shooting Threat: This Isn't a Game." *Disrupting Dinner Parties*, November 10, 2014. https://disruptingdinnerparties.com/2014/11/10/usu-shooting-threat-this-isnt-a-game/#more-29965

Scarry, Eddie. "Trump Defends Roger Ailes from Sexual Harassment Accusations." *The Washington Examiner*, July 14, 2016. http://www.washingtonexaminer.com/article/2596510

Schilt, Kristen, and Laurel Westbrook. "Doing Gender, Doing Heteronormativity: 'Gender Normals,' Transgender People, and the Social Maintenance of Heterosexuality." *Gender & Society* 23, no. 4 (August 1, 2009): 440–64.

Schlafly, Godfrey, and Fitzgerald. "Lawsuit Filed against Commission on International Women's Year," April 9, 1976 (Archives of the Library of Congress, Collection League of Women Voters, Box 133, File opposition anti-ERA literature 75–77).

Schlafly, Phyllis. "What's Wrong with Equal Rights for Women?" *The Phyllis Schlafly Report*, February 1972. https://eagleforum.org/publications/psr/feb1972.html

Schlafly, Phyllis. *The Power of the Positive Woman*. New Rochelle, NY: Arlington House Publishers, 1977.

Schlafly, Phyllis. "E.R.A. Suffers 1978 Defeat." *The Phyllis Schlafly Report*, March 1978 (Archives of the Schlesinger Library, Collection Phyllis Schlafly Report, Book 1: 75–78).

246 Bibliography

Schlafly, Phyllis. "Changing Social Security to Hurt the Homemaker." *The Phyllis Schlafly Report*, June 1979a (Archives of the Schlesinger Library, Collection Phyllis Schlafly Report, Book 2: 1978–1979).

Schlafly, Phyllis. Letter to STOP ERA leaders. August 16, 1979b (Eagle Forum Archives, Collection Phyllis Schlafly, Series ERA, miscellaneous, Box 2, File 2).

Schlafly, Phyllis. "Testimony to the Senate Labor and Human Resources Committee," April 21, 1981a (Archives of the Schlesinger Library, Collection Carabillo, Box 15.9).

Schlafly, Phyllis. *The Power of the Christian Woman*. Cincinnati, OH: Standard Pub, 1981b.

Schlafly, Phyllis. "Ten Years of ERA Is Enough!." *The Phyllis Schlafly Report*, April 1983 (Archives of the Schlesinger Library, Collection Phyllis Schlafly Report, Book 4: 82–84).

Schlafly, Phyllis. "Statement by Phyllis Schlafly to the Compensation & Employee Benefits Subcommittee of House Post Office and Civil Service Committee," May 1985 (Archives of the Library of Congress, Collection Winn Newman, Box 406, File 8).

Schlafly, Phyllis. *Feminist Fantasies*. Dallas: Spence, 2003.

Schlafly, Phyllis. *The Flipside of Feminism: What Conservative Women Know—and Men Can't Say*. Washington, DC: WND Books, 2011.

Schlafly, Phyllis. *Who Killed the American Family?*. Washington, DC: WorldNetDaily, 2014.

Schmitz, Rachel, and Emily Kazyak. "Masculinities in Cyberspace: An Analysis of Portrayals of Manhood in Men's Rights Activist Websites." *Social Sciences* 5, no. 2 (2016): 18. https://doi.org/10.3390/socsci5020018

Schneider, Anne L., and Helen M. Ingram, eds. *Deserving and Entitled: Social Constructions and Public Policy*. Ithaca: State University of New York Press, 2004, 221. Accessed January 6, 2021. ProQuest Ebook Central.

Schreiber, Ronnee. "Is There a Conservative Feminism? An Empirical Account." *Politics & Gender* 14 (2018): 56–79.

Seltzer, Rick. "Cal State to Pay $240,000 to Settle Anti-abortion Speaker Lawsuit." *Inside Higher Ed*, February 6, 2020. https://www.insidehighered.com/quicktakes/2020/02/06/cal-state-pay-240000-settle-anti-abortion-speaker-lawsuit

Serwer, Adam, and Katie J. M. Baker. "How Men's Rights Leader Paul Elam Turned Being a Deadbeat Dad into a Moneymaking Movement." *Buzzfeed News*, February 6, 2015. https://www.buzzfeed.com/adamserwer/how-mens-rights-leader-paul-elam-turned-being-a-deadbeat-dad?utm_term=.bvY2OY9yl#.ukPZzDNx6

Sharp, Walt. "At Home with the Schlaflys." *Alton Telegraph*, February 18, 1978 (Eagle Forum Archives, Collection Phyllis Schlafly, Series ERA, subjects, Box 26, File 8).

Sheldon, Sally. "Unwilling Fathers and Abortion: Terminating Men's Child Support Obligations?" *The Modern Law Review* 66, no. 2 (2003): 175–94.

Shemla, Meir, and Anja Kreienberg. "Gender Quotas in Hiring Drive Away Both Women and Men." *Forbes*, October 16, 2014. http://www.forbes.com/sites/datafreaks/2014/10/16/gender-quotas-in-hiring-drive-away-both-women-and-men/

Shuurman, Bart, Masse Lindekilde, Stefan Malthaner, Francis O'Connor, Paul Gill, and Noémie Bouhana. "End of the Lone Wolf: The Typology that Should Not Have Been." *Studies in Conflict & Terrorism* 42, no. 8 (2019): 771–78.

Simon, Rita J., and Jean M. Landis. "A Report: Women's and Men's Attitudes about a Woman's Place and Role." *The Public Opinion Quarterly* 53, no. 2 (Summer 1989): 265–76.

Skocpol, Theda, and Vanessa Williamson. *The Tea Party and the Remaking of Republican Conservatism*. Oxford: Oxford University Press, 2011.

Skowronek, Stephen. *Presidential Leadership in Political Time: Reprise and Reappraisal* (2nd ed.). Lawrence: University Press of Kansas, 2011.

Smith, Greg M., *Film Structure and the Emotion System*. Cambridge: Cambridge University Press, 2003, 41.

Smith, Tom W., Peter Marsden, Michael Hout, and Jibum Kim. "General Social Surveys, 1972-2016." *NORC at the University of Chicago*, 2018. http://gssdataexplorer.norc.org/

Solem-Pfeifer, Chance. "An Oregon-Bred Actor Takes on One of the Most Challenging Roles of His Career." *Willamette Week*, October 15, 2019. https://www.wweek.com/arts/2019/10/15/an-oregon-bred-actor-takes-on-one-of-the-most-challenging-roles-of-his-career/

Soloman, Akiba. "Another Day, Another Race-Baiting Abortion Billboard." *Colorlines*, March 29, 2011. https://www.colorlines.com/articles/another-day-another-race-baiting-abortion-billboard

Sommers, Christina Hoff. "Title IX: How a Good Law Went Terribly Wrong." *Time*, June 23, 2014. http://time.com/2912420/titleix-anniversary/

Sommers, Christina Hoff. "'Amoral Masculinity': A Theory for Understanding Trump from Feminist Contrarian Christina Hoff Sommers." *American Enterprise Institute*, November 2, 2016. https://www.aei.org/publication/amoral-masculinity-a-theory-for-understanding-trump-from-feminist-contrarian-christina-hoff-sommers/

SPLC. "Male Supremacy: Male Supremacy Is a Hateful Ideology Advocating for the Subjugation of Women." Accessed February 10, 2021. https://www.splcenter.org/fighting-hate/extremist-files/ideology/male-supremacy

Staggenborg, Suzanne. "Social Movement Communities and Cycles of Protest: The Emergence and Maintenance of a Local Women's Movement." *Social Problems* 45, no. 2 (May 1998): 180–204.

Stanley, Amy Dru. "Conjugal Bonds and Wage Labor: Rights of Contract in the Age of Emancipation." *The Journal of American History* 75, no. 2 (1988): 471–500. Accessed January 12, 2021. https://doi.org/10.2307/1887867

Stanley, Amy Dru. *From Bondage to Contract: Wage Labor, Marriage, and the Market in the Age of Slave Emancipation*. Cambridge: Cambridge University Press, 1998.

STOP ERA. "You Can't Fool Mother Nature." (Archives of the Schlesinger Library, Collection Memorabilia, Box 23 O'Reilly).

STOP ERA. *Participation Form to the Annual Conference*, June 25–26, 1975, Springfield, IL. (Archives of the Schlesinger Library, Collection Carabillo, Box. 15.10).

Stuart TV. *Abortion Conspiracy*. YouTube. Video. November 8, 2010.

Swim, Janet K., Kathryn J. Aikin, Wayne S. Hall, and Barbara A. Hunter. "Sexism and Racism: Old-Fashioned and Modern Prejudices." *Journal of Personality and Social Psychology* 68, no. 2 (1995): 199–214.

Tesfaye, Sophia. "Donald Trump will adopt Heritage Foundation's 'Skinny Budget': Arts, Violence against Women Funding to be Cut." *Salon*, January 19, 2017. http://www.salon.com/2017/01/19/donald-trump-will-adopt-heritage-founda

Turner, Ralph H. "Sponsored and Contest Mobility and the School System." *American Sociological Review* 25, no. 6 (1960): 855–67.

Tyler May, Elaine. *Homeward Bound: American Families in the Cold War Era*. New York: Basic Books, 2008 [1988].

Valerius, Karen. "A Not-So-Silent Scream: Gothic and the US Abortion Debate." *Frontiers* 34, no. 3 (2013): 27–47.

248 Bibliography

Valizadeh, Roosh. "No One Would Have Died If PUAHate Killer Elliot Rodger Learned Game." *Return of Kings*, May 25, 2014. http://www.returnofkings.com/36135/no-one-would-have-died-if-pua-hate-killer-elliot-rodger-learned-game

Van Kersbergen, Kees. "The Politics of Welfare State Reform." *Swiss Political Science Review* (2002): 7. Accessed at: https://onlinelibrary.wiley.com/doi/pdf/10.1002/j.1662-6370.2002.tb00392.x

Van Syckle, Katie. "Here's What a Trump Administration Could Mean for Campus Sexual Assault." *New York Magazine*, January 18, 2017. http://nymag.com/thecut/2017/01/what-a-trump-administration-means-for-campus-sexual-assault.html

Van Valkenburgh, Shawn P. "Digesting the Red Pill: Masculinity and Neoliberalism in the Manosphere." *Men and Masculinities* (2018): 1097184X1881611. https://doi.org/10.1177/1097184X18816118

Venker, Suzanne. "The War on Men." *Fox News*, November 26, 2012. http://www.foxnews.com/opinion/2012/11/24/war-on-men.html

Vinograd, Cassandra. "Breitbart's Michelle Fields and Three Others Resign over Trump Incident." *NBC News*, March 14, 2016. http://www.nbcnews.com/news/us-news/breitbart-s-michelle-fields-ben-shapiro-resign-over-trump-incident-n537711

Vito, Christopher, Amanda Admire, and Elizabeth Hughes. "Masculinity, Aggrieved Entitlement, and Violence: Considering the Isla Vista Mass Shooting." *NORMA* 13, no. 2 (2018): 86–102. https://doi.org/10.1080/18902138.2017.1390658

Walsh, Joan. "Meet the 'Feminists' Doing the Koch Brothers' Dirty Work." *The Nation*, August 18, 2016. https://www.thenation.com/article/archive/meet-the-feminists-doing-the-koch-brothers-dirty-work/

Warf, Barney. "Usenet." In *The Sage Encyclopedia of the Internet*, edited by Barney Warf. Thousand Oaks, CA: SAGE Publications, 2018: 891.

Weinberg, Jill, Jeremy Freese, and David McElhattan. "Comparing Data Characteristics and Results of an Online Factorial Survey between a Population-Based and a Crowdsource-Recruited Sample." *Sociological Science* 1 (2014): 292–310.

Weir, Margaret. "States, Race, and the Decline of New Deal Liberalism." *Studies in American Political Development* 19, no. 2 (October 2005): 157–72. Accessed https://doi.org/10.1017/S0898588X05000106

Welch, Liz. "6 Women on Their Terrifying, Infuriating Encounters with Abortion Clinic Protesters." *Cosmopolitan*, February 21, 2014. http://www.cosmopolitan.com/politics/news/a5669/abortion-clinic-protesters/

Whitley, Bernard E. "Gender-Role Variables and Attitudes toward Homosexuality." *Sex Roles* 45, no. 11–12 (2001): 691–721.

Williams, H. Howell. "'Personal Responsibility' and the End of Welfare as We Know It." *Political Science and Politics* 50, no. 2 (April 2017): 379–83.

Wills, Gary. *Heart and Head: American Christianities*. New York: Penguin Press, 2007.

Wilson, Chris. "Nostalgia, Entitlement and Victimhood: The Synergy of White Genocide and Misogyny." *Terrorism and Political Violence* (2020): 1–16. https://doi.org/10.1080/09546553.2020.1839428

Wilson, Jason. "What Do Incels, Fascists and Terrorists Have in Common? Violent Misogyny." Accessed February 10, 2021. https://www.theguardian.com/commentisfree/2018/may/04/what-do-incels-fascists-and-terrorists-have-in-common-violent-misogyny

Wilson, Laura C., Alesha D. Ballman, and Theresa J. Buczek. "News Content about Mass Shootings and Attitudes toward Mental Illness." *Journalism & Mass Communication Quarterly* 93, no. 3 (2016): 644–58.

Winter, Jessica. "The Link between the Capitol Riot and Anti-abortion Extremism." *The New Yorker*, March 11, 2021. https://www.newyorker.com/news/daily-comment/the-link-between-the-capitol-riot-and-anti-abortion-extremism

Woolf, Nicky. "'PUAhate' and 'ForeverAlone': Inside Elliot Rodger's Online Life." *The Guardian*, May 20, 2014. https://www.theguardian.com/world/2014/may/30/elliot-rodger-puahate-forever-alone-reddit-forums

Woolford, Jessica, and Andrew Woolford. "Abortion and Genocide: The Unbridgeable Gap." *Social Politics: International Studies in Gender, State and Society* 14, no. 1 (2007): 126–53.

Wright, Scott, Verity Trott, and Callum Jones. "'The Pussy Ain't Worth It, Bro': Assessing the Discourse and Structure of MGTOW." *Information, Communication & Society* 3, no. 1 (2020): 1–18. https://doi.org/10.1080/1369118X.2020.1751867

WSYX (Sinclair). "Caught on Cam." *16 KMTR*, July 10, 2014. https://nbc16.com/news/nation-world/caught-on-cam-pro-life-activists-confronted-attacked-by-woman

Zaikman, Yuliana, and Michael J. Marks. "Ambivalent Sexism and the Sexual Double Standard." *Sex Roles* 71, no. 9–10 (2014): 333–44.

Zeigler, Sara L. "Wifely Duties: Marriage, Labor, and the Common Law in Nineteenth-Century America." *Social Science History* 20, no. 1 (Spring 1996): 63–96.

Zuboff, Shoshana. "Big Other: Surveillance Capitalism and the Prospects of an Information Civilization." *Journal of Information Technology* 30 (2015): 75–89.

Zuckerberg, Donna. *Not All Dead White Men: Classics and Misogyny in the Digital Age.* Cambridge, MA and London: Harvard University Press, 2018.

INDEX

Page numbers in **bold** indicate tables, page numbers in *Italics* indicate figures and page numbers followed by n indicate notes.

#MeToo movement 25, 44

A Voice for Men (AVFM) 6, 58
abortion: anti-abortion homicide 97; antisemitic myth of blood libel 103, 105, 113n46; antisemitism and Holocaust denial 97–8; and child support 149–51, 154, 158, 160; "Choice for Men" (C4M) 149–51, 154, 158, 160; morality of 150–1; rights to and race 54, 57–8; *Roe V. Wade* 4, 97, 149
abortion clinic, bombings 97
"abortion malpractice" (ABMAL) 106
Abrams, Laura S., and Curran, Laura 159
Act of Marriage, The (LaHaye and LaHaye) 50
Activist Radio: The Mark Harrington Show 100
Aid to Families with Dependent Children (AFDC) 146, 150, 156
AIDS, neonazis exploited anti-gay fear 55
Ailes, Roger 12
Alana's Involuntary Celibacy Project 166
Alliance Defending Freedom 107
alpha females 192
alpha males 208, 217n35
alt lite 188

Alt Right 3; abortion and race 57–8; assertions of women's inferiority 11; ideology 57; and manosphere 58; online harassment of women (by) 12; quasi-feminism 60–1; rejection of homosexuality 57; revitalization of politics 57–61; Trump support 167; video games 9–11, 167; women activists 60–1
Alternative Right 10
alt.mens-rights 147, 149, 152
Alton Telegraph, media image performance/marketing (Schlafly) 83
Ambivalent Sexism Index 27
American College of Obstetricians and Gynaecologists 102
American dream, "nuclear family" 70, 82, 88n15
American National Election Studies (ANES) 34
American Nazi Party 55
Anderson, Dianna 7
"androphilia" (Donovan) 59, 61
Antifa 191
Aryan civilization, Greg Johnson's comments (homosexuality) 61
Aryan Nations 55
Atlanta lesbian bar, Eric Rudolph's bombing 54–5
Atlas Shrugged (Rand) 7

Index **251**

Bannon, Stephen 10, 12
Bard, Christine 79
Barnett, Rosalind C., and Rivers, Caryl 6
Beatie, Thomas 222
Beckett, Emma 208
Beesley, Francis, and McGuire, James 185
Bernard, Michelle 5, 11–2, 206
Bhabha, Homi K. 119
'biblical' gender roles 7
biblical patriarchy movement 51–3, 59
"Big Sister Federal Tyranny" 96–7
birth control, federal funding 51
Black history appropriation, Created Equal (CE) 99
Black labor, exploitation 158
Black Lives Matter (BLM), Created Equal (CE) 100
"Black Pill" mentality: misogynist incels 131, 165, 172–3; suicide 173
Black population, police kill rates/abortion rates 100
Black poverty, Created Equal (CE) 100
Blair, Anita 5
Blee, Kathleen 56–7
Bokhari, Allum 9
Bomberger, Ryan 100
Bourdieu, Pierre 69, 74
Bozell, L. Brent Jr. 99
"bra-burning feminist" 79
Braine, Naomi 8
Bray, Michael 96, 97
Breitbart 9, 10, 12
Bridges, Tristan, and Pascoe, C. J. 119, 121
Britain, misogynist incel violence 176
Brown, Sarah 221
Burnham, Linda 10

campus sexual assault 6, 22
Capitol Attack (January 6) 188, 191, 211
Carian, Emily K. 21–47; and Johnson, Amy 22
Carlson, Gretchen 12
Catholicism: motherhood (prestige) 72; *Order of the Knights of Columbus* 186
Center for Bio-Ethical Reform (CBR) 98
Cernovich, Mike 9, 12
Chafe, William H. 74
Chamberlain, Pam 4
Charleston church shooter (2016) 8, 202
Child Support Enforcement Program 146
"Choice for Men" (C4M) 149–51, 154, 158, 160
Chowdhury, Romit 184

Christian feudalism 52
Christian International Ministries 53
Christian masculinists 7
Christian Reconstructionists 51–3, 62
Christian Right 48; biblical patriarchy movement 51–3; complementarianism 52; feminist language use 50; and Proud Boys 192; Trump-Pence administration 14; women's false accusation of sexual assault 5
Cleveland International Film Festival (CIFF), *Cuck* (film by Lambert) 202, 203
Clinton, Bill, "New Democrats" 145
Clinton, Hillary 3, 12; appreciation by IWF 12, 13; presidential elections (2016) 11–3, 25; tweets attacking during campaign 9; voting behaviors and inversive sexism 42–3, 44
Collier Township gym shooter 7–8, 166–7
Concerned Women for America (CWA) 5, 50–1
Connell, Raewyn 118, 119, 185; and Messerschmidt, James W. 119
Conscience of a Conservative, The (Goldwater) 99
conservative movement: after World War II 68, 86n3; and feminism 68, 87n7; women in 68; *see also* Eagle Forum
contemporary sexism 23–5; hostile and benevolent sexism 23–4, 27, 29, 31, 42; types **24**
Conway, Kellyanne 13
Cooper, Cloee, and Jenkins, Daryle Lamont 188
Costello, Jef 59
Coulter, Ann 107
Counter-Currents 57–8, 59, 60
Covington, Harold 55
Created Equal (CE) 94–114; *Abortion*; antisemitic myth of blood libel 103, 105, 113n46; Black history appropriation 99; Black Lives Matter (BLM) 100; civil rights rhetoric 98–9, 100, 109; college campus filming/protests 95, 101–2, 105–7, 108; digital film projects 95–6, 101–5, 107–9; feminist stereotypes 108; free speech legal claims lawsuits 106–7; Genocide Awareness Project (GAP) 97–8, 106; gothic themes of gore, injury, and dismemberment 98, 103–5, 110; historical, religious, and racial contexts 96–101; jumbotron presentation 94, 105; Lexington campus (Adrienne Rogers) 105–6; life is God's dominion

252 Index

102–3; and manosphere 107, 108; Martin Luther King Jr. (use of) 98, 99, 100, 108; organization's revenue 106, 113n55; overview 94–6; patriarchal traditionalism 96; Promise Keepers (PK) 96, 98; University of Kentucky 94, 108; victimhood 109–10; video archive website 101–3; video clips for news media 107–9
Crenshaw, Kimberlé 96, 144
Cross, Katherine 9, 219–25
Crowe, Lonnie 53
Crown Spa erotic massage, incel terrorism 176
Crutcher, Mark 106
Cuck (film by Lambert) 202–18; alpha males 208, 217n35; anti-hero's death 214–15; Bill 209, 211; Bill as cuck 209–10; Candy 209, 210; Candy's webcam videos 209, 210, 218n45; "Chad" 208; Chance Dalmain 204–5, 208, 210, 211; characters showing goodwill to Ronnie 209, 210; Charleston church shooter (2016) 202; Christchurch shooter 211; Cleveland International Film Festival (CIFF) 202, 203; cuckold 202, 215n2; dating (transactional view) 208–9; "deep state" 204, 206, 216n15; intended audience 202–3; Kant quote 204, 205; Lambert's nonpolitical claim 212, 215; Lone Wolves (so-called) 203, 205, 211–12, 213, 215, 216n18; "mommy dearest" 207–8, 217n34; "myths of victimhood" 206, 209; online communities (Ronnie's involvement) 211, 212; online date 208–9; opening sequence 204–5; Red Pill philosophy 202, 204, 215n1; right-wing identity and ideology 205–7; Ronnie Palicki (father's suicide) 214; Ronnie Palicki (mother's abuse) 207–8, 217n34; Ronnie Palicki (radicalization) 205; Ronnie Palicki (Red Pilling) 202, 204; Ronnie Palicki (sympathy for) 203, 210; Ronnie Palicki (violent rampage) 214; Santa Barbara perpetrator (2014) 202, 208; sex transactional view 210; "silent scream" 207; suicide by cop 214; surveillance capitalism 204, 216n16; Trump rally 210, 211, 212, 213, 218n44; Van Nuys, Los Angeles 204; victimhood and white male anti-hero 205, 206, 207–10, 212; visual and digital culture of far right 212–14; "visual reciprocity" 213–14; VlogTubes (Chance Dalmain) 204–5, 208; VlogTubes (Ronnie) 208, 209, 210, 213, 214
Curran, Laura, and Abrams, Laura S. 159

Daily Stormer, The 60
Dangerous Speech Project 168; *Daughters of the American Revolution* 68, 86n5
Davis, Angela 96
de Beauvoir, Simone 74, 220
de Coning, Alexis, and Ebin, Chelsea 142–63
Death of Cool, The (McInnes) 186
Deckert, Paige, Gill, Paul and Horgan, John 211, 212
Declaration of Independence 99
DeCook Julia R. 213; DiBranco, Alex and Kelly, Megan 164–80
DeLuca, Kevin Michael, and Peeples, Jennifer 213
Demetriou, Demetrakis 118, 119
demographic nationalism: eugenics programs 49, 55, 57–8; neonazis 55; Quiverfull 53
DePue, Mark 82, 84
DeVos, Betsy 143
DiBranco, Alex 3–20; DeCook Julia R. and Kelly, Megan 164–80
digital hate culture 117; online content analysis 118, 138n13; *see also* manosphere
Donovan, Jack 7, 58–60, 61, 62
Doyle, Richard F. 81
Drayer, Seth 109
Dupuis-Déri, Francis 75
Dworkin, Andrea 50, 76

Eagle Forum: annual conference 78; applications to be president state chapter 72, 88n25; beginnings 68; "Eagle Award" 84; Equal Rights Amendment (ERA) 69, 80, 82, 84, 85, 87n8; "Fred Schlafly Award" 81–2; "Fulltime Homemaker Award" 84; Gayle Ruzicka's husband 81–2; political training for right-leaning women 85; "positive woman" (rhetoric of female power) 74; vector of oppression and emancipation for women 84; women's forum supported by husbands 80–2, 91n72, 91n75, 91n82
Earle Cabell Federal Building in Dallas, misogynist incel violence 176
Ebin, Chelsea, and de Coning, Alexis 142–63
Elam, Paul 7–8, 58

Index

employment practices: Black labor 158; "comparable worth" 77; family wage 156, 158; homo/transphobic 223; husband-breadwinner integrity 76–8, 90n51, 157; mommy-tracked 223; stay-at-home mothers 192; time with children 23; wage equality 51; women as privileged class 22

Equal Pay Act (1963) 77

Equal Rights Amendment (ERA) 4, 67–8; Eagle Forum 69, 72, 75, 80, 82, 84, 85, 87n8; as "a men's lib amendment" 76, 89n49; "equality feminism" 5, 6–7, 15n17

eugenics programs: demographic nationalism 49, 55, 57–8; people of color 222

Family Law Quarterly 146

family wage 156, 158

far right's politics of gender 48–64; Alt Right revitalization 57–61; Blee study of women in far right groups 56–7; Christian Reconstructionists 51–3, 62; Christian Right 48, 50, 53–4, 59; demographic nationalism 49, 55, 57–8; feminist language use 50–1; homosexuality 54–5, 57; male bonding through warfare 49; male tribalism 58–60, 61; New Apostolic Reformation (NAR) 53–4, 62; overview 48–50; patriarchal traditionalism 48–9; quasi-feminism 49, 51, 56, 60–1; visual and digital culture 212–14; warriors and bearers of the race 54–7

Farrell, Warren 6, 190

FathersManifesto.net 152, 162n35

"Feminist Counseling Column" (Gill) 56

feminist language, use by far right 50–1

feminist stereotypes: Created Equal (CE) 108; "man-hating feminist" 76; *Phyllis Schlafly Report, The* 79; Proud Boys 193; welfare, MRAs and personal responsibility 158

Fields, Michelle 12

Fiorina, Carly 12

Fisher, Robert 122

Fiske, Susan, and Glick, Peter 23

Fluke, Sandra 4

Forney, Matt 10, 13, 58, 60

Fox and Friends 108

Fraser, Nancy, and Gordon, Linda 156, 157

Fraternal Order of Alt-Knights (FOAK) 187

Futrelle, David 11

Game, The (Strauss) 166

"Gamergate" 9, 11, 167

Ganesh, Bharath 206

"geek masculinity" 120

gender hierarchy (Schlafly's defense) 67–93; antifeminist cause/negotiation of boundaries 79–85; countermovement structure 69, 87n11; emancipation in subjugation 83–5; emasculating men 75, 89n47; Equal Rights Amendment (ERA) 67–8, 69, 72, 75, 80, 82, 84, 85; feminine women (in favor of) 78–9, 90n65; feminist myth of an oppressive patriarchy 70–4; gender essentialism 74–6; gender roles 70–1, 72, 82; housewife-activist model 82–3, 92n93; husband-breadwinner integrity 76–8, 90n51, 157; influence and mobilizing capacity 68–9; language changes (genders) 75, 89n44; media image performance/marketing (Schlafly) 83; and men's rights movement 86; motherhood (prestige) 71–2; overview 67–8; patriarchal marriage 70–1; "positive woman" (rhetoric of female power) 73–4, 75; social fabric (cost of feminism) 74–9; Social Security and working women 76–7, 90n55; STOP ERA 68, 75, 82–3; study data and method 69–70; women's forum supported by husbands 80–2, 91n72, 91n75, 91n82; *see also* Eagle Forum

gender roles: 'biblical' 7; Christian ideology 4; combat 190; emasculating men 75, 89n47; patriarchal traditionalism 70, 71–2, 82, 87n14

General Social Survey 34

Genocide Awareness Project (GAP) 97–8, 106

Gilder, George 76

Gill, Molly 56

Gill, Paul, Horgan, John and Deckert, Paige 211, 212

Ging, Debbie 120

Gingrich, Newt 145

Glick, Peter, and Fiske, Susan 23

Goldwater, Barry 85, 99

Good Morning America, media image performance/marketing (Schlafly) 83

Gordon, Linda, and Fraser, Nancy 156, 157

Hansen, Janine 85

Hardisty, Jean 4

Harrington, Mark 98, 99, 106, 108

254 Index

Harris, Kamala 25
Hays, Charlotte 8, 12
hegemonic masculinity: manosphere 118, 119–21, 136; Proud Boys 185; Helms, Jesse 84, 92n105
Hill, Anita 5
homosexuality: Alt Right rejection 57; Greg Johnson's comments 61; Jack Donovan 59; and race (TYN) 61; violent anti-LGBT attacks 54–5
Horgan, John, Deckert, Paige and Gill, Paul 211, 212
HoSang, Daniel Martinez, and Lowndes, Joseph E. 99, 188
Hyde, Henry 84, 92n105
hypermasculinity: manosphere 120; Proud Boys 185

Illinois Congress, feminist raid 79
Illinois Rape Myth Acceptance (IRMA) Scale 34, 42
incels 107; Alana's Involuntary Celibacy Project 166; term 165, 166, 167; see also misogynist incels
Independent Women's Forum (IWF) 5, 11, 12; support for Hillary Clinton 12, 13
Independent Women's Voice (IWV) 13
Institute for Research on Male Supremacism 165
intactivists (anti-circumcision activists) 143
International Conference on Men's Issues (2019) 159–60
Internet Archive Usenet Historical Collection 147
interracial sex 54
inverse sexism 24–5
inversive sexism scale 21–47; Amazon Mechanical Turk 26, 27, 33; Ambivalent Sexism Index 27; beliefs related to gender **38–9**; contemporary sexism 23–5, **24**; corporate/government polices related to gender **36–7**; developing 25–7; discussion 43–4; foundational beliefs (male supremacist groups) 21; hostile and benevolent sexism 23–4, 27, 29, 31, 42; individuals who identify as female 31, 46n39; inversive sexism (endorsement) 29–30; men's rights forum 21–2, 25; method and sample 27–9, **28–9**, 33–5; modern sexism 24, 27, 31; modified grounded theory 26, 45n28; ordinary least squares (OLS) regression **32**, 35; overview 21–3; participant questionnaire 34; political attitudes and behaviors

40–1; predictive utility 33–43, **36–41**; scale items **26**; sexism scores (average) *30*; sexism scores (distribution) *31*; sexual assault accusations 35; sociodemographic predictors 30–3; statements characteristics 26; study demographic characteristics **28–9**, 34; study results 29–33, *30*, *31*, **32**, 35–43, **36–7**; voting behaviors for Hillary Clinton 42–3, 44; Wald tests *31*, **32**; women as privileged class 22

Jacobs, Cindy 53
Jasser, Greta, Kelly, Megan and Rothermel, Ann-Kathrin 117–41, 177
Jenkins, Daryle Lamont, and Cooper, Cloee 188
Joe Rogan Experience (JRE), Proud Boys 186, 189, 193, 200n44
Johnson, Amy, and Carian, Emily K. 22
Johnson, Greg 57–8, 60, 61
Justice Rides 98

Kant, Immanuel 204, 205
Kayzak, Emily, and Schmitz, Rachel 120
Kearl, Michelle Kelsey 98, 102
Kelly, Megan: DiBranco, Alex and DeCook Julia R. 164–80; Jasser, Greta and Rothermel, Ann-Kathrin 117–41, 177
Kelly, Megyn 12
Kentucky Kernal 105
Kessler, Jason 188
Kimmel, Michael 6
King, Zachary 103
Klansmen 96
Koch brothers 13

La domination masculine (Bourdieu) 69
labor: Black 158; sexual division 159; wives' houshold 157–8
LaHaye, Beverly 4, 5; and LaHaye, Timothy 50
Lake, Diane 53
Lambert, Rob 211, 212, 215, 215n2; Lone Wolves (so-called) 202, 211
Larson, Nathan 172
Las Vegas shooting (2017) 171
Ledeen, Barbara 5
Legler, Paul 146
Lerner, Gerda 69
Lewandowski, Corey 12
Life Dynamics 106
Limbaugh, Rush 4

Linder, Alex 55
Lone Wolves (so-called) 8, 202, 203, 205, 211–12, 213, 215, 216n18; *see also* Santa Barbara perpetrator (2014)
Lowndes, Joseph E., and HoSang, Daniel Martinez 99, 188
Lukas, Carrie L, 11
Lye, Matthew 58
Lyons, Matthew N. 10, 48–64

MacKinnon, Catharine 219
male supremacist groups, foundational beliefs 21
male tribalism 49; O'Meara 61; "Way of the Gang" (Donovan) 58–60
"man-hating feminist" stereotype 76
manosphere 117–41; and Alt Right 58; analyzing 123–33, **124**, 141n68; and Created Equal (CE) 107, 108; digital hate culture 117; hegemonic masculinity 118, 119–21, 136; history of 121–3; hybrid masculinities 119–21, 136; hypermasculinity 120; masculinities of 133–6, **133**–5; men going their own way (MGTOW) 118, 122, 127–9, **134**; men's rights activists (MRAs) 118, 120, 124–5, **133**; misogynist incels 118, 120, 122, 131–3, **135**, 136, 138n14; nonhegemonic masculinities 118, 119, 120, 121, 136, 138n16; overview 117–18; pick-up artists (PUAs) 118, 125–7, **134**; PUAHate.com 122; Red Pill, The (TRP) 122, 129–30, **135**; Reddit 120, 122; toxic masculinity 136
manospherians: Greg Johnson 60; homophobia and transphobia 58
Marantz, Andrew 9
March Upcountry, The (Covington) 55
Martin, Judith N., and Nakayama, Thomas K. 207
Martinez, Brian 160
Mason, Carol 94–114
Massanari, Adrienne 120
masturbation (opposing) 187
McGuire, James, and Beesley, Francis 185
McInnes, Gavin 183, 186, 187; analyzing his rhetoric 197; Joe Rogan Experience (JRE) 186, 189, 193, 200n44; YouTube videos 187, 189, 190, **197–8**
men going their own way (MGTOW) 7, 22; "creators of civilization" 127; manosphere analysis 118, 122, 127–9, **134**; mgtos.com website "About" section 128

men's rights activists (MRAs): manosphere analysis 118, 120, 124–5, **133**; offline movements 121; *see also* welfare, MRAs and personal responsibility
Men's Rights Association 81
men's rights movement (MRM) 121; beginnings 142, 160n1, 160n2; human rights movement term 144; overview 143–4
Messerschmidt, James W., and Connell, Raewyn 119
Messner, Michael 77
Metzger, Tom 56
misogynist incels 164–80; access to sex as right 131–2; "Becky" 170; "Black Pill" mentality 131, 165, 172–3; "Chads" 131, 132, 169, 170, 174, 208; Collier Township gym shooter 7–8, 166–7; "copes" 131, 173; "cucks" 170; "currycel" 174; dangerous speech 168–9, 170; "ethniccels" 174; "femoid" / "foid" 170; forum member survey (2020) 174–5; history 165–8; "Incel Rebellion" 174, 175; incel term 164, 165, 166, 167; "JBW" (Just Be White) 174; "landwhales" 171; Las Vegas shooting (2017) 171; "LDAR" (lay down and rot) 173, 175; manosphere analysis 118, 120, 122, 131–3, **135**, 136, 138n14; mass violence and terrorism after Sata Barbara 175–7; media awareness 175, 177; memes 169; "NEET" (not in employment, education, or training) 174–5; nihilism 131, 133; "noodlewhores" 171; "normies" 170, 171, 172; pedophilia (rhetoric supporting) 172; race and class intersections 174–5; Red Pill philosophy 165, 166, 172–4; rhetoric of dehumanization 169–74; "rice-cel" 174; "roasties" (vulgar for labia) 170–1; "role" 173; Santa Barbara foundational manifesto 168–9, 170, 173, 176; Santa Barbara perpetrator (2014) 164, 165, 167, 171, 174, 175, 176; "Scientific Blackpill" 174; sex for money or benefit to women 132, 141n73; "sexual market value" (SMV) 166, 175; sexual objectification 168–9, 170–1; "Stacys" 169; strain of dehumanizing subject 177; Swedish Defence Research Institute 176; Toronto attack (2018) 165, 170, 173, 174, 175; "Tyrone" 170; violence (promotion and glorification) 171–2; *see also Cuck* (film by Lambert)

256 Index

misogyny (mobilizing) 3–20; equity, feminism and men's rights 5–7; male supremacist harassment and violence 7–8; patriarchal traditionalism 3–5; post-election (2016) gender justice 13–4; presidential elections (2016) 11–3; video games and Alt Right 9–11
Miss America Pageant, protests (1968) 79
Mitchell, W. J. T. 213–14
modern sexism 24, 27, 31
Montreal École Polytechnique 166
Montreal mass shooter (1989) 7
Moonshot CVE 171
motherhood (prestige) 71–2
Mudde, Cas 11
Myth of Male Power (Farrell) 6
"myths of victimhood" 206, 209

Nagle, Angela 121
Nakamura, Lisa 213
Nakayama, Thomas K., and Martin, Judith N. 207
Nance, Penny 50
National Alliance 55
National Anarchist 60
National Center for Men 149
National Socialist Movement 55
"NEET" (not in employment, education, or training), misogynist incels 174–5
neonazis: demographic nationalism 55; exploited anti-gay fears (AIDS) 55; quasi-feminism 56; racial ideology 54
New Apostolic Reformation (NAR) 53–4, 62
New Deal program 144, 161n13
New Gay Liberation, The (Lye) 58
New Soft War on Women : The (Rivers and Barnett) 6
New Yorker 9
nonbinary people 220, 222
nonhegemonic masculinities, manosphere 118, 119, 120, 121, 136, 138n16
Norway attacker (2011) 8
"nuclear family," American dream 70, 82, 88n15

Oklahoma City bomber 171
O'Meara, James 61
Order of the Knights of Columbus 186

Palin, Sarah 12, 51
Paquette, Danielle 6
Park, Meadhbh 183–201

Parsons, Talcott 70
Pascoe, C. J., and Bridges, Tristan 119, 121
patriarchal marriage 70–1; English common law 71, 88n19; "gendered class interest" 71; tamed men 76, 89n49
patriarchal traditionalism 48–9; Created Equal (CE) 96; gender roles 70, 71–2, 82, 87n14; Proud Boys 191–4; and sexual rules 55; white supremacy to Christian Right 3–5
patriarchy, definition (Gerda Lerner) 69
Payne, Diana L., et al. 42
pedophilia (rhetoric supporting) 172
Peeples, Jennifer, and DeLuca, Kevin Michael 213
Pence, Mike 5
Personal Responsibility and Work Opportunity Reconciliation Act 1996 (PRWORA) 145–6
Peterson, Jordan 172
Phillips, Doug 51
Phyllis Schlafly Report, The 68, 79
Pick-Up Artist, The (VH1 show) 166
pick-up artists (PUAs) 7, 13, 107; alt. seduction.fast 166; beginnings 121–2; "bootcamp" training 167; economic language of "investment" 126; "Game" 130, 166, 167; "last-minute resistance" (LMR) 167; manosphere analysis 118, 125–7, **134**; "negs" 126; offline movements 121; pop culture 166; "seduction techniques" 125; self-help ideology 126; "sexual marketplace" 166; Valizadeh 58
Pierce, William 54
Planned Parenthood 5, 222–3
Political Research Associates (PRA) 4, 8
Potok, Mark 8
Power of the Positive Woman, The (Schlafly) 73, 75
presidential elections (2016) 11–3; Proud Boys 183
Promise Keepers (PK) 96, 98
Protestant evangelicals, complementarianism 52
Proud Boys 183–201; "America-first" nationalism 188; American warrior hero vision 191; beginnings 186–7; Capitol Attack (January 6) 191; Christian Right views 192; crisis of masculinity 184–5; crypto-fascism 186, 213; degrees of membership 186–7; divorce (topic of interview) 193; feminism (intense vitriol against) 191, 194, 195; feminist stereotypes 193; hegemonic

masculinity 185; hybrid masculinities 191; "hypermasculinity" 185; Joe Rogan Experience (JRE) 186, 189, 193, 200n44; "JQ" ("Jewish Question") 187; masturbation (opposing) 187; McInnes rhetoric (analyzing) 197; men of color 192, 197; multiracial and white supremacist 187–8, 197; overview 183–4; Parler page 197; patriarchal traditionalism 191–4; plausible deniability 188, 193; presidential debate Trump/Biden 183; Proud Boys' creed 186; Proud Girls 185; Red Pill, The (TRP) 195; romantic relationships 192–3; stay-at-home dad (mocking) 192, 193; stay-at-home mothers 192; street brawls 187, 190; study analysis (deductive thematic) 189; study method 188–90; suicide (males) 195; violence and manhood 190–1; Wisconsin Proud Boys 196–7; YouTube videos 187, 189, 190, **197–8**

Pruden, Meredith L. 202–18

PUAHate.com 8, 122, 167

QAnon Trump supporters 103–4, 184

quasi-feminism 10, 49; Alt Right 60–1; Concerned Women for America (CWA) 51; neonazis 56

Quiverfull 52, 53

racial ideology, neonazis 54

Radiance Foundation 100

Rand, Ayn 7

Rape of the Male, The (Doyle) 81

Reagan, Ronald: presidential campaign 85; "welfare queen" 4, 144–5, 154–5, 158; welfare state reform 145

Red Pill, The (TRP) 7; "enforced monogamy" 172; manosphere analysis 122, 129–30, **135**; *The Matrix* (film) 172, 215n1; Proud Boys 195; "sexual marketplace" 129, 141n72

Reddit 120; America First subREADIT 212; r/ForeverAlone 167; r/MensRights 22; r/TheRedPill 122

Register-her.com 7

Reno, Janet 97

reproductive health care: attacks on professionals 97; Planned Parenthood 5, 222–3

reproductive rights: abortion 54, 57–8; birth control 51; far right's politics of gender 54, 57–8; homo/transphobic 220–1,

222–3; "morning after pill" 4; people of color 222; pro-choice women 13; *Roe V. Wade* 4, 97, 149; state anti-abortion bills (2011) 4; Trump 3, 5; women of color 220–1; *see also* Created Equal (CE)

"Republican Motherhood" 72

Republican National Convention, Illinois delegate (Schlafly) 85, 93n106

Republican Party, gender factionalism 84

Return of Kings 8, 58

Rewire 7, 14

Ribieras, Amélie 67–93

Rivers, Caryl, and Barnett, Rosalind C. 6

Roberts, Dorothy 96

Roe V. Wade 4, 97, 149

Rogers, Adrienne 105–6

Romano, Aja 11

Roose, Joshua M. 185

Roosevelt, F. D., New Deal program 144, 161n13

Ross, Loretta 14, 96

Rothermel, Ann-Kathrin, Kelly, Megan and Jasser, Greta 117–41, 177

Rudolph, Eric, Atlanta lesbian bar bombing 54–5

Rymph, Catherine 12

Salter, Michael 120

same-sex marriage 58

Sanders, Bernie 105

Santa Barbara perpetrator (2014) 8, 164, 165, 167; *Cuck* (film by Lambert) 202, 208; dangerous speech 168–9; foundational manifesto 168–9, 170, 173, 176; glorification 171; race and class intersections 174, 175; sorority target 168; suicide 173; violence/terrorism 176

Sarkeesian, Anita 9

Sasour, Linda 194

Schlafly, Phyllis 4, 5, 13, 73, 87n6; enrolment in law school 83; media image performance/marketing 83; Republican National Convention delegate 85, 93n106; Republican Party work 85; *see also* gender hierarchy (Schlafly's defense)

Schlesinger, Arthur Jr. 6

Schmitz, Rachel, and Kayzak, Emily 120

Schreiber, Ronnee 84

Schuurman, Bart, et al. 211

Second Sex, The (de Beauvoir) 74

Seelhoff, Cheryl 52

Sessions, Jeff 14

258 Index

sexual assault/harassment allegations: campus sexual assault 6, 22; pick-up artists (PUAs) 167; "She lied" 42; Trump 11; women's false 5, 6; workplace 81, 153
"sexual marketplace": misogynist incels 131, 166, 175; pick-up artists (PUAs) 166; Red Pill 129, 141n72
Sexual Suicide (Gilder) 76
Sherman, Zachary Ray 203, 210
Silent Scream, The (Nathanson) 104
single-parent households: paternity DNA tests 146; and welfare 146
SisterSong 10, 18n55
Skowronek, Stephen 144
Sledd, Tisha (Pastor) 53–4
SlutHate.com 167, 171, 174
Smith, Helen 7
Social Security and working women 76–7, 90n55
social welfare in US 144–6, 161n9; Child Support Enforcement Program 146; Clinton (Bill) 145–6, 159; "good" and "bad" dependency 157; New Deal program 144, 161n13; "New Democrats" 145; "New Right" 144; payroll taxes 156; Personal Responsibility and Work Opportunity Reconciliation Act 1996 (PRWORA) 145–6; Reagan reforms 145; single-parent households 146; women's bad behavior (incentives) 160; work for welfare 146; *see also* welfare, MRAs and personal responsibility
Sommers, Christina Hoff 6, 7, 12
Sotomayor, Tommy 159–60
Southern Poverty Law Center 14; hate group listings 187; *Intelligence Report* 8
Spencer, Richard 11, 107, 204
Steven, Liam 149
STOP ERA 68, 75, 82–3
Stormfront 60
Strauss, Neil 166
Students for Life 107
studying the Right and male supremacism: Created Equal (CE) 109–10; strain of dehumanizing subject 177
suffragists 157, 165–6
suicide: "Black Pill" mentality 173; by cop 214; rate in males 195; Santa Barbara perpetrator (2014) 173
Supplemental Nutrition Assistance Program 156
Swedish Defence Research Institute, misogynist incel violence 176
Swim, Janet, et al. 24, 27

Tallahassee yoga class attack, misogynist incel violence 175
Taylor, Linda 145
Temporary Assistance for Needy Families (TANF) 146, 150
'Think Progress' 9
Thirteenth Amendment 157
Thomas, Clarence, sexual harassment allegations 5
Tiller, George 97
Title IX, rewriting 143
Traditionalist Youth Network (TYN): homosexuality 61; "western women" leadership roles 61; women activists 60–1
trans women (invisible sisterhood) 219–25; bodies (controlling ideology) 220, 222, 224; bodies (meaning society gives) 219, 220–1, 223; feminism's promise none win unless all do 224; myths 219, 221; natural reproductive capacity 222, 223; patriarchal myth that women are all the same 220, 223; police abuse 223; and racism 224; reproductive rights/justice 220, 221–3; sperm bank requests 222–3; sterilisation and ID gender markers 222, 223, 225n4; trans women (natural occurrence) 221, 223; transition denial 222; "woman" as white supremacist construct 224–5; "woman" (essentialising and universalising) 220, 221; women are not wombs 223–4; women, becoming not born (de Beauvoir) 220
Trump, Donald: Alt Right support 167; Christian Right 3, 14; misogyny 13; presidential elections (2016) 9, 11–3, 122; QAnon supporters 103–4; reproductive rights 3, 5; sexual assault allegations 11
Turner Diaries, The (Pierce) 54

Umpqua Community College shooter 175, 179n46
Unite the Right Rally 188, 211
U.S. Constitution: sex equality 70, 87n13; Thirteenth Amendment 157
U.S. Department of Health, Education, and Welfare 76–7, 90n55

Valenti, Jessica 7
Valerius, Karyn 104
Valizadeh, Daryush ("Roosh V") 8, 58, 60
Vanguard News Network (VNN) 55–6
Vice magazine 186
"victim mentalities" 7

video games and Alt Right 9–11, 167
Violence Against Women Act (VAWA) 5
Virginia Tech shooter 171
Voice of Montreal 186
Vox 11

wage discrimination 77
War against Boys:, The (Sommers) 7
"Way of the Gang" (Donovan) 58–60
welfare, MRAs and personal responsibility
142–63; child support 149–51, 154;
"Choice for Men" (C4M) 149–51,
154, 158, 160; equal and corollary
rights 148–51, 159; family wage 156,
158; FathersManifesto.net 152, 162n35;
feminist capture of the state 151–4, 158;
"good" and "bad" dependency 157;
husband-breadwinner integrity 76–8,
90n51, 157; Internet Archive Usenet
Historical Collection 147; labor (sexual
division) 159; men's rights movement
(MRM) 143–4; overview 142–3;
parasitical women 154–5; personal
responsibility narratives 147, 156, 159;
single and divorced mothers 156–7;
social welfare in US 144–6, 161n9;
study data and method 146–8; study
results 148–60; Thirteenth Amendment
157; "welfare queen" 158; wives'
household labor 157–8; women's need
for extra support 155; workplace sexual
harassment 153; *see also* social welfare
in US

"welfare queen" 4, 144–5, 154–5, 158
Westgate shopping center in Arizona,
misogynist incel violence 176
"What Is Neomasculinity" (Valizadeh),
pick-up artist 58
White Anglo-Saxon Protestant (WASP)
nativism 3
White Aryan Resistance (WAR) 54, 56
white knighting 209, 217n42
Who Killed the American Family (Schlafly) 73,
88n30, 89n31
Why Men Are the Way They Are (Farrell) 6
Who Stole Feminism? (Sommers) 6
Williams, Howell 145
Wisconsin Proud Boys 196–7
wives' household labor 157–8
woman: becoming, not born 74, 220; as
white supremacist construct 224–5
"Women for Judge Thomas" 5
women in far right groups: activists in Alt
Right 60–1; Blee study 56–7
workforce, wives in the 1950s 6
workplace sexual harassment: guidelines
153; Schlafly's testimony to the Senate 81

Yeoman, Andrew 60
Yiannopoulos, Milo 9, 107
YouTube videos, Gavin McInnes (Proud
Boy) 187, 189, 190, **197–8**

Zohrab, Black poverty 100
Zohrab, Peter 147, 152, 153

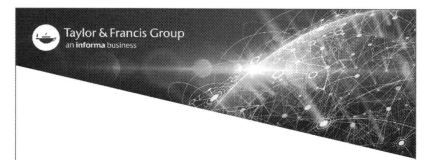

Printed in the United States
by Baker & Taylor Publisher Services